T0301420

Jewish Radicals

THE GOLDSTEIN-GOREN SERIES IN AMERICAN JEWISH HISTORY
General Editor: Hasia R. Diner

*We Remember with Reverence and Love: American Jews
and the Myth of Silence after the Holocaust, 1945–1962*
Hasia R. Diner

Is Diss a System? A Milt Gross Comic Reader
Edited by Ari Y. Kelman

*All Together Different: Yiddish Socialists, Garment Workers,
and the Labor Roots of Multiculturalism*
Daniel Katz

Jews and Booze: Becoming American in the Age of Prohibition
Marni Davis

Jewish Radicals: A Documentary History
Tony Michels

Jewish Radicals

A Documentary History

EDITED BY TONY MICHELS

NEW YORK UNIVERSITY PRESS
New York and London

NEW YORK UNIVERSITY PRESS
New York and London
www.nyupress.org

References to Internet websites (URLs) were accurate at the time of writing.
Neither the author nor New York University Press is responsible for URLs that
may have expired or changed since the manuscript was prepared.

Library of Congress Cataloging-in-Publication Data

Jewish radicals : a documentary history / edited by Tony Michels.
p. cm. -- (The Goldstein-Goren series in American Jewish history)
Includes bibliographical references and index.
ISBN 978-0-8147-5743-7 (cl : alk. paper) -- ISBN 978-0-8147-5744-4 (pb : alk. paper) -- ISBN
978-0-8147-6345-2 (ebook) -- ISBN 978-0-8147-6346-9 (ebook)
1. Jewish socialists--New York (State)--New York--History--Sources. 2. Immigrants--Polit-
ical activity--New York (State)--New York--History--Sources. 3. Jews, East European--New
York (State)--New York--History--Sources. 4. Working class Jews--New York (State)--New
York--History--Sources. 5. Labor movement--New York (State)--New York--History--
Sources. 6. New York (N.Y.)--Ethnic relations--History--Sources. I. Michels, Tony.
HX550.J4J49 2012
331.88'608992407471--dc23
2011052290

New York University Press books are printed on acid-free paper,
and their binding materials are chosen for strength and durability.
We strive to use environmentally responsible suppliers and materials
to the greatest extent possible in publishing our books.

Manufactured in the United States of America

c 10 9 8 7 6 5 4 3 2 1
p 10 9 8 7 6 5 4 3 2 1

Contents

Acknowledgments   xi

Introduction: The Jewish-Socialist Nexus   1
    Tony Michels

PART I: AWAKENINGS   25

1. "When I Went Home I Was Aflame" (memoir; c. 1925)   27
    Abraham Bisno

2. "I Saw a New World Opening Before Me" (memoir; 1931)   41
    Emma Goldman

3. The World of Socialism and Revolution (memoir; 1963)   49
    Alexander Bittelman

4. "Rebellion Raged within Me" (memoir; 1948)   59
    Lucy Robins Lang

5. "It Wasn't Difficult for Me to Reject Judaism" (memoir; 1965)   70
    Paul Jacobs

PART II: IN STRUGGLE   81

6. "Strong, Firm, and Correct Propaganda" (1886)   83
    Di nyu-yorker yidishe folkstsaytung

7. "Socialism Is Not a Dream" (1888)   86
    Dovid Edelshtat

8. The Birth of the Knee-Pants Makers' Union (memoir; 1924)   88
    Bernard Vaynshteyn

9. "The Whole City Seethed" (1892)   91
    Di arbeter tsaytung

10. Working Women Unite (1893–1894)   93
    Women's Societies

11. The Attempted Assassination of Henry Clay Frick (memoir; 1912)   95
    Alexander Berkman

12. The Prophet Karl Marx (c. 1910s)   97
    Abraham Shiplacoff

13. "Our Mecca" (memoir; n.d.)   99
    Isadore Wisotsky

14. "The Right to Control Birth" (1916)   104
    Rose Pastor Stokes

15. A Personal and Confidential Letter to Louis Marshall (1917)   109
    Abraham Cahan

16 Gangsters and Socialists on Election Day (memoir; 1944)   111
    Louis Waldman

17. "If I Were a Colored Man What Would I Do?" (1919)   120
    Louis Michel

18. The Meaning of Labor Day (1921)   124
    Justice

19. An Encounter with a Klansman (memoir; n.d.)   126
    Sam Darcy

20. Communist "Criminals" in Los Angeles (1929)   129
    Upton Sinclair

21. "Unions with Brains" (1930)   133
    The Nation

22. In Defense of the Kentucky Miners (1932)   135
    Workmen's Circle, Branch 417

23. "The Obligations of Youth Today" (1932)   137
    Isadore Bernick

24 ."Some Vital Problems of Negro Labor" (1935)   140
    Frank Crosswaith

25. "Charlatans and Gangsters and Pompous Racketeers" (1938)   144
    Jennie Cohen

26. "With Nazism We All Are at War" (1942)   146
    J. B. S. Hardman

PART III: LIFE OF THE MIND   151

27. "Their Intense Desire to Study" (1893)   153
    Ida Van Etten

28. The Power of Speech and Education (1893)   157
    Education Societies

29. "For That, We Found Time" (interview; 1965)   159
    Pauline Newman

30. A Lower East Side Vacation (1903)   162
    Bernard G. Richards

31. "Jewish Working People . . . Have Lost All Interest
    in the Synagogue" (1905)   168
    Phillip Davis

32. "Peripatetic Philosophers" (1910)   174
    New York Times

33. Yiddish Lectures in Philadelphia (1916)   179
    A. Faynman

34. "A Language That He Wants to and Must Forget" (1918)   183
    B. Sheyfer

35. "America's Most Interesting Daily" (1922)   185
    Oswald Garrison Villard

36. "The Strongest Weapons in the Hands of Jewish Workers" (1924)   191
    United Jewish Workers' Cultural Society

37. The Aims of Workers' Education (1926)   194
    International Ladies' Garment Workers' Union

38. Sexual Relations from a Communist Standpoint (1928)   198
    N. Glass

39. "Sow the Field of Yiddish Cultural Tradition" (1939)   199
    United Council of Yiddish Women's Reading Circles of Detroit

40. "The Responsibility of English-Speaking Jewish
    Intellectuals" (1946)   204
    Nathan Ausubel

PART IV: THE RUSSIAN REVOLUTION   209

41. In Honor of Red Sunday (1906)   211
    New York Times

42. Leon Trotsky on Second Avenue (memoir; 1944)   214
    Louis Waldman

43. "These Glad Days of Russian Freedom" (1917)   219
    Katherina Maryson

44. New York Socialists Contribute to Chaos in Russia (1917)   221
    New York Times

45 "The New Man" (1921)   224
    Moissaye J. Olgin

46. Communism and Freedom of Speech (1925)   228
    Workers' (Communist) Party; Roger Baldwin and Earl Browder

47. A Revolutionary Returns (1929)   239
    Nokhum Khanin

48. Building Communism in the Ukraine (interview; 1981–1982)   249
    Max Granich

49. "G.P.U. Intrigues in America" (1938)   254
    Vanguard

50. Fighting Stalinists and Chasing Girls (memoir; 1965)   258
    Paul Jacobs

51. The Murder of Ehrlich and Alter (1943)   264
    The New International

52. The Soviet Union Reappraised (1956)   268
    Jewish Life

PART V: THE QUESTION OF ZIONISM   277

53. "The Whole Thing Is Ridiculous" (1906)   279
    Jacob Milch

54. "The Jewish Militant" (1906)   286
    Der yidisher kemfer

55. Zionism and Transnationalism (1916)   288
    Randolph Bourne

56. "Should We Change Our Stance toward Zionism?" (1918)   294
    Herts Burgin

57. "The Pogroms in Palestine" (1929)   298
    The Forverts

58. A Revolt of the Oppressed Arab Masses (1929)   301
    Di morgn frayhayt

59. "Jew and Arab" (1934)   304
    Hayim Greenberg

60. "Give Up the Illusion of Building a Jewish Homeland" (1936)   308
    Samuel Weiss

61. Jewish Upbuilding Is Revolutionizing Palestine (1939)   312
    Bezalel Sherman

62. "The Jewish Problem Will Be Solved as Soon as
    the Jews Again Become a Normal Nation" (1943)   316
    Arthur Rosenberg

63. The Final Emancipation of the Jews Is the Struggle
    for Socialism (1946)   319
    Ernest Mandel

64. Jewish National Aspirations Are Not a Violation
    of Marxist Principles (1947)   322
    Albert Glotzer

65. Israel and the World Struggle for Peace and Democracy (1948)   327
    Alexander Bittelman

Recommended Reading   333

Index   335

About the Editor   349

Acknowledgments

I would like to thank a number of people who played important roles in the publication of this book. I am especially grateful to New York University's Goldstein-Goren Center for American Jewish History, under the directorship of Professor Hasia Diner, for inviting me to spend the academic year 2005–2006 as a fellow of the Center. I completed much of the research for this book during that time. Shira Kohn provided valuable and diligent research assistance during my fellowship. At my home university in Madison, Wisconsin, Jeff Broxmeyer, Joel Feingold, and Shira Roza helped locate and transcribe documents. Professor Melissa Klapper generously donated the document by Rose Pastor Stokes. Dr. Alisa Braun translated two documents from the Yiddish. Ariel Eisenberg helped with many of the annotations. Professors Jill Fields, Daniel Katz, and Sarah Stein offered insightful comments on the book's introduction, as did the anonymous readers for New York University Press. Finally, I wish to thank my editors, Ciara McLaughlin and Eric Zinner, who patiently and carefully shepherded the book through all its stages.

Introduction

The Jewish-Socialist Nexus

──────── TONY MICHELS ────────────────────────

1890: New York City's knee-pants workers go on a general strike, forcing their bosses to sign union contracts for the first time. 1892: an anarchist attempts to assassinate one of America's leading industrialists. 1916: eight hundred workers assemble in a Philadelphia hall to hear a Yiddish lecture on "Revolutionary Motifs in World Literature." 1919: an up-and-coming labor lawyer is elected to the New York State Assembly on the Socialist Party ticket, only to be expelled, along with four other Socialists, a year later. 1929: a Los Angeles judge sentences five women to San Quentin for flying the Soviet flag at a summer camp in the San Bernardino Mountains. 1947: the Communist Party USA calls for the establishment of a Jewish state in Palestine. These disparate events provide glimpses into the long, complicated involvement of Jews in American socialism, a history in which class conflict, political repression, revolutionary fervor, and universalistic visions of humanity collided into and intermixed with faith in American democracy, striving for economic success, and commitment to Jewish group solidarity. Along the way, Jews redefined who they were, as both individuals and a community, as they joined with like-minded people of all backgrounds to remake American society. What produced this convergence between Jews and socialism? And what were its ramifications? The story begins in the late nineteenth century.

As a distinct phenomenon in the United States, Jewish socialism came into existence in the 1880s with the birth of the Jewish labor movement.[1] The movement arose from the masses of Yiddish-speaking Jews who immigrated to the United States from the Russian Empire, Austria-Hungary, and Romania between the 1880s and 1920s. Numbering more than two million, they crowded into America's major urban centers, where they encountered harsh working and living conditions. Long workdays, low pay, mistreatment by bosses (usually other immigrant Jews who had worked their way up), dirty sweatshops, and substandard dwellings provided the ingredients of collective hardship. In response, many immigrants took to protest and self-organization, building a movement that had, at its inception, few antecedents in eastern European Jewish life.

The Jewish labor movement encompassed an array of trade unions, political parties, and voluntary associations centered in New York City, home to the world's largest Jewish population, but active in cities across the country. Organizationally decentralized, the Jewish labor movement was also ideologically diverse. Within its ranks, proponents of various brands of socialism—social democracy, communism, anarchism, and left-wing versions of Jewish nationalism—vied for popular support. They often differed fiercely and occasionally violently with one another, but Jewish socialists of all persuasions occupied common ground in their desire to create a cooperative, egalitarian society, freed from poverty and bigotry.

The Jewish labor movement was arguably the largest upsurge of activism in American Jewish history. Although we cannot determine precisely how many joined its ranks, statistics provide some measure. A quarter of a million Jews belonged to the socialist-led United Hebrew Trades, an umbrella organization composed of union locals (especially, but not only, located within the garment industry) with predominantly Jewish memberships. The socialist daily *Forverts*, the most widely circulated Yiddish newspaper in the world and a powerful actor in American Jewish life, boasted more than two hundred thousand readers in the years following World War I. The Arbeter Ring (Workmen's Circle) fraternal order counted eighty-seven thousand members at its peak in the 1920s.[2] Beyond the realm of formal institutions, an untold number of individuals marched in parades, participated in rent strikes and consumer boycotts, crowded around soapboxes, and flocked to celebrations and fund-raisers for one cause or another.[3] How many of those men and women considered themselves dedicated socialists or just casual participants? Historians will never know exactly. What we do know is that tens of thousands of immigrant Jews accepted the leadership of radicals, joined organizations they founded, and absorbed many of their ideas, not so much as doctrines but as "a whole climate of opinion that cemented, both socially and intellectually, a Jewish world in turmoil," to quote the historian Moses Rischin.[4] In deed and thought, Jewish radicals challenged established customs, ways of thinking, and dominant institutions within the Jewish community and American society broadly.

The Jewish labor movement did not arise in a vacuum. It emerged in cooperation with the general American socialist movement, which, in the nineteenth century, was dominated by German immigrants, the most numerous immigrant group to the United States between 1840 and 1890. Germans imported two main schools of thought from their country of origin. One was social democracy, which had developed a formidable theoretical literature stretching back to Karl Marx. In its broad outlines, social democracy held that class conflict, advanced by unions and labor-based political parties (the relative importance of each was a matter of debate), would lead to the abolition of capitalism through either revolution or gradual social transformation (another matter of contention). The other, less popular, school of socialist thought was anarchism, which, in the German case, grew out of social democracy. Anarchists rejected social democracy's emphasis on practical organizational work and instead proclaimed violent confrontation—not at some future point but immediately—the best method to topple capitalism. Anarchists also differed from social democrats in the ideal society they wished to create. Whereas social democrats sought to harness the means of production under the control of a strong state, anarchists wanted to destroy the state altogether and replace it with decentralized forms of government and economic production.[5] Anarchism and, to a greater extent, social democracy exerted strong influences on late-nineteenth-century immigrant Jews, despite the fact that few of them had any prior exposure to socialism in their countries of origin. (Not until the 1900s did socialism become a mass movement among Jews in eastern Europe.) German immigrant socialists, most of them Gentiles, provided ideological tutelage and, beyond that, financial assistance and organizational models to immigrant Jews.[6] They helped to launch the Jewish labor movement and link it permanently to broader American labor and socialist organizations.[7]

The Jewish labor movement reached mass proportions during the first two decades of the twentieth century, coinciding with socialism's greatest successes in U.S. history. During this time, the Socialist Party, founded in 1901, emerged as the political focal point of American radicalism, encompassing a number of ideological currents from agrarian populism to Marxism to anarcho-syndicalism. The Socialist Party reached far beyond German immigrants. At its high point in 1912, the party had almost 118,000 members across the country: native-born Americans and immigrants, blacks and whites, proletarians and farmers, members of the middle class and the poor. Eugene V. Debs, the party's leader, garnered 915,000 votes, or 6 percent of the popular vote, in his 1912 presidential bid. Socialists scored twelve hundred election victories across the country and controlled a number of city governments, including those of Milwaukee, Wisconsin; Butte, Montana; Flint, Michigan; and Berkeley, California. The Kansas-based Socialist newspaper

Appeal to Reason was, for a time, the most popular political weekly in the United States, with a peak circulation of 750,000. In the realm of organized labor, Socialists controlled a number of important unions, including the Brewery Workers, the United Mine Workers, the International Association of Machinists, and the predominantly Jewish International Ladies' Garment Workers' Union (ILGWU).[8] Such advances boosted the confidence of Jewish radicals. As immigrant outsiders, they understood that they could not go it alone; their ultimate success or failure depended on the fortunes of socialism as a whole. During the first two decades of the twentieth century, many thousands of Jews had reason to believe that a socialist society could be achieved in their lifetimes.

A number of factors thus converged to render socialism a potent force among immigrant Jews: the sudden appearance of a large and rapidly growing Jewish working class, the early support of German radicals, and the general growth of socialism in American society. One could cite other factors. There was the leading role played by left-wing intellectuals, idealistic men and women who established the Jewish labor movement and shaped it in a socialist mold. Another factor was the predominantly Jewish composition of the garment industry in New York City, the locus of the Jewish labor movement. On the Lower East Side in 1897, 75 percent of the workforce in clothing manufacturing was Jewish. Over time, a greater number of non-Jewish immigrants, Italians especially, entered the garment industry, but Jewish bosses and employees continued to predominate. In this mostly Jewish context, the socialist message of class against class resonated strongly. As Eli Lederhendler has argued, Jewish workers tended to believe that "it was not their Jewishness but their status as immigrant labor that determined their plight. They were therefore willing to see Jewish issues as subsidiary to class issues."[9] Yet another factor was the absence of traditional structures of Jewish communal authority capable of acting as a restraining force. Unlike Catholic priests, rabbis lacked any real power to check socialism's strength. Intellectuals, activists, and labor leaders thus enjoyed a wide-open field in the Jewish community. And, finally, most immigrant Jews were relatively young and eager to learn new ways of thinking and behaving, which further worked to the benefit of socialists. For all these reasons, and probably still others, socialism found fertile soil in urban Jewish neighborhoods.[10]

Although a product of American conditions, the Jewish labor movement evolved within a transnational context. Organizations, publications, individuals, and ideas moved from country to country, following Jewish migration patterns. During the 1890s, New Yorkers helped give rise to the Russian

Jewish workers' movement by shipping thousands of Yiddish publications to their comrades hampered by censorship in "the old country."[11] After the collapse of the 1905 revolution, thousands of Jewish revolutionaries came to the United States and transplanted new ideologies to their adopted home. Members of the Bund, Russia's first Jewish political party, founded in 1897, were the most numerous.[12] The Bund's program combined Marxism with a form of Jewish nationalism demanding the right of Yiddish-speaking Jews to govern their cultural and educational affairs, or what the Bund called "national cultural autonomy." Less numerous but still significant were the socialist-Zionists. They agreed with Bundists that Russian Jewry constituted an oppressed nation but believed the problems of anti-Jewish violence, discrimination, and poverty could only be solved through the creation of a Jewish homeland in Palestine. Other Jewish socialist parties wanted to establish a Jewish homeland wherever feasible, not necessarily in Palestine, and/or full-fledged Jewish communal autonomy in Russia, not just in the realm of culture and education (as the Bund would have it) but in all communal affairs. Finally, some revolutionaries rejected independent Jewish politics altogether. In the name of "internationalism," they opted for all-Russian parties that advanced no specifically Jewish goals and subsumed the problem of anti-Semitism under the larger struggle against capitalism and autocracy. Such internationalists (a label that should be used advisedly given that many Bundists and socialist-Zionists also laid claim to internationalism) argued that the removal of legal restrictions on Jews within a framework of equal rights for all Russian citizens would lead to the demise of anti-Semitism. "Internationalists" regarded Jewish political parties as reactionary and accused them of perpetuating divisions between Jews and Gentiles.[13] Whatever their differences, members of all these parties swelled the ranks the American Jewish labor movement and introduced new ideas, all the while reinforcing connections between Jews across national boundaries.

Jews were one of many immigrant groups involved in American socialism, but they played a particularly significant role in it during the first half of the twentieth century. They joined socialist unions, voted for radical parties, and read left-wing publications in numbers far out of proportion to their fraction of the general population. As early as 1904, 60 percent of New York City's Jewish voters—more than twice their percentage of the city's overall population—in largely Jewish assembly districts cast their ballots for Socialist Party candidates. Between 1908 and 1912, Jews made up 39 percent of the Socialist Party's membership in New York City, the party's largest demographic component. By 1918, the major needle-trade unions—the ILGWU, the Amalgamated Clothing Workers of America (ACWA), the United Cloth, Hat, and Cap Makers' Union, and the Fur Workers' Union—endorsed the Socialist Party. And between 1914 and 1920, Jewish voters elected nineteen Socialists to city, state, and national offices, thus consummating "a successful political marriage," to quote the historian Melvyn Dubofsky, between the Jewish labor movement and the Socialist Party.[14] Jews, in short, formed the backbone of New York socialism.

Few other immigrant groups contained a comparable number of Socialists during the first two decades of the twentieth century. Italians constituted only 3 percent of the party's New York membership, and Irish immigrants only 1 percent. Indeed, socialism scored no significant "material political gains outside of New York's Jewish precincts," as Dubofsky has found.[15] This is not to suggest that socialism was entirely alien to other immigrants but to note its limited appeal. The predominantly Irish Boot and Shoe Workers Union, for instance, rallied behind the Socialist Labor Party (a forerunner of the Socialist Party) in New England during the 1890s. This alliance, however, lasted only a handful of years before the shoe workers turned in a conservative direction typical of most Irish trade unionists.[16] To cite another example, the Socialist Party's Polish federation numbered less than eighteen hundred members nationwide in 1913, and in Chicago the circulation of the sole Polish-language Socialist newspaper was just eight thousand, not even one-third that of the city's leading Polish paper.[17] Italian immigrants formed hundreds of anarchist groups around the country, but this vibrant sub-culture, whose members participated in countless labor struggles, constituted a small minority within the overall Italian community. By the 1920s, the Red Scare and the upsurge in nativism left Italian immigrant radicalism "profoundly crippled" and soon eclipsed by fascism.[18] German immigrants, the standard bearers of socialism in the nineteenth century, represented the major exception among European immigrants in the United States. Yet Germans ceased playing that role after 1900 when immigration from Germany greatly declined and no longer included large numbers of socialists. As of 1910, Germans made up just 23 percent of New York City's Socialist Party (the second-largest group after the Jews), and the circulation of the German Socialist *Volkszeitung* stood at fifteen thousand, a small figure compared to that of the Yiddish *Forverts*.[19] Pockets of German ethnic socialism survived, most notably in Milwaukee, but most German-Americans had come to situate themselves squarely within the political mainstream by World War I. Finnish immigrants provide a final point of contrast. No group surpassed the Finns in their enthusiasm for radical ideologies. The Socialist Party's

Finnish federation was the party's first and largest foreign-language organization, with 12,600 members in 1913. Furthermore, Finnish radicals developed an all-encompassing social and cultural life fostered in Finnish Halls, a wide network of consumer and farming cooperatives, and a solid Finnish-language press. According to one historian, between 25 and 40 percent of Finnish immigrants identified in some way with the Socialist or Communist parties.[20] Yet the Finns, a small community numbering some 177,000 permanent residents located mainly in mining areas of the upper Midwest, exerted a mainly regional influence.[21] Immigrant Jews, by contrast, outnumbered Finns more than tenfold and settled in major cities close to centers of economic and political power. Sixty percent of Jews lived in Chicago, Philadelphia, and, above all, New York, where they numbered 1.75 million, or almost 30 percent of Gotham's population by 1914. Jews, furthermore, dominated New York's readymade-clothing industry, the largest part of the city's manufacturing sector, and its pro-Socialist trade unions. Jews' large numbers, concentration in major cities, and predominance in a key industry meant that they occupied strategic economic and geographic positions, which served to magnify their already significant presence on the Left.

Jews further differentiated themselves from most other immigrants by their long-term ties to socialism, even during periods when the Left as a whole was weak. This became evident in the 1920s, when the Socialist Party entered the decade nearly decimated by political repression and internal schisms, from which it never fully recovered.[22] In 1920, the year Republican William Harding won the presidency on a promise to return America to "normalcy," a remarkable 38 percent of Jewish voters cast their ballots for Debs, a percentage ten times greater than his overall national vote.[23] True, in later years, the Socialist Party failed to maintain comparable electoral strength among Jews, but the Jewish labor movement's major institutions—the *Forverts*, many Arbeter Ring branches, and the needle-trade unions—remained loyal to the Socialist Party during this otherwise conservative decade.[24] Jewish labor donated large sums of money to the Socialist Party and to myriad causes beyond the immigrant-Jewish world. When the party could no longer afford to maintain its radio station, WEVD (named in honor of Eugene V. Debs), the *Forverts* assumed ownership. When the party decided to launch a weekly newspaper in English, the *Forverts*, the ILGWU, and the ACWA began funding *The New Leader*.[25] And when the party's national office faced insurmountable operating costs, the Yiddish daily once again came to the rescue with a monthly $500 subsidy. "[W]ithout this help," writes one historian of the Socialist Party, "it is doubtful that the office could have remained open."[26]

African American labor leaders also discovered that they could depend on Jewish labor for financial and moral support. The garment unions readily admitted black workers and encouraged their organizing efforts. At the ILGWU's 1922 convention, to cite just one of many examples, the union donated $300 to the *Messenger*, the esteemed radical black labor magazine, and praised African American women, who had entered the waist and dress trade in significant numbers since 1917. Such support to black workers, Hasia Diner writes, "departed quite dramatically from the traditional practice of American organized labor."[27]

The ILGWU and the ACWA also distinguished themselves by their innovative approach to unionism. Whereas most American trade unions sought merely to protect the bread-and-butter interests of their members in terms of wages, length of workday, hiring procedures, and the like, the ILGWU (with 88,000 members in 1924) and the ACWA (with 110,000 in 1929) pursued a broad agenda. Viewing their organizations as instruments of social change, the major garment unions built medical clinics, workers' banks, vacation centers, summer camps, cooperative housing developments, and extensive educational programs for their multilingual memberships.[28] For these experiments, *The Nation* magazine commended the garment unions and their "Jewish socialist theories" for giving "fresh hope to those who believe that labor organization is essential to a modern democratic society."[29] Strictly speaking, the garment unions were not "Jewish," inasmuch as their memberships, especially outside of New York City, included a growing number of members from a variety of immigrant and racial groups. In Chicago, for example, Jews comprised only 25 percent of the eight hundred members belonging to the ACWA's Coat Makers Local. Even so, Jews continued to play the leading role. The "active members were overwhelmingly Jewish," and a "strong Jewish labor consciousness continued to hold sway over an ethnically diverse constituency," as Lizbeth Cohen found in her study of the Chicago working class.[30] The garment unions, in other words, retained a Jewish character even as their ethnic composition changed. This corresponded to the self-perception of Jewish socialists as "tone setters" for the American labor movement. In the words of David Shub, editor of a Yiddish weekly allied with the Socialist Party,

> [Jews] are better acquainted with social-political questions than the average leader of American unions, they have a broader view of labor politics than the average American, and they are also better acquainted than the average American with the history of the socialist and labor movements in

other countries. Every radical and progressive movement in America will be able to recruit its most inspired and enthusiastic adherents from the Jewish masses for a long time.[31]

To be sure, many American labor leaders and union activists did not share Shub's viewpoint. They looked upon Jews not as inspiring visionaries but as troublemakers out of step with the spirit, customs, and authentic purpose of American labor. Such perceptions all too often contained anti-Semitic overtones, but that did not always hold true. Some American labor leaders viewed Jews as simply misguided. As John Frey, editor of the *International Molders' Journal* and an important official in the American Federation of Labor, wrote to Benjamin Schlesinger, the ILGWU president, in 1920,

> You are aware from conversations with me that I have an interest in the large number of Hebrew workers affiliated with the American Federation of Labor. I have not been in agreement with some of them on more than one question, but I felt that this disagreement was due to the fact that the trade-union movement itself did not appeal to them in the same way that it did to me. . . . Many of the Hebrews of my acquaintance were more familiar with the various political, social and economic theories which have been advanced for the welfare of mankind than they were with the practical lessons to be learned from trade-unionism and they looked upon trade-unionism as something which had little more than passing value.
>
> I have believed that, if some of the unions composed largely of Hebrews became familiar with the history of trade-unionism, the conditions under which it developed, the methods it adopted and the sure and certain things which it accomplished, this would be beneficial as it would lead them more and more to give attention to the practical considerations so far as their terms of employment and conditions of labor were concerned.
>
> There is something very active and eager in the Hebrew mind . . . a greater willingness perhaps to study and to analyze than we find among some other peoples, and the danger is, and in fact has been so far as my observations go, that the mental activity has been given over more to the speculative than to the practical.[32]

Frey's perspective, representative of the American Federation of Labor's mainstream, posed a problem to Jewish socialists. Jews could remain "tone setters" only for so long. If the majority of American workers could not be persuaded to choose Schlesinger's view over Frey's, then what would become of socialism? It would either remain narrowly "Jewish" or disappear altogether. Thus, while Jews and the American Left grew inextricably intertwined during the 1920s, this provided no cause for celebration, for it reflected socialism's overall weakness. Shub, for one, recognized this predicament.

No phenomenon better indicated both the persistence of radicalism among Jews and its simultaneous isolation within American society than the rise of the Communist Party. Inspired by the Bolshevik Revolution, the Communist Party resulted from a series of splits within the Socialist Party between 1919 and 1921. The early Communists wanted to create a "vanguard" party that would prepare the most militant workers for an imminent seizure of power and the establishment of a "dictatorship of the proletariat" modeled after Soviet Russia. The party, in reality, fell far short of sparking a revolution and counted only around twenty thousand members during the 1920s. Around 90 percent of the members were immigrants, and among them Jews and Finns once again stood out. The party's Yiddish-speaking section hovered around two thousand members, second in size only to the Finnish section, but that figure hardly conveys the extent of Jewish involvement with Communism. To begin with, Jews joined other foreign-language branches (Russian and Polish, for instance), as well as English-speaking ones. Moreover, Communism's influence extended well beyond the precincts of party organizations. The Communist Yiddish daily *Di frayhayt* reached a readership of twenty to thirty thousand, a higher circulation than any other Communist newspaper, including the English-language *Daily Worker*. Jewish Communists built a network of summer camps, schools, cultural societies, and even a housing cooperative in the Bronx that, all told, encompassed tens of thousands of Communist Party members, sympathizers, and their families. Of greatest potential consequence was the Communist-led insurgency that nearly took over the ILGWU during the mid-1920s and succeeded in gaining full control over the Furriers Union.[33] Communists, in other words, commanded wide support among Jewish workers, including many who did not join the party. Communism's promise to put an immediate end to capitalism, imperialism, and all forms of inequality tapped into utopian longings and fervent emotions evident among immigrant Jews since the early labor strikes of the 1880s. At the same time, however, Communists introduced previously unknown levels of invective in their battles against the Jewish labor movement's established leadership, causing tremendous bitterness and unbridgeable divisions. Furthermore, the Communist Party's blind loyalty to Soviet Russia, a source of prestige during the early, heady years of the Bolshevik Revolution, eventually discredited it and ensured Communism's marginality within the Jewish labor movement. By 1930, it became clear that Communists would not win over most Jewish workers, even as a hard core of Jewish Communists formed a highly organized, Yiddish-speaking subculture that persisted for decades. They, along with the Finns, proved to be the Communist Party's most dedicated supporters over the long term.[34]

Our discussion of Jews and radicalism has, so far, focused on immigrants, but the story does not end with them. Socialism also held strong appeal for second-generation, American born or raised Jews, and this served to differentiate them once again from other ethnic groups, including even the Finns, who generally failed to pass on radical political beliefs to their English-speaking children.[35] Immigrant Jews were unique in their ability to bequeath a radical legacy to the next generation, whose members played an increasingly prominent role across the terrain of the American Left. The second generation did not displace immigrants altogether, but its growing presence signaled a shift in the composition of the Left following Congress's decision in 1924 to cut off mass immigration from Europe. After the nation's doors all but closed, the number and proportion of second-generation Jewish socialists (in the generic sense of the term) grew markedly into the 1940s.

Differences between the generations were substantial. To begin with, most of those who came of age after World War I did not work in sweatshops or factories. Many, in fact, were students, college-educated professionals, and would-be professionals who found their career paths narrowed or blocked by the Great Depression and anti-Semitism.[36] Of course, Americans of any number of ethno-religious backgrounds turned leftward during the "red decade" of the 1930s, when socialism enjoyed its second great upsurge in twentieth-century America. What differentiated second-generation Jews from other Americans was their disproportionately high numbers on the Left, a phenomenon already witnessed among Yiddish-speaking immigrants. In part, this continued disproportionality resulted from a disturbing rise in hostility toward Jews between the two World Wars. Already in the 1920s, Jews suffered growing discrimination in employment, higher education, and myriad social arenas, but these restrictions grew even tighter during the Depression and were accompanied by occasional, yet alarming, outbreaks of violence. Escalation of anti-Semitism within the context of the general economic crisis skewed Jews leftward. Whereas many white Americans could and did respond to the Depression by moving to the political Right, no Jew could make common cause with the assorted isolationist, fascist, and anti-Semitic groups—the Christian Front, the German American Bund, the America First Committee, the Silver Shirts, and on and on—that gained significant followings during the 1930s.[37] While the political Right was patently inhospitable to Jews, the Left held a special attraction. In a socialist organization, one's Jewish background carried no stigma. Anybody with talent and motivation could excel as a writer, orator, theoretician, or organizer and do so for the lofty goal of creating a new America, where outsiders from all backgrounds could one day enjoy equality. This was a powerful ideal for children of immigrants, such as Irving Howe, whose roots were "loose in Jewish soil, but still not torn out, . . . lowered into American soil, but still not fixed."[38] Hostile to all forms of bigotry, socialism offered a universalistic solution to a specifically Jewish predicament.

As Howe's comment implies, American-born radicals differed from immigrants with regard to their Jewish identity. Members of the second generation certainly possessed an awareness of their roots in Jewish families and communities, but they viewed Jewishness as merely part of their backgrounds and of little relevance to their political identities.[39] Rarely did they join self-defined Jewish organizations. With the important exception of socialist-Zionists, American-born radicals usually viewed Jewish affairs as a parochial distraction from the class struggle and other matters of seemingly larger significance. This desire to escape Jewish particularity had antecedents in the immigrant experience. During the early years of the Jewish labor movement, activists used to unfurl banners declaring, "We are not Jews, but Yiddish-speaking proletarians," lest they be mistaken for Jewish nationalists. Still, those "Yiddish-speaking proletarians" participated in entirely Jewish organizations, so that their internationalism amounted to a statement of ideals, not an actual break from the bonds of ethnicity. In any case, such negations of Jewish identity diminished over time, often in direct correlation to persecutions of Jews in Europe. After all, railing against Jewish ethnocentrism hardly seemed the most appropriate way to respond to a pogrom. But among second-generation Jewish radicals—American raised, English speaking, removed from Europe—the desire to trade Jewish ethnicity for the international proletariat ran strong during the interwar period. Not until they confronted the full dimensions of the Holocaust did Irving Howe's generation undertake their own reassessment of Jewish identity.[40]

It may seem dubious, therefore, to include under the rubric of "Jewish radicals" people who rejected Jewish ethnic identification. If such "non-Jewish Jews," to use Isaac Deutscher's famous designation, considered their Jewishness irrelevant, why should historians treat it otherwise?[41] A number of reasons may be cited for doing so. To understand why a disproportionately high number of Jews embraced socialism over an extended period of time,

The East-Side Jew That Conquered Europe

Cartoon of Leon Trotsky, The Liberator, 1920.

historians must consider their ethnic backgrounds: the families, neighborhoods, and communities in which they were raised. Countless young American Jews absorbed socialism at their kitchen tables, in the streets, in summer camps, on school playgrounds, and in working-class housing cooperatives where the atmosphere was thick with socialist ideologies. "Socialism was a way of life, since everyone else I knew in New York was a Socialist, more or less," the writer Alfred Kazin recalls. "I was a Socialist as so many Americans were 'Christians.' I had always lived in a Socialist atmosphere."[42] Family and neighborhood, in other words, predisposed many Jewish children to the Left, even as socialism's universalistic vision offered a path—an "exit visa," in the words of one sociologist[43]—away from the Jewish people. Ethnicity thus served as both a formative influence and a target of rebellion.[44]

A second rationale for including alienated "non-Jewish Jews" in the history of Jewish radicalism is the need for flexible categories. The socialist movement did not divide neatly into discrete Jewish and non-Jewish spheres, even though contemporaries often thought in such terms. Organizations overlapped with one another or were interconnected. One might pay dues both to a Jewish organization and to a non-Jewish one simultaneously. Individuals crossed between Yiddish and English, and sometimes Russian and German. A person with no interest in Jewish affairs or the Jewish people per se often interacted with other Jews primarily. The Russian revolutionary Leon Trotsky, who lived in New York City for two months in early 1917, illustrates the point. Trotsky always insisted that he was not a Jew or a Russian but "a Social Democrat and only that."[45] Yet, in New York, Trotsky moved in Jewish circles, addressed Jewish audiences, and frequented cafés popular with Jews, not because he harbored a special desire to associate with them but because Jews dominated socialism in New York. (The fact that many of them could speak Russian provided further common ground.) Understandably, Jews and Gentiles alike identified Trotsky as a Jew, regardless of his own preference. In March 1920, *The Liberator* magazine ran a cartoon of Trotsky in his role as commander of the Soviet Red Army, with the caption, "Trotsky, the East Side Jew that conquered Russia." Trotsky would have surely cringed at *The Liberator*'s label (and not because he had lived in the Bronx, not the Lower East Side), but the cartoon reflected something important about the intersection of politics and ethnicity in New York. The Left and the Jews were so thoroughly enmeshed that one could not necessarily discern where one ended and the other began. Certain organizations contained so many Jews, and so few Gentiles, that they assumed a quasi-ethnic character. The writer and activist Paul Jacobs discovered this when he joined the Young Communist League (YCL) in the early 1930s. Conversations among Young Communists, mostly children of eastern European immigrants, "were so strewn with the rich Yiddish phrases they had learned from their parents" that the organization acquired a "pronounced Jewish flavor." This appealed to Jacobs, who had recoiled from his parents' bland, middle-class, Reform Judaism. Whereas Jacobs's German-born parents scorned Yiddish, he happily acquired as much of it as he could in the YCL. Communism thereby enabled Jacobs to "reject being Jewish without any feelings of guilt" and, indeed, become more culturally Jewish, in a certain way, by virtue of the company he kept.[46] Rigid divisions between "Jewish" and "non-Jewish" fail to capture such complexities of lived experience.

Finally, many radicals changed their minds about "the Jewish question" over time. Depending on events, circumstances, and ideological trends, an individual might shift directions from one extreme to the other. The Russian Revolution had the effect of pulling Jews toward internationalism, as defined by Moscow, after 1917. Alexander Bittelman, for instance, associated primarily with Bundist émigrés until he became a founder of the American Communist Party in 1919, at which point he renounced the Bund's Yiddish cultural nationalism. Three decades later, following the Holocaust and the Soviet Union's diplomatic support for the establishment of Israel, Bittelman touted Jewish culture and the Jewish state.[47] Albert Glotzer, one of Trotsky's former guards, reached a similar rapprochement with Zionism after World War II.[48] Such trajectories away from and return toward Jewish identification recurred across decades and generations. This back-and-forth dynamic reflected a deep tension between the competing ideological poles of socialist internationalism and Jewish nationalism, both of which had made strong claims on Jewish politics since the nineteenth century. Understanding the long encounter of Jews with the Left is impossible without an appreciation of that tension.

Thus, self-identified Jews and "non-Jewish Jews" should be studied together, not in order to collapse distinctions but because categories of "Jewish" and "non-Jewish" shifted over time and were blurry from the outset. They existed as types in relationship to one another along the same spectrum of socialist politics.

During the 1930s and 1940s, Jews populated the breadth of the American Left, from moderate social democrats to self-proclaimed revolutionaries. Within the Communist Party, they accounted for anywhere between 32 and 45 percent of the Central Committee between 1921 and 1950,[49] perhaps 50 percent of the party's cultural apparatus (those who contributed regularly to Communist-affiliated publications and were members of the John Reed Club, League of American Writers, and National Council of the Arts, Sciences, and Professions), and the "great majority" of party members in New York County, where party membership was highest during the 1940s.[50] Many more Jews could be found in the YCL (which reached a peak membership of twelve thousand) and the constellation of organizations—"front groups," professional associations, civil rights organizations, and fraternal orders—allied with the Communist Party but formally independent of it.[51] The Jewish People's Fraternal Order, the Jewish affiliate of the International Workers Order, reached a membership of fifty thousand at its peak in the mid-1940s, far larger than any other IWO affiliate.[52] And, finally, there was an unknown number of individuals who never joined a formal organization but identified with Communism nonetheless. "[O]ne never needed to hold a membership book to be a YCL or Party member," recalls William Herrick, an American-born Jew who grew up in New York City during the 1930s. "I was a Communist, that was my creed, my religion, my blood."[53] The sociologist Nathan Glazer was certainly correct to point out in 1961 that "no detailed understanding of the impact of Communism on American life is possible without an analysis of the relationship between American Jews and the American Communist Party."[54]

Further out on the left-wing fringe, Jews commanded an even more visible presence in the small Marxist-Leninist parties that grew out of the Communist Party but rejected its authoritarianism and fealty to the Soviet government. These sects rarely numbered more than a thousand members, and usually fewer. The Workers' Party, led by a Polish-born Jew named Max Shachtman, counted around five hundred members, mostly Jews and almost none of them actual factory workers by trade. A Lithuanian-born Jew named Jay Lovestone, a former general secretary of the Communist Party, led a similarly small group of activists and intellectuals, based mainly in the ILGWU. Notwithstanding the small size of the Marxist-Leninist groups, some of them established close ties to unions and exercised influence within broader intellectual circles. They may have been sects, but they were not necessarily irrelevant, and sometimes were even significant, actors in the events and debates of their time.[55]

Yet the largest number of Jews eschewed revolutionary Marxism in favor of moderate forms of socialism. An important part of the Communist Party's appeal in the second half of the 1930s and in the 1940s had to do with its willingness to tone down revolutionary rhetoric and cooperate with liberals and Socialists. The party's slogan, "Communism Is Twentieth Century Americanism," reflected its aim (directed by the Soviet Union) of creating a broadly based, antifascist "Popular Front" starting in 1935. This strategy blurred the line between radicalism and reformism as Communists rallied behind President Franklin Roosevelt and adopted positions that sometimes differed little from those of liberal Democrats. Many members of the Socialist Party also moved toward the Democratic Party. In 1932, the Socialist leader, Norman Thomas, won almost nine hundred thousand votes for president, but, four years later, the party's "Old Guard" concluded that Roosevelt's New Deal reforms, albeit inadequate in and of themselves, nonetheless opened the door to a more expansive social democratic program. Members of the Old Guard broke away to form the American Labor Party (ALP), with the goal of pressuring Democrats to institute a comprehensive welfare state, to increase government regulation of business, and to implement labor and consumer legislation. The ALP's brand of social democracy was considerably more mild than its nineteenth-century forebear, but it possessed real political weight. The ALP (and its successor, the Liberal Party) fielded its own, sometimes victorious, candidates and supported liberal candidates from the two major parties. In doing so, the ALP played a significant role as power broker in city, state, and federal politics.[56] The ALP was not officially a Jewish party, but its strength "rested upon the social base and political culture of distinct New York City Jewish neighborhoods," according to Kenneth Waltzer, author of the ALP's definitive history.[57] Garment unions donated the bulk of financial and organizational assistance to the ALP (the ILGWU alone gave nearly $142,000 to the ALP's 1936 campaign),[58] the *Forverts* gave the party its blessings, and Jews provided most of the votes. Between 20 and 40 percent of Jewish voters cast their ballots for the ALP in the late 1930s.[59] In short, from social democracy to revolutionary Marxism, large numbers of Jews found a political home on the American Left during the 1930s and 1940s.

How, if at all, did the disproportionate involvement of Jews on the Left matter? Did they influence or affect left-wing politics or culture, or American society, in any particular way? Based on existing evidence, we can offer several tentative conclusions. First of all, it seems that Jews played a crucial role in maintaining organizational continuity, especially during the "lean years" of the 1920s. No doubt, the Communist and Socialist parties would have existed without the Jews, but would they have amounted to anything more than small, unimportant sects? Could they have marshaled enough money, personnel, organizational capacity, and ties to mass-membership organizations to have been able to mobilize popular discontent during the economic crisis of the 1930s? There is good reason for doubt. What seems clear, though, is that Jews buoyed membership rolls, financed institutions, and granted both the Communist and Socialist parties an important base in organized labor via the needle trades.[60] During the 1920s, when the Socialist Party found itself in disarray, the Communist Party was stuck in near isolation, and the bulk of organized labor was pushed into retreat, Jews kept radicalism alive and functioning.

The literary historian Alan Wald identifies a specific Jewish contribution in the antifascist crusade of the 1930s and 1940s. "What was perhaps singular in Jewish American left-wing anti-fascism was the political form it took," Wald writes. "Jewish Americans called for unified armed resistance [against fascist and colonial powers] among all the oppressed and expressed a sense of sympathy and solidarity with other non-Jewish groups suffering persecution, especially through colonialism and white supremacism."[61] The high number of Jews engaged in the Communist Party's antiracist work during the 1930s and 1940s reinforces Wald's perception. Consider the case of Harlem. Although Harlem was home to Communists of Finnish, German, Hungarian, Italian, and Latin American backgrounds, Jews accounted for the majority of activists involved in interracial work. As Mark Naison has found, "Jewish-Americans provided many of the shock troops around the Scottsboro issue and constituted the bulk of the white administrators and education directors sent in to the Harlem section," and "almost all of the

Communist teachers and relief workers in Harlem were of Jewish ancestry."[62] In far-away Alabama, Jewish Communists played a similarly conspicuous role in organizing African Americans.[63]

Culture can be identified as a third arena in which Jews made a special mark. Jewish intellectuals, writers, and artists enlarged the cadre of cultural workers in the Communist Party and secured the prominence of theater, music, and literature in party life. Furthermore, Jewish Communists and fellow travelers enjoyed access to the art and entertainment industries, where Jews already had a strong presence. Thus well-situated, Jewish leftists infused mainstream popular culture with prolabor, antifascist, and antiracist themes between the 1930s and 1950s, a phenomenon that the historian Paul Buhle has explored at length. If American popular culture became "labored," to use Michael Denning's term, then this owes much to the links Jews provided between the political Left and the culture industries.[64]

Finally, the sheer size and political strength of Jewish labor enabled it to play a leading role in social reform efforts. In New York City, Jews stood at the forefront of what Joshua Freeman describes as its unique "social democratic polity": an ethnically diverse, working-class-oriented political community committed to affordable housing, decent health care, civil rights, amenable labor laws, and access to the arts and education. The ILGWU's health center, for instance, served as a model of socialized medicine imitated by thirteen other unions serving half a million New Yorkers by 1958. The Arbeter Ring and garment unions provided the seed money for the nonprofit City Center for Music and Drama "to meet the demand for cultural entertainment at reasonable prices." And, perhaps most notably, the ILGWU and the ACWA built large-scale housing cooperatives, containing some 120,000 residents in nearly forty thousand units, constructed between the 1930s and 1960s.[65] On the national level, the ACWA innovated in industrial organization and industrial relations. As the historian Steve Fraser argues, the Amalgamated and its leader, Sidney Hillman, "prefigured the essential ideological assumptions, programmatic reforms, and political realignments characteristic of the New Deal. On the eve of the depression, the Amalgamated was already a leading exponent of social-welfare liberalism, committed to a policy of state-managed capitalism and to the distributive reforms suggested by Keynesian monetary and fiscal theory. Moreover, it had established working relationships with that broader network of liberal businessmen, scientific management technocrats, lawyers, economists, and social workers, and Progressive political reformers which functioned as a kind of shadow government until it actually assumed power during the 'second' New Deal."[66] Indeed, Hillman served as President Roosevelt's primary adviser on labor issues. Clearly, much more research is needed, but these examples suggest ways in which Jews exercised specific influences on the development of the American Left and American society more broadly.

Jewish Radicals comes to an end in the 1950s. This was a decade of crisis for American socialism, when memberships dwindled and leftist ideologies lost their appeal amid renewed economic prosperity, the Cold War, McCarthyism, and the aftermath of Soviet totalitarianism and Nazism. By this time, the majority of American Jews had moved into the middle class, a process that contributed to political deradicalization. Yet the story of Jewish radicalism continued beyond the scope of the present volume. Even during the 1950s, sufficient numbers of Jews retained old affiliations and sympathies so as to provide a bridge to the next generation of radical Jews who appeared in the 1960s.[67] The New Left may be considered a legacy—tenuous in some instances, direct in others—handed down by earlier generations going back to the founding of the Jewish labor movement in the 1880s.[68]

This book attempts to uncover the increasingly remote voices of immigrant Jewish radicals and their children. The documents collected here reflect various perspectives: those of Jews and Gentiles, leaders and rank-and-file activists, outside observers and insiders, and radicals of all sorts. The book's geographic scope stretches from Los Angeles to Soviet Russia, New York to British Mandatory Palestine. The events encompass the obscure and the well-known. Taken together, the documents provide a window onto the world of Jewish radicals. To understand their dreams of equality and happiness for all, to appreciate how these ideals seemed perfectly obtainable, even inevitable, we must turn to the articles, speeches, letters, proclamations, debates, and recollections that Jewish radicals have left behind.

NOTES

1. Individual Jews had previously participated in movements for radical social change but they did not create self-defined Jewish organizations. The feminist leader Ernestine Rose (1810–1892) and the abolitionist August Bondi (1833–1907) provide two such examples. Morris U. Schappes, ed., *A Documentary History of the Jews in the United States, 1654–1875*, 3rd ed. (New York: Schocken Books, 1971), pp. 187–194, 324–332, 352–363.

2. Joseph Brandes, "From Sweatshop to Stability: Jewish Labor between Two World Wars," *YIVO Annual of Jewish Social Science* 16 (1976): 16.

3. Dana Frank, "Housewives, Socialists, and the Politics of Food: The 1917 New York Cost-of-Living Protests," *Feminist Studies* 11, no. 2 (Summer 1985): 255–285; Hadassa Kossak, *Cultures of Opposition: Jewish Immigrant Workers, New York City, 1881–1905* (Albany: SUNY Press, 2000), pp. 131–157; Tony Michels, *A Fire in Their Hearts: Yiddish Socialists in New York* (Cambridge: Harvard University Press, 2005), pp. 69–124; Beth S. Wenger, *New*

York Jews and the Great Depression: Uncertain Promise (New Haven: Yale University Press, 1996), pp. 106–127.

4. Moses Rischin, introduction to *The Spirit of the Ghetto*, by Hutchins Hapgood, ed. Moses Rischin (Cambridge: Belknap Press of Harvard University Press, 1967), p. xxvi.

5. On German immigrant socialists, see Tom Goyens, *Beer and Revolution: The German Anarchist Movement in New York City, 1880–1914* (Urbana: University of Illinois Press, 2007); John H. M. Laslett, *Labor and the Left: A Study of Socialist and Radical Influences in the American Labor Movement, 1881–1924* (New York: Basic Books, 1970), pp. 9–53; Stan Nadel, "The German Immigrant Left in the United States," in *The Immigrant Left in the United States*, ed. Paul Buhle and Dan Georgakas (Albany: SUNY Press, 1996), pp. 45–76; Dorothee Schneider, *Trade Unions and Community: The German Working Class in New York City, 1870–1900* (Urbana: University of Illinois Press, 1994); Elliott Shore, Ken Fones-Wolf, and James P. Danky, eds., *The German-American Radical Press: The Shaping of a Left Political Culture, 1859–1940* (Urbana: University of Illinois Press, 1992).

6. An apparently small number of German-speaking Jews participated in the German-immigrant socialist and labor movement, but they did not form separate Jewish organizations.

7. Michels, *A Fire in Their Hearts*, pp. 41–49.

8. Laslett, *Labor and the Left*, pp. 98–226; David Shannon, *The Socialist Party of America* (Chicago: Quadrangle, 1967), pp. 1–42; James Weinstein, *The Decline of Socialism in America: 1912–1925* (New Brunswick: Rutgers University Press, 1984), pp. 1–118.

9. Eli Lederhendler, *Jewish Immigrants and American Capitalism, 1880–1920: From Caste to Class* (New York: Cambridge University Press, 2009), p. 72. As Lederhendler points out, Jews constituted a minority of garment workers in the state of New York (25 percent in 1897) and the country as a whole (just under 40 percent in 1909). For a discussion of tensions between Italian and Jewish women garment workers, see Susan Glenn, *Daughters of the Shtetl: Life and Labor in the Immigrant Generation* (Ithaca: Cornell University Press, 1990), pp. 188–194. According to Glenn, Jewish women expressed frustration over their Italian co-workers' reluctance to go on strike and join unions in the 1900s and 1910s. Glenn writes, "Typically, Jewish women stressed their own militance and class consciousness in contradistinction to the values and behavior of other groups of women. This was a powerful ethnic myth Jews constructed about themselves and outsiders believed about them" (p. 192). In this case, ethnic divisions did not inhibit but rather reinforced a commitment to socialism on the part of Jews. By the 1920s, however, Italians played an increasingly active role in the garment unions, suggesting that socialism's unifying message overcame interethnic prejudices.

10. For a longer discussion of these factors, see, Michels, *A Fire in Their Hearts*, pp. 6–16.

11. Tony Michels, "Exporting Yiddish Socialism: New York's Role in the Russian Jewish Workers' Movement," *Jewish Social Studies* 16, no. 1 (Fall 2009): 1–26.

12. The party claimed more than thirty thousand members by 1903 and was one of the largest in Russia.

13. Jonathan Frankel, *Prophecy and Politics: Socialism, Nationalism, and the Russian Jews, 1862–1917* (Cambridge: Cambridge University Press, 1981), pp. 90–364, 453–560; Jack Jacobs, *On Marxists and the Jewish Question after Marx* (New York: NYU Press, 1992), Ezra Mendelsohn, *On Modern Jewish Politics* (New York: Oxford University Press), pp. 3–36; Michels, *A Fire in Their Hearts*, pp. 125–178; Enzo Traverso, *The Marxists and the Jewish*

Question: The History of a Debate, 1843–1943, trans. Bernard Gibbons (Atlantic Highlands, NJ: Humanities, 1994).

14. Melvyn Dubofsky, "Success and Failure of Socialism in New York City, 1900–1918," *Labor History* 9, no. 3 (Fall 1968): 363; Charles Leinenweber, "The Class and Ethnic Bases of New York City Socialism, 1904–1915," *Labor History* 22, no. 1 (Winter 1981): 43.

15. Dubofsky, "Success and Failure of Socialism in New York City," p. 365.

16. Laslett, *Labor and the Left*, pp. 54–97; Leinenweber, "The Class and Ethnic Bases of New York City Socialism," 43.

17. That same year, the Polish-language federation of the Socialist Party claimed 1,870 members nationwide. Mary E. Cygan, "The Polish-American Left," in *The Immigrant Left in the United States*, ed. Paul Buhle and Dan Georgakas (Albany: SUNY Press, 1996), p. 159.

18. Jennifer Guglielmo, *Living the Revolution: Italian Women's Resistance and Radicalism in New York City, 1880–1945* (Chapel Hill: University of North Carolina Press, 2010), p. 6. Guglielmo stresses the strength and influence of radicalism, especially anarchism, among Italian immigrants. However, given the fragmented nature of the anarchist movement, the generally small memberships of anarchist groups, the often informal nature of participation, and low circulations of anarchist newspapers (none surpassed fifteen thousand copies), it is difficult to assess the extent to which anarchism enjoyed a popular following in the Italian-immigrant community. The sharp decline in anarchism after World War I suggests that it may have been weaker than it appeared before the world war. Ibid., pp. 141–155, 199–229. Likewise, Philip Cannistraro and Gerald Meyer provide a wide survey of Italian American radicalism, but their data inadvertently reinforces the impression that radicalism among Italian immigrants was weaker than it might seem. Philip V. Cannistraro and Gerald Meyer, "Italian American Radicalism: An Interpretive History," in *The Lost World of Italian American Radicalism: Politics, Labor, and Culture*, ed. Philip V. Cannistraro and Gerald Meyer (Westport, CT: Praeger, 2003), pp. 1–48.

19. Leinenweber, "The Class and Ethnic Bases of New York City Socialism," 43, 48. Nadel, "The German Immigrant Left in the United States," p. 63.

20. Paul C. Mishler, "Red Finns, Red Jews: Ethnic Variation in Communist Political Culture during the 1920s and 1930s," *YIVO Annual* 22 (1995): 142–147.

21. In 1920, there were 149,824 Finnish-born residents in the United States. Many more, perhaps as many as 350,000, came to the United States between 1883 and 1920, but an estimated 30–40 percent returned to Finland or emigrated elsewhere. Tauri Aaltio, "A Survey of Emigration from Finland to the United States and Canada," in *The Finns of North America: A Social Symposium*, ed. Ralph J. Jalkanen (Hancock: Michigan State University Press, 1969), p. 65.

22. Shannon, *The Socialist Party of America*, pp. 99–125; Weinstein, *The Decline of Socialism in America*, pp. 177–233.

23. Ira N. Forman, "The Politics of Minority Consciousness: The Historical Voting Behavior of American Jews," in *Jews in American Politics*, eds. L. Sandy Maisel and Ira N. Forman (Lanham, MD: Rowman & Littlefield, 2001), pp. 152–53.

24. By contrast, "Through the 1920s, Polish-American socialists saw their newspapers and organizations shrink, fold, or merge." Cygan, "The Polish-American Left," p. 169.

25. Ari Kelman, *Station Identification: A Cultural History of Yiddish Radio in the United States* (Berkeley: University of California Press, 2009), p. 96; Paul Kessler, "History of the New Leader" (Columbia University thesis, 1949), p. 3.

26. Shannon, *The Socialist Party of America*, p. 186.

27. Hasia Diner, *In the Almost Promised Land: American Jews and Blacks* (1977; repr., Baltimore: Johns Hopkins University Press, 1995), p. 200; Laslett, *Labor and the Left*, p. 121.

28. Brandes, "From Sweatshop to Stability," 43–48; Steve Fraser, "Dress Rehearsal for the New Deal: Shop-Floor Insurgents, Political Elites, and Industrial Democracy in the Amalgamated Clothing Workers," in *Working-Class America: Essays on Labor, Community, and American Society*, eds. Michael H. Frisch and Daniel J. Walkowitz (Urbana: University of Illinois Press, 1983), pp. 212–255; Bernard Mergen, "'Another Great Prize': The Jewish Labor Movement in the Context of American Labor History," *YIVO Annual of Jewish Social Science* 16 (1976): 394–423.

29. See document 21.

30. Lizbeth Cohen, *Making a New Deal: Industrial Workers in Chicago, 1919–1939* (New York: Cambridge University Press, 1990), p. 47.

31. D. Shub, "Di yidn un di sotsyalistishe bavegung in Amerike," *Der veker*, Sept. 20, 1924, p. 25.

32. John Frey to Benjamin Schlessinger, July 26, 1920, Benjamin Schlessinger Collection, box 1, folder 8, Kheel Center, Cornell University. On relations between Jewish labor and the American Federation of Labor, see Robert Asher, "Jewish Unions and the American Federation of Labor Power Structure," *American Jewish Historical Society* 65, no. 3 (Mar. 1976): 215–227; and Irwin Yellowitz, "Jewish Immigrants and the American Labor Movement, 1900–1920," *American Jewish History* 71, no. 4 (Dec. 1981): 188–217.

33. John Holmes, "American Jewish Communist and Garment Unionism in the 1920s," *American Communist History* 6, no. 2 (Dec. 2007): 171–195; Laslett, *Labor and the Left*, pp. 127–129; Arthur Liebman, *Jews and the Left* (New York: Wiley, 1979), pp. 305–325; Stanley Nadel, "Reds versus Pinks: A Civil War in the International Ladies Garment Workers Union," *New York History* 66 (1985): 49–72: Robert D. Parmet, *The Master of Seventh Avenue: David Dubinsky and the American Labor Movement* (New York: NYU Press, 2005), pp. 31–53.

34. A comparison with Polish immigrants is instructive. In Chicago, Poles were the city's largest immigrant community and made up slightly more than 17 percent of the city's population. However, only 6.5 percent of the Communist Party's members in that city were Poles as of 1930–1931. Jews, by contrast, constituted perhaps 16 percent of the overall population yet 22 percent of the party's membership—the largest portion of its membership. Randi Storch, *Red Chicago: American Communism at Its Grass Roots, 1928–1935* (Urbana: University of Illinois Press, 2009), p. 40. According to a 1925 report by two Polish Communists, "The Poles in this country . . . are more interested in the church than in class-war. . . . All the large Polish organizations in this country are either clerical or nationalistic." B. K. Gebert and M. Marek, "Problems Confronting [the] Polish Section [illegible] Reorganization," Records of the Communist Party of the United States in the Comintern Archives (Fond 515), microfilm edition compiled by the Library of Congress and the Russian State Archive of Social and Political History, reel 15, delo 233, Tamiment Library, New York University. In Los Angeles, according to one Communist source, 90 percent of the Communist Party was Jewish in 1929. Nathan Glazer, *The Social Basis of American Communism* (New York: Harcourt, Brace & World, 1961), p. 221.

35. "The differences in the development of Jewish and Finnish communism were significant in each group's efforts to maintain a radical political culture in an English-speaking context. For the Finns, the identity of radical politics with ethnicity made it difficult to maintain the strength of their culture into the next generation. For the Jews, radical politics became an expression of ethnicity and thus helped define ethnic identity even among English-speaking working-class Jews during the latter part of the 1930s. . . . The Finnish-American Communist culture was unable to pass on the political beliefs and values of the Communist movement to the English-speaking generations; the relationship between Finnish language and radicalism seemed too tight." Mishler, "Red Finns, Red Jews," pp. 148–149.

36. Thus, Harvey Klehr writes, "Many Jewish teachers, social workers, and office workers, facing the double handicap of discrimination and the Depression, were attracted to the CPUSA." Harvey Klehr, *Communist Cadre: The Social Background of the American Communist Party Elite* (Stanford, CA: Hoover Institution Press, 1978), p. 40. Also see Daniel J. Walkowitz, *Working with Class: Social Workers and the Politics of Middle-Class Identity* (Chapel Hill: University of North Carolina Press, 1999), pp. 141–160.

37. Henry Feingold, *A Time for Searching: Entering the Mainstream, 1920–1945* (Baltimore: Johns Hopkins University Press, 1992), pp. 125–154; Howard Sachar, *A History of the Jews in America* (New York: Vintage Books, 1992), pp. 428–464; Beth Wenger, *New York Jews and the Great Depression: Uncertain Promise* (New Haven: Yale University Press, 1996).

38. Irving Howe interview with Grace Schulman, Feb. 10, 1977, printed in *Society* 45 (2008): 355.

39. Alan M. Wald, *The New York Intellectuals: The Rise and Decline of the Anti-Stalinist Left from the 1930s to the 1980s* (Chapel Hill: University of North Carolina Press, 1987), pp. 27–100.

40. Irving Howe, *World of Our Fathers: The Journey of the East Europeans to America and the Life They Found and Made* (New York: Harcourt Brace Jovanovich, 1976), p. 255.

41. Isaac Deutscher, *The Non-Jewish Jew and Other Essays* (Boston: Alyson, 1968), pp. 25–41.

42. Alfred Kazin, *Starting Out in the Thirties* (Boston: Little, Brown, 1965), p. 4.

43. Zygmunt Bauman, "Exit Visas and Entry Tickets: Paradoxes of Jewish Assimilation," *Telos* 77 (1988): 45–77.

44. Arthur Liebman, "The Ties That Bind: Jewish Support for the Left in the United States," *American Jewish Historical Quarterly* 66, no. 2 (Dec. 1976): 285–321.

45. Quoted in Robert Wistrich, *Revolutionary Jews from Marx to Trotsky* (New York: Barnes and Noble Books, 1976), p. 189.

46. See document 5.

47. See document 65.

48. See document 64.

49. The exception was 1940, when the percentage fell to 23 percent. Klehr, *Communist Cadre*, pp. 45–46.

50. Alan M. Wald, *Trinity of Passion: The Literary Left and the Antifascist Crusade* (Chapel Hill: University of North Carolina Press, 2007), p. 180; Glazer, *The Social Basis of American Communism*, p. 221.

51. Glazer, *The Social Basis of American Communism*, p. 220.

52. This amounted to 25 percent of the IWO's total membership.

53. William Herrick, *Jumping the Line: The Adventures and Misadventures of an American Radical* (Oakland, CA: AK Press, 1998), p. 78.

54. Glazer, *The Social Basis of American Communism*, p. 131.

55. Peter Drucker, *Max Shachtman and His Left: A Socialist's Odyssey through the "American Century"* (Atlantic Highlands, NJ: Humanities, 1994), pp. 150–213; Ted Morgan, *A Covert Life: Jay Lovestone: Communist, Anti-Communist, and Spymaster* (New York: Random House, 1999), pp. 105–140.

56. New York's electoral laws permitted more than one party to endorse the same candidate, thus allowing a voter to choose a third party without "throwing away" his or her vote.

57. Kenneth Waltzer, "The American Labor Party: Third Party Politics in New Deal–Cold War New York, 1936–1954" (Ph.D. diss., Harvard University, 1977), p. 182.

58. Parmet, *The Master of Seventh Avenue*, p. 156.

59. Deborah Dash Moore, *At Home in America: Second Generation Jews in New York* (New York: Columbia University Press, 1981), p. 221.

60. Referring to the Trade Union Educational League, a pro-Communist organization led by the union organizer William Z. Foster, James Barrett writes, "The TUEL built its strongest and most durable movement in the needle trades—the International Ladies Garment Workers Union (ILGWU) and the Amalgamated Clothing Workers of America (ACWA), as well as the capmakers' union, the fur workers' union, and other smaller unions." James R. Barrett, *William Z. Foster and the Tragedy of American Radicalism* (Urbana: University of Illinois Press, 1999), p. 126.

61. Wald, *Trinity of Passion*, pp. 181–182.

62. Mark Naison, *Communists in Harlem during the Great Depression* (New York: Grove, 1985), p. 321.

63. Robin D. G. Kelley, *Hammer and Hoe: Alabama Communists during the Great Depression* (Chapel Hill: University of North Carolina Press, 1990), pp. 16, 25, 48, 61–62, 128–129.

64. Paul Buhle, *From the Lower East Side to Hollywood: Jews in American Popular Culture* (London: Verso, 2004); Wald, *Trinity of Passion*, pp. 1–45, 74–145, 176–257. Unlike Buhle and Wald, Denning assigns Jews no special place in the "laboring" of American culture; rather, he includes them among other "plebians" (working-class ethnics and racial minorities) who made their way into the center of American culture starting in the 1930s. Among the forty names he lists as examples, half were Jews. Michael Denning, *The Cultural Front: The Laboring of American Culture in the Twentieth Century* (London: Verso, 1997), pp. 60–62.

65. Joshua Freeman, *Working-Class New York: Life and Labor since World War II* (New York: New Press, 2000), pp. 67, 105–124, 129–142.

66. Fraser, "Dress Rehearsal for the New Deal," pp. 212–213.

67. Maurice Isserman, *If I Had A Hammer . . . : The Death of the Old Left and the Birth of the New Left* (New York: Basic Books, 1987); Judy Kaplan and Linn Shapiro, eds., *Red Diapers: Growing Up in the Communist Left* (Urbana: University of Illinois Press, 1998).

68. On Jews and radicalism during the 1960s, see Stanley Rothman and S. Robert Lichter, *Roots of Radicalism: Jews, Christians, and the Left* (New York: Oxford University Press, 1982); Michael E. Staub, *Torn at the Roots: The Crisis of Jewish Liberalism in Postwar America* (New York: Columbia University Press, 2002).

Awakenings

How did young men and women first encounter socialism? What did socialism mean to them? To shed light on these questions, this section features excerpts from the autobiographies of five prominent radicals. The Communist leader Alexander Bittelman became radicalized as a thirteen-year-old boy in his hometown of Berdichev in the Russian Empire. His father, although a pious man, had grown close to the Bund and enrolled the young Usher, Alexander's given name, in the local party organization. Bittelman originally perceived socialism as "dream-images of some bright and joyful future, something like what would happen when the Messiah arrived." He soon discarded his religious beliefs and became a wholehearted revolutionary, a process familiar to many eastern European Jews who made the leap from traditional Judaism to socialism.

Unlike Bittelman, who immigrated to the United States in 1912, most of the Jewish labor movement's early participants became radicalized in the United States. The seminal event was the Great Upheaval of 1886, the largest strike wave hitherto in America's history. One person swept up by the unrest was a young cloak maker in Chicago named Abraham Bisno. From German-immigrant radicals Bisno learned about capitalism and the capacity of ordinary workers to change the system. Bisno converted to socialism and went on to become a union activist in Chicago. A different narrative of discovery comes to us from the anarchist firebrand Emma Goldman. According to her autobiography, she turned to the radical movement not out of economic misery but in search of emotional and intellectual fulfillment. Anarchism "offered an escape from the grey dullness" of her life in Rochester, New York, where she felt stifled by "the everlasting talk about money and business." Another anarchist, Lucy Lang, discovered in Chicago's radical circles access to interesting people, opportunities for education, and a means to protest social injustices. Lang describes her political awakening as a product of the inequities of work and family life.

Paul Jacobs's account departs from the conventional trope of conversion. The only native-born American included in this group of autobiographers, Jacobs encountered socialism not on a picket line or in the streets or in an underground movement but among classmates in his Bronx high school. Those intellectually precocious sons of eastern European immigrants led Jacobs to the Young Communist League and, later, the Trotskyist Socialist Workers Party. Jacobs experienced socialism not as a sudden discovery but as a gradual coming of age. Many more autobiographies exist, and they undoubtedly describe various trajectories. If the five accounts included here contain a common theme, it is a sense of awakening to a world of new ideas and possibilities, initiating a process of self-discovery that would lead to an understanding of themselves as actors in a world-historical movement for liberation.

"When I Went Home I Was Aflame" (memoir; c. 1925)

ABRAHAM BISNO

Born in Russia, Abraham Bisno (1866–1929) immigrated to Chicago in 1881. He worked as a cloak maker and joined the local labor movement in 1886 amid the massive, nationwide strike wave known as the Great Upheaval. Bisno later worked as a factory inspector for the state of Illinois and as an official in the Chicago Cloakmakers' Union, among other unions. His autobiography appeared posthumously in 1967.

One fine day—it must have been in the month of April [1886]—Mother came from the butcher shop and informed us all at the shop that there was going to be a meeting in De Koven Street Hall. I asked her what the meeting was and she said she didn't know but it was her understanding that everybody would come together in that hall on Saturday afternoon. I asked her who told her and she said she didn't know except the women in the butcher shop spoke about it.

On the next Saturday afternoon I went over along with other people from our shop and a few other shops to that meeting. When I came there I found that there were a great many people assembled around the hall, that the hall was closed and the Bohemian who owned the saloon and the hall was at the door explaining to everybody that nobody rented a hall and that he knew nothing about the meeting. Some of us assembled thought that we had better make up a purse of a few dollars to rent the hall. He said he wouldn't open the door for less than three dollars, that that was cheap but that he figured that we were going to patronize the saloon downstairs in addition to that. We chipped in a nickel apiece and had three dollars and even more on short notice. The man opened the hall and within fifteen or twenty minutes we packed the hall to capacity, standing room, mainly. The hall was ordinarily used for a Bohemian dance-hall so there was only standing room.

There was a great tumult; everybody was talking and nobody knew quite what this whole thing was about until one of our men asked everybody to be quiet and began to speak. He thought that the price for labor was very low; that the treatment we were receiving in the shops was very undignified; that the examiners were exacting very fine work and were sending the work back over and over again; and that the operators wanted too much money for their work and since he was a contractor, he couldn't pay it because the employers downtown wouldn't pay him enough to pay it; that he didn't know who called this meeting together and intimated that even if he did know, he wouldn't say, because he believed that somebody would carry the message to the employers. But anyway he didn't know, but no matter who called it, it is good that we are here to jointly talk matters over and see if we can't find any way to remedy conditions as they are.

Next to him another man got up, said that he was a sewing-machine operator, that all he was able to earn was seven dollars a week, that it was hard to support his family on that income, that he didn't have steady work, that in between seasons there was a great deal of slack,[1] that he hardly earned enough in busy seasons to be able to live during the slack seasons. He assaulted vigorously the conduct of the contractors. "Who tells you to bring work home when it don't pay enough?" he asked. "Why do you bring work home without knowing how much you are going to be paid for it; don't take that kind of work; never mind about the independence of the employers; if they don't need you, they'll give you no work anyway. Since they are giving you work, they evidently need that work and if they need it, you can be independent too. Tell them just how much you want for the work, don't take it unless you get your price; then you will not kick if we want a decent wage for our work."

An old presser got up to talk. He described how hard he worked; he made motions with his hands showing how hard it was to work with a twenty-two-pound iron, that he was all in after a day's work, that the hours were too long, that those operators wanted to eat up everything, that nothing was enough for them, and that unless they worked for less there wouldn't be enough left for the presser, and that he was afraid he was going to contract consumption like other people that he knew from the charcoal gas in the burner and from too hard work.

To make a long story short, we continued that meeting all along until very late at night. I remember I got up, too, to say something, but when I noticed everybody looking at me my knees began to bend, blood rushed into my head and I would have collapsed right then and there if it wasn't for a friend of mine who evidently sensed my predicament and got ahold of me, led me to a chair, and sat me down. One of the men, an operator, finally took the floor. He was a very healthy-looking chap, rather raw and rough in appearance, and in a loud voice shouted something to this effect, that tomorrow nobody goes to work and that Monday we will select a committee to visit the manufacturers and tell them that the foremen and superintendents should treat us decently and that the examiners should not be so "stuck up."

Someone in the audience asked him what we were going to do in case some of our people would not abide by the decision and would work tomorrow. He answered in an even louder voice than before, raising his first, "If they work we'll break their heads for them." Our young fellows thought it would be quite fun to have a fight with those that would work and before very long there was quite an understanding amongst the young fellows as to where and when they would meet, early in the morning, to visit shops and see whether or not they were closed.

On Sunday morning I got up quite early and with quite a mob we spread out to the numerous shops in the neighborhood. Most of them did not work, but we did find some that did; they were afraid that if they stopped working the employers would not give them any work at all, and we threatened with violence, took off the thread from the machine, shut off the fire in the coal grates, abused them very vigorously, made fun of them, and stationed a committee there to watch right in the shop and see that nobody worked. In those days there were not shops separated from the homes; they were all in homes; homes and shops were all together. The casual entrance of strangers into one of these shops was quite a normal proceeding; we had as yet not acquired the habit of knocking at the door before we went in.

Later on Sunday we met again in the same hall and selected spokesmen to visit the manufacturers. I remember that we had great difficultly in selecting the spokesman; everybody was afraid that he would be considered by the manufacturers as the ringleader of the fight and, therefore, wished to be excused from the appointment. Those that were the most vigorous spokesmen, though, were the men who did not get work to do directly from the manufacturer but were working for the contractors in their outside shops. They did not mind going because the manufacturers would not reach them individually by boycotting them.

After great efforts a committee was constituted; it wasn't appointed by anybody nor was it self-appointed. Simply the consensus of opinion formed itself on a group of men who, while they represented the people and knew the interests of the people, were at the same time not within the reach of the employers for purposes of employers' retaliation. The point that the committee itself might be bribed by the manufacturers was quite an item of discussion in our group. It was said that, as for the contractors, they might be offered more work and better work and be induced to line up on the side of the manufacturers. The element of personal honestly was an item of consideration, and after a great deal of haggling and discussion, the committee was formed.

By that time the manufacturers themselves organized into a group to fight the strikers, and when the committee appeared before the manufacturers, they were told that in the judgment of the manufacturers the people had no grievance to complain of, that they had better go back to work. And after that report was brought back to our mass meeting we felt quite forlorn and bitter, and resolved to continue the strike. When I say resolved, I don't mean that a vote was taken, not even a pro-and-con discussion. It was simply a sort of consensus of opinion to continue the strike without anyone in the group questioning its being so.

This situation took place in the month of April, 1886. By that time the preparation of the Knights of Labor[2] for the eight-hour strike in May [had begun] and the agitation was conducted very rigorously. Someone in our group had invited the authorities of the Knights of Labor to appear before our meeting and advise us to join the Knights of Labor. A delegation from the Knights of Labor did appear before our meetings and advised us to join their organization, and we did join their organization. All I then knew of the principles of the Knights of Labor was that the motto of the Knights of Labor was, One for All, and All for One. I think they did require us to pay a dollar per man for membership and when we paid our membership we were all initiated with great ceremony, took an oath of allegiance to the organization, and were made full-fledged members.

All this was done while the strike was going on and we had plenty of time to elect our officers, formulate our demands for the manufacturers, and establish some kind of an organization. As I think of the matter now, I am still very much puzzled. As I said before, nobody knew who called the first meeting, nor did anyone know who called the Knights of Labor to send us a delegation. Prior to our entry as members of the Knights of Labor we had not even selected a secretary or a chairman of our meetings. None of us knew that an organization must have a chairman, a secretary, rules of order, a mode of proceeding by which one man will get the floor while the other man will have to sit quietly and wait until he is through—all of that was unbeknown to us. When we went out on strike we didn't have a vote; when we agreed to join the Knights of Labor we didn't have a vote; when we sent a committee to the manufacturers we didn't have a vote. This whole thing was done in a way that appeared to us spontaneous with no objecting voice. In rare cases somebody did say something; nobody knew whether he agreed or dissented with the established public opinion, but there were no men or issues discussed. As I think it over now after so many years have elapsed, I am satisfied that there must have been someone who did, with premeditation and intent, help to cause that whole movement; first causing the rumor to be spread that the meeting was to be held; after that meeting was held, he must have so informed the authorities of the Knights of Labor and caused them to send a delegation to our meeting. It must also have been the same party that suggested that we join the Knights of Labor, but if anyone did all these things at all, he did it very cleverly, because up to now, our people do not know how it all came about.

Under the rules of the Knights of Labor, the only people authorized to negotiate with the employers were those selected by the Knights of Labor themselves, members out of their own central committee. It was those appointed who undertook the job of visiting the employers again and negotiating with them the settlement of our strike. I remember the personnel in that committee, a bricklayer and an Irish blacksmith and a man that was in business of some kind, not a working man at all. The rules of the Knights of Labor were that every man was entitled to membership except a saloon-keeper and a lawyer, so that there did belong to the Order, storekeepers, landlords, clergymen, and all kinds of people. It was not a labor organization in the strict sense of the word. Its claim was not made based purely on the claim of labor and their interests, but it was based on the claim of ethics, morality, justice, etc.

When this commission went over to our employers, they were received very well, but were informed that we were being led by a lot of anarchists, men who do not know what they want, and since this commission didn't understand our trade nor the nature of our complaint, they came back quite converted to the side of the employers. There was a complete misunderstanding between ourselves and the committee of the Knights of Labor. As I can formulate it now after so many years have passed, I think the following would set this complicated situation in order. We wanted to establish a regular day's work; while there was some movement for an eight-hour day, we would have been glad to agree with the manufacturers for a ten-hour day, because we were working unlimited hours and we would even give in to a comprehensive regulation of overtime, but we knew we couldn't do it ourselves, we couldn't establish a uniform work day by our own authority and wanted the manufacturers to agree on the justice of our claim and co-operate with us to enforce that regulation by failing to send or give work to the shop that failed to live up to that standard.

The manufacturers made fun of us and the delegation of the Knights of Labor saw it in the same light. They claimed, which was true, that we were not working directly for them at all; they said, we give work to a contractor and he can do what he darn pleases; he can work four hours a day so far as we are concerned. But we knew that unless there was an agreement betwcen manufacturers, contractors, and working men on this standard of ours, competition among ourselves would cause in the future, as it did in the past, a condition making for an unlimited working day. On that point this committee of the Knights of Labor ridiculed us, saying, "Can't you fellows take care of yourselves, establish your own rules in your shops?" so that they even made some of our own people believe it was true. The argument was: if you want to work ten hours, work ten hours; don't work any more if you don't want to. But since the work was distributed in a large number of separate shops, especially homes where a union cannot possibly keep control on the time their members work, we knew we were right, but at the same time, we could not possibly convince the authorities in the Knights of Labor of the justice of our claim.

Substantially the same argument was made in reference to wages. The argument was made by the employers in something of the following manner: it isn't us that make you work cheap; you're working piecework. If you don't want to make a certain garment for a certain price, don't take it out from the shop; we don't force you to take it. And that was true. They couldn't force us; this was a free country. But our poverty, our want, and our need did force us and we ourselves competing with each other reduced our wages below a living point. It was the intention, through the organization, to enter into an understanding with the employers to mutually cause contractors and working people to set the price for labor before the merchandise left the factory so that the price for the labor would not be subjected to competition between ourselves, but that a standard of wages would be set and maintained in the interests of all concerned. It was this point that the manufacturers would not agree to and made our committee themselves believe they were right.

There was another point at issue and that was, we claimed that work should not be given to anyone in a shop that did not belong to the union. The manufacturers maintained that meant they were to become organizers for our union and they said to the committee, if these fellows want to organize a union they can do it themselves without calling on us to organize them. On this point we were even more vitally interested than on both of the previous points because we sensed the intent of the employers. We knew that unless that point was acquiesced to on the part of the employers, shops that didn't belong to the union would get all the work; union shops would be left in the cold, which would disintegrate our organization and destroy whatever we had accomplished. On this point, too, the committee agreed with the employers. They said, if you fellows want to belong to the Knights of Labor, nobody interferes with you—this is a free country. And it is. Except that freedom to starve militates against freedom to belong to a union, and that the right to be a member of a union must be accompanied by the right to get work and earn one's living while he is a member.

The Knights of Labor commission did not convince us, but did encourage materially the scab element amongst our people; it encouraged the contractors; it encouraged such relatives of the contractors who were working in the shops and constantly, by agitation and persuasion, threw cold water on our enthusiasm. But the bulk of our membership was solid on all these three points, and after four weeks or so on strike, we did take a vote on the subject and the majority in favor of the strike were more than three to one.

Something else happened in the course of the life of that strike that may be recorded now as being of significance.

A mass meeting was called to explain the nature of the strike and encourage our membership. By that time there were already a great many of us that were in actual want for food, house wants, etc., and when that meeting was called a man was invited to speak to us in the German language and he made a wonderful speech. August Spies[3] was his name. He was the editor of a German socialist or anarchist newspaper. He was then engaged in the agitation for the eight-hour movement, but he didn't only advocate an eight-hour movement. He advocated something much more significant. He told us that we were experiencing now in the modern industrial life a class struggle; that we, all of us, were on the side of the poor; that the capitalists, the employers of all kinds, traders and storekeepers of all kinds, the government, legislators, judges and policemen and clergymen were all classed as either capitalists or their henchmen and were arrayed against us; that humanity was suffering because humanity was disinherited, that the property of the country belongs all to that one class and their henchmen; that the great body of the people, the working man and the poor, had no property, and depended for their living only on wages that they received from the employing classes; that under the present economic order of things there was such a thing as an iron law of wages which meant that no working man got more than bare subsistence for his work so that he might be able to live and work for his boss and reproduce, in his children, working men for ever after to keep his employer in wealth, nay, he said, even in riotous luxury; that the employers were maintaining their horses and their dogs in better houses than their men; that the employers worked their horses less than they did their men and that was because when a horse died because of being exhausted the employer lost something, while if the working man died, he was easily replaced with no damage to the boss.

August Spies went on to say that we are now living in an industrial age that keeps on developing itself, that working men are acquiring more and more significance as the real producers of all wealth; that the employers, tradesmen and their henchmen, clergymen and government officials, are all a useless lot, bound to be overthrown by labor in the course of time, and that historically labor was assigned the mission to overthrow the capitalist class, and that while he wished us good luck in our strike to establish a regular working day, raise the price for our work, and enforce decent treatment on the part of the employers, he thought that this was only a minor effort and that the real effort to be made by us [was] to destroy root and branch the present capitalist order of things and establish a co-operative commonwealth. He advised us to read anarchist and socialist newspapers and books on the labor movement; there were then and there in the hall a number of German socialists and English socialists and anarchists who distributed amongst us appeals, leaflets, newspapers, in both German and English, and we were advised to read them so that we might educate ourselves in the cause of labor, the theories of socialism and anarchism, and on the general labor movement. He spoke in very plain German, and since Yiddish is only a dialect of German, I understood almost every word he said and it made a great impression on me.

On that night when I went home I was aflame; the whole argument struck me like lightning and went all through me. I had heard ideas that I had never heard before in my life and they seemed to express the very thoughts that were in my inner consciousness. He's right, I thought; we are disinherited, the property of the country does belong to the rich; all we get out of it is a bare living for very hard work; there must be a chance to improve conditions; there are so many of us, there ought to be no division of opinion amongst us; we ought to all unite, all the working people from all trades, and support what he calls the Labor Movement for the purpose of getting redress. [...]

On May the fifth, 1886, an event happened that had a great influence on the fortunes of our strike. It was known to us that the manufacturers had taken into their own downtown shops a number of our own people to do the work inside instead of in the outside shops. In doing so, they were able to satisfy their trade and prolong the strike for an indefinite time. When we got together in the hall in conversation between ourselves, it was made clear that unless we could go downtown and stop those shops, we would be obliged to lose the strike; but that was a big job. The manufacturers had their factories on the upper floors of great big buildings. To break into these buildings it would be necessary to have a great many men. It was necessary to overawe the non-union people in the shops, and make them come down in the hope that we might win the strike.

A consensus of opinion was formed that in this special case the committee to stop those shops must be composed of our entire membership. About six hundred of us left the De Koven Street Hall, which was about a mile or more distant from the factory, and walked in a body downtown. When we crossed the Van Buren Street bridge, something happened that we had not expected to happen at all, namely, patrol wagons came in on us from all sides of the city in large numbers; hundreds, probably thousands of policemen were unloaded in very short order in the cloak district; every policeman had a billy and they began to chase us and beat us unmercifully. Within ten or fifteen minutes the whole neighborhood there was cleared; none of us were arrested, none of us had time to do anything that would warrant an arrest. We simply were there, but a great many of us were beaten up very badly, and we ran for our lives.

When we finally got back into the hall, and got over our astonishment at the treatment we received at the hands of the police, we bound up the wounds of those of us that were badly hurt and tried to find some explanation for what had happened. We found the following. One of our men was able to read German. He said that he read in the newspaper that there was a great big factory about a mile away called the McCormick Harvester Works; that the people over there were out on a strike for an eight-hour day; that two or three days past they had had a meeting near the factory; that the policemen had tried to disperse them and they killed a number of men; that yesterday these men held a meeting at Haymarket Square and the policemen there, too, tried to disperse them; that someone threw a bomb under the policemen's patrol wagon, which killed a number of policemen and wounded a great many more; that the police were out to stop those gatherings and were looking for the men who threw the bomb; that it was said in the newspapers that the men who threw the bomb were anarchists; that one of them was this same August Spies who had lectured before us, and because of that, any assembly on the street by working men was prohibited, and the fact that so many of us had gone downtown at the same time made the police think we were anarchists prepared to throw bombs and make riots and therefore they treated us the way they did. Now if this man that knew German had told us about it before we went, we probably would not have gone, because we were not a fighting crowd in the real sense. Most of the people were elderly tailors who had never had a fight in their lives, but we didn't know anything about it and therefore got ourselves into trouble. That event, too, demoralized materially the strike.

After May 1, 1886, picketing became absolutely impossible. The police arrested all pickets, even two or three. The attitude on the part of the police was practically the same as though the city was under martial law. Labor unions were raided, broken up, their property was confiscated, the police used their clubs freely. Arrests were made without any cause, and the life of a working man was not quite safe when out on strike. [. . .]

The experience I had during the strike and the speeches we heard in these six weeks left a great impression on me. The vision of a united labor party and labor unions held out to me great possibilities. Life was very hard then; in busy season we worked almost to death; in slack season we suffered great want; the American atmosphere influenced our people much. As we became more and more Americanized we noticed the difference between the standard of living of the Americans and that of ourselves, and we suffered by comparison. The stores were full of merchandise, the streets of downtown were filled with well-dressed crowds, healthy-looking, neat-appearing people, while we, during our busy season, were unwashed, unkempt, ill-dressed and overworked and, during the slack season, underworked and underfed. The housing, too, we noticed was much better amongst the older emigrants and the American families. They didn't have to keep their shops in their houses; they were able to keep their homes straight, while we, who had the shops in our living room, had pretty poor places to live in. We had to rent poor houses, too, because for shop and business purposes they wouldn't rent us any decent houses, and so a sense of rebellion found its way into our minds. We didn't know much about the labor movement except what we learned from the strike, but enough was left from the strike to cause us a great deal of thinking and dissatisfaction.

Two years after the strike, in 1888, the sense of this dissatisfaction began to take shape. The more intelligent of us, especially the younger people, began to talk when we visited each other about the labor movement. We didn't know very much what it was, but we talked about it anyway. In those two years I [had] learned to read English and had already read a number of radical papers and some pamphlets on the labor movement. Some I got in the public library, and some I got from friends.

There was a young doctor in the neighborhood, who I was told was a revolutionary in Russia, named Knopfnagel. It was to his house that I went to ask him what socialism was and what was a revolutionist. He gave me some pamphlets and some explanation which frankly I didn't understand well. He spoke to me abut the French Revolution in the eighteenth century; about the nobility and the bourgeoisie; how the nobility had outlived their usefulness and through the development of the town, and the merchant, the bourgeoisie had acquired social power; how they had become able to function in social life in competition with the nobility when a struggle ensued which made for the French Revolution, and modern capitalism was born; that modern capitalism now is outliving its usefulness; that the proletariat is acquiring social significance and social power, and that there will be a revolution in the immediate future overthrowing capitalism, expropriating the expropriators and establishing socialism.

What is socialism—a co-operative commonwealth, a partnership of all people, mainly the working people, the abolition of rate, interest, and profit, the establishment of a brotherhood of men, and that may only be done through the class struggle. Something in the line of the same thing was the talk that August Spies delivered in 1886 and for which he and his friends were tried and sentenced to be hung, and were hung on November the 11th, 1886. Somehow to me the social problem wasn't as simple as all that, and I said to him that I only vaguely understood what he was thinking about, and that I would have to read up on the subject. He advised me to read and study the science of political economy, books by Adam Smith, David Ricardo, Karl Marx, Proudhon, and others. He also advised me to read up on natural science, Darwin's books and Herbert Spencer's. He told me to read the history of the world and special histories of Rome, England, France, Germany, and Italy. He suggested to me that I form a club to be called an educational organization by which we would invite lecturers, establish a reading room, and establish a center for labor unions, etc.

There were about seven or eight men, friends of mine, to whom I first submitted the idea of forming that club. Most of them felt like myself about life; the work was too hard, remuneration too small, and general living conditions unbearable. We got together one night at our house after work and formed an organization called the Workingman's Educational Society. We taxed ourselves some thirty-five or forty dollars to rent a floor of rooms on

Canal Street, painted and hung out the sign on the front door, had circulars printed both in Yiddish and English announcing the formation and establishment of that club, and on the back of the circulars was a statement of its aims and objectives. All eight of us circulated around the Jewish community and distributed about a thousand copies announcing a meeting on a certain Saturday night. We bought forty chairs all told and we had a mob of several hundred people on the first night. They couldn't all get in and they crowded themselves into these rooms so that we were almost choked. Knopfnagel made the first speech; honestly, none of us understood a word of what he said, but we appreciated the spirit in which he said it and were quite enthusiastic and applauded him to beat the band.

After this response we were very much encouraged; we took in forty members on the first night; each man paid a dollar initiation fee and promised to pay twenty-five cents a meeting. We thought we had lots of money. We formed all kinds of committees; a committee to reorganize the coatmakers, and a committee to organize a branch of the Socialist Party[4] but some of us disagreed right then and there on the Socialist Party. They were inclined to be anarchists by saying that political action was all a mistake; that it was simply a source for corruption; that the state was the property of the capitalists, was in the hands of the capitalists, was the tool of the capitalists, that we couldn't get it even if we had a majority, that the institution of the state could not be for purposes other than capitalist purposes; that labor didn't need a state; that labor simply needed an industrial co-partnership, a brotherhood, for purposes of living and producing together, only for needs and not for sale. And so a discussion arose that lasted for months and months, until finally we separated, the anarchists separate, and the socialists separate, and some in between, but others neither anarchists or socialists, were desirous of belonging to our club for purposes of education and sociability. [. . .]

The group in the Educational Society assumed upon themselves the duty of advance guard and considered it about time to organize the coatmakers again, because in 1886 and 1887 their union was destroyed. I remember once some such experience as this: "Moisha," said I, to one of the men working in the same industry, an operator, "over in the Educational Society we are going to have a meeting tonight on Canal Street right near Bunker. You'll see a sign at the door, go right up about eight o'clock at night."

"What's the meeting for?" said he.

"We are going to increase the membership in our socialist society," I said to him, "and I want you to be a member."

"Socialist society? What do these fellows want?"

"Well, we want to establish a co-operative commonwealth; we want to make a revolutionary change in society; we want to abolish rent, interest and profit; we want to have the working man acquire the entire property of the country and abolish private property and other means of production and distribution; we will then be able to work shorter hours and earn more money and live better. You know how you live, now. When your children are sick, you haven't any money for a doctor; you very seldom can pay your rent on time; you always owe money to the grocery store; you're damn glad to get credit; both you and your family never are well clothed or well dressed or well housed. The people who employ you think of you as just so much labor power; they care for and are interested in you less than in their cattle; the same is true of your landlord and the entire class of parasites; hangers-on, etc. That's why we want working men to join the Socialist Society, to establish a condition of things making life worth living."

Moisha listened to me patiently and when I was through he said to me, "Tell me, will we have to convert everybody to that? All the Jews?"

"Yes," said I.

"What about the Germans? Them, too, won't we?"

"Yes."

"And the Irish, the French, everybody in Chicago?"

"Yes."

"And then the people all through the state, won't we?"

"Yes."

"And the people of all other states, won't we?"

"Yes."

"You're crazy," says Moisha.

"Why?" says I.

"You won't live long enough to see it and your children's children won't live long enough to see it. Why should I worry my head about the distant future when I've got all I can do to take care of the troubles I am facing today? Haven't I got enough worries now? So that you want to put me next to some more. You're crazy, I tell you, I won't come." And Moisha didn't come.

Some weeks afterwards, I met the same Moisha. "Moisha, over at that Educational Society on Canal Street," I said to him, "there is going to be a meeting tonight. I want you to come."

"What's it for," says Moisha, "socialism? To take care of my great-grandchildren?"

"No, Moisha, this time you're wrong. It is to organize the cloak-workers into a labor union."

"A labor union, what's that?"

"Well, you know the season is approaching; those manufacturers pay almost nothing for work, and when we have no union, even when the season is in full blast, we won't get enough out of it to be able to live decently. Then we work too damn hard—fifteen to eighteen hours a day. But if you organize into a union now before the season is on, we will stop work just before the season develops and make the manufacturers give us decent prices for our labor and establish some rules in the industry under agreements with the manufacturers making for our benefit—work less hours, get more money, get better treatment, and what not."

"Are we going to do it this season or wait like you socialists will?"

"No," I said, "we'll go to it right away."

"That sounds reasonable," he said. "You can count on me; I'll be there."

Source: Abraham Bisno, *Union Pioneer* (Madison: University of Wisconsin Press, 1967), pp. 67–89.

NOTES

1. The period during the year when little or no work was available.

2. Originally a secret society founded in 1869, the Knights of Labor became the country's largest labor organization, open to women and African Americans as well as white men. In its push for an eight-hour workday, the Knights emphasized peaceful negotiations and boycotts over strikes, believing the former to be more effective strategies. After the collapse of the eight-hour movement in 1886, the organization began to decline and was superseded by the American Federation of Labor as the premier labor organization in the United States.

3. August Spies (1855–1887), prominent Chicago labor activist, working, first, within the Socialist Labor Party and, later, as editor of the German-language anarchist newspaper *Arbeiter-Zeitung*. Spies is perhaps best known for his involvement in Chicago's 1886 Haymarket Square incident, which led to his conviction of conspiracy to commit murder and his execution by the state of Illinois.

4. Bisno must mean the Socialist Labor Party; the Socialist Party was not established until 1901.

"I Saw a New World Opening Before Me" (memoir; 1931)

EMMA GOLDMAN

Emma Goldman (1869–1940) was one of America's most famous proponents of anarchist thought, free speech, sexual freedom, and homosexual rights. Amid the Red Scare of 1919, the federal government deported Goldman to Soviet Russia, then in the throes of revolution and civil war. Goldman soon became disillusioned with the Bolshevik Revolution and left the country for western Europe. She was barred from returning to the United States for the remainder of her life.

It was the 15th of August 1889, the day of my arrival in New York City. I was twenty years old. All that had happened in my life until that time was now left behind me, cast off like a worn-out garment. A new world was before me, strange and terrifying. But I had youth, good health, and a passionate ideal. Whatever the new held in store for me I was determined to meet unflinchingly.

How well I remember that day! It was a Sunday. The West Shore train, the cheapest, which was all I could afford, had brought me from Rochester, New York, reaching Weehawken at eight o'clock in the morning. Thence I came by ferry to New York City. I had no friends there, but I carried three addresses, one of a married aunt, one of a young medical student I had met in New Haven a year before, while working in a corset factory there, and one of the *Freiheit*, a German anarchist paper published by Johann Most.[1]

My entire possessions consisted of five dollars and a small hand-bag. My sewing-machine, which was to help me to independence, I had checked as baggage. Ignorant of the distance from West Forty-second Street to the Bowery, where my aunt lived, and unaware of the enervating heat of a New York day in August, I started out on foot. How confusing and endless a large city seems to the new-comer, how cold and unfriendly!

After receiving many directions and misdirections and making frequent stops at bewildering intersections, I landed in three hours at the photographic gallery of my aunt and uncle. Tired and hot, I did not at first notice the consternation of my relatives at my unexpected arrival. They asked me to make myself at home, gave me breakfast, and then plied me with questions. Why did I come to New York? Had I definitely broken with my husband? Did I have money? What did I intend to do? I was told that I could, of course, stay with them.

"Where else could you go, a young woman alone in New York?" Certainly, but I would have to look for a job immediately. Business was bad, and the cost of living was high.

I heard it all as if in a stupor. I was too exhausted from my wakeful night's journey, the long walk, and the heat of the sun, which was already pouring down fiercely. The voices of my relatives sounded distant, like the buzzing of flies, and they made me drowsy. With an effort I pulled myself together. I assured them I did not come to impose myself on them; a friend living on Henry Street was expecting me and would put me up. I had but one desire—to get out, away from the prattling, chilling voices. I left my bag and departed.

The friend I had invented in order to escape the "hospitality" of my relatives was only a slight acquaintance, a young anarchist by the name of A. Solotaroff,[2] whom I had once heard lecture in New Haven. Now I started out to find him. After a long search I discovered the house, but the tenant had left. The janitor, at first very brusque, must have noticed my despair. He said he would look for the address that the family left when they moved. Presently he came back with the name of the street, but there was no number. What was I to do? How to find Solotaroff in the vast city? I decided to stop at every house, first on one side of the street, and then on the other. Up and down, six flights of stairs, I tramped, my head throbbing, my feet weary. The oppressive day was drawing to a close. At last when I was about to give up the search, I discovered him on Montgomery Street, on the fifth floor of a tenement house seething with humanity.

A year had passed since our first meeting, but Solotaroff had not forgotten me. His greeting was genial and warm, as of an old friend. He told me that he shared his small apartment with his parents and little brother, but that I could have his room; he would stay with a fellow-student for a few nights. He assured me that I would have no difficulty in finding a place; in fact, he knew two sisters who were living with their father in a two-room flat. They were looking for another girl to join them. After my new friend had fed me tea and some delicious Jewish cake his mother had baked, he told me about the different people I might meet, the activities of the Yiddish anarchists, and other interesting matters. I was grateful to my host, much more for his friendly concern and *camaraderie* than for the tea and cake. I forgot the bitterness that had filled my soul over the cruel reception given me by my own kin. New York no longer seemed the monster it had appeared in the endless hours of my painful walk on the Bowery.

Later Solotaroff took me to Sachs's café on Suffolk Street, which, as he informed me, was the headquarters of the East Side radicals, socialists, and anarchists, as well as of the young Yiddish writers and poets. "Everybody forgathers there," he remarked; "the Minkin sisters will no doubt also be there." For one who had just come away from the monotony of a provincial town like Rochester and whose nerves were on edge from a night's trip in a stuffy car, the noise and turmoil that greeted us at Sachs's were certainly not very soothing. The place consisted of two rooms and was packed. Everybody talked, gesticulated, and argued, in Yiddish and Russian, each competing with the other. I was almost overcome in this strange human medley. My escort discovered two girls at a table. He introduced them as Anna and Helen Minkin. They were Russian Jewish working girls. Anna, the older, was about my own age; Helen perhaps eighteen. Soon we came to an understanding about my living with them, and my anxiety and uncertainly were over. I had a roof over my head; I had found friends. The bedlam at Sachs's no longer mattered. I began to breathe freer, to feel less of an alien.

While the four of us were having our dinner, and Solotaroff was pointing out to me the different people in the café, I suddenly heard a powerful voice call: "Extra-large steak! Extra cup of coffee!" My own capital was so small and the need for economy so great that I was startled by such apparent extravagance. Besides, Solotaroff had told me that only poor students, writers, and workers were the clients of Sachs. I wondered who that reckless person could be and how he could afford such food. "Who is that glutton?" I asked. Solotaroff laughed aloud. "That is Alexander Berkman.[3] He can eat for three. But he rarely has enough money for much food. When he has, he eats Sachs out of his supplies. I'll introduce him to you."

We had finished our meal, and several people came to our table to talk to Solotaroff. The man of the extra-large steak was still packing it away as if he had gone hungry for weeks. Just as we were about to depart, he approached us, and Solotaroff introduced him. He was no more than a boy, hardly eighteen, but with the neck and chest of a giant. His jaw was strong, made more pronounced by his thick lips. His face was almost severe, but for his high, studious forehead and intelligent eyes. A determined youngster, I thought.

Presently Berkman remarked to me: "Johann Most is speaking tonight. Do you want to come hear him?"

How extraordinary, I thought, that on my very first day in New York I should have the chance to behold with my own eyes and hear the fiery man whom the Rochester press used to portray as the personification of the devil, a criminal, a bloodthirsty demon! I had planned to visit Most in the office of his newspaper some time later, but that the opportunity should present itself in such an unexpected manner gave me the feeling that something wonderful was about to happen, something that would decide the whole course of my life.

On the way to the hall I was too absorbed in my thoughts to hear much of the conversation that was going on between Berkman and the Minkin sisters. Suddenly I stumbled. I should have fallen had not Berkman gripped my arm and held me up. "I have saved your life," he said jestingly. "I hope I may be able to save yours some day," I quickly replied.

The meeting-place was a small hall behind a saloon, through which one had to pass. It was crowded with Germans, drinking, smoking, and talking. Before long, Johann Most entered. My first impression of him was one of revulsion. He was of medium height, with a large head crowned with grayish bushy hair; but his face was twisted out of form by an apparent dislocation of the left jaw. Only his eyes were soothing; they were blue and sympathetic.

His speech was a scorching denunciation of American conditions, a biting satire on the injustice and brutality of the dominant powers, a passionate tirade against those responsible for the Haymarket tragedy[4] and the execution of the Chicago anarchists in November 1887. He spoke eloquently and picturesquely. As if by magic, his disfigurement disappeared, his lack of physical distinction was forgotten. He seemed transformed into some primitive power, radiating hatred and love, strength and inspiration. The rapid current of his speech, the music of his voice, and his sparkling wit, all combined to produce an effect almost overwhelming. He stirred me to my depths.

Caught in the crowd that surged towards the platform, I found myself before Most. Berkman was near me and introduced me. But I was dumb with excitement and nervousness, full of the tumult of emotions Most's speech had aroused in me.

That night I could not sleep. Again I lived through the events of 1887. Twenty-one months had passed since the Black Friday of November 11, when the Chicago men had suffered their martyrdom, yet every detail stood out clear before my vision and affected me as if it had happened but yesterday. My sister Helena and I had become interested in the fate of the men during the period of their trial. The reports in the Rochester newspapers irritated, confused, and upset us by their evident prejudice. The violence of the press, the bitter denunciation of the accused, the attacks on all foreigners, turned our sympathies to the Haymarket victims.

We had learned of the existence in Rochester of a German socialist group that held sessions on Sunday in Germania Hall. We began to attend the meetings, my older sister, Helena, on a few occasions only, and I regularly. The gatherings were generally uninteresting, but they offered an escape from the grey dullness of my Rochester existence. There one heard, at least, something different from the everlasting talk about money and business, and one met people of spirit and ideas.

One Sunday it was announced that a famous socialist speaker from New York, Johanna Greie,[5] would lecture on the case then being tried in Chicago. On the appointed day I was the first in the hall. The huge place was crowded from top to bottom by eager men and women, while the walls were lined with police. I had never before been at such a large meeting. I had seen *gendarmes* in St. Petersburg disperse small student gatherings. But that in the country which guaranteed free speech, officers armed with long clubs should invade an orderly assembly filled me with consternation and protest.

Soon the chairman announced the speaker. She was a woman in her thirties, pale and ascetic-looking, with large luminous eyes. She spoke with great earnestness, in a voice vibrating with intensity. Her manner engrossed me. I forgot the police, the audience, and everything else about me. I was aware only of the frail woman in black crying out her passionate indictment against the forces that were about to destroy eight human lives.

The entire speech concerned the stirring events in Chicago. She began by relating the historical background of the case. She told of the labour strikes that broke out throughout the country in 1886, for the demand of an eight-hour workday. The centre of the movement was Chicago, and there the struggle between the toilers and their bosses became intense and bitter. A meeting of the striking employees of the McCormick Harvester Company in that city was attacked by police; men and women were beaten and several persons killed. To protest against the outrage a mass meeting was called in Haymarket Square on May 4. It was addressed by Albert Parsons, August Spies, Adolph Fischer, and others, and was quiet and orderly. This was attested to by Carter Harrison, Mayor of Chicago, who had attended the meeting to see what was going on. The Mayor left, satisfied that everything was all right, and he informed the captain of the district to that effect. It was getting cloudy, a light rain began to fall, and the people started to disperse, only a few remaining while one of the last speakers was addressing the audience. Then Captain Ward, accompanied by a strong force of police, suddenly appeared on the square. He ordered the meeting to disperse forthwith. "This is an orderly assembly," the chairman replied, whereupon the police fell upon the people, clubbing them unmercifully. Then something flashed through the air and exploded, killing a number of police officers and wounding a score of others. It was never ascertained who the actual culprit was, and the authorities apparently made little effort to discover him. Instead orders were immediately issued for the arrest of all the speakers at the Haymarket meeting and other prominent anarchists. The entire press and *bourgeoisie* of Chicago and of the whole country began shouting for the blood of the prisoners. A veritable campaign of terror was carried on by the police, who were given moral and financial encouragement by the Citizens' Association to further their murderous plan to get anarchists out of the way. The public mind was so inflamed by the atrocious stories circulated by the press against the leaders of the strike that a fair trial for them became an impossibility. In fact, the trial proved the worst frame-up in the history of the United States. The jury was picked for conviction; the District Attorney announced in open court that it was not only the arrested men who were the accused, but that "anarchy was on trial" and that it was to be exterminated. The judge repeatedly denounced the prisoners from the bench, influencing the jury against them. The witnesses were terrorized or bribed, with the result that eight men, innocent of the crime and in no way connected with it were convicted. The incited state of the public mind, and the general prejudice against anarchists, coupled with the employers' bitter opposition to the eight-hour movement, constituted the atmosphere that favoured the judicial murder of the Chicago anarchists. Five of them—Albert Parsons, August Spies, Louis Lingg, Adolph Fischer, and George Engel—were sentenced to die by hanging; Michael Schwab and Samuel Fielden were doomed to life imprisonment; Neebe received fifteen years' sentence. The innocent blood of the Haymarket martyrs was calling for revenge. [. . .]

Johanna Greie spoke of Parsons, Spies, Lingg, and the others as socialists, but I was ignorant of the real meaning of socialism. What I had heard from the local speakers had impressed me as colourless and mechanistic. On the other hand, the papers called these men anarchists, bomb-throwers. What was anarchism? It was all very puzzling. But I had no time for further contemplation. The people were filing out, and I got up to leave. Greie, the chairman, and a group of friends were still on the platform. As I turned towards them, I saw Greie motioning to me. I was startled, my heart beat violently, and my feet felt leaden. When I approached her, she took me by the hand and said: "I never saw a face that reflected such a tumult of emotion as yours. You must be feeling the impending tragedy intensely. Do you know the men?" In a trembling voice I replied: "Unfortunately no, but I do feel the case with every fibre, and when I heard you speak, it seemed to me as if I knew them." She put her hand on my shoulder. "I have a feeling that you will know them better as you learn their ideal, and that you will make their cause your own."

I walked home in a dream. Sister Helena was already asleep, but I had to share my experience with her. I woke her up and recited to her the whole story, giving almost a verbatim account of the speech. I must have been very dramatic, because Helena exclaimed: "The next thing I'll hear about my little sister is that she, too, is a dangerous anarchist."

Some weeks later I had occasion to visit a German family I knew. I found them very much excited. Somebody from New York had sent them a German paper, *Die Freiheit*, edited by Johann Most. It was filled with news about the events in Chicago. The language fairly took my breath away, it was so different from what I had heard at the socialist meetings and even from Johanna Greie's talk. It seemed lava shooting forth flames of ridicule, scorn, and defiance; it breathed deep hatred of the powers that were preparing the crime in Chicago. I began to read *Die Freiheit* regularly. I sent for the literature advertised in the paper and I devoured every line on anarchism I could get, every word about the men, their lives, their work. I read about their heroic stand while on trial and their marvelous defence. I saw a new world opening before me.

Source: Emma Goldman, *Living My Life*, vol. 1 (1931; repr., New York: Dover, 1970), pp. 3–10.

NOTES

1. Johann Most (1846–1906), former Reichstag deputy in Germany and the foremost leader of the anarchist movement in New York during the 1880s and 1890s.

2. The person Goldman refers to is probably Hillel Solotaroff (1865–1921), a prominent anarchist who frequently lectured and wrote in Yiddish.

3. Alexander Berkman (1870–1936), Russian-born Jewish anarchist, who served fourteen years in prison for an attempted assassination of Henry Clay Frick, the chairman of the Carnegie Steel Company (see document 11). He was deported with Goldman to Russia in 1919.

4. Goldman refers here to the Haymarket Square incident. On May 4, 1886, an anarchist-led demonstration in Chicago's Haymarket Square became violent when the police attacked the rally and a bomb subsequently exploded. In the ensuing chaos, eight police officers and a larger, though undetermined, number of demonstrators died. Though the source of the bomb remained unknown, police swiftly arrested eight prominent labor

leaders and convicted them of conspiracy to murder, largely on the basis of their authorship of revolutionary texts and their association with anarchism, rather than on any direct connection to the May 4 bombing. Of those eight men, four of them—August Spies, Albert Parsons, George Engel, and Adolph Fischer—died on the gallows. Louis Lingg committed suicide the night before his scheduled execution. The final three men—Oscar Neebe, Samuel Fielden, and Michael Schwab—had their death sentences commuted to life imprisonment and were released from prison in 1893 by Illinois's newly elected governor, John Peter Altgeld, who acknowledged the grave miscarriage of justice to which the men had been subjected.

5. A German immigrant active in the Socialist Labor Party, Johanna Greie (b. 1864) lectured frequently on women's rights and other subjects.

3

The World of Socialism and Revolution (memoir; 1963)

ALEXANDER BITTELMAN

Born in the Ukraine, Alexander Bittelman (1890–1982) joined the Bund at an early age and immigrated to the United States in 1912. He became a founding member of the Communist Party in 1919 and remained a high-ranking official over the following four decades. Between 1953 and 1957, Bittelman served a three-year prison term for violating the Smith Act, a federal statute making it illegal to advocate the overthrow of the U.S. government. The Communist Party formally condemned his planned memoir, excerpted here in print for the first time, and expelled him in 1960.

[. . .] The Bund, of which I became a member on a certain memorable day, was an underground organization of Jewish workers of a socialist and revolutionary nature. Its full name was The General Jewish Labor Alliance of Lithuania, Poland and Russia. The "Bund" is the Jewish [word] for "Alliance."

I was 13 years old at the time. Naturally, I couldn't yet know or fully understand the program and theory of the "Bund." But I knew Isaak—the man who enrolled me into membership. I knew him as the man who used to come to my father's house, usually in the evening, to speak to the shoeworkers about their grievances and their needs. These were secret meetings, to be protected from the curiosity of the police and the gendarmery, at which Isaak tried to organize a shoeworkers' trade union. This was something that the Czar's government considered a crime against the state and punished accordingly. Isaac knew this and so did the shoeworkers. But they went ahead and actually organized a trade union. This was in the summer of 1902, the first organization of its kind in my own city, the place of my birth, the city of Berdichev, the province of Kiev.

Isaak was also the man I used to hear at these nightly meetings agitate the shoeworkers to go out on strike to rectify their grievances against their employers. And strike they did, later the same summer, which was the first shoeworkers' strike in the history of Berdichev. So, when Isaak enrolled me into the "Bund," I knew I was joining something that was trying to help improve the conditions of life of my father and my father's friends. And those conditions, as I already knew them all too well, needed lots of betterment to make them bearable.

But there was much more to Isaak's nightly talks than the organization of a trade union and preparations for a strike. He spoke of all the injustices and brutalities of the entire existing social and political systems. He did so in plain words, as I remember, but very feelingly. About the doings of the Czar's government to the workers, the Jews and all the people, he spoke with anger but in a quiet and low voice. He was no orator and the immediate environment of these meetings didn't lend itself very well to oratorical performances.

The audiences usually consisted of about 20 people, shoeworkers, of course. Most of them were seated on the floor of our living room. The rest made themselves comfortable on the few available chairs and on the floor of the kitchen, these being all the rooms we had. These two rooms were however much more spacious and livable than the other two little rooms in which I found my family when I rejoined them in Berdichev. We had moved to another part of town, called in Jewish "The Peskes," probably from the Russian "Pesky," the Sands. This was a much poorer neighborhood than the other, the poorest in Berdichev, but the dwelling was better.

Now, Isaak would sit by the small table all by himself. He would gaze into the faces of his listeners in the poorly lighted room which had only one small kerosene lamp hanging on the wall, and talk to them as man to man and from heart to heart.

My own position during these meetings was on the bed, my father's and mother's bed, the only bed in the house, which stood by one of the walls in the living room. My younger sister and brother would be sleeping in the one corner and I would be reclining in the opposite corner. Father and mother would sit on the edge of the bed facing the audience.

I was intensely interested in Isaak's talks and tried not to miss a word. From him I first heard elaborate explanation of the meaning of such words as socialism, revolution, democratic republic; also class struggle, exploitation, capitalists and proletariat. These latter four words already had to me concrete meanings at the time: workers fighting their exploiters—the capitalists. But socialism, revolution and republic these were to me then only dream-images of some bright and joyful future, something like what would happen when the Messiah arrived.

It is quite possible that this was the way Isaak himself spoke of socialism and revolution. But then it may have been my own way of understanding it. Now, I also remember very distinctly that Isaak used to speak of Abe Lincoln and of the slaves whom he liberated; and this was supposed to have some very close relation to what he was urging his listeners to do—to overthrow their slavery and become free men. Since then Abe Lincoln became one of my heroes.

And another thing that impressed me in Isaak's talks. That was the way he would speak of the sufferings of the Jewish workers as Jews. According to him, the Jewish workers in Czarist Russia were carrying a double burden: the burden of exploited workers which they shared with all other workers in Russia and the burden of an oppressed and discriminated and persecuted nationality. Never before have I seen the special Jewish miseries in the Czar's empire in quite that light.

Well, this was Isaak. So, when my father brought me to Isaak's house on a wintry Saturday afternoon, with the intention of having him enroll me into the Young "Bund," I already knew that Isaak was one of the leaders of the local organization of the "Bund" and that the "Bund" itself is something very good and important.

Perhaps I should say right here that Isaak was a "Litvak," that is, he was born and brought up in Lithuania. One could tell that by the way he spoke his Yiddish. Mother especially used to comment on this somewhat critically since Isaak's Yiddish had overtones and undertones that sounded very strange to her Ukrainian-Jewish ears. But she also respected Isaak for, like all Litvaks, he was a scholarly person and a man with a keen mind. Here, in passing, I would note that the "Bund" leaders in Berdichev that I came to know at the time were all Litvaks. Why so? Possibly, because the "Bund" was born in the Lithuanian part of the Czar's empire.

I also found later that Isaak was a workingman, a gloves maker and that he was working in a small shop operated by a relative of Sholem Aleichem, a brother or brother-in-law. The shop was located on Bielopol street, I believe. Isaak lived by himself, in one spacious room, with lots of books in it, which he rented from a family of friends.

Isaak greeted us, father and me, with restrained friendliness. He asked us to sit down and inquired of father how things were going with him after the strike. The strike was successful in many ways. It reduced the workday to ten hours from twelve and increased various piece rates. Father said things were much better than before but the bargaining for the piece rates was quite a job. The shoeworkers' strike lasted about a week. During the strike, the police arrested a number of strikers, father among them, releasing them shortly.

Of me Isaak wanted to know how things were after the printers' strike, which took place a couple of weeks before the shoeworkers'. I remember feeling a bit embarrassed but I did answer that there is now a little more free time in which to read, to meet friends, and earnings too are somewhat better. But the change from before isn't very great.

Father was pleased with my answer. Isaak agreed. Of course, he said, really great improvements couldn't be gotten while the Czarist regime lasts. Say, you want an eight-hour day and wages to make a decent living and similar things. How are you going to get it? First of all you need political freedom. You need the right to organize legal trade unions, to hold meetings openly and freely, and to strike for your demands without the government trying to suppress the strike. But how can you get political freedom, which the workers in the West are enjoying, without getting rid of the Czar and establishing in Russia a democratic Republic, like in France and in America?

That reminded me of what Yachnis used to tell me about the trade unions and short workday in the western countries. And I liked the idea very much. Well, said Isaak, that's what the "Bund" is trying to accomplish, together with the other organizations of socialists and revolutionists.

But the democratic Republic isn't yet Socialism, is it? That was my question and father looked rather proudly at me. Isaak said: Oh, no. That isn't Socialism at all. France had a revolution, got rid of its Kings, and established a democratic Republic but they still have capitalism. And, in America, they had a revolution, kicked out the English king, made themselves a democratic Republic but the capitalist system is still there. Socialism is still to come.

That answer didn't quite satisfy me. I wanted Isaak to explain why can't we go straight ahead and get Socialism instead of a democratic Republic? Isn't Socialism the only way to a happy and joyful life? Sure, said Isaak, sure. Socialism is the only true answer to our needs. But without a democratic Republic the working class of Russia could not organize itself and become strong enough to overthrow the capitalist system together with the Czarist regime. We need political freedom for that.

This did make sense but my dreams were of Socialism. Now I knew that, when I saw the poverty and suffering of my parents, of their friends and relatives, and as a boy of 9 or 10 pleaded with God, in my prayers, for justice and fairness, tears flowing down my cheeks, I knew now, in talking with Isaak, that I had been pleading for Socialism. I also knew now that Socialism was not only a dream. Workers all over the world were fighting for Socialism, that's what Isaak impressed on me, and some day they are bound to win.

Alright, I said to myself, let's get the democratic Republic so we can go ahead and win Socialism for ourselves. I thought at the time of "The International," the song I learned lately and loved so much to sing.

I knew, of course, that father had brought me to Isaak to have him enroll me into the "Bund." Isaak knew that, too. Turning to me, he said: Well, Usher [*Ed.*—Alexander's given name], I see you are a class-conscious worker and a Socialist. I think you ought to join the "Bund." Father gave me a loving and encouraging look. I said I was ready to join. The fact was I have been dreaming about joining some day ever since I learned about the "Bund." Isaak smiled and said we ought to have some tea and cake and went out of the room to bring the refreshments.

Father was standing behind my chair and patted my head.

Thus, at the age of 13, I became a member of the "Bund." I became a Socialist and a revolutionary and, shortly, afterwards, I found a new hero. His name was Karl Marx.

Looking back I can't help but wonder how it was possible for this event to take place only a few weeks after my family celebrated my Bar Mitzvah, with a holiday meal and myself delivering the Derashah, the special address which the Bar Mitzvah (the son of the Commandment) has to give on this occasion. I thus assumed the responsibilities of a man within the Jewish religious tradition. And, then, several weeks later, I become a member of a socialist and revolutionary organization in which, I knew even then, there was no room, for either God or religion.

More than that. Following my Bar Mitzvah, I began to wear the Tefillin (phylacteries) whenever I had a chance to do my prayers which I continued to do quite often, after I joined the "Bund."

Was I in contradiction here with myself? Or was I a hypocrite? And what about my father? He was not a pious man but he lived with the Jewish religious tradition and, at the same time, he was a devoted sympathizer of the "Bund," if not a real member.

My mother, I knew, was more deeply religious than father. Even though she was totally illiterate, couldn't read or write in any language, she knew by heart the standard prayers for women and followed strictly the regulations and rules prescribed by religious tradition.

Interestingly enough, she was somewhat dubious about my joining the "Bund." Not that she objected or criticized; she was just wondering whether a young fellow like me ought to get mixed up with something that don't believe in God and, besides, smells of arrests and imprisonment. But, on the whole, my impression was that she felt rather proud that her first-born is already a "ganzer mench" (a full-grown human being) recognized as such by people whose judgment she respected—Isaak, for instance.

And, speaking of mother: she was a regular mathematician, great with numbers. She helped me a good deal when I began to study arithmetic, at home, by myself. She operated the four rules of arithmetic with the greatest of ease, and everything in her head, because she couldn't read or write, and that included numbers. She was especially good with fractions, dividing and multiplying, which to me looked rather formidable at first. Father, too, had great respect for her mathematical gifts.

Well, to come back to my contradictions. It didn't look quite right to me to continue paying tribute to the Almighty—rendering prayers with the Tefillin on me, going to synagogue on Saturdays and holidays, and observing various religious rules—and at the same time participating in a socialist organization which was non-religious and atheist. True, the "Bund" didn't ask of its members to cease being religious. In fact, I couldn't recall Isaak ever discussing God or religion at any of the nightly meetings in my father's house when they were organizing the shoeworkers' trade union and strike. Hence, I did not transgress against any rules of membership. But what about the spirit of the thing? How does the ideal of socialism make peace and live together with God and religion? This bothered me a lot.

Besides: I asked myself this question: what sense is there in observing religious rites and rules when you have already broken relations with God Himself? When you pray, you pray to God. But you have broken with Him? You abstain from having any relations with Him? Aren't you behaving foolishly and non-sensically?

Yes, I would reply to myself: but He exists. He is God—the Almighty, the Creator of the World, Who had chosen the Jews (and I am a Jew) as his Own people and has made a Covenant with them. Moses was the intermediary and Moses is still my hero, "Bund" or no "Bund."

How do I square all these things?

At the time, I had no answer. However, gradually these questions ceased to bother me. I was getting involved more and more in the new life around me: the underground circle to which I was assigned, the educational classes—also illegal—which I attended, the daily affairs of our printers' organization, a sort of trade union.

Above all I was becoming aware of an approaching revolutionary storm in the country. One could sense it in the atmosphere. I used to hear of big strikes taking place everywhere—strikes against the capitalists, strikes against the government: strikes for political freedom, the thing Isaak used to talk about. I also heard about anti-government street demonstrations of large numbers of workers in many parts of the country. Also of collisions of these demonstrations with the Czar's police and troops, resulting in the killing of many demonstrators.

Strikes were also taking place in Berdichev at that time, in the years 1902 and 1903 and 1904. We also had the first anti-government street demonstration in Berdichev, on May Day, 1903. That was quite an event. It was organized by the "Bund" and, I believe, the local organization of the Social-Democratic party. Of the latter I am not sure because it was quite small and played little part, at that time, in the revolutionary life of Berdichev.

The city was expecting it. So did the police and the gendarmery. A week or so before May Day, the "Bund" issued and spread proclamations throughout the city, especially in working-class quarters, calling upon the people to come out into the streets on May Day to demonstrate for the 8-hour day, for the Democratic Republic, for Socialism. The proclamation had slogans for the overthrow of the anti-Semitic and pogrom-making Czarist government and for the expression of solidarity with the international working class.

Naturally, I participated in spreading the proclamation. Together with a friend of mine, a boy of about the same age who was a jeweler's apprentice. Feldstein was his name. We were assigned by the "Bund" circle to which we both belonged, a certain part of the city. It was called "Unter der Greblie" (Behind the Dam). Twice, at about midnight, Feldstein and I went out on our assignment and cautiously and quietly we stuck copies of the proclamation into the opening of pretty nearly all houses in the neighborhood.

The "Bund" also made sure that its members understood well the full meaning of this international working-class holiday. In our educational classes, we had several sessions, prior to May Day, devoted to a discussion of this very important matter. There I learned a good deal about the world abroad, the West, about its labor and socialist movements, its political systems and—above all—the international meaning of the struggle for socialism. That latter point was impressed upon us very strongly. I also learned that May Day as the symbol and banner of the international working-class struggle for the 8-hour day—that this originated in the United States of America.

May Day arrived and with it came the demonstration. It was a great event. Under the leadership of specially assigned captains, small groups of demonstrators assembled early in the morning in various side streets around the square from which the demonstration was to start. I forgot the name of the square. It was in the very center of the city, where its two main thoroughfares met—Bielopol street and Machnovskaya street—and where the water-tower was located.

At a pre-arranged signal, the various groups with their captains began to converge on the square, singing revolutionary songs in Yiddish. So did my group. But this one had a special function to perform. It was to march beside the banner-bearer, a sort of honor guard, following the first four or five rows of demonstrators who were to lead the procession and who were made up of the physically strongest so that they would protect the banner and the bearer from the expected attack of the police. I was the youngest in the banner-carrying group, 14 years, while the banner-bearer, my good friend Peisach Mandel, was almost 20.

Despite the presence on the square of numerous policemen and gendarmes, all stationed around the water-tower, we were able to assemble on the square in good order, several hundred of us, listen to a one- or two-minute speech, reciting the May Day slogans, and start singing the "International," in Yiddish, of course. The few non-Jewish participants may have sung it in Russian or, perhaps, Ukrainian. The police did not interfere. But the moment Peisach Mandel raised the banner, a beautiful red banner, the police and the gendarmery charged into us, forcing us to break up and disperse. They went particularly after the banner. A sharp fight, only a fist fight, ensued between the police and the strong-arm comrades of the front several rows. Most of the demonstrators rushed to the defense of the banner and the banner-bearers.

It was the general impression that we acquitted ourselves with honor. The police did succeed in breaking up the demonstration. We were never able to move out of the square and start the procession which was scheduled to proceed along Bielopol street. But we saved the banner and prevented the police from making arrests on the square, although they did manage to arrest many people in the side streets after the break-up of the demonstration. Only one policeman used his revolver, firing at Peisach Mandel, the banner-bearer, at close range and wounding his right arm. But this was the only serious casualty of the encounter.

The big thing to me, and to most everybody else, was the fact that, for the first time in the history of Berdichev, an open anti-government demonstration took place. The prestige of the "Bund" rose very high, among its own membership and among the masses of the people generally. The demonstration was the talk of the town for weeks. And, of course, I, as one of the participants, felt awfully proud of myself, and must have begun to behave with greater authority and self-assertion.

To mother this was a day of anguish. She had known that there would be a demonstration on May Day and was fearful of the consequences to father and myself if we participated. Father gave in to her pleas not to go. I couldn't, even though it was terribly hard to bear her pleadings. She was therefore very happy, to put it mildly, to see me come back home all in one piece. And when I began to describe the demonstration with all the particulars, putting the best light, naturally, on my own accomplishments, she seemed rather pleased with the thing. Father was all smiles.

In subsequent days, whenever neighbors happened to talk about the demonstrations—which took place quite often—mother would go as far as to approve certain things. For example: she thought saving the banner from those "Khamooles," the bums and blockheads, meaning the police, was a fine thing. She also thought it a good idea to tell the Czar exactly what we thought of him and his pogrom-makers and let the whole world know about it. And she would add: but it is dangerous.

As to myself, this really was a milestone in my life. I felt I was doing something worthwhile for the revolution, which I could feel coming, and for Socialism which became the ideal of my living. I felt part of something big and great and good. I studied socialism in my classes; also the Russian language, and the history of culture, and also elementary physics and chemistry. New worlds were opening up before me. Among them was a world of ideas and evidence that there is no such thing as a God the Creator of the world and no need for any religion. I was beginning to learn something about Marxism.

Not that I was studying Marx himself. Even though I already knew of his *Das Kapital* and of the *Communist Manifesto*, I had not yet seen any of his own works nor could I have understood them. But in the classes we were given an extended and popular exposition of the theory of scientific socialism of Marx and Engels.

We were also given in these classes various Yiddish pamphlets to read. They were illegal, of course, bound in black paper covers, as I remember. Two of these pamphlets stuck in my mind. One was called "The Four Brothers." It was written for the purpose of introducing the reader to the Marxist theory of society. The other, whose title I don't recall, was devoted to the origin of religions and religious beliefs, and its author, I vaguely remember, was a man by the name of Berman.

That there was a Bundist leader by that name, I learned in later years. One of the delegates to the convention at which the "Bund" was founded, in Vilna (Lithuania), in 1897, was a man by the name Pavel Berman. Whether he was the author of the pamphlet on religion, I am not certain.

Anyway, this pamphlet had played a major role in my intellectual and spiritual development. Imagine me finding out that religious beliefs have a history and that it is possible to know how and why people began to believe in various Gods. This was what the pamphlet was about. From it I learned that primitive men, fearful of the forces of nature, which they did not understand and didn't know how to cope with, were seeking to placate these forces and to pacify them. Primitive men endowed nature and natural conscious forces with a will and power to be good to men or be bad to men. The way to deal with these forces—rivers, seas, mountains, forests, storms, earthquakes, etc., etc.—is to try to win their goodwill. And this was what primitive man tried to do by offering sacrifices of various kinds, by prayers, by committing his loyalties to these forces. And from all this men came to endow these forces with God-like qualities. One more step in the history of civilization and these forces of nature become Gods, all knowing and all powerful. Through epochs of many Gods, men came to worship one God, that is, the idea of one God.

Having learned all of that, I was pretty nearly ready to consider myself a complete freethinker and atheist. I felt convinced that here lies the truth. Still there were some questions yet to which I had no answer. How did our world come into being? Nature, the heavens, men? Who or what makes it run? If it isn't God, who is it? If God is the invention of men, as I learned from the origin of religious beliefs, who has invented men?

The educational classes which the Berdichev Committee of the "Bund" provided for its members, especially the young ones, had also courses in the history of culture. I remember all of us using a particular text-book and its author, if I am not mistaken, was a man by the name of Lippert. Well, from the study of this book I found out that the world had no creator and that the Biblical version of creation was just a legend, a beautiful story. I also learned that the origin of man has a long history, too; and here I made my acquaintance with Charles Darwin.

Thus I took leave of my religious ideas and beliefs. And I can say that I had acquired a new confidence in life and in living, a greater respect for the human being and his creative capacities. This meant also greater respect for and confidence in myself. And all of that was an intimate and inseparable part of my membership in the "Bund," my participation in the revolutionary movement, my dreams of a new, a better, a socialist world.

Source: Alexander Bittelman, "Things I Have Learned," typed manuscript (1963), pp. 46–58, Alexander Bittelman Papers, box 1, folder 5, Tamiment Library, New York University.

4

"Rebellion Raged within Me"
(memoir; 1948)

LUCY ROBINS LANG

Born outside of Kiev, Lucy Lang (1884–1962) immigrated to the
United States at the age of nine. She joined the anarchist movement in Chicago by the age of fifteen and devoted the rest of her
life to the labor movement and the cause of free speech. Lang
directed various regional and national committees in support
of persecuted anarchists, labor organizers, and antiwar activists.
She eventually became an adviser to Samuel Gompers, president of the American Federation of Labor, although without
renouncing her anarchist ideals.

Father had lived in Chicago during his first, brief stay in America.
My mother's brother, whom Father had helped across the border, was living
there, and so were other relatives, pioneers who had blazed the trail from
Korostyshev to the metropolis of the Middle West. The dominant figure on
the group was Aunt Yente Chave, a sister of Grandmother Broche's scholarly
husband.

On his second arrival in the United States, Father remained in New York.
Here he had no relatives and no friends. By trade he was a silversmith, and
frequently he could find no job. He felt helpless and terribly lonely in the
great city.

It was then that Chaye the *peddlerke*[1] took him in hand, as she was to take
the rest of us in hand when we reached New York. Chaye had a stand on Mott
Street, where Father was boarding with a poor Jewish family that lived in a
couple of dark rooms. The stand consisted of two empty fruit boxes propped
against the wall of a tenement house. Here she displayed her wares: halves of
damaged oranges, the decayed parts cut away, four pieces for a penny; old
squashed apples, two for a penny; small, round, brightly colored gum candy,
each piece about the size of a pea, ten for a cent; salted pumpkin and sun-
flowers seeds, a small tin cup measure for a penny.

Chaye always wore the same clothes, a great many at the same time, one skirt over another and more than one waist. Aprons hung on every side of her, and a multitude of shawls and kerchiefs were draped over her head and shoulders, with the ends of each passed under her arms and tied on her back.

Father stopped now and then at her stand, permitting himself the extravagance of a measure of sunflower seeds, and Chaye talked to him. "What are you so scared of?" she challenged him. "This isn't Fonia's Russia. You should be ashamed, going about with your nose on the sidewalk." She found jobs for him, told him how to buy steamship tickets for his family on the installment plan, located a flat he could afford, and picked out second-hand furniture for it.

Although she herself could not speak English, Chaye interpreted America to countless Jewish immigrants. She refused to encourage their longings for the old country. "Everybody should run away from Russia," she told them indignantly; "everyone should come to America. What did you have in Russia?" she would ask. "Pogroms you had! Why don't you read the papers and see for yourself? So you don't like America? Woe is me and woe is to Columbus!" [. . .]

Our tenement was in back of another tenement that faced on Mott Street, and was reached by a long dim corridor. The two houses were owned by the same landlord, and the tenants of both felt a certain community interest. In both tenement houses the sink was in a niche in the wall along the stairs between two floors. The sinks were black, and the water had to be pumped. Tenants stood in line waiting their turns to get water. After supper a crowd of women would gather to wash their dishes, and then they would air their complaints against the New World and their hopes for the future.

The smaller and darker of our two rooms was our parents' bedroom, and had a bed and a chair. The other room, which had two windows facing the yard, was the sleeping room for all the children and served as a kitchen, dining room, living room, and parlor for receiving guests. Chaye was our most frequent visitor.

Mother became ill. It was necessary to call a doctor, and we feared that Father's wages would not suffice. The whole burden of looking after the household fell on my shoulders. Willie was lame because of an attack of infantile paralysis while he was a baby, and I accompanied him and Beckie to school each morning. Then I hurried home to clean the rooms, keep watch over Sam, and prepare lunch. The school was near by, and I could hear the children singing as I went about my chores. My heart was heavy with my longing for school.

When father returned home from work, he would embrace me tenderly for my day's toil and, after dinner, when the dishes were washed and the house put in order, he would braid my hair. Then I would put on my new American dress, which Mother had made just before she fell ill, and go down to the street for my recreation. I never went away from the house. Enviously, I would stand before the door and watch other girls of my age. An Italian often came by with a hand organ, and the children danced while I stood mute and lonely by the door.

The day Father was paid he gave us a penny each, and I would lead Beckie and limping Willie to Chaye the standkeeper. She had been so kind to us that, of course, we went to her stand, and in any case it paid, for invariably she gave us six instead of four halves of orange for a penny.

A secret was being whispered in our two rooms. At first only my parents spoke of it, and then Chaye was initiated: Mother was bringing another child into the world, an American child. Chaye told me. To her way of thinking I was already grown-up, and I had to know it and be prepared for a bigger share of the housework.

Just at this time we suffered a great blow: because of the slow season, Father lost his job and could find no other. Daily he went to look for work, even going far into the East Side, where the unemployed congregated to hear news of jobs from one another. Late in the afternoon he would return crestfallen. Chaye suspected that his shyness and reserve were partly responsible for his failure to find work, and she began to look for a job for him. Not a person passed her stand without her asking if he knew of employment for a man "with golden hands and a heart of silk." And still there was no job.

But the overcast skies were suddenly penetrated by a ray of light. A letter came from Chicago in which my Uncle Fox and Aunt Yente Chave stated that Father could get work there. They suggested, however, that he come alone, for they could defray traveling expenses for only one person. Later they would help him to bring the rest of the family.

Chaye was called in for consultation, and at once she said that Father must go. She also recommended that I go with him, for then our relatives would have to take steps as quickly as possible to bring Mother and the other children.

The trip lasted a very long time, for we traveled on a slow local train in order to economize. It was cold, and the passengers huddled together around the coal stove in the center of the car. Water was boiled on this stove, and tea was brewed, to be drunk with the food brought from home.

This trip gave me an insight into Father's gentle character. When we descended from the train to stretch our legs, I would stride along beside him, my coat thrown over my shoulders capewise, and he would praise me for being so grown-up. Dominated by his father, oppressed by the burden of a family while still so young and dependent, he felt inadequate to the demands of life in America. He wanted me to be independent and fearless, as he could never be. He tenderly looked after all my needs on the trip, yet treated me as an adult, and I responded to his confidence and encouragement with all the ardor in my childish breast.

Aunt Yente Chave immediately wanted to know why I had been brought to Chicago. She, too, was a matriarch, ruling over a large clan and offering advice to strangers as well as kin. She was capable, and she did much good, but her virtues were overshadowed by her fanatical faith in her own rightness. She had hardly patted my head when she began to scold me. Such a big girl, almost ten years old! I should have had more sense than to come along.

This outburst injured the pride that Father had aroused in me during the trip. I felt that my lips were trembling, and I must have answered her sharply, for she told me not to have such a big mouth. I wept, and after that I would not speak to her but spoke only to Father, telling him that I would not be a nuisance but would work and help him.

"Look at her!" Aunt Yente Chave said. "Some person! This will go to work!" But perhaps she was moved by my words, for she looked at me in a maternal fashion, and she arranged that I should stay with her daughter, who was married to Uncle Fox, while Father lived with her. She impressed upon me that I must live up to the name of Fox, which we bore, prophesying that it would some day be an important name in America.

With $50 Aunt Yente Chave had established Uncle Fox in a cigar store on Chicago Avenue. He made his own cigars on a little table on the sill of the store window, and he and his wife and two small children lived in a room separated from the store by a curtain. Later he became an important figure in the tobacco industry, but he was far from prosperous in those days, and I had to earn my bread in his house. I took care of the two children, who were not much younger than myself; I helped with the cooking and laundry behind the curtain; and I swept the store.

With Aunt Yente Chave's aid, Father immediately found a job on a piecework basis in a concern manufacturing picture frames. He inserted gold leaf into the frames, and he earned about $5 a week working twelve hours a day. His employer, who came from Korostyshev, knew our family, and he promised that Father would earn more as soon as he gained speed.

Father found a job for me as a tobacco stripper in a cigar factory owned by the Spector brothers. They had come from Kiev, too, but were of a lower social status there, and considered it a privilege to give a job to the grand-daughter of Reb Chaim. They even paid me $1 a week, whereas most children who learned the trade in cigar factories worked without pay in the beginning and sometimes had to pay tuition for the privilege.

With my earning capacity added to his, Father borrowed money and brought Mother and the children from New York. For $4.50 a month Aunt Yente Chave rented rooms for us in the basement of the house on Morgan Street in which she lived, and she also found for us an unsteady table, some lame chairs, a rusty bed, and an ancient sofa.

The basement was divided in two, and we lived in the part toward the street. The front room had a barred window, through which we could see only the feet of passers-by and the rats that thronged under the wooden side-walk. The second room was the kitchen, and in it was a smoky stove. Then there was a half room, like a cave dug into a black cliff, and the bed was placed there, near the windowless wall. The other half of the basement contained the toilet and the coal bins, which were infested with rats as big as cats. When the tenants came to get coal, they had to fight the rats, which fled towards our apartment. Mother, who was very unwell, lived in dread of the rats.

Mother was taking this pregnancy hard. Her beauty and buoyancy, which had survived so many hardships, now began to fade. As soon as Father and I returned from work, she would lie down on the bed in the half room, while we prepared the food and did the dishes. As the time of her labor approached, a doctor was provided through Jane Addam's Hull House.[2] In fear and anguish Mother awaited the event. Father could not afford to miss a day's work, and I stayed at home.

Soon Mother's agonized screams sent me running for the doctor. He came, accompanied by a visiting nurse, and I had to watch carefully every-thing the nurse did so that I could take over when she left. Despite Mother's outcries, the doctor and the nurse paid little attention to her. Probably they knew that there was plenty of time, but I trembled with exasperation at their seeming indifference. Was it because we were poor immigrants that they treated Mother so callously? Humiliated and outraged, I began to weep, and the younger children followed my example.

At last the doctor and nurse approached Mother's bed and in our presence performed the mysterious act of removing a child from its mother's body. Mother's last inhuman scream was followed by the wail of the baby. It was a big baby, a boy with reddish fuzz on his head and full lips. I suddenly felt as if he had been living with us all along.

At this same time Uncle Fox's wife, Beckie, was giving birth in the clean, well lit apartment of her mother, Aunt Yente Chave, on the fifth floor. She came from Chicago Avenue to be delivered under her mother's watchful care, and though Aunt Yente Chave was far from rich, she provided all possible conveniences. A private doctor and nurse were engaged, and Aunt Yente Chave's other daughters were on hand to help. The baby and its mother on the fifth floor were tenderly cared for, while in the basement, once the charity doctor and the nurse had departed, the new mother had only her frightened, weeping children.

The celebrations that introduced the babies into the fold of their people and their faith brought added humiliation for the baby in the basement. On the fifth floor there was a dignified ceremony, with a prominent rabbi, many well dressed guests, a table laden with wine, brandy, and home-baked cakes. On the barren table in the basement stood a small bottle of whisky with two tiny glasses, one for Father and the other for the impoverished and unknown *mohel* who came to perform the ceremony[3] as an act of charity. There was a plate with salted beans, the only dessert after the drink. The wishes of good luck to Mother were voiced only by the half-starved *mohel*, by Father, whose heart was crying out with shame and pain, and by me, her oldest child, who was feeling the stirrings of revolt against this poverty. The baby on the fifth floor was given an American name, Sydney. Our baby was named Hymie, in good immigrant style, after Grandfather Reb Chaim. When the baby was returned to Mother, she turned her head to the wall so that we should not see her tears.

Rebellion raged within me. Why should others have all the things we didn't have? My indignation became mixed with a great devotion and love for the baby. Had anyone asked me to give my life for Hymie, I would have gladly done so.

My mother was greatly changed. Her body was contorted, and in place of the smile that her lips had so constantly worn was an expression of vague, dark regret.

I worked from seven in the morning to six in the evening, with a half-hour interval for lunch. Since carfare would have consumed the greater part of my week's dollar, I walked to the factory on Jackson Boulevard, and the walk took an hour each way. I was small for my age and slight of build, and the harsh wind would whip me along or hold me back. The Chicago of those days was overridden with rats, and they actually scampered about my feet as I trotted along of a wintry morning under the flickering gas lamps. I hated mice and rats, and I was deeply grateful to the stray dogs that chased them away.

Aunt Yente Chave feared that I might be thought even younger than I was, and so she insisted that I wear a long dress of green wool that she found among the cast-off clothes of her grown daughters. This dress, many years out of style, was short enough in front to expose my laced, high-top shoes, but in back it trailed on the ground. Aunt Yente Chave also devised a plan to make my figure seem more mature by wrapping me in an ancient corset with whalebone ribs. Thus padded and uncomfortably dressed, I went to work in the cigar factory.

I made friends with older girls in the factory, Americanized Irish and Poles, and they taught me to speak English. I also learned from them the intimate "secrets of life."

Jake, one of the bosses who looked after the factory, was constantly demanding higher production, and I was always afraid of losing my job. I must have proved satisfactory, however, for Jake decided to make me a stock-keeper. A stockkeeper had to spray a certain liquid on the dry tobacco leaves to give them a special aroma. Another part of my job was to sweep the factory during the half hour that the employees had for lunch. This made me very unhappy, for the other workers gathered in a big room upstairs, ate their lunches quickly, and had fifteen minutes or so for talking, reading, or dancing. I was barred from all this, and ate in weary solitude the food I had brought from home.

More and more I began to resent the fact that I had not been able to go to school. My younger sister, who was attending school, spoke English almost all the time, and that meant that she was rising out of the squalor of immigrant life. My Irish and Polish friends in the factory had had some schooling before they went to work. I suffered because of my ignorance.

Then Rose Aron, a new girl in the factory, told me about night school. She had been graduated from high school, and dreamed of becoming a doctor. When I began talking about attending one of the night classes held for immigrants, Mother objected strenuously: wasn't I tired enough when I returned from work? But Father won that round for me.

The class was made up of older people, and I was like a child among them. Perhaps because of this, the teacher, who had a kind of missionary zeal, took a special interest in me, and I made rapid progress. I would stay up late every night, preparing my lessons by the light of a small candle, and then would rise even earlier than I had done before, in order to have time to stop and read the posters and signs in store windows on my way to work.

I asked my boss for a raise, and, of course, he shouted out his refusal, but he did me a favor just the same. There were many cigar stores in Chicago, mostly operated by Germans, that did contract work, and when one of these stores needed a tobacco stripper, Jake would send me. My wages on such an occasion were paid by my temporary employer, and Jake arranged that I should get $1.50 a week. Sometimes, however, my employers ordered me to sweep the store or even to do housework, and then I was humiliated.

Encouraged by Rose Aron, I kept at Jake, and finally he agreed to pay me an additional twenty-five cents a week. I felt now that I was a full-fledged worker, and I mingled with the other workers on terms of equality. They accepted me as a younger sister to be encouraged and helped and taught the facts of life.

One of the best of my teachers was Tony, an Irishman whose right leg had been amputated above the knee. He had a crude wooden stump, and he carried a crutch, but he was strong and agile, and he refused to admit that he was handicapped in any way. When Chicago welcomed President McKinley and Admiral Dewey, the latter fresh from his triumphs over the Spaniards, we had a half holiday. I was caught in the great crowd that thronged the streets for the parade, and felt that I was about to suffocate. Suddenly I was seized by a pair of strong hands, and I heard Tony's gay voice. "Sit, little one," he said, as he swept me to his shoulder. "Look and see what's going on." And there he stood, as if his wooden leg had been welded to the sidewalk, and while the crowd laughed at us, he told me who Admiral Dewey was and what it meant to be President.

This was only the first of many lessons in politics that Tony gave me. A little later, when the news came that President McKinley had been shot by an Anarchist named Czolgosz, Tony bitterly denounced the assassin and his associates. The Anarchists were not only disloyal to the country, Tony argued; they hurt the cause of labor. For Tony was both a staunch patriot and a great believer in the rights of workingmen. These two sentiments, as I discovered in time, were not incongruous: only the well paid worker can be a good patriot and a positive force in the life of the nation. As for my own feelings about McKinley's death, they were simpler than Tony's: here was I, a poor greenhorn girl, who had a chance to see the President, and suddenly somebody killed him.

From Rose Aron I learned that there was another side to the story. Her older sisters and their friends were radicals, some of them Anarchists. They regretted that the President had been shot, but they were not bitter against the man who had committed the crime. From Rose I learned how Emma

Goldman, whom the police were hunting on a charge of complicity in the shooting, had voluntarily surrendered herself. When I repeated to Tony what Rose had told me about the Anarchists and their ideals, he muttered something about Jewish girls being too radical. It was not so very much later that he married one of these radical Jewish girls, and learned to depend on her vitality and strength.

Romance as well as politics played a part in the life of the cigar factory. My cousin Abe, a son of Aunt Yente Chave, worked at the same table as gracious, attractive Jenny. Soon he announced that he had chosen a bride and wished to bring her to his home to receive his mother's blessing. Of course Aunt Yente Chave would not consent. She was shocked that a son of hers should even propose such indecent behavior. Summoning the clan, she expressed her indignation. To Abe she said: "You are not to have anything more to do with this Jenny. You will marry the girl that I choose, a girl with a good dowry." To the members of the clan it was inconceivable that Abe should oppose the will of the matriarch. Why, he would be banished from the family, from Chicago, from the world! And Abe could only see things as the clan saw them. Although he continued to adore Jenny, he never again spoke of her at home, and in the end he married that girl Aunt Yente Chave selected.

I had been enchanted by the romance between Abe and Jenny, and I was filled with righteous indignation against Aunt Yente Chave. I called her an old tyrant, and denounced her on every possible occasion. When she heard of this, she said that I, "big as a pea and old as a drop of dew," had better stop meddling in her affairs or she would take me in hand.

She was as good as her word. Her opportunity came just before Christmas. I passed night-school examinations with honors, and the teacher, praising me before the class, presented me with a book. Of course Father and Mother boasted of my triumph, and Aunt Yente Chave heard of it. She shook her head. My teacher was a man? A goi?[4] She shook her head again. Obviously his intentions were dishonorable. But I was only twelve. So much the worse. She convoked a family council, and solemnly asked what should be done. Her husband, her sons and daughters, their wives and husbands, and a host of more distant relatives, all trained to obey her every word, were properly horrified. They surrounded my parents as if some unspeakable calamity had befallen them, and I almost became convinced that I really had committed some terrible sin. My mother and father had no choice but to agree: I must drop out of night school.

What was even worse, I was forbidden to go to Hull House. I had recently been asked by motherly Jane Addams to assist a girls' dancing class, and this little recognition filled me with joy. Aunt Yente Chave wanted to know what I did at Hull House, and when she heard that I was connected with a dance group, she cocked her head and put on an expression of deep significance, as she always did when she was investigating sins. "So that's it!" she said. "No good will come of her!"

Seething with rage, I ran to tell Jane Addams. After listening patiently to my story, she agreed to talk with Aunt Yente Chave. When these two met, the contrast was magnificent. They were both strong-willed women, but their backgrounds were utterly different. Behind Aunt Yente Chave were generations of men and women who had suffered every kind of hardship and persecution in order to live in the way they believed to be right. To her, the least deviation from the established code threatened the whole structure. Jane Addams, on the other hand, the product of generations of freedom and security, believed that standards of conduct could and should be based on reason.

Aunt Yente Chave, wearing a black peruke that formed bangs over her high forehead, was not in the least humble or apologetic when she confronted the founder of Hull House. Nor was Miss Addams in any way critical or condescending. She knew the strength and validity of the way of life Aunt Yente Chave represented, and she did not seek to destroy it, but she also knew that the younger generation in America had to adapt itself to new ways of living, and she was trying to aid in the adjustment.

Hardly speaking the English language, the matriarch from the Russian Pale understood the lady from Cedarville, Illinois, and made herself understood. "Traditions of the home," said Aunt Yente Chave, "and commands of the parents must be the basis of training the young."

"The young must be free to experiment," Miss Addams replied. "They must learn to understand the meaning of right and wrong. Life should be interesting and joyful for them."

"Ah," said the matriarch, "we have joy in our homes. We have our celebrations, our weddings. And we know the needs of girls. First, they need loving, watchful parents. Then early marriage and a happy home of their own. I have daughters, so I know this."

"I cannot speak from experience," Miss Addams interrupted. "I have no daughters."

"Only boys?"

"No children at all."

"God have mercy."

"I have never married."

"So you don't know nothing at all."

It was funny, and yet it was sad. Poor Aunt Yente Chave knew how easily a family could be destroyed, its members set to wandering along the highways and byways of exile, never safe from persecution, never secure. What greater opportunity could America offer her than the chance to build an abiding home for her tribe for generations to come? How could she tolerate the least weakening of her power, which was the essential instrument of the only kind of survival she could understand.

Jane Addams could not budge Aunt Yente Chave, but she convinced my parents, and I was grudgingly permitted to return to Hull House. But by now my eyes were dazzled by a brighter vision of freedom, and my feet were set on paths of which Jane Addams might not have approved.

Source: Lucy Robins Lang, *Tomorrow Is Beautiful* (New York: Macmillan, 1948), pp. 15–26.

NOTES

1. Yiddish: a female peddler.

2. Hull-House was Chicago's first settlement house, founded by Jane Addams and Ellen Gates Starr in 1889 with the intention of improving urban life for working-class people, mainly immigrants. In addition to providing medical support to community members, Hull-House also offered social events and lectures for adults.

3. The *bris*, or ritual circumcision.

4. Yiddish: a Gentile male, often derogatory in connotation.

5

"It Wasn't Difficult for Me to Reject Judaism" (memoir; 1965)

PAUL JACOBS

Born into a middle-class, German-Jewish family in New York City, Paul Jacobs (1918–1978) became a "professional revolutionist" after his graduation from high school, participating in Communist and, later, Trotskyist organizations. Jacobs abandoned sectarian politics in the 1940s but continued to work as a union organizer, journalist, and activist until his death.

I didn't become a radical because my early childhood was unpleasant or because I suffered from anti-Semitism. My parents were nonintellectual middle-class German Jews who had emigrated to the United States in the years before World War I and spoke English with only a faint accent. Both of them came from the mercantile rather than the scholarly tradition, and when I was born in 1918 my father was prospering in the import-and-export business. The standards held up for us to emulate were always those of the rich and prominent German-Jewish families of New York, who were envied models for my parents. We never quite made it, though, and so instead of going to private schools I went to nice middle-class public schools and played with nice middle-class boys—and girls, too, whenever I could cajole them into empty lots or back yards.

We lived in an apartment house on a quiet tree-lined street in the upper Bronx, just off the Grand Concourse. Most of the houses on the block were one-family homes, two or three stories high with stoops in front and yards in back. For a few years, until it burned down, I went to a wooden school located right across the street from our house. One block away there was a church and down the street an Orthodox synagogue, which we didn't attend; for my parents were Reform Jews who belonged to a brick temple on the Concourse. [. . .]

The most joyful discovery of my early childhood was the public library, with its whole top floor full of children's books. I became a voracious reader, taking out as many books at a time as the rules allowed, reading them as quickly as I could, then returning for another batch. I discovered the joys of the city at the same time: the firehouse just a block or two away, where I stood gaping at the engines for hours on end; the empty lots where my friends and I roasted potatoes over forbidden fires; Van Cortlandt Park with hundreds of acres for us to roam, pretending to be explorers; and, best of all, the street games we played until it was so dark we had to go home. [. . .]

And every Sunday except during the summer I walked to a Sunday School in a nice polite middle-class temple, where we didn't learn Hebrew or much of anything else that made any impression except about sex, which wasn't on the formal curriculum. The girl who sat next to me for two years gave me private lessons in that as we sat in the last row of the classroom, our busy exploring hands hidden from the teacher's view.

I remember one other thing about Sunday School: the Happy Days Club, a great gimmick to raise money for the temple. If you or someone in your family had a happy day during the week, you got up on the platform in the temple vestry during the assembly period; when your turn came, you stepped forward to tell what the day had been—maybe a very good report card, a new baby in the family, your mother's birthday—and made a contribution (of an unspecified amount) to the temple.

Now, all this was very boring to hear week after week until I realized that I could tap my father for a contribution every Sunday and then split it with the temple fifty fifty. I didn't keep my half of the money all for myself, but instead impressed my fellow students by distributing free candy bars and peanuts.

When I was thirteen I became a "bar mitzvah boy." In a Reform temple at your bar mitzvah, which took place on a Saturday morning, you sat up on the pulpit with the rabbi in front of your family and your own friends. At the appropriate time during the service you read a section from the Torah in painfully memorized and badly mispronounced Hebrew. This was followed by a short speech in painfully memorized and stiltingly elocuted English. All bar mitzvah speeches in my youth began with "Dear Parents, Relatives, and Friends," continued with proper obeisance to the magnificent religious education you had received at the hands of the rabbi (who, incidentally, always wrote the speeches), and ended with a stirring peroration wherein you described how you would now take your place in the ranks of the Jewish people. After the rabbi had placed his hands on your head and mumbled, as in my case, a few platitudinous phrases as a blessing, the ceremony was concluded with the rabbi preaching, in rolling organ tones about the spiritual content of "Joodeyism." Then you took you place among the Jewish people by being the guest of honor at a reception hosted by your parents at which all of your relatives and friends presented you with gifts of ten-dollar gold pieces and fountain pens.

So I grew up, nominally Jewish on Sundays and on the Jewish holidays, like Rosh Hashanah and Yom Kippur, when we stayed away from public schools. My being Jewish didn't make much of an impression on me or my friends. I don't know how many of my childhood friends were Christians, since we lived in a neighborhood where there were many non-Jewish families. At grade school, too, I must have known many children who were not Jewish and while I was in the first grades, I would drop my eyes to steal furtive glances at the Christian boys when they stood at the urinal next to me, for then I was still curious about how a foreskin looked. But the really acute sense of difference between Christian kids and myself focused on the Catholic boys and girls who attended parochial school. I was very much aware of them, partially because they were associated with nuns who taught in the parochial school and who frightened me with their black habits, their faces all squinched together under them as if they had no ears or hair. There was a flourishing folklore about nuns among non-Catholic children: "Hold your buttons when you pass one or they'll fall off" was one such bit of wisdom, and so we fearfully clutched the buttons on our clothes. We were equally convinced, of course, that if you stepped on an ant it would rain the next day, and the fact that the buttons didn't fall off our clothes or that the rain did not come had no effect on our beliefs.

There were no Christmas-Chanukah festivals when I went to grammar school, and even in our home Christmas was a more important holiday than Chanukah. It's only in recent years that Chanukah has been endowed by some Jews with significance by being transformed into a Jewish Christmas so that their children won't feel discriminated against when it's time to pass out the gifts. But when we were kids my brother and I always hung up Christmas stockings, although we didn't have a tree. Every year we were given lots of Christmas presents, too: an erector set, a chemistry outfit, books, sleds, clothes, and all the other things that make Christmas the nice greedy holiday it is for children. At Easter time we got chocolate eggs, and it didn't seem to disturb my parents that the eggs were a Christian symbol. Indeed, the atmosphere in our house was as much German as it was Jewish, since we were Reform Jews. I said my nightly prayers in German, my parents didn't observe the kosher dietary laws, and my mother didn't light candles on Friday night (on the contrary, it was more likely that she and my father would play bridge with their friends on Fridays).

So although we were Jewish, we weren't "Jews," like the men with beards and earlocks or the women with brown wigs who embarrassed me when I saw them on the street or on the subway reading Yiddish newspapers. Sometimes during the Passover holiday a Seder was held either at our home or in some relative's house; it was usually arranged with some difficulty because so few in our family were capable of reading the Hebrew service. To us, Hebrew was a language only the rabbis understood. There was a Hebrew printing in the Reform temple prayer book, on the page opposite the English, but so few prayers were said in it that it was possible to memorize them or mumble a few words. Yiddish was almost as unfamiliar to us, since neither of my parents, nor anyone else we knew well, spoke the language except for the argot that had already become part of New York's own slang.

As a middle-class American Jewish kid, I also knew very little about Yiddish culture. Yiddish was the tongue of the unassimilated Eastern European Jews, towards whom my parents had inherited a contemptuous attitude as part of the German-Jewish assimilationist tradition.

The gap between families like mine and the East European Jews was nearly as great as the one separating my parents from their Christian friends. Yiddish was a lower-class language, spoken by people who didn't play bridge or mah-jongg, as my mother did, or read the New York *Sun*, as my father did. Yiddish-speaking Jews didn't call their children Clifford or Paul, but Saul or Isadore or Hyman. In the Gentile world, a "kike" may have been descriptive of any Jews, but to my parents and their friends it was any East European Jew, especially the noisy ones. "Stop acting like a kike" was a frequent admonition to noisy, badly behaved children—or adults as well—who offended the middle-class mores of the German Jews.

At high school, though, I came into contact with a different group of Jewish kids from the ones I had met at home. When I was about twelve and half I entered an accelerated high school—Townsend Harris—for obnoxiously smart youth. Harris was almost a prep school for the City College of New York, although no one at either place would have recognized it as such. If you passed the difficult qualifying entrance examination, you were graduated in three years and almost guaranteed admission to any college in the United States, although most of the graduates naturally went on to the City College, on whose campus Harris was located.

If you were thirteen when you first went to Harris and sixteen when you graduated, you were considered almost moronic. The school, which had a great academic reputation, drew its youthful wizards from all of New York City, in contrast to most other high schools, whose student body lived in a single geographic area. Before Harris was abolished by Mayor LaGuardia during World War II (because he believed it too expensive to operate in the interests of an "elite" group) it had a long and honorable history of students who became writers, lawyers, teachers, and so on. During my years there and afterward, Harris also turned out boys who became Communists, Socialists, and Trotskyists, like me.

The student body at Harris was very small and mostly Jewish. This fact, which at the time didn't strike me as being odd, coupled with the self-conscious young-genius atmosphere of the school, gave Harris a high degree of intellectual homogeneity. We talked about politics a great deal, both in the classrooms with teachers and, even more, outside among ourselves. This was probably inevitable, considering the time—the depression—and the fact that many of the students came from Yiddish Socialist homes, where politics was constantly discussed.

Politics at Harris was also compensation for the lack of sports. It was our proud boast that the school had no football team. Even those teams we had, like tennis and baseball, distinguished themselves by never winning. There was one exception: chess. We were very big on chess and usually won all the interschool tournaments. Every noon you could find a few chess games going in the school cafeteria—two boys hunched over a chess board, one usually wearing knickers and the other looking like an owl with big glasses perched on his nose. Around them would be clustered a group of silent kibitzers[1] munching on their sandwiches, while off at the other tables heated arguments went on about the "real meaning" of the Nazi rise to power in Germany.

"Mit Sozialismus"[2] was the way one of my fifteen-year-old classmates at Harris signed his yearbook picture at graduation, and it seemed a perfectly normal salutation to me. Since neither family background nor geography were factors in determining the make-up of the student body, Harris had quite a few poor boys and just as many rich boys mixed in with the bulk of the student body, who came from middle-class homes like mine. At Harris I encountered boys whose voices carried faint echoes of the Yiddish their parents spoke at home. In dealing with them, it took me a long time to overcome the phony pride inculcated in me because of my German-Jewish background—pride which even survived the effects of the 1929 depression on our family. [. . .]

I discussed politics and religion perpetually with Bob, who was still my best friend. Although we hadn't gone to the same schools or lived in the same neighborhood after a while, we had remained close. We were devoted to each other as boys, as adolescents, and as young revolutionists, and I guess that if he hadn't died in 1941 we might still be friends. Together we first discarded "Joodayism" and, later, capitalism.

It wasn't difficult for me to reject Judaism. Whatever content it had was completely lacking in the pallid diet of pap I was fed every Sunday at temple. And all I learned about being Jewish at home was a set of defensive standards. There were limits, for example, to what Jews could expect from Gentiles, and proper behavior for Jews was based often on the fear that the Gentile world might respond badly to other patterns of action if taken by Jews. All of this knowledge was encompassed in one of the few Yiddish phrases I learned at home: a Jew did not make "rishis."

To "make rishis" was to stir up a fuss of some kind, and it was a cardinal sin, for it supposedly made Jews vulnerable to the potential wrath of the Christian world. This world was conceived of as something like a potentially evil sleeping giant who, if awakened by a loud noise, might, and probably would, turn on the disturber of his peace and do him harm. Even my parents, assimilated as they were to American middle-class patterns and coming from an assimilated German middle-class background, never completely lost their fear of what must have seemed to them a dominant Christian culture. Thus they were caught in not just one but a number of conflicts, two of which created great tensions in the family. One lay in the strain between the German tradition and the American reality about the proper way to rear children, and the other involved the difficulty of retaining some aspects of Jewishness without being conspicuous Jews. [. . .]

Everything about Reform Judaism grew more and more repellent to me. In the summer the Saturday services in the temple were canceled, as was Sunday School, as if going to religious services was less important during July and August than at other times of the year. Obviously there was a reason for canceling temple activities; either most of the families were away in summer houses, as was ours, or at the beaches, or the children were away at camp. Nevertheless, since so much of Jewish life centered around the temple, the minimal temple activity all summer was proof to me that being a Jew wasn't nearly as important as my parents had said. What seemed like hypocrisy filled me with contempt for those people, like my parents, who, I believed, perpetuated the deceit by being religious Jews once a year, when they got all dressed up for the High Holiday services.

However, religion was only one of the strains that made life hell between my parents and myself during that period—and it was perhaps the least important. Other conflicts—about sex, money, how late I could stay out at night—sent me into stomach-knotting fits of rage to which my parents responded with their own shouts and threats. The final and most painful rupture between us was caused by my increasing involvement in radicalism: after I had been graduated from Townsend Harris, I simultaneously entered City College and joined the Young Communist League.

The precise circumstances under which I joined the Young Communist League are very hazy in my mind—as vague as the names and faces of the other branch members, shadows drifting on the outskirts of my memory. [. . .]

When people ask now why I became a radical then, my answers are somehow always unsatisfactory, at least to me. I assume that my bitter quarrels with my parents and my brother, my father's business difficulties that deprived me of achieving my childish fantasies, and my contempt for the values of the family, especially what I believed to be their hypocritical attitude toward religion, all pushed me into rebellion. But children have always rebelled against their parents and not all of them join the Young Communist League. So I must turn to the times as they were to make myself and my actions understandable.

The depression wasn't something that happened in another country or to other people: it was all around us. The Roosevelt-Hoover campaign wasn't an ordinary election; it was a passionate quarrel between life and death. The shabby men selling apples were on every street corner, and the clusters of flimsy shacks grimly named "Hoovervilles" were not just along the banks of the Hudson River but on every river. And in faraway Europe, Hitler was becoming an ever more menacing and sinister figure and I would scream with impatience at my parents when, like most of their contemporaries, they pooh-poohed him as a clown whom the German people would quickly reject.

Even without the domestic crisis of the 1930s, without the New Deal and the Blue Eagle, without the Emergency Relief Administration and the Works Progress Administration, Hitler forced politics on us and dominated our lives. His name was on everyone's tongue, on every front page, in every newsreel. At Harris we had openly taunted a German professor we suspected of being a Nazi sympathizer and had mocked the Nazi goosestep and the cadenced shouting of "Heil, Sieg Heil!" Then, suddenly, almost overnight, those ludicrous stormtroopers were beating up Jews in the streets. Thus, Hitler became an enemy even in our house as my parents, like many Jews of German descent, began a feverish attempt to help their relatives get out of Germany.

So Hitler was everywhere and forced us to talk continually about politics.

Arguing excitedly about politics, about the depression, about anti-Negro prejudice, about anti-Semitism, and how to fight against German and Italian fascism took up a lot of time at City College, too, where informal student life centered in an area known as The Alcoves, underneath one of the main buildings. There, in huge recesses set around the perimeter of the building, I watched the other students eating their sandwiches from paper bags, studying and playing chess, and, among the politicals, always arguing. Each political group had its own alcove, and an informal understanding existed that no other group would attempt to dispossess it. Very often, though, the "members" of one alcove drifted over to another, either for a discussion if there was any common political bond between them or for a violent argument when the groups were as widely separated as, say, the Stalinists and the Trotskyists.

As far as I was concerned, those alcove discussions were the most important part of life at City College. I knew there were classes, for I had to attend them, and I knew there were other student activities, for the posters advertising the clubs and lectures were everywhere; but for me there was only one world into which I wanted to be taken and accepted: the radical atmosphere which dominated City College in those years. [. . .]

I have a hunch, too, that for me one of the unconscious pressures toward radicalism was that the movement provided an atmosphere in which I could reject being Jewish without any feelings of guilt. One of the first rituals in the radical movement was the adoption of a party name by which one was to be known in the organization. The origin of the custom was legitimate enough: revolutionists in Europe and Russia always took false names as a device to handicap police persecution. The same technique in American radical organizations may not have been justified by that reason, but it did give us a link, a romantic identification, with the revolutionary heroes of the past. Even granting the legitimate need we felt to change our names in order to escape possible consequences, why was it that so many of the Jewish radicals took as their cover names ones that were conspicuously non-Jewish? No comrade Cohen ever adopted Ginsberg as a party name; instead he became Green or Smith or Martin, or something equally bland. So, too, when for a short time I became Paul Jackson in the little red membership book, it was because Jackson was a less Jewish name than Jacobs and therefore somehow more American.

Yet many of the comrades I met then came from Yiddish-speaking homes, and their conversations were so strewn with the rich Yiddish phrases they had learned from their parents that I, too, began to absorb them into my vocabulary. But the pronounced Jewish flavor which permeated the New York radical movement had nothing religious about it. Quite the opposite: the entire Yiddish Socialist and radical milieu was militantly atheist or agnostic.

My interest in the YCL was also stimulated when Bob left New York to attend Ohio State University and began writing me about radical activities in which he became involved. In addition, I had made a new friend who lived in the same apartment house as I in upper Manhattan. He, too, was a City College student, and although he was a few years older, we sat for hours in a nearby park talking about the books I was reading—Roland's *Jean Christophe* and John Reed's *Ten Days That Shook the World*. It was he, I think, who took me to my first YCL meeting.

The YCL episode turned out to be a very short one, for within six months after joining I was expelled. I got kicked out for being a Trotskyite, although at the time I hadn't the foggiest notion of what a Trotskyite was.

The specific circumstance that led up to my expulsion was the break-up by Communists of a Socialist meeting in Madison Square Garden addressed by Norman Thomas.[3] The small-scale riot that disrupted the Thomas meeting was considered a great success by the YCLers, who reported it at one of the meetings I attended, but it left me rather confused, for when my father and I got into our usual violent arguments about politics, he always denounced Thomas as a wild-eyed and even dangerous visionary. My father's business reverses had no effect on his political outlook, and even during the period of his most painful financial embarrassment he continued to vote Republican and to read the New York *Sun*. So I couldn't understand why, if my father, who was such a conservative, hated Thomas, the YCL was attacking him too. Impatiently the leader of the branch explained the Communists were just beginning to shift from the view that leadership of the socialist parties all over the world were the equivalent of the fascists: a major effort of the Communist movement had been directed toward breaking away the membership of the socialist groups from their leaders in what was called "The United Front from Below."

But I understood very little of all this and continued asking what were obviously very naïve questions of my more and more impatient comrades. Finally, at one of the weekly meetings I was told that I had been expelled from the branch for Trotskyist leanings. It was a measure of my ignorance about the hatred the Communists felt toward Trotskyism that I went downtown to the Communist party building on Thirteenth Street and climbed the stairs to the top of the seven- or eight-story building looking vainly on each floor for the headquarters of the Trotskyists.

It was again through Bob at Ohio State that I finally did find the Trotsky-ist headquarters in New York. At the time I was expelled from the YCL, he had become a member of the Spartacus Youth League, the Trotskyist youth group, and had written me urging me to join the SYL also. He sent me the address of the adult organization known then as the Communist League of America, and one night I went to my first meeting at its national headquar-ters, a loft someplace in the Union Square district of Manhattan.

I walked into a large bare room next to some dingy offices and was greeted by a dark-haired and attractive girl with slightly protruding teeth who turned out to be the stepdaughter of a prominent Trotskyist leader. Bob's name brought me a warm welcome, and she took me around the room introducing me to other people, including her husband, a good-looking young man with a very pleasant voice.

The whole evening was much less grim than the atmosphere of the Young Communist League, where the omnipresent, omniscient, and frightening party line had been so much in evidence as the standard against which all my actions were judged. It was this difference that set apart the SYL from the YCL, for the procedures of the meeting were the same and the discus-sions just as confusing to me. The same kind of reports were given by the same kind of committees: the chairman of agitation-propaganda (agitprop for short) reported the number of copies of the weekly newspaper sold in door-to-door visits, the number of people who had attended the street-cor-ner meetings held in the city, and the success of the educational classes in the theories of Marxism and Trotskyism; the trade-union chairmen discussed the efforts of the members who were young workers to influence the poli-cies of the unions to which they belonged; the head of the student fraction (as these caucuses were called) reported on the ideological struggle being waged at City and Brooklyn Colleges against the Communists; and, finally, the social committee chairman told of the money-raising parties that were to be held in the next two weeks. After that, someone produced an accordion and we stood to sing revolutionary songs, but the same as those I had been learning in the YCL except that Trotsky's name was substituted for Stalin's. I sang along loudly, faking the words I didn't know and hoping no one could tell the difference.

I discovered other, more important, differences between the Spartacus Youth League and the Young Communist League as I attended more meet-ings. In the absence of the awesome and frightening party line, the discus-sions in the SYL seemed more free to me. The arguments between comrades were open, and although some members of the group were clearly more influential than others, political differences were sharply discussed. Somehow, too, the SYL members seemed more friendly, more interested in me as a person, than the YCL group had been, and I did feel more comfortable in this comparatively free atmosphere than I had within the rigid frame of the YCL. In a few weeks, without knowing very much about Trotskyism, I joined the Spartacus Youth League. [...]

Source: Paul Jacobs, *Is Curly Jewish? A Political Self-Portrait Illuminating Three Turbulent Decades of Social Revolt, 1935–1965* (New York: Atheneum, 1965), pp. 5–23.

NOTES

1. Yiddish: an observer who offers unsolicited or unwanted advice.
2. German: "with socialist greetings."
3. Norman Thomas (1884–1968), an ordained Presbyterian minister, pacifist, and standard-bearer of the Socialist Party from 1928 until his death.

Part II

In Struggle

A hopeful conviction radiated from the very core of socialism and roused people to action. This was a belief in the capacity of the poor and exploited to rebel and create a just society. The imperative to act could lead in any number of directions, and with mixed results. A socialist-Zionist named Louis Michel, outraged by the plight of African Americans, became a proponent of pan-Africanism in Los Angeles. Sam Darcy, a Communist from New York, preached racial equality in Indiana, and it almost cost him his life. Jennie Cohen, a garment worker in Philadelphia, was expelled from her union for insisting on enforcement of overtime rules. The Socialist Party activist Louis Waldman successfully campaigned for the New York State Assembly on a platform of high ideals only to learn that a notorious gangster had given him unsolicited help. How does one adapt lofty beliefs to everyday realities? It was a perennial question radicals had to wrestle with amid heroic strikes, grand parades, and epic campaigns.

6

"Strong, Firm, and Correct Propaganda" (1886)

DI NYU-YORKER YIDISHE FOLKSTSAYTUNG

The weekly *Di nyu-yorker yidishe folkstsaytung* (1886–1889) was the first radical Yiddish newspaper of consequence in the United States. The following program, a blend of socialism and what could be called proto-Jewish nationalism, appeared in the debut issue of the newspaper. Its somewhat awkward prose reflected the editors' lack of experience with Yiddish journalism, then in its infancy.

The Jewish worker, who makes good use of what little free time he has, spends a few cents on a Yiddish newspaper.

What does he look for in a newspaper? What does he wish to find there?

As a worker, his situation is directly connected to all workers of the world; his destiny hinges on the destiny of other workers; his future is the future of all his comrades; his hopes are the same as theirs. He sees, knows, feels that in the chain that binds the labor world together, he is a ring equal to all others, and that he is supported by the same power that holds all of the rings together. He understands that as the rings become forged more strongly, the chain becomes harder to break. He sees the chain becoming larger, heavier, and longer all the time, and, with it, the power that holds them together becomes greater and stronger.

On the other side, he sees the power of capitalism, which uses all means to break the chain of labor, to break it and scatter its rings. The worker understands all too well the capitalists' mind-set: a single person is much easier to squeeze and oppress than a unified group of people.

Such divergent goals form a war in the struggle between two conflicting classes: the workers and the capitalists. The longer the war goes on, the larger and fiercer it becomes; the more the capitalists persist, the more the workers bind themselves together, clasping their hands more firmly and becoming brothers in arms.

What can result from such a war? How long can it last, when did it begin, who is becoming the victor, the winner? What is the class struggle's current situation? What means do the workers possess? What do the leaders of the labor movement, the educated men who understand the class struggle very well, think about all of this? What do they advise? On the newspaper page, which the Jewish worker is just becoming accustomed to reading, he searches for the correct answer to all of these important questions.

As a Jew, the situation of the worker is entirely different. The Jewish Question is still wide open. It separates the Jewish worker from the entire world. When it comes to The Jewish Question, the Jewish worker still has very old and large accounts to settle. In the field of struggle as workers, the Jewish worker has many allies; in the field of struggle as a Jew, he has very few. The Jewish Question is very important, and one should consider it well so as to be able to answer it. The Jewish worker can give an answer only when he becomes familiar with Jewish history.

As a man, the Jewish worker has the right to know the state of contemporary education, civilization, and culture, to know about all scientific discoveries and about each step in human progress.

It is also important for him to read various important and fine original stories, as well as good translations.

As a part of the United States, it is very important for the Jewish worker to know the political issues in America and also know of various other peoples [. . .] and of distant countries. [. . .][1]

These are the main points, which should and must be the foundation of a newspaper read by Jewish workers.

When we consider the foundations upon which various American Yiddish newspapers are built, we see large holes among the stones, very many irregularities, and considerable negligence. The strength of any building depends on the strength of its foundation. A weak foundation shows that the architect has very little understanding of the art of construction. Thus, we hold that it is right and good to familiarize the Jewish public with the program and foundation of our newspaper.

The program is the following:

1. The labor question, its entire evolution from beginning to the present, all steps workers in various countries have made in order to improve their situation, and all means recommended by the experts and most of the important labor leaders, in order to solve the labor question.

2. Strong, firm, and correct propaganda and explanation of the truths and ideals, which must be implanted in the hearts and thoughts of all workers, who want ultimately to bring equality, freedom, and brotherhood to the world.

3. The situation of Jewish workers in the world generally and in America particularly.

4. The Jewish Question in connection with the evolution of the civilizations among various peoples.

5. The general development of culture and civilization in various stages throughout the world from the ancient period through to the present.

6. The major chapters and moments in Jewish history assembled by the best and most important Jewish historians.

7. Interesting, original stories and good translations from the latest writers.

8. The political situation and questions among various peoples.

The development of this program is the edifice of our newspaper; pure truth and the correct critique is its foundation; and both of them together will be a mirror in which the Jewish worker will see his image in the old world, his physiognomy in the current period, and many aspects of his future.

Source: "Di program," *Di nyu-yorker yidishe folkstsaytung*, June 25, 1886, p. 1. Translated by Tony Michels.

NOTES

1. The remainder of this paragraph is illegible.

7

"Socialism Is Not a Dream" (1888)

DOVID EDELSHTAT

Dovid Edelshtat (1866–1892) immigrated to the United States in 1882 in response to the pogroms that broke out in the Ukraine in the previous year. Edelshtat initially settled with his family in Cincinnati, Ohio, where he found work as a buttonhole maker. He moved to New York City around 1887 and became active in the nascent Jewish labor movement. A native Russian speaker, Edelshtat learned Yiddish in New York and was considered among the best Yiddish poets at the time of his premature death from tuberculosis at the age of twenty-six.

Dear parents, beloved brothers, and dear Sonia![1]

We in New York live at a remarkably fast pace. In a single day you often experience so much, as much as you would experience and ponder in five whole years in the calm, peaceful city of Cincinnati. In this letter, I want to share with you all the impressions that have flooded into me, like a boiling hot southern storm, from nearly the first day I came here. A new life, new energies, new truths, self-education, and an avid striving for light are noticeable here, especially in Jewish circles. But I'm not going to speak about that now. I want to tell you about the memorial event for the Chicago anarchists[2] that took place here in New York. This was a grand, historical event, which I'll never forget in my life and will never be forgotten, I think, in world history. Knowing that there would be a large crowd at the Cooper Institute, I got there at 7 o'clock in the evening, but by then there was already a mass of 1,000 people. And a group of our Russian Jews was standing in a corner bickering in Russian about some writer, and they shouted so loudly that the Germans and Americans looked astonished, like they wanted to send them to an insane asylum.

Finally, the Institute opened, and the mass of people lurched forward, shoulder to shoulder, into the hall. . . . When I recovered from all the pushing, I was standing in the middle of the hall, squeezed among thousands of people, who went there to show the world that the ideas of anarchism, the ideas of people's freedom, are far from dead; they live in the hearts of hundreds of thousands of people, who assembled in all corners of the world to protest bourgeois oppression. This mass of thousands, which gathered in this gigantic hall, covered with red banners of the revolution, found tribunes in the persons of [Johann] Most[3] and [Sergius] Schewitch,[4] whose grand speeches I cannot convey to you. I will only say that when Schewitch spoke, I felt tears streaming from my eyes, and, afterward, when the band played the Marseillaise and the gigantic mass of people let out cries of unadulterated enthusiasm, I felt that socialism is not a dream, not an illusion, that it is the real future of the people, and that the time is not far off when this mass will grow to be hundreds of thousands of people, who will consciously struggle for their stolen human rights. Most was greeted by the audience with thundering applause, which lasted ten minutes. [. . .] It was remarkable that our Russian Jews stood at the forefront with their dedication to humanity's great strivings. There were Russian Jews everywhere.

Source: Reprinted in the Russian original alongside a Yiddish translation in Kalman Marmor, *Dovid Edelshstat* (New York: IKUF, 1950), pp. 189–190. Translated by Tony Michels.

NOTES

1. Edelshtat's sister, then living in Cincinnati with his other family members.

2. Edelshtat refers here to the five men who were sentenced to death—unfairly, many in the radical community believed—for their alleged role in the Chicago Haymarket riot of May 1886.

3. Johann Most (1846–1906), German immigrant and foremost anarchist in late-nineteenth-century New York.

4. Sergius Schewitsch (1835–1912), the son of Latvian nobility, editor of the German-language daily *New Yorker Volkszeitung*, and a leading figure in the Socialist Labor Party. Both Schewitsch and Most had a strong influence on Jewish radicals during the 1880s and 1890s.

8

The Birth of the Knee-Pants Makers' Union (memoir; 1924)

BERNARD VAYNSHTEYN

Bernard Vaynshteyn (1866–1946) immigrated to New York City from Odessa in 1882. He worked as a cigar maker during his early years in New York and helped to build the institutional foundation of the Jewish labor movement. As secretary of the United Hebrew Trades, established in 1888, Vaynshteyn earned a reputation as a tireless and effective organizer. The following recollection of the knee-pants makers' strike of 1890, a year of nearly constant unrest among Jewish workers, comes from his Yiddish memoir published thirty-four years later.

Of all the most important and exciting strikes by Jewish workers in 1890, the most interesting and characteristic one was the knee-pants makers' strike.

Nine hundred knee-pants makers went on a general strike with the demand that bosses and contractors provide sewing machines for their work. Until then, every knee-pants maker had to bring, in addition to their own feet and hands, their own "katerinke" [sewing machine], needles, thread, and so on to work. You used to work in sweatshops for small contractors who would get work from large clothing manufacturers. The knee-pants operators had to change bosses all the time, and then the operators had to take their "katerinkes" and carry it on their shoulders from one boss to the next. This was terribly taxing on the workers. So, to put an end to it, they went out on strike. The most capable members of the union organized a strike committee. The United Hebrew Trades selected an aid committee, made up of Morris Hillquit, his brother, Louis Miller, Michael Zametkin,[1] and the writer of these lines.

The headquarters of the strike was in a cellar on 165 East Broadway. A large demonstration was immediately organized in the middle of the day, in which 900 knee-pants makers, in addition to workers from other trades then on strike, marched through the streets of the Lower East Side. The slogans were very strong and effective. Everyone greeted the marching workers warmly.

The knee-pants contractors, who themselves were no great rich men, began to settle after the first week. Tragicomic scenes took place at the settlements. There was a total of over a hundred bosses against whom the workers struck. The bosses arrived all at once. They were brought to the strike committee, one by one, and when the boss consented to sign the union agreement, the poor bosses, being illiterate ignoramuses, sweated profusely until they figured out how to sign the paper.

At one point, the following incident happened:

The strike committee was in the middle of negotiating with a boss, when a girl operator came in and turned to the strike committee with these words: "Please brothers of the strike committee, do not allow my boss to sign the agreement until he also agrees in writing to stop his wife from beating me with a broom."

There were many similar such demands that showed what a sad situation the workers from that trade, and all trades, found themselves in back then. The bosses were forced, one by one, to concede to the demands of their workers. Only a small number of the knee-pants shops remained scab[2] shops. It is important to note that the rich clothing manufacturers gave out all the work for children's short pants to contractors in sweatshops. Inside, in the warehouses, only cloth was cut. Sweatshops were also places where small-time bosses and their families lived. Some of the operators also used to board there, and they ate and slept in the same place where britches were made day and night.

By the time the strike came to an end, the knee-pants union had become strong. The workers were revived. They didn't have to haul the sewing machines on their shoulders every time they went to work. But it didn't take long, and the knee-pants workers looked around and saw that although the bosses had given machines to the workers, the wages for making a dozen pairs of shorts were still very small, and one could earn only 6–7 dollars per week doing piecework. The result was that, four months later, in July 1890, a second general strike broke out among the knee-pants workers. That strike was for higher wages.

Over a thousand workers went out on strike. This time the struggle was difficult because [. . .] it was hard to get the workers to walk out of the open shops. The bosses did not rush to settle, as they did the previous time during the strike for sewing machines. The contractors expected the manufacturers to raise wages, but they did not. On the contrary, they incited the contractors to try to hire scabs.[3] Some contractors hired scabs from among those they worked with in the sweatshops, and when the strikers would cross paths with the scabs, they would come to blows. The struggle was bitter.

One Saturday afternoon the strikers held a mass meeting at 165 East Broadway. The hall was packed, and the audience strongly applauded the speakers. Suddenly an uproar started, and people began pushing their way into the hall as policemen came after them with their clubs in the air. It soon turned into a terrible riot. The policemen worked their clubs left and right. A bold female striker treated a policeman to a ringing slap in the face, which caused a stir in all the New York newspapers. The policemen immediately arrested her, together with the secretary of the union, Levin, and another member.

The riot happened after the union committee went to a sweatshop and demanded that the scabs join the union. The boss readied the policemen, and when the strikers saw them, they ran into the hall and the policemen came after them, and that resulted in a clash at the mass meeting. The arrested workers had a difficult trial, which lasted for a considerable time. The strike was lost, and the union collapsed.

The United Hebrew Trades took on the defense of the three arrested workers. The trial cost a lot of money. The striker, Ida Ginzburg, was the first to be prosecuted. The jury declared her "not guilty," and she went free. The other two, Levin and Shereshevsky, were sentenced a year later, and a jury found them guilty of "assaulting an officer." They received a prison sentence of two years. But the judge, after the two innocent workers sat in The Tombs[4] for six weeks, gave them suspended sentences, and they went free.

The knee-pants workers union was resurrected later with the help of the United Hebrew Trades.

Source: Bernard Vaynshteyn, *Fertsik yor in der yidisher arbeter bavegung* (New York: Farlag Der Veker, 1924), pp. 134–138. Translated by Tony Michels.

NOTES

1. Hillquit, Miller, and Zametkin were leading organizers, lecturers, and journalists in the early Jewish labor movement. Hillquit later became a successful attorney and a leader in the Socialist Party, Zametkin a popular staff writer for the *Forverts*, and Miller editor of *Di varhayt*, a nonsocialist daily.

2. That is, nonunion shops.

3. Strike-breakers.

4. The colloquial name for the New York Halls of Justice and House of Detention, as well as other detention centers in lower Manhattan.

9

"The Whole City Seethed" (1892)

——— DI ARBETER TSAYTUNG ———

The Marxist weekly *Di arbeter tsaytung* debuted in 1890 and enjoyed a respectable circulation of six to eight thousand. The following report on a campaign rally in support of the Socialist Labor Party, with which *Di arbeter tsaytung* was aligned, may have been authored by Abraham Cahan, the newspaper's editor.

The socialist demonstration in New York, which took place on Saturday evening, was a glowing success. The whole city seethed with marching workers who walked to the huge gathering in Union Square under the red flag. According to the newspapers, between 8,000 and 10,000 people assembled. The demonstration of Jewish workers was especially successful. At 6:00 p.m., Rutgers Square was black with people who arranged themselves into columns for the parade. At 7:30 p.m. the procession left Rutgers Square. Marching in the first division were the organizations of Districts 2, 3, 4, and 5 of the Socialist Labor Party, the Socialist Labor Campaign Club, the Brotherliness Society, the Jewelers' Union, and the Purse Makers' Union. Marching in the second division were the Knee-Pants Workers' Union, which was represented by 500 members with red badges, the Socialist Tailors' Campaign Club, the Yiddish-Speaking Section of the Socialist Labor Party, the Proletariat Society, the Bookbinders' Union, and the Shirt Makers' Union. Members of all the organizations carried transparencies with various slogans, such as, "Down with the Sweating System," "The Best Strike Is through the Ballot Box," "We Demand the Abolition of Wage Slavery," "Don't Be Blinded by the Swindle of Free Trade and Protective Tariffs," and "Vote for the Candidates of the Socialist Labor Party." Devoted members of the Cap Makers' Union carried the flag. There were 1,500 men in this procession, illuminated by 400 lamps. The marchers were received with great merriment and enthusiasm on almost every street the parade went. Many houses were decorated. The marchers were greeted with lights and fireworks. The Labor Lyceum at 91 Delancey St. was richly decorated, and when the procession crossed Delancey, past the Lyceum, the merriment and enthusiasm was indescribable. The entire block was lit up by fireworks and deafened by shouts of hurrah. At 8:00, the procession arrived at the German Labor Lyceum on 4th St., where it joined the procession of the German- and English-speaking trade unions and the assembly districts of the SLP. The many musical orchestras filled the streets with the Marseillaise and other labor songs. At 8:00 the entire procession arrived at Union Square. The Square was already strongly occupied by people who warmly greeted the marchers. At 9:00 the procession from the West Side arrived. The chairman on the main platform was Comrade Matchet, candidate for vice president. He was greeted with great applause. The other speakers were comrades Salsbury, Seniel, Abe Cahan, Balkom, and Gintner. Those speakers spoke in English. Speaking on the other two platforms were comrades Bennet and Wilson Sheffer (each in English), Faygnboym and Pollack (in Yiddish), and Kuno (in German).

Comrade Shteynberg was arrested for distributing socialist literature on the way to the demonstration. The judge fined him three dollars. Aside from that, everything succeeded in the finest fashion and left an impression that will not long be forgotten.

Source: *Di arbeter tsaytung*, Oct. 28, 1892, p. 3. Translated by Tony Michels.

10

Working Women Unite
(1893–1894)

WOMEN'S SOCIETIES

Among the countless *fareynen*, or voluntary societies, established during the 1890s were those dedicated to promoting
socialism among women. The following three announcements,
published in *Di arbeter tsaytung* and the anarchist newspaper
Di fraye arbeter shtime, provide glimpses into their activities.

Progressive Women's Society, Paterson, NJ

Under this name, a group of more or less goal-oriented women have
established a society in Paterson to cultivate the spirit of freedom in working women. The first meeting took place at the Proletariat Club, 59 Hamburg
Ave. It was decided that, on every Saturday evening, formal readings and
business meetings should take place at the Proletariat Club. All women are
invited to the large mass meeting on Sunday, July 2, where Comrade Leontieff[1] will hold a lecture on The Women's Question.

Source: *Di fraye arbeter shtime*, June 23, 1893, p. 4.

Workingwomen's Society, New York City

Last Friday evening, the Workingwomen's Society held its first mass meeting at 165 East Broadway and had an unexpectedly great success. The hall
was packed with five or six hundred women and men, as well, and many
people had to be turned away because of lack of space. The well-known German orator Mrs. Kantsius and Comrade Zametkin[2] gave inspired lectures in
which they explained the goals and aspirations of the new society, namely,
the organization of the women's trades and the achievement of political
rights by struggling hand in hand with the male proletariat for the liberation
of all of humanity regardless of sex. The speeches were greeted with strong

applause, and 20 new members joined the society. The first lecture will be given by Dr. Ingerman[3] at 412 Grand St. next Friday evening on the topic: "Women in the Past, Present, and Future." All are welcome.

Source: *Di arbeter tsaytung*, Dec. 15, 1893, p. 3.

"A Women's Gathering"

The cloak makers have hit upon an outstanding plan. Everybody knows that the greatest enemies of strikes are often the wives of the strikers themselves. That which the bosses cannot achieve with money, policemen, and Pinkertons,[4] they achieve much easier by hiring people to incite the wives against their striking husbands. This inadvertent alliance is usually the greatest danger for all strikes. In order to avoid this danger, the cloak makers yesterday took their wives to Walhalla Hall, where S. Miller, S. Pollack, and M. Sheynfeld gave them moral instruction. Over 500 wives of the strikers listened with great attentiveness to the speeches, and, at the end, they fervently swore not only not to chastise their husbands anymore for striking but, on the contrary, to allow the men not to return to work until the bosses give in to the union's demands.

Source: *Di arbeter tsaytung*, Nov. 7, 1894, p. 3. Translated by Tony Michels.

NOTES

1. Pseudonym of Leon Moisseiff (1872–1943), Yiddish writer and lecturer associated with the anarchist movement. A suspension-bridge engineer, Moisseiff gained a national reputation as a designer of the Manhattan Bridge.

2. Adele Kean Zametkin (1864–1931), socialist activist and cofounder of the Workingwomen's Society.

3. Dr. Anna Amitin Ingerman (1865–1931), frequent lecturer in English, German, Russian, and Yiddish, cofounder of the Workingwomen's Society, and active in the Socialist Labor Party, the Socialist Party, and Russian-émigré politics.

4. Private detectives hired to break strikes.

11

The Attempted Assassination of Henry Clay Frick (memoir; 1912)

ALEXANDER BERKMAN

Born in Russia, Alexander Berkman (1870–1936) immigrated to the United States in 1888 and rose to prominence in the anarchist movement. In 1892, he attempted to take the life of Henry Clay Frick (1849–1919), chairman of the Carnegie Steel Company, to avenge the deaths of seven steel workers killed by Frick's detectives during the great Homestead Strike. Berkman served fourteen years in prison for his deed. The following account appears in Berkman's prison memoir.

The door of Frick's private office, to the left of the reception-room, swings open as the colored attendant emerges, and I catch a flitting glimpse of a black-bearded, well-knit figure at a table in the back of the room.

"Mistah Frick is engaged. He can't see you now, sah," the negro says, handing back my card.

I take the pasteboard, return it to my case, and walk slowly out of the reception-room. But quickly retracing my steps, I pass through the gate separating the clerks from the visitors, and, brushing the astounded attendant aside, I step into the office on the left, and find myself facing Frick.

For an instant the sunlight, streaming through the windows, dazzles me. I discern two men at the farther end of the long table.

"Fr——," I begin. The look of terror on his face strikes me speechless. It is the dread of the conscious presence of death. "He understands," it flashes through my mind. With a quick motion I draw the revolver. As I raise the weapon, I see Frick clutch with both hands the arm of the chair, and attempt to rise. I am at his head. "Perhaps he wears armor," I reflect. With a look of horror he quickly averts his face, as I pull the trigger. There is a flash, and the high-ceilinged room reverberates as with the booming of cannon. I hear a sharp, piercing cry, and see Frick on his knees, his head against the arm of the chair. I feel calm and possessed, intent upon every movement of the man. He is lying head and shoulders under the large armchair, without sound or motion. "Dead?" I wonder. I must make sure. About twenty-five feet separate us. I take a few steps toward him, when suddenly the other man, whose presence I had quite forgotten, leaps upon me. I struggle to loosen his hold. He looks slender and small. I would not hurt him: I have no business with him. Suddenly I hear the cry, "Murder! Help!" My heart stands still as I realize that it is Frick shouting. "Alive?" I wonder. I hurl the stranger aside and fire at the crawling figure of Frick. The man struck my hand,—I have missed! He grapples with me, and we wrestle across the room. I try to throw him, but spying an opening between his arm and body, I thrust the revolver against his side and aim at Frick, cowering behind the chair. I pull the trigger. There is a click—but no explosion! By the throat I catch the stranger, still clinging to me, when suddenly something heavy strikes me on the back of the head. Sharp pains shoot through my eyes. I sink to the floor, vaguely conscious of the weapon slipping from my hands.

"Where is the hammer? Hit him, carpenter!" Confused voices ring in my ears. Painfully I strive to rise. The weight of many bodies is pressing on me. Now—it's Frick's voice! Not dead? . . . I crawl in the direction of the sound, dragging the struggling men with me. I must get the dagger from my pocket—I have it! Repeatedly I strike with it at the legs of the man near the window. I hear Frick cry out in pain—there is much shouting and stamping—my arms are pulled and twisted, and I am lifted bodily from the floor.

Police, clerks, workmen in overalls, surround me. An officer pulls my head back by the hair, and my eyes meet Frick's. He stands in front of me, supported by several men. His face is ashen gray; the black beard is streaked with red, and blood is oozing from his neck. For an instant a strange feeling, as of shame, comes over me; but the next moment I am filled with anger at the sentiment, so unworthy of a revolutionist. With defiant hatred I look him full in the face.

"Mr. Frick, do you identify this man as your assailant?"

Frick nods weakly.

The street is lined with a dense, excited crowd. A young man in civilian dress, who is accompanying the police, inquires, not unkindly:

"Are you hurt? You're bleeding?"

I pass my hand over my face. I feel no pain, but there is a peculiar sensation about my eyes.

"I've lost my glasses," I remark, involuntarily.

"You'll be damn lucky if you don't lose your head," an officer retorts.

Source: Alexander Berkman, *Prison Memoirs of an Anarchist*, 2nd ed. (New York: Schocken Books, 1972), pp. 33–35. First edition published in 1912.

12

The Prophet Karl Marx (c. 1910s)

ABRAHAM SHIPLACOFF

A leading activist in the Socialist Party, Abraham Shiplacoff (1877–1934) was elected to the New York State Assembly in 1915 and to the New York City Board of Aldermen in 1920. His opposition to U.S. involvement in World War I led to his indictment under the Espionage Act. The following is the surviving fragment of a speech delivered by Shiplacoff in Yiddish, probably in the 1910s.

Marx was a prophet, no less so than Isaiah, Jeremiah, or Ezekiel. With honest conviction and courage he proclaimed the economic liberation of humanity. He appealed to the workers of the world and inspired them with his conviction that they are destined to fulfill the great task of abolishing poverty, thus putting an end to wars between nations and classes, and, in doing so, realize the great thousands-year-old dream of human brotherhood. Basically, Marx's vision of a social order rooted in justice and equal opportunity for all, and whose blossoms are the joy of fellowship and brotherliness, were no less a holy prophecy than the social prophecy called God's Kingdom on Earth by the great Jewish Prophets.

We who call ourselves students of Marx unfortunately forget quite often the intellectual significance of our movement. Marx never forgot it. True, he strongly underscored the inevitability of the class struggle as a fact of social development and called on the workers of all countries to unite in order to vanquish the ruling class. But his idea was much deeper. He never forgot that the ultimate purpose of victory is not to make the workers into rulers over the class under which they had been subjected. Rather, it was to put an end, once and for all, to class domination by abolishing those circumstances that make possible the division of society into various classes. Only thus can a fellowship of humanity become possible.

Marx bitterly attacked economic enslavement and struggled to liberate the world from material poverty, unhappiness, and oppression. But this was only his short-term goal, not his final goal. Marx was too great a man and too deep a thinker to consider material satisfaction and comfort the highest goal in life. He realized that the spiritual life of man was strongly dependent on his physical life and that the highest development of spiritual life is a flower that sprouts from the highest development of material life. He knew full well that the chains that bind the body also bind the soul and that the liberation of the soul can be enriched by breaking the chains that bind the body.

Source: A. I. Shiplacoff Papers, box 5, folder 3, Tamiment Library, New York University. Translated by Tony Michels.

13

"Our Mecca" (memoir; n.d.)

ISADORE WISOTSKY

Born in Latvia, Isadore Wisotsky (1895–1970) immigrated to the United States with his family at the age of four. He worked in the garment industry and joined the Industrial Workers of the World, perhaps the most militant labor organization in the United States during its heyday in the years running up to World War I. The following portrait of Union Square, a hotbed of radical activity in the early decades of the twentieth century, comes from Wisotsky's unpublished autobiography.

Properly speaking, Union Square—where Broadway meets Fourth Avenue and crosses 17th and 14th Streets—is not a part of the Lower East Side. But it was the Lower East Side that gave it life.

The Square was our Mecca; the place where East met West, . . . where Uptown came Downtown. We gathered to make revolution and stayed to talk. And how we talked—anarchism, atheism, against the military, for birth control, against injustice, for socialism, for the rights of the workers to organize. Hardly a subject was left untouched by our excitement, by our passions, by our sincerity.

I first came to the Square as a teenage immigrant boy. On tip-toe, I strained to hear and see everything. In those days, the Square was a bubbling hub with spokes reaching out into every neighborhood of the city. A rally in the Square frequently was preceded by scores of community meetings, a clustering around street corners that would turn into one large stream of human traffic moving onto it. People came there from the Lower East Side, from Williamsburg and Brownsville in Brooklyn, and from the far reaches of the Bronx, to talk, to listen, to learn. They were, in the main, working men and women, mostly young, dressed neatly as for an outing. A demonstration in Union Square was a holiday, an escape from the long hours of drudgery and the grim realities of a dull, crowded tenement life.

Many in the crowd were immigrants. But not all. The Square also attracted every kind of radical and nonconformist intellectual from Greenwich Village, as well as the diletanti and just plain spectators and rubbernecks. But the heart of the assembly was that of the labor force, working people, registering their awareness of the troubles of the world.

The speakers, ah, the speakers! What attractions we had. Out of the west came big, tanned men with powerful and persuasive voices and intoxicating ideas to stand on a common platform with the thin, hungry-looking, pale figures from the slums. There was "Big Bill" Haywood,[1] a one-eyed giant, who on closer meeting was a soft-spoken gentle fellow beneath a wide-brimmed battered hat. On the stand, he was a roaring firebrand, denouncing war and capitalism with fervor.

Or Elizabeth Gurley Flynn,[2] who later turned Communist. She was then a ravishing, black-haired rebel girl of the IWW. She, too, burned with an inner fire on the soapbox. And Ed Louis, the finest orator of them all, a freelancer without any organization affiliation but ready to speak up for the "victims of capitalism." He was just as ready to discuss labor, war, or politics over a friendly glass of spirits. From the sidewalks of New York came Harlem's atheist-Socialist agitator Hubert Harrison,[3] who later found God in Tammany Hall; and the brilliant, crippled Bohemian poet from Brooklyn Charley Sunshine, who talked his young life away against the war on the one hand and for "brotherhood" on the other.

Those valuable speakers had sharpened their thinking and had strengthened their voices on soapboxes in mining towns and lumber camps and on city street corners. They had traveled in freight cars, slept in poor homes of friends, and raised grubstakes through the sale of literature at these spirited meetings. After they had passed such tests, they were eligible and ready for the important engagements at Webster or Carnegie Hall. But only the very best could expect to make it to the speakers' stand at the north end of famous Union Square facing 17th Street.

There, they were central figures in the dramas that opened and closed with "hymns" frequently from the acid pen of the Wobbly poet Joe Hill,[4] who was executed on a framed-up charge of murder in Salt Lake City, Utah. "Long-Haired Preachers," my favorite, includes these lines:

> Longhaired preachers come out every night,
> Try to tell us what's wrong and what's right
> But when asked how about something to eat
> They will answer with voices so sweet
> You will eat, bye and bye
> In the glorious land above

the sky,
Work and pray, live on hay
You'll get pie in the sky
when you die.

Almost any issue could draw a sizeable crowd, 20,000 or more, to Union Square. Sometimes, the police made surprising sneak arrests at these great mass demonstrations. Dr. Ben Reitman, a physician, was arrested there for distributing forbidden birth control information and sentenced to sixty days in jail. I remember the time the Birth Control League conducted a protest meeting in the Square. When it was over, attorney Jessie Ashley and Bolton Hall, a prominent and respected advocate of the Single Tax, were arrested for distributing birth control literature.

But most of the meetings in that World War I period, however, dwelt on labor questions. On high-flung banners waving over the crowd could be read our demands, as speakers swayed the crowd with their oratory.

Our slogans were simple and to the point.

War is murder.
Down with capitalism, long live the social revolution.
An injury to one is an injury to all.
Down with craft unionism, long live one big union.
The eight-hour day—today.
Capitalism is the cause of all evils.

In 1914, during that bitter winter when many thousands waited long hours in bread lines and slept in drafty flophouses or wherever they could find shelter, we of the IWW led our followers into churches. We argued that Christ had urged the starving to come unto him. [. . .] But as was the case with most events of the day, we did end up in Union Square. As the "respectables" protested in Carnegie Hall, we of the IWW marched on Union Square despite the prevailing police ban.

I recall quite vividly the day that "Wild Joe" O'Carroll, one of the more eloquent of our speakers, mounted the stand.

"Why," he cried out, "are you standing here? Go into the stores," he roared, sweeping his hands around the Square. "Take what you need. If they ask for money, tell them to send me the bill." He could say no more, for the police dragged him bodily from the platform. The cops started swinging their clubs at the crowd while the women screamed. Many fled in terror. Joe Carroll got his head split open and would have been killed on the spot had not Beckie Edelson, "sweetheart of the anarchists," thrown herself across his prostrate body. Unhappily, her sacrifice was not in time. Joe Carroll died several months later as a result of this beating. Arthur Caren, half Indian, half white, and all Wobbly, was pulled into a car by detectives and beaten beyond recognition. The crowd was chased off the Square.

But this kind of violence was rare. For most of its history, Union Square was a place of peaceful assembly; noisy with cheers, boisterous with enthusiasm, but peaceable. Actually, there might have been even fewer incidents of conflict except for the attitude of the authorities and the actions of the police.

Times changed along with the issues. Speakers and organizations changed, too. The Communists came into the Square and tried to monopolize it. When they weren't staging their own rallies, they were heckling others. During the 1920s, and most of the '30s, their favorite target was Norman Thomas, who, along with other Socialists and labor leaders, relentlessly exposed Communist lies and hypocrisies. For a brief respite in the late '30s, during the Popular Front, there was an uneasy truce. That ended with the infamous Hitler-Stalin Pact.

World War II spelled the end of the Square as a haven for free speech and as a political forum, except for a few Communist sorties. It has been years now since radical issues and nonconformist speakers could find large and interested audiences there. The old generation has moved on and lost interest. The Lower East Side changed with the times and now no longer marches on the Square. Permission for meetings in the Square is rarely asked for and more rarely given.

Source: Isadore Wisotsky, "Such a Life," pp. 134–144, Isadore Wisotsky Autobiographical Typescript, box 1, folder 9, Tamiment Library, New York University.

NOTES

1. William "Big Bill" Haywood (1869–1928). From 1915 until 1917, Haywood served as leader of the Industrial Workers of the World. The U.S. government arrested him in 1917 for calling for strikes during wartime, and he fled to Soviet Russia after his final appeal was rejected by the U.S. Supreme Court in 1921.

2. Flynn (1890–1964) was a leader in the Industrial Workers of the World and, later, a founding member of the American Civil Liberties Union and chairperson of the American Communist Party. Among the many causes she championed were birth control and women's suffrage.

3. Harrison (1883–1927) was a West Indian immigrant to Harlem whose writings and speeches on socialism and race-consciousness helped to spawn the "New Negro" movement of the 1920s.

4. Hill (1879 or 1882–1915) was a Swedish immigrant, poet-songwriter, and member of the Industrial Workers of the World. Many of his songs and sayings became rallying cries of the radical labor movement. Hill was arrested and charged with the murder of a butcher and his son in 1915; although he pled innocent (and evidence supported that plea), he was nevertheless executed for the crime in 1915.

"The Right to Control Birth" (1916)

ROSE PASTOR STOKES

Rose Pastor Stokes (1879–1933) emigrated from Poland to Cleveland, Ohio, where she worked as a cigar roller during her teenage years. Pastor Stokes's career as a labor advocate began in 1903 when she took a job in New York City writing for the English pages of the *Yidishes tageblat*. Her marriage in 1905 to James Graham Phelps Stokes, a social reformer from a wealthy Anglo-Protestant family, generated much public attention. Pastor Stokes joined the Socialist Party a year later and became a popular lecturer and writer for party publications. Stokes delivered the following speech at a birth control rally in honor of Emma Goldman, who was present at the occasion. Stokes was later arrested, in 1916, for passing out leaflets on the subject of birth control.

We have met here in protest against the law which operates to keep the knowledge of contraception from the mothers of the poor and blinks the fact that the comfortable classes obtain that knowledge from their highly-paid physicians and from one another. We demand that the law which is a dead letter for the rich also become a dead letter for the poor, and declare that we shall continue in ever-increasing numbers to honor this law by breaking it. The poor and the physicians of the [poor], and those who realize the immediate necessity of spreading contraceptive knowledge, will not continue to respect a law that is negatively responsible for so much misery among the masses of the people.

The absurdity of the situation is clear to everyone. Some of the administrators of the law are being privately ridiculed for their hypocrisy. For it is widely known—and discussed (although not in print)—that not among the least of those who have persecuted the poor law-breakers in this respect have rich law-breaking friends and do themselves break the law and benefit by the scientific knowledge they are instrumental in sending others to prison for disseminating.

What a travesty of justice! Here is material for a Shavian comedy and will surely find an enterprising author to do the theme justice.

Again, we find the authorities setting a Comstockian[1] detective to catch William Sanger,[2] for instance, in the act of giving out contraceptive information. Why (is the question being asked everywhere), to be consistently legal (or equally unjust), do they not send a Comstockian detective to catch a society doctor or put themselves in jail? No one condemns the society doctor. He is thought to be both wise and humane. But so too in this respect are William Sanger, Emma Goldman, Ben Reitman.[3] Why, then, this discrimination? Is it possible that according to the law of our economic autocracy to be poor is to be obscene and to have property is not to be obscene? Ah, but these propertyless agitators who are spreading this scientific knowledge among the poor and the propertyless must be suppressed. For it is the business of our greedy capitalist society to prevent the poor from regulating the size of their families in order that the size of unearned incomes might not also thereby be automatically regulated—downward. The overburdened mothers of the poor must not be given food for thought, when overburdened capitalism (overburdened with the unconsumed surplus of its exploited peoples) needs food for cannon.

The reformer could, and indeed tries to, convince the capitalist class of its short-sightedness by pointing to the high death rate which, in present conditions, is a concomitant of the high birth rate. He points to the incalculable economic waste this fact indicates: the cost of the births: doctors, nurses, special expenditures for food and clothing, hospitals, clinics, lost work days, loss of physical and mental efficiency, the cost of sickness in those periods, long or short, between birth and death; then the cost of the deaths: the funeral expenses and again the loss of work days and of mental and physical efficiency for those most intimately concerned. Marshalling these facts, which speak in terror of dollars and cents, (the language best understood by the ruling class), the reformer tries to make some impression upon the dull brains of the exploiters. But the thing that impresses the "impractical" radical most is not so much the cost in money as the cost in human life, the toll paid in human suffering, the agony millions of mothers endure when sickness or poverty or other unfavorable conditions (needlessly forced upon them by a maladjusted system) brings them a coffin and carries away the cradle, or—as frequently happens—leaving the cradle, leaves with it something more tragic than a coffin.

Recently an editor commented on this birth control movement. The climax of his editorial was that the distribution of contraceptive literature is not only against the law of man but of the Almighty. The old cry of superstition against science. Do these men who claim to be so intimately acquainted with God ever announce what the will of God is with regard to crushing little children in the mills, the mines, the factories? One does not hear much concerning God's decision in this respect. Yet when they do speak up, it is usually to impress upon us the thought that in child labor there may be hidden some divine purpose. In their hearts they must know that it exists to fill the pockets of greedy mill and mine and factory owners and stockholders.

These junior partners of the Lord seem to know it is God's will that children should come indiscriminately into the world; and that a large percentage of them should also be forced out of the world by humanly preventable conditions. Science comes to regulate life and prevent needless death. But, say the bigots, these conditions exist by God's will and must therefore be borne in a meek and humble spirit.

From the day that the light of science began to break upon the mind of men, superstition has attempted to place a black curtain of fear between man's mind and the light. If man had heeded what Superstition has always chosen to call the "will of God," we should still stand little higher than the ape. It is only because Science has been, since its earliest youth, reversing the "decisions of the Lord," that man has been enabled to struggle up to what light he has in the present and to feel in his breast the hope of perfection in the future. The battle between Science and Superstition is by no means over, but for Science it has been and continues to be a winning fight.

Believing as I do, that humanity progresses rapidly through science, I have done and will do all I can to spread its light. If the master-class chooses for its own greedy purposes to side with bigotry and superstition by this law, so much the worse for the law. It will be broken and ignored.

Since the dinner at the Brevoort I have had scores upon scores of letters pleading for information on methods of contraception. I have spent a good deal of my time answering them, refusing no one. Letters from mothers with over-large families and a small surplus of strength and hardly any income. Women whose several children have died at birth because of constitutional inability to bring children into the world able to survive. Letters from young mothers with two or three or four children who, because of sickness or temporary worklessness on the part of the wage earner, desire to wait for a time when they can decently and safely take care of more children before bringing them into the world. Letters from mothers who have been warned by their physicians that another child birth would mean the mother's death, but to whom those same doctors denied contraceptive information. Letters from mothers already burdened with large families, who frankly confess that they have resorted, from time to time in their desperation, to abortion, begging for the knowledge that would make unnecessary a prepetition of the horrors they have passed through. Such and many more have come to me day after day and are still coming. Some of them too tragic and too terrible to quote or to mention. Very many of them barely literate, with addresses that lend to some of the worst living sections of the city. Letters from farmers' wives, letters from women of the middle class, letters from the farthest ends of the country. Requests even from Catholic women. And from all, the God bless yous and the words of thankfulness and encouragement that indicate the deep, the crying, the immediate need, and the widespread revolt against the law which declares the giving out of contraceptive information a crime.

Frankly, then, I have broken the law over and over, because I believe that since science has shown the way, the mothers of the world should have the power and the right to control birth—to have as many or as few children as the conditions of their health or their particular material environment coupled with a decent standard of living, shall dictate.

My chief interest is not birth control, but Socialist propaganda, which aims to place land and industry within the reach of all the people upon terms of equal opportunity—which purposes to eliminate poverty and insecurity by eliminating the waste and robbery of Capitalism. But pending the day when the Socialists have sufficient control to effect these basic changes, there are lesser causes to meet immediate vital needs that I believe to be worth fighting for, and birth control is such a cause.

You, gentlemen, who earn your living by hunting down the victims of a maladjusted society, and you, gentlemen of the club, if you are here to interfere with, or arrest, or provide the authorities with evidence against anyone ignoring this unjust section of the law, I address myself to you. I should be truly sorry to place you under so mean an obligation, for I know your hearts well enough to know that you do not always relish the job your economic insecurity forces you to hold on to.

But I can not do other than again take the opportunity afforded me here of passing out information to wives and mothers in need.

I do not, of course, want to go to jail, and, again, I am not bidding for arrest. I wish to be saved all that, naturally. But I am not afraid. For twenty-three years, Capitalist Society has done its worst to me. It gave me an underfed childhood, hemmed me in on all sides by the stone walls of No Opportunity, and, when I was hardly old enough to bear the burden, it began to turn my very heart's blood into gold for others—sometimes for people I never saw and who never saw me. Whole seasons at a time it worked me not only the long day but also far into the night, giving me in return semi-starvation, a starved body upon it, a few indecent rags, no schooling, frequently the hard floor for a bed, and the weight of an unnamable nightmare as each succeeding year added another mouth to feed, then eliminated the father of those six little ones, in the unequal struggle for bread. (Oh yes, don't look at the *one* who has somehow chanced to survive but look down into the pit where the millions struggle weakly, and where millions have succumbed.)

Capitalist society has not succeeded in making me bitter, but it has succeeded in making me unafraid.

Therefore, be the penalty what it may, I here frankly offer to give out these slips with the forbidden information to those needy wives and mothers who will frankly come and take them.

Source: Speech delivered at Carnegie Hall, New York City, on May 5, 1916, Rose Pastor Stokes Papers, Film R-7124, reel 67, frame XIX, 7, Tamiment Library, New York University. Special thanks to Melissa Klapper for sharing this document with me.

NOTES

1. Stokes refers here to the Comstock Law (full name: Act for the Suppression of Trade in, and Circulation of, Obscene Literature and Articles for Immoral Use), which was named after Anthony Comstock, a leading vice crusader. Since its passage in 1873 until it was struck down in 1938, the law was widely used to curb the distribution of information on birth control and contraceptive devices.

2. William Sanger was the husband of birth control activist Margaret Sanger from 1902 until 1913. During Margaret's exile from the United States in 1915, William inadvertently delivered a copy of his former wife's publication "Family Limitations" to an undercover agent of Anthony Comstock. He was arrested, tried, and served thirty days in prison for the offense.

3. Ben Reitman (1879–1942), an anarchist and "hobo physician," treating drifters, prostitutes, and other marginal people in industrial urban America. He performed abortions at a time when the practice was illegal. Reitman and Emma Goldman, who was his lover, were both arrested in 1916 under the Comstock Law for advocating birth control; Reitman was imprisoned for six months.

15

A Personal and Confidential Letter to Louis Marshall (1917)

ABRAHAM CAHAN

In 1917, the postmaster general threatened to rescind the *For-verts*'s second-class mailing privileges because of its opposition to America's entry into World War I. This penalty probably would have bankrupted the Yiddish daily, as it did many antiwar newspapers. However, the *Forverts* was saved by the intercession of Louis Marshall, prominent attorney and head of the American Jewish Committee, who solicited the following statement of loyalty from the *Forverts*'s editor, Abraham Cahan. Cahan separately promised the postmaster general that he would henceforth refrain from commenting on the war.

Dear Mr. Marshall:

In reply to your kind inquiry of this date concerning the policy of the Jewish Daily Forward, I wish to say that it has been its desire to stand for strict obedience to the laws of the land. Whatever its policy may have been before the enactment of any particular law, it regards it to be its duty as well as that of its readers to observe unreservedly any and every law after its enactment. This policy has not been intentionally departed from.

As the editor of the paper I propose in its future management to continue this policy and to do nothing or permit nothing to be done that may be interpreted as advocating or encouraging disobedience or defiance in any shape, way or form of any law promulgated by the government of the United States.

To state the matter more definitely and concretely, it will be my policy from this time forth to see to it that the Forward is kept entirely free from anything that could either in letter or in spirit, be interpreted as breach or disregard of any of the laws enacted by our government for the purpose of prosecuting the war, or which might be regarded as inimical to our government.

The Forward, as you undoubtedly know, is by far the largest and most important Jewish newspaper not only in this country but in the world. It is not only the avowed and accepted spokesman of the hundreds of thousands of Jewish workers in all parts of the country, but the general cultural center of the great immigrant Jewish population. The Forward has a very large mail circulation, and the withdrawal of second class mailing privileges would seriously cripple if not destroy the publication. It would inflict a severe blow not only upon the publishers of the paper, but upon a large section of the Jewish population of the country.

Yours sincerely,
Abraham Cahan

Source: Abraham Cahan to Louis Marshall, Oct. 8, 1917, Benjamin Schlesinger Records, box 3, folder 2, Kheel Center, Cornell University.

16

Gangsters and Socialists on Election Day (memoir; 1944)

LOUIS WALDMAN

The labor lawyer Louis Waldman (1892–1982) immigrated to the United States from the Ukraine in 1909. He was twice elected to the New York Sate Assembly on the Socialist Party ticket. Although the Republican-controlled Assembly expelled Waldman and the other four Socialist Assemblyman on the first day of the 1920 legislative session, Waldman continued to run for office into the 1930s, polling over one hundred thousand votes in his gubernatorial campaigns. Waldman served as counsel for the Amalgamated Clothing Workers Union, the New York Central Trades and Labor Council, and other unions.

Election Day in this age of the voting machine is the day when a popular candidate, even if he belongs to a minority party, casts his vote to the click of news cameras and relaxes from the strain of his campaign. But when I first encountered politics, New York elections were often dirty and unsavory things, and a Socialist candidate on Election Day went through the experiences of a minor war.

The polling places were generally in some untidy barbershop or in the elevating atmosphere of a funeral parlor. It was a common occurrence for toughs and gangsters to lounge about the polls, intimidating and browbeating voters. The polling inspectors and watchers for the two dominant parties were usually people to whom election of their candidates meant a job of some kind. Unscrupulous conduct at elections was, therefore, frequently a matter of economic self-preservation.

In each district the political organizations, Republican as well as Democratic, were geared to take advantage of the existing inadequate election machinery. The captain of each block knew every resident voter, his needs, interests, and weaknesses. On Election Day, before noon, he would have before him a last-minute list of all registered voters who were not likely to vote that day—the sick, the dead, and the absentees. In some sections, a stream of strangers would then flood the polls and, under the tolerant eyes of the party regulars, cast votes in the names of those who were absent, according to previous instructions. "Cemetery voters," "mattress voters," people who moved into a district overnight, all these weighed heavily against an honest poll.

"Counting out" a candidate was an easy matter before the advent of the voting machine. With a small piece of lead concealed under a fingernail, the skillful ballot-counter would "mutilate" an opposition ballot and thus have it discredited as "spoiled." Sometimes he would tear it slightly in the handling, to put it out of the count. These were only a few of the opposition tactics with which Socialist candidates had to contend.

To guard against such dishonest practices, the Election Law authorizes each political party to appoint two official watchers for each polling place. But not a few of our watchers, under the threat of guns and blackjacks, had to abandon their posts on Election Day for fear of bodily harm. And many a time I had to storm the entrance of a polling place to which, as a candidate, I had legal right of entry.

Among our most ardent watchers were Harry Donnenfeld and his young bride, Gea. By no fantastic stretch of the imagination could anyone have then guessed that cheerful, short, thin Harry would ever have any connection with the type of strong, invincible super-manhood that is today glorified by the fabulous Superman. He is now, however, that super-hero's owner and publisher, and enjoys the affectionate nickname of "Superman" Donnenfeld.[1]

One Election Day during this period, Donnenfeld and I shared a typical experience that had all the elements of a Superman thriller except one. The setting was one of the East Side's toughest polling places, a dingy, crowded, smoke-filled barbershop on Fourteenth Street. The villains were two political thugs whose task it was to keep out the Socialist watchers. The "heroes" were Harry and myself. Like Superman, we were crusaders, but there ended all similarity between us and the miracle-working foe of the underworld.

Four of our watchers had already been persuaded to leave this polling place, and had numerous lumps, bruises, and contusions to prove it, when Donnenfeld and I set forth to establish the party's legal rights there. A special reception awaited us. Hardly were we in the place when we were shoved into a corner and found ourselves staring into two evil-looking automatics and two pimply but equally grim and evil-looking faces.

"Are you gonna get outta here," remarked one of these guardians of the sanctity of the ballot, out of the side of his mouth, "or are we gonna drill ya fulla holes?" The invitation was seconded by the noses of the automatics, which had established intimate contact with our ribs.

Superman, as Donnenfeld pointed out to me ruefully at a recent New Year's party at his home, when he reminded me of the incident, might have extricated himself from this tight spot by lifting himself out of it perpendicularly, probably laying low the two plug-uglies en route. But we were no supermen. We looked at those faces, and reasoned. Unlike the mercenary members of Murder, Incorporated, who, it has since been revealed, undertook their homicidal chores at fifty dollars a head, the artists who stood before us that day, we knew, were eager to do the job in hand out of sheer esthetic pleasure. Being sensible men, we rejected the alternative of becoming the martyred victims of another unsolved East Side murder, and beat an ignominious retreat.

Back at headquarters we found other watchers who had been mauled and thrown out of the polls. When one of them displayed the black eye he had received from the welcoming committee at his appointed polling place, a gray-haired, cultured, distinguished-looking woman, who had been listening with obvious indignation, asked to take his place. She was one of many liberals who had responded to our public appeal for volunteers. The name she gave me was Harriot Stanton Blatch.

I had of course heard of this noted women's suffrage leader and, though I was grateful for her offer, I tried to dissuade her from taking the particular polling place because of the indignity to which I was afraid she might be subjected.

"You give me the credentials and I'll get in and stay in," she said firmly.

In less than a hour she was back at headquarters, flushed and furious, yet somehow retaining all the dignity for which she was famous.

"I was told to go back where I came from," she fumed, "by a man with a European accent. And a policeman stood right there and laughed when they shoved me out of the place!"

As she described her experience, there was mounting anger among the men and women in the club room, who resented bitterly the fact that this great lady, the daughter of the famous Elizabeth Cady Stanton,[2] should be subjected to the same insults which they themselves had become used to. But Harriot Stanton Blatch was not a woman to let anyone else fight her battles for her.

"I'm going to move into this district," she declared amid cheers, "and fight side by side with you against this sort of thing!" That was the beginning of a long friendship which I valued highly, though in the years that followed I disagreed sharply with Mrs. Blatch in her opposition to protective labor legislation for women.

When, years later, on August 1932, I testified before the State Legislative Committee investigating New York election malpractices, and told them of our experiences on Election Day, Senator Cosmo Cilano, chairman of the committee, commented, "What you describe was more like a little war than an election!"

Since my early campaigns, over twenty-five years ago, some progress has been made in the improvement of our election machinery. But we have yet to win the final victory for the honest ballot: the elimination of political local election boards and the substitution of boards selected from Civil Service lists, with emphasis on honesty, integrity, and reputation.

Mrs. Blatch was as good as her word. Soon afterwards she became a resident of my district, and the party made her one of its local candidates. It was in this way that she became one of the growing group of public lecturers and educators to whom many of us referred as the "faculty" of the "Second Avenue University." They included Algernon Lee, educational director of the Rand School of Social Science; Scott Nearing, author and teacher of economics and sociology in the University of Pennsylvania and the University of Toledo, Mrs. Blatch, and myself. At that time Scott Nearing had not yet embraced the extreme left-wing doctrines which he now advocates.

The so-called Second Avenue University was born on the corner of Second Avenue and Tenth Street early in the campaign of 1918. It was there, before a street corner crowd of about five thousand people, that I introduced Scott Nearing as our candidate for Congress in the Fourteenth Congressional District. Scott had just been fired from the University of Toledo because of his political and economic views.

"Toledo University," I said, "may not want Scott Nearing on its faculty, but we welcome him to the Second Avenue University of the Open Air." The idea caught the crowd's fancy, and they cheered for several minutes.

Young, vigorous, and with an engaging personality, Scott stepped forward to receive the acclaim of his new "students" in this open-air assembly, students who came back to listen to him for many weeks. As if to make good my introduction, he launched his campaign, not with a political speech, but with a lecture on economics which delighted the audience. Instead of the crowd dwindling—which is usually the case at a street meeting when the hour grows late—by the time he was through his audience had swelled to a number which police estimated to be over seven thousand.

During these years, all of us among the "faculty" and guest speakers made our campaigns the occasion for lectures on street corners on the subjects of philosophy, history, politics, economics, the science of government, literature, and art. And we tried to make these subjects vivid to our listeners by using as concrete examples the lives and environment of the people in the audience. Each evening there were four or five of these meetings, which we sometimes called "classes," and which were attended by hundreds; but the grand finale usually came at Tenth Street and Second Avenue, which was our university's assembly hall. Toward ten o'clock the smaller meetings would adjourn, and their audiences would drift toward the assembly. These final meetings, frequently several thousand strong, had a deep spiritual content almost like that of revival meetings. There the candidates would get together on one platform, there the tense emotions we had accumulated throughout the evening would be released in a final appeal to our constituents. And there, under the stars, we pleaded with thousands of men and women, black and white, Americans, Irish, Poles, Russians, Scandinavians, Jews, for comradeship, understanding, friendship, democracy.

In the campaign of 1919 we had a fusion of Republicans and Democrats against us. We also had to contend with the Communists, who had just split away from the Socialist Party. But, although it made for a tough political fight, this was a welcome change from the underhanded inner struggle that had been precipitated by the left-wingers within our own ranks. Now, at last, the political atmosphere had cleared. Well, temporarily at least. . . .

The Assembly fight that year was an exciting one, and the crowds that attended our Second Avenue University were bigger than ever. We were plagued by a great deal of heckling, but the more hecklers our opponents sent over, the larger the crowd and the better we liked it. Members of the opposition parties employed a type of heckling that we had never encountered before. Invariably at my meetings a cavalcade of passing automobiles would appear, breaking into the overflow crowd while the drivers vigorously honked their horns. This went on repeatedly. We appealed to the police without results.

But support materialized from an unexpected quarter. One evening, when the usual parade of automobiles began, a few men in the audience jumped on the running boards and began roughing up the drivers. This happened several times that evening and for several nights thereafter. Then, suddenly, the plague of our hecklers was over, as unexpectedly as it had begun. And although I deplored the violence, my heart swelled with pride at this evidence of stout civic consciousness. Evidently the people were determined to hear my message and would brook no interference.

A favorite subject during my meetings at that time was the question of the criminal and crime prevention. My district contained, in addition to thousands of hard-working, underprivileged citizens, a number of notorious gangsters who had made the East Side their habitat. I knew something of the lives of these gangsters. They were young men, immigrants or the children of immigrants, who had grown up in poverty, in the overcrowded, ugly, dangerous tenements such as I had known on Orchard and Allen streets. Escaping from the ugliness of slum homes, these boys traveled the familiar path of crime: the neighborhood poolroom, saloon, or speak-easy, bad company, gambling dens, the lure of "easy money," step by step into gangsterism. I knew that ordinary police methods were not sufficient to cope with such a social phenomenon.

At several of my meetings I pointed out that some politicians actually thrived on gangsterism, protecting the gangster in return for the services of strong-arm squads during elections. However, when, as the result of public pressure, action was inescapable, the politicians selected one of their colleagues as yet untouched by public suspicion, to conduct the anti-gangster crusade. I discussed this situation a number of times during the 1919 campaign.

Election Day finally came around. We were confident and yet fearful. I felt that my vote would be increased, but I shared the apprehension of many of my co-workers that the opposition would stop at nothing to count me out at the polls.

As usual, the crucial moment came when the vote was in. Reports trickled into headquarters about two o'clock in the morning that watchers in some of the polling places had been beaten up and thrown out. One messenger who brought us this news was a specimen victim; he had a black eye and a bloody nose. He described the method of counting as "murder" to our cause.

Putting in a call for volunteers, I set out in a car with three husky co-workers. As we swung into the traffic it seemed to me that another car was following. We pulled up before a polling place, a barbershop with drawn shades. I went up to the door. It was locked, and I banged on it.

A shade was drawn up slowly and a tough face peered out.

"Who is it?" the face rasped.

"I'm a candidate for Assembly in the district," I answered, "and I demand admission."

The face withdrew. The shades went down, and that was all there was to it. The policeman inside made no effort to enforce the law.

At this moment the car I had noticed following us drew up to the curb. Five men leaped out, and, without a word, strode to the door. Their leader, a dapper and flashily dressed young man, took out a coin and rapped authoritatively on the window with it. The shade was drawn up again and the same face appeared. After one glance it withdrew, apparently for consultation with the men inside. Then the door was opened and the five men were allowed to enter. I followed with our own men from headquarters.

Inside, I found paper ballots lying on the table, face up, in several piles. The time had come for consultation as to how to count the votes.

"Under the election law," I reminded the cigar-chewing election board, "the ballots should be placed in one pile, face downward. Please put those ballots in a single pile and start counting!"

For a moment nothing happened. The tellers looked at each other. Then, to my amazement, the dapper young man took a hand in the proceedings.

"Y'hoid what the man said, didncha?" he said sharply. "Put them ballots on the table face down an' start countin' right, like Mr. Waldman toldja."

Reluctantly, but evidently in fear, the tellers obeyed the astonishing command of my newly found supporter.

Since there was other work to be done that night, and since I knew the situation was well in hand at this particular polling place, I left, too excited to ask the name of my champion. On the way out I remarked to one of my co-workers that it was a pleasure to see public-spirited citizens acting in defense of the honesty of the ballot box.

It was not until eleven o'clock Wednesday morning, November 5, that the last vote was recorded. I had won in the Eighth Assembly District after an election in which trickery and violence had done their best to defeat me. We had made up for our defeat in the campaign of 1918 by electing five Assemblymen: August Claessens, Samuel Orr, Charles Solomon, Samuel A. DeWitt, and myself.

In those days a run-of-the-mill election gave no particular distinction to being known as an Assemblyman. Voters were asked to choose between two machine candidates, and in the lower East Side, as a rule, the election results were virtually a foregone conclusion. However, in our Socialist campaign a unique and vital relationship existed between voter and candidate. Our party was a minority party, and we were looked upon as crusaders. We had challenged the champions—the Democrats and Republicans—and we had won. It was no mere personal tribute to walk down Second Avenue and to receive from everyone, at almost every step, pleasant smiles, friendly nods, and the good wishes of people on the street. These were tributes to a fight well fought against heavy odds, a fight conducted on issues that vitally concerned everyone living in those teeming streets.

Sauntering down Second Avenue one evening shortly after the election, I came face to face with a man who looked familiar. It wasn't until he had passed me that I remembered, suddenly, who he was. I turned around and called to him.

"Aren't you the man who helped me with those toughs at the barber-shop on election night?" I asked.

"Yeah," he answered with a shamefaced grin.

We shook hands, and this time I asked him his name, telling him, "I feel proud at having a public-spirited man like you in my district."

"My name?" he hedged. "That makes no difference."

I persisted. He seemed unwilling to talk about himself and tried to edge away. I ignored his reluctance and continued to press him.

"Well, if you must know," he said finally, "I'm Dropper."

I stared at him.

"Not *Kid* Dropper?" I exclaimed. He nodded.

"Kid" Dropper was one of the most notorious gangsters of his day. His name was one to inspire fear and terror in the hearts of the inhabitants of the East Side, and yet here he had been apparently fighting to uphold the idea of the clean ballot. I was amazed.

"Why did you do it?" I asked.

"Well, I'll tellya," he said earnestly, with a distinct East Side accent. "I listened to you at a couple meetings an' I remember what you said about us guys in gangs, how we was all right an' had nice mothers and hard workin' fathers, but we used to be poor kids an' never had a chance. I liked what you said about them politicians that take us for a double ride, first they hire us an' then they ride us. Well, Mr. Waldman, that hit the nail on the head."

We stood there on the sidewalk talking for some time: I, a Socialist reformer, and he, a notorious gangster. Incongruous though it sounds, we stood there discussing crime and crime prevention!

"Remember them guys in cars that tried to break up your meetings?" Dropper asked.

I certainly did. Those noisy cavalcades had almost completely broken up my street campaign.

"I told my boys it hadda stop," he informed me. "We fixed 'em."

Another illusion crashed. So these were my public-spirited citizens!

"But aren't you fellows hired to fix elections?" I asked, bewildered. "Didn't you lose business by helping me?"

"Naw," he said. "It didn't cost me a cent. As soon as I seen you was okay, I said, 'Waldman has gotta win.' I wouldn't let 'em count you out."

"But what was the pay-off?" I persisted.

"You see," Kid Dropper explained patiently, "it was this way. Me an' the boys put up a bet of ten grand on you against twenty for the palooka runnin' against you. We *hadda* see that you got every vote that was comin' to you!"

Source: Louis Waldman, *Labor Lawyer* (New York: Dutton, 1944), pp. 79–88.

NOTES

1. A Romanian immigrant who came to the United States at the age of five, Harry Donnenfeld (1893–1965) was owner of National Allied Publications, the distributor of Action Comics and Detective Comics. These publications are best known for originating the comic book characters Superman and Batman, respectively.

2. Elizabeth Cady Stanton (1815–1902) was a prominent women's rights advocate. In addition to agitating for women's suffrage, Stanton fought for more liberal divorce laws and for better educational opportunities for women.

17

"If I Were a Colored Man What Would I Do?" (1919)

LOUIS MICHEL

Little is known about Louis Michel. He enters the historical record as an active supporter of Marcus Garvey's United Negro Improvement Association and a contributor to the *California Eagle*, the leading newspaper of Los Angeles's African American community. A socialist-Zionist, Michel wrote this article on the need for black empowerment against the backdrop of more than two dozen race riots in cities around the country.

If I were born of Negro parentage, either full blooded or only mixed in part with the blood of other races, [. . .] I would hold high my head and steady my feet and say very proudly, very happily, very plainly: It is my best fortune to be counted one of those that are not the exploiters, the commercial robbers, the arrogant persecutors, the malicious egoists, but rather one of those that are the offspring and progenitors of the downtrodden, the unjustly persecuted, the dusky skinned or lighter skinned children of the persecuted Negro people.

I would deem myself glorified and hallowed not to belong to the minions of tyranny, the upholders of race prejudice and unjust racial persecution. I would thank God that I was greatly fortified in my position to be in the right, whilst my foes were in the weak position of the wrong and in the final analysis of justice and fair play would be on the losing, but my comrades with myself, on the justly vindicated and finally winning side of the future!

But I would not merely think so in a meek and only prayerful mood, but like a true man. I would fight a good and strenuous fight to win my place under the sun for myself and my fellow racemen and here is a short summary of what I would do, or at least, what I would aim to accomplish.

I would urge upon my people to organize for their realization of their fondest hopes and dreams to be for all times full-fledged and sovereign citizens of the United States. [. . .]

1. political. No candidate of any political party could get my vote on any occasion of public struggle unless I would know fully and undoubtedly whether or not he were sound and true on the race question. I would not take the word of his mouth only, he would have to come out boldly in public writings and speeches, where thousands could see, hear and gauge him in his manifestos upon the race question, how he stood, what he thought of my people, etc.; and if he failed to come out in this true, straight, undeceiving way, he would never get my vote, whether he was the blackest Republican [. . .] or the most alluring Democrat that ever smiled with a Colored man, but never did anything else. [. . .]

2. economical. I would, if I were a Colored man, try to organize my brethren and sisters into a strong union that would press for the opening of the mills and shops in this city for the Colored toilers in all branches. Delegations after delegations of strong intellectual Colored men and women should go before the manufacturing heads of these concerns, augmented and assisted by the right-minded friends of the white race and with this proper organization courageously, with word and pen, fighting a brave local battle that would in time call forth National attention, the good big fight can surely be made and won.

On the other hand the 30,000 Colored inhabitants of Los Angeles could probably raise Thirty Thousand Dollars ($30,000) and start a factory of their own—first one and, perhaps later on another one, and thus prove by superabundant efforts that the virile Colored people can no more be kept down than the wandering, but hard-fighting Jew. Only progressive, even aggressive, action can win the way; cowardice and submission are the handmaids of drudgery and persecution and cannot be resorted to for freedom's sake and justice's glory.

I would help no merchant, stand by no storekeeper, however reasonable they would sell their wares, unless [I] was fully convinced that they were real, not merely pretending friends of my race. I would organize the members of my race to do vigilant picket duty for the purpose of a strenuous boycott of every theatre or other place of amusement that would segregate and discriminate against my people, and I would keep such an effective organization of vigilance a-going in Los Angeles that soon the best members of my race and the bulk of the rank and file of my people would be hugely benefited and encouraged by such a needed association of powerful effort. Only in this way can the foes of the Colored people be brought to their senses, not by dove-like tranquility, nor yet by the acquirement of just a single exceptional job for one member of the race, but only by universal, fundamental struggle over the entire city battle line, until the mouths and stomachs of my people would be recognized. [. . .]

3. education. In as much as the Colored folks have the National Association for the Advancement of Colored People and the Progressive Businessmen's League already in existence here, it may be a very useful and fruit-bearing proceeding on their part to distribute leaflets and pamphlets setting forth the proper statistics concerning our Colored people here and how needful it were for the proper welfare of the whole city that the Colored elements must share in the production, distribution and consumption of things, so equitable and fair, that they no longer can be classed as industrial outcasts and economic Pariah of this city. Prejudice must be routed, malice must be undone in this educational campaign, the industrial freedom of the Colored man in Los Angeles must be won!

The whole political system of both parties in this city is rotten and the quicker the Colored leaders of thought and action make this fact known the better for the race, the better for the city. The industrial freedom of the race can never be achieved by permitting a few Colored men or women to be allowed to hand tickets around on primary or election days—such work is thralldom, not freedom, new enslavement, not liberty! [. . .]

I advise the Colored people to drop the Democrats and Republicans in a party sense and associate only with such elements as will help the race to get a square deal in this city. Republicans as well as Democrats have been industrial boycotters of the Colored man's bones and sinews, of his labor and muscles, and the Colored race should wake up and treat them just the same as they have treated him. All these things and others equally pointed should be thoroughly explained in booklets and a thorough campaign for educational purposes efficiently conducted to gain these economic concessions. There are brainy Colored men and women here who can carry on this campaign, once they break away from the old parties that steal the race-members to perpetuate their own system of political stealth and industrial duplicity.

If I were a Colored man I would put the economic independence of my race first and foremost over personal political advancement, because the economic battlefield decides the bread and butter of the masses and masses count most, leaders in politics least! The mill, the shop, the mine work for the Colored man are more important than an old party political speech or a pre-ferred political delegate at a newly-fettering convention. If I were a Colored man I would think of my freedom in Los Angeles first, before I would fight until my last breath would leave me, until this freedom would be attained.

And at all times as a Colored man I would be very proud of my race, for it is a very noble feeling to know that the Colored race is really the honestest, the truest and the most imposed upon racial element here in Los Angeles and in a larger sense in all America! Let anyone deny this fact, if they dare!

Source: Louis Michel, "If I Were a Colored Man What Would I Do?," *California Eagle*, Sept. 13, 1919.

18

The Meaning of Labor Day (1921)

As socialists, the ILGWU's leaders considered May Day the day of international workers' solidarity. Yet they also urged members to honor Labor Day, the more accepted labor holiday in the United States. At the time this editorial appeared in *Justice*, the ILGWU's English-language newspaper, the union had seventy-three thousand members and was the third-largest union belonging to the American Federation of Labor. It was authored by the veteran journalist Shoel Yanovsky (1864–1939), who also edited the ILGWU's Yiddish newspaper and the anarchist weekly *Di fraye arbeter shtime*.

In point of fact, the radical labor unions in this country have two labor holidays to celebrate. On May First they demonstrate their solidarity with the workers of the entire civilized world who adopted the first day of Spring as the day of demonstration and protest, a day on which they reassert their determination to wrest from life all they are rightfully entitled to as the builders and producers of all social wealth. Our second labor day is the first Monday in September, chosen many years ago by organized labor in America as a day for demonstrating its power, its importance and its firm determination to gain a greater measure of happiness for the workers of this land.

Our radical unions are taking part in both these demonstrations. They are ever mindful of the fact that the great stretches of water which separate this continent from other lands mark no fundamental division of interest between the workers of America and the workers of Europe. The greater the strides made by European labor in their fight for "a place in the sun," the greater are our own chances of progress and advancement. We also take part in the Labor Day of the organized workers of America because we are part and parcel of this movement. True, we have our compunctions about the philosophy and the point-of-view of the American labor movement. True, we believe that the American labor movement ought to be more radical and more class-conscious. We are, nevertheless, far removed from the thought that because of its shortcomings we must keep aloof from it. Such a policy would have been the height of folly and would condemn us to total impotence.

It is equally true that Labor Day in America has heretofore been pale and inexpressive of its true purpose and has degenerated into a day on which petty politicians grind, with cheap solemnity, their petty grist. This, however, is not essentially the fault of the Labor Day idea. Originally, Labor Day was designed to be a true labor holiday, a day when the growing strength of the working class is demonstrated throughout the land. The fact that Labor Day was not heretofore used for its proper and original purpose should not, in the least, deter the workers this year from converting it into a day of great mass meetings, parades and demonstrations from one end of the country to the other.

The workers of America have today on their hands a very bitter and determined defensive struggle. Labor Day this year has therefore an earnest and grave message for the workers of America. Impressive demonstrations must be held in every city of the country and to serve notice upon organized capital that labor is determined not to permit itself to be crushed by its enemies and that it stands ready in spite of these adverse conditions, to fight with the old vigor and enthusiasm until the exploitation of labor will totally disappear from the face of the earth.

Such must be the meaning and the character of the coming Labor Day. And this meaning and message should be made clearer and clearer from year to year, as organized labor in America gradually, though slowly, opens its eyes to the true situation in the land. Of course, our radical unions will not fail to participate in such celebrations of America's Day of Labor.

Source: Editorial, *Justice*, Sept. 2, 1921, p. 6.

An Encounter with a Klansman
(memoir; n.d.)

SAM DARCY

Born Samuel Dardeck in the Ukraine, Sam Adams Darcy (1905–2005) was an organizer, orator, and official in the Communist Party for more than twenty years. He served as head of the Young Workers League, the Communist youth organization, between 1925 and 1927; organized the first mass demonstration of the unemployed in New York City in 1930; and was a major strategist of the San Francisco general strike of 1934, while directing the Communist Party's California organization. For several years during the late 1920s and again in 1930s, Darcy worked for the Communist International in Moscow, where he led the South African Secretariat, in addition to holding other posts. Darcy was expelled from the Communist Party in 1945 for predicting (accurately, as it turned out) that harmonious relations between the United States and the USSR would come to an end in the years following World War II. Darcy later became a successful furniture merchant and activist in the Democratic Party. The following reminiscence is drawn from his unpublished autobiography.

At the end of 1925, following the Fifth Convention of the Worker's (Communist) Party,[1] I was invited to remain in Chicago where the National headquarters was situated, to serve as a member of the National Committee of the Communist youth movement. I found the atmosphere unbearable. The intrigue and the conniving of one group against the other occupied the entire time of the National leadership. The Communist youth movement was not growing. In the course of one of the meetings the question arose of doing more work in the field. Most members of the National Committee refused to leave Chicago for fear someone would get a factional advantage over them through winning a convert and changing the balance of power. I seized on the opportunity and volunteered.

There was very little money available for such work. However, I was given five dollars with which to launch a national organization tour and was told in a solemn discussion that to make up for the deficiency of funds I would be given four States as an initial territory, namely, Indiana, Ohio, Pennsylvania and New York.

I procured my old hiking clothes from my home in New York and a knapsack and set out.

My method of operation was very simple. There were practically no contacts with whom I could begin in any town. I used the morning for hitch-hiking from town to town. During the afternoon I read the local newspapers and informed myself on the local political situation. At approximately seven o'clock I set up a box in the public square or in a congested shopping district and depended upon the Lord and the volume of my voice to guide people towards me. After an hour's speech I asked for those who were interested to step up to the platform and help me set up a local organization of the Communist youth movement. Usually one, two, or three people did step forward. With their help we would draw up a list of young people in the town who might be interested to join and they would visit them with a proposal to hold a meeting a few days to a week later when I would return and if the preliminary work was successful would set up a branch of the youth movement. I carried a small amount of literature for sale and some dues stamps and membership books, out of which I was allowed a small percentage which I used for traveling expenses. I averaged $1 a day in income. It was therefore impossible to sleep in hotels. After the meeting therefore I would hike out of town and sleep in a barn or hay-pile in the field. When it got too cold for this I sometimes asked one of my new friends for hospitality for the night or occasionally squandered a half dollar at some cheap hostelry.

During the first few weeks I inquired for contacts in other towns and on occasion had the rare good luck to run into someone who not only suggested people to approach in other towns but also—heaven of heavens—had access to a mimeograph machine. Then we would proceed in grand style. A leaflet would be mimeographed, for example, in Sandusky, which I would distribute the following morning in Lorraine for a meeting that evening. And in Lorraine I succeeded in having a leaflet mimeographed for distribution in Ashtabula, for a meeting the night after. After months of pedestrian activity of this sort I succeeded in organizing 32 functioning branches of the Young Workers Communist League and sent several hundred dollars in dues and literature sales and paid for my own food, since I had almost no other expenses.

In the course of the activity there were many exciting experiences. One of the fundamental theses of the Communist program is the poor section of the farmers are the natural allies of the workers, and since the Communists identified ourselves with the working class, we regarded every poverty stricken farmer as our closest and intimate friend. One day, while I was hitch-hiking through Ohio, an old and broken down Ford (old and broken down even for 1925) came along. A shriveled up old farmer, the toil of years upon him, his hands gnarled on the wheel, was its only occupant. He stopped for me. This, I thought, was surely my opportunity to make headway amongst the agricultural folk. Remembering the Party program on the question of the farmers, I looked for an opening to begin a discussion with him on social questions, hardly doubting for a minute that he was my natural friend. The Ku Klux Klan was then growing very powerful and all the roads had signs painted on them announcing "klaverns" or meetings of their followers. This was excellent subject matter. I commented upon the signs and launched into an extended description of the follies, crime and general unworthiness of the Ku Klux Klan. My farmer friend never said a word. This I took as confirmation that he listened to what I had to say with favor, for I had heard of the taciturnity of farmers. Suddenly the farmer turned off the main highway. "This is where I get off, I want to stick to the main road," I said to him. He still said nothing. After a few minutes of not getting a reply it occurred to me that he was hard of hearing. I repeated in a loud voice that he should stop because every foot he drives forward I will have to walk back to the main highway. He kept his face forward and if anything his hands tightened on the wheel and the Ford fairly trembled in response to his effort to get more speed. I was beginning to sense something wrong when he swerved into a dirty, badly littered farmyard, jumped out of his car and ran into the broken down old shack which apparently served as his home. I jumped off the car, threw my knapsack over my shoulders and ran for the gate. As I reached the gate the old man rushed out of the door, shouting "you s.o.b., you lousy Nigger-lover, I will teach you to talk against the Ku Klux Klan!" and bang, bang, went the shotgun he had gotten hold of. Fortunately, a few pellets entered my knapsack but did not hurt me. He had, however, shattered in my mind the thesis previously fixed there that the poorest sections of the farmers were automatically the best friends and allies of the workers. After that I knew we would have to win them one by one.

Source: Sam Darcy, "The Storm Must Be Ridden," autobiographical typescript (c. 1945), Sam Adams Darcy Papers, box 3, folder 15, Tamiment Library, New York University.

NOTES

1. The official name of the Communist Party at that time.

Communist "Criminals" in Los Angeles (1929)

UPTON SINCLAIR

The following case of political repression reported by the novelist and journalist Upton Sinclair (1878–1968) appeared in *The Nation*, the oldest liberal magazine in the United States. At the time, Jews made up an estimated 90 percent of the Communist Party's membership in Los Angeles.

Southern California has acquired another lot of political prisoners. What a sense of security and relief must have been in the homes of the "orange belt" when they opened their beloved *Times* and read that five Russian Jewish working women have been sentenced to San Quentin, one for a period of from one to ten years, and the other four, from six months to five years, for the felony of conducting a summer camp for working children with the flag of Soviet Russia flying over it!

I witnessed the scene in the courtroom, full of court officers and strict attorneys and detectives and "red squad" and Better America Federation[1] agents and reporters of Los Angeles newspapers, and it pleased me so that I wish to spread its fame to the farther corners of the civilized world. Friends and comrades in New York and London and Paris and Berlin and Stockholm and Amsterdam and Moscow and Tokyo and Sydney and Johannesburg who will read these words, join with me in acclaiming the courage and loyalty to duty of our "heaven-born band" of patriots who saved the orange country from the peril of five Russian Jewish working girls and a little piece of red silk, home-cut and home-sewed by the fingers of working-class children! Many glorious events are set forth in our patriotic annals—Concord, with its shot heard round the world, and Bunker Hill, where we trusted in God but kept our powder dry—but nothing, I am sure, can claim a higher place in history's roll than the raid upon the Yucaipa Camp by the Better American Federation of Southern California. It seems that some working people of the east side of Los Angeles, Communists or sympathizers, wanted a place to send their children for a glimpse of the country in summer time, at a cost not too far beyond their means. They rented a shack at Yucaipa in the mountains of San Bernardino County, sixty-five miles from Los Angeles, and a group of half a dozen women, with one man to chop wood and do the heavy work, took care of two score children at a price of six dollars a week each. The teacher of the camp was Yetta Stromberg, nineteen years of age, recently a student of the University of California. The name "comrade Yetta" comes with a familiar sound, because Arthur Bullard wrote a novel by the title some twenty years ago;[2] now here is the heroine—except that times have changed and she calls herself Communist instead of Socialist.

She is, I should estimate, something less than five feet in height, and if she weighs a hundred pounds I am a bad guesser. She has quaint little old-fashioned features of delicate loveliness which would charm a painter of miniatures; and she has a faith which has caused some to hail her as the "Joan of Arc of Los Angles." Now she will no longer study social problems in the University of California, but in a more realistic school, the women's department of San Quentin Prison, along with the hammer murderesses and bootleg queens and dope fiends. She received a double sentence because of the very special and aggravating series of crimes which were proved against her in the Superior Court of San Bernardino County.

Yetta, it seems, taught the children history. She taught them that there had been various stages in the development of human society—tribalism, barbarism, feudalism, capitalism. She had got almost through with the first two, so she testified, and intended to go to the others, and wind up with her conception of communism, which she hopes will be the next stage of human evolution. As a preliminary, to prepare the children's minds, she got some red cloth and they made a flag, and with water colors painted on it a hammer and a sickle. The red symbolized human brotherhood, because of the fact that all human blood is red—excluding, of course, that of patriots and supporters of the Better America Federation which is blue. The hammer stood for the workers and the sickle for the peasants of Russia—it being the idea that farmers and workers should unite to have a government for their own benefit, instead of for the benefit of landlords, capitalists, and bankers, as in America. Every morning the children raised the flag and made a pledge—which was read over and over in court, and constituted the special aggravation which brought the double conviction by the brave jury, and the double sentence by the conscientious judge. The pledge read as follows:

> I pledge allegiance to the worker's red flag
> And to the cause for which it stands:

One aim throughout our lives,
Freedom for the working class.

So long as Yetta and her children were let alone, the above words were heard only by some fifty persons. But news of her doings leaked out to the noble bands of American Legion men who guard the cause of patriotism in San Bernardino. From them it spread to the Better America Federation of Los Angeles, with the result that the camp was raided, and the evil words were prepared before a crowded courtroom day after day, and were published in all our Southern Californian newspapers. They are now reproduced in this narrative and will be read in New York, London, Paris, Berlin, Stockholm, Amsterdam, Moscow, Tokyo, Sydney, and Johannesburg. A campaign in defense of Comrade Yetta will go on in all these cities, and the formula which she taught to a handful of children will be recited and discussed by a countless million of workers. Here is a singularly beautiful illustration of what happens when we set out to suppress ideas by means of policemen's clubs and jails! The demonstration should be of the greatest help to the Better America Federation in its next campaign to raise funds among our bankers and businessmen.

To get on with the story; a gallant band of strapping six-footers, county sheriff's men, American Legion heroes, and red-hunters of the "Intelligence Bureau" of the Los Angeles police department, swooped down upon that little camp and carried half a dozen children off to a detention home. The six women and the man who chopped the wood were shut up in the San Bernardino jail. When Mr. Leo Gallagher, an attorney of Los Angeles, member of the executive committee of our Civil Liberties Union, went to arrange for their bail, a deputy sheriff seized him by the throat and choked him. (I took occasion to report this assault to the so-called "Constitutional Rights Committee" of the Los Angles Bar Association, which referred the matter to the similar committee in San Bernardino Country, which in turn did nothing.)

In due course the prisoners were brought to trial before Judge Charles L. Allison. John Beardsley, another attorney of Lost Angeles—not a radical, but a member of our Civil Liberties group—defended the prisoners, and after a trial lasting nine days, "Comrade Yetta" was convicted on two counts, and four women and one man upon one count, of "conspiracy to display a red flag or other emblem of opposition to organized government." The women are Emma Schneiderman, Jennie Wolfson, Ester Karpeloff, and Bella Mintz. It is interesting to note that there was one man from Holland on the jury, C.F. De Meyere, and he held it up for the twenty-three hours and forced the acquittal of Mrs. Schneiderman's mother, who had arrived at the camp just a few hours before the raid. The mother then applied to be allowed to take her daughter's place in jail.

As a sample of the fairness of the trial it should suffice to record that the sole man at the camp was a veteran of the World War, severely injured by gas in the trenches and partly incapacitated as a result; and that the jury of patriots of the orange country were denied an opportunity to know that this man was a war veteran. Isidor Berkowitz would now be on his road to San Quentin, save that he found a way to deliver himself from the clutches of patriotism. On the night before he was scheduled to be sentenced to San Quentin, he took a rope and hanged himself.

Picture the band of five female felons, assembled in court to hear their fates: all of them frail, and only one of them what we should call a woman of normal stature. They face the stern judge and he questions each in turn. All but one were born in Russia, only two have had a school education, two or three are mothers of children who were in the camp, and the others are self-supporting. None of them uses dope, they state in answer to questions, and none has ever been previously convicted of a felony. The two who are members of the Communist Party, of course, refuse to apply for probation; the other three do apply, and the judge turns down the application of the group on the ground that they are not persons who would be reformed by receiving a new chance. Then he sentences them, and I observe the signs of satisfaction among the four representatives of the Los Angeles "red squad" who have supervised the entire procedure.

Source: Upton Sinclair, "Communist 'Criminals' in California," *The Nation* 129, no. 3359 (Nov. 20, 1929): pp. 582–583.

NOTES

1. The Better America Federation was founded in 1920 by conservative business leaders who opposed organized labor and Progressive politics.

2. Albert Edwards, *Comrade Yetta* (New York: Macmillan, 1913). Albert Edwards was the pseudonym of Arthur Bullard (1879–1929), journalist, novelist, and statesman.

21

"Unions with Brains" (1930)

THE NATION

While most American trade unions clung to conventional methods and narrow aims during the 1920s, the Amalgamated Clothing Workers of America and International Ladies' Garment Workers' Union stood out as innovators in the areas of education, social welfare, racial integration, and industrial relations. At the dawn of the Great Depression and amid renewed organizing efforts in the clothing industry, liberal observers hoped that the garment unions and their "Jewish socialist theories" would revivify the American labor movement.

The two most interesting trade unions in the United States today are in the garment trades. The Amalgamated Clothing Workers in the men's clothing industry and the International Ladies' Garment Workers' Union in the field of women's wear have consistently applied brains to the solution of the practical problems facing them and have at the same time kept untarnished the social idealism of their Jewish socialist theories. As a result they have managed to give fresh hope to those who believe that labor organization is essential to a modern democratic society.

The older union technique consisted in organizing the workers by hook or crook, and then taking the employer by the throat and compelling him to give up the most that he could be made to yield in the wages and hours. The technique worked fairly well until the employers learned the trick of organizing themselves into groups to fight the unions or until industries became organized into great trusts under unified management. Then the old union leadership was bankrupt. It had no tactics to meet the new conditions and no ideas by which to live. Consequently, despite the great growth in numbers that came with the war, American unionism has gone through a long period of intellectual sterility and practical impotence. A powerful organization like the United Mine Workers, failing to adjust itself to the new conditions, has been broken to pieces on the rock of stubborn economic facts; while the building trades, the heart of the American Federation of Labor, though managing by various devices to maintain a high wage scale for their limited membership, have yet lost all significance for the great body of workers whom they can see no way of organizing.

Among the clothing workers we behold a different scene. The International Ladies' Garment Workers have just called a great strike in New York to bring about the organization of the dressmaking industry, having successfully accomplished the result for the cloak and suit industry by the strike of last summer. Faced with the fact that their earlier success in forcing union standards on the big factories by the older methods was simply hastening the process of driving the industry out of those factories into the little subcontracting shops and sweatshops, they broadened their conception to the actual organization of the whole industry, so that no one should be able to take advantage of sub-standard labor conditions. Further, they succeeded in having impartial machinery set up for the protection of employer and employee alike against unreasonable demands, thus obtaining for themselves a position of power and partnership in the industry.

To those who fear the destructive effect of "radical" ideas, we commend a consideration of the activities of the International Ladies' Garment Workers. Without surrendering their socialist principles these hard-headed unionists, who have consistently remained in good and regular standing with the American Federation of Labor, have come forward with a series of constructive plans for the stabilization and upbuilding of the industry in which they make their living. What "conservative" organization can show an equally good record?

Source: "Unions with Brains," *The Nation*, Feb. 19, 1930, p. 209.

22

In Defense of the Kentucky Miners (1932)

The Workmen's Circle (Arbeter Ring, in Yiddish) was a nation-wide, fraternal order established in 1900. A mass-membership organization, the Workmen's Circle did not adhere to a single ideology but maintained a broadly socialist orientation reflecting the diverse ideological commitments of its members. Over the years, the Workmen's Circle offered generous financial and moral support to myriad labor and socialist causes. The following resolution in defense of imprisoned strikers in Harlan County was issued by members of the Workmen's Circle hailing from the Russian city of Bielotzerkov.

Comrades:

The following is a resolution unanimously passed at our Special Meeting held on Jan. 15, 1932, at Aristocrat Hall, 69 St. Marks Place, at which our Delegates reported about the Conference for the Defense of the Kentucky Miners[1] called by the General Defense Committee, held on Jan. 6, at the Labor Temple, 14th St. and Second Ave., New York, N.Y.:

"We endorse the stand taken by our delegates to invite all other Labor organizations, regardless of their political beliefs, to join in the defense of the Kentucky Miners as well as of all political prisoners. We believe—as [do] our delegates—that in order to make the struggle really effective, labor must unite its forces in the struggle against the oppression by the ruling class.

"We express our hope that the Conference for the Kentucky Miners Defense will make an honest attempt in that direction."

Fraternally yours,

Bielotzerkover Br. 417, Workmen's Circle

Source: Labor Age 21, no. 2 (Feb. 1932): p. 25.

1. The "Kentucky Miners" refers to a group of seven imprisoned coal miners and mine union officials from Harlan County, Kentucky. In 1931, Harlan County's miners, faced with starvation wages and inadequate housing, struck for the right to organize under the auspices of the United Mine Workers. They were met with violent resistance from local authorities and mine owners. An incident on May 5 left three coal company guards and one striking miner dead and led to the conviction—on questionable legal grounds—of the seven Kentucky Miners. The Kentucky Miners received publicity and financial support from national and local labor unions of all political persuasions. Most of the defendants were convicted of "conspiracy to murder" or lesser crimes, and the coal miners' battle for unionization continued until 1939, when the United Mine Workers won the right to organize in Harlan County.

23

"The Obligations of Youth Today" (1932)

ISADORE BERNICK

Born on the west side of Chicago to Russian-immigrant parents, Isadore (Paul) Bernick (1914–2001) joined the Communist Party's Young Pioneers in the mid-1920 and participated in party youth organizations until he was expelled in the early 1930s for Trotskyist sympathies. Bernick remained active in various Trotskyist organizations through the 1930s and 1940s. From 1952 to 1981, he served as executive director of American ORT (founded in Russia to provide vocational training to Jewish men and women) and helped to develop it into the largest private technical-training organization in the world. Bernick delivered the following, previously unpublished, speech to the party's Youth Week Assembly shortly before his expulsion.

Slaves, working, sweating, dying from the strain. This was the period when the Jews who were slaves in Egypt called for a leader. The Youth, the militant section of a people of a class realized that something was wrong. When a situation calls for a leader—a leader comes. Moses came. The Jews with their militant, thoughtful youth and a leader solved the problem before them. They became free again.

Leaders and practical, thinking people are needed today more than ever before. Today we find that the people know something is wrong but there are few who know how to correct these defects.

We, the youth, must study why the people of our class suffer. We, the youth must build our bodies so that we can carry on through the bumpy road of life. We, the youth, must educate ourselves now so that we will be capable of the tasks before us. We, the youth, have the task of making a new world based on the experiences, failures, and struggles of you, the parents.

These are the obligations of the youth of today, so that when we take the reins of life into our hands, we—as capable, educated people, with capable leaders—will be able to eradicate the decaying systems and build a new society that will serve not a few, but all.

Most of the audience has been affected by the present crisis. You, parents, our breadwinners, worry daily of how to give the elements of life, food, clothing and shelter to us. We, your children, your dependents, realize this fact. We not only realize but feel its clutches by having our allowances cut and more than that, there are many who haven't any money for lunches and other school necessities.

This has made us think. We ask ourselves, "What can be done to remedy the situation?" To remedy not only this present depression but to do away with the causes of all crises. These experiences are training us for future life.

You, parents, teachers, and other adults sitting in this audience listening to this speech will say, "Well, he spoke well but will the young really learn?" You say that it is easy to talk, but we forget quickly. True! It is too true. But it is the obligation of the youth of today more than ever before not to forget. You parents, and teachers, must not forget our duties to society.

Did you ever see a female dog with her puppies? Sure you did! The puppies watch very closely how their mother is acting. Why are dogs afraid of fire? He learns that to touch it pains him. Did you ever see a puppy put his paw on a hot stove? He never puts it there again.

If the puppy tries to do anything wrong the she-dog bites the pup. No you must not, you must keep on the right track.

We, the youth, also learn from experience, and when we stray from the right track you must check us just as the female-dog checks the puppy by biting when it strays.

The Spartan youth went through vigorous exercises, out-of-door life, endurance of pain, strenuous physical combats. These were some of the difficult tasks that the Spartan boy was confronted with so that he would profit from his experiences and knowledge in order to become strong, alert and clean when he would reach manhood.

Today our sufferings are giving us experience. Today our sufferings are making us fight to do away with the rottenness that makes us suffer. Today our sufferings are developing real leaders. Today our sufferings are making us realize that we belong to a certain class that has suffered most in periods of a depression; that has always been given the smallest share of prosperity.

Therefore we will no longer sit idle and let this injustice continue but will join with our parents into the fighting ranks of our class.

Joan of Arc ended the hundred years war and gave a "soul" to France. Before her time, France was slowly but surely losing her independence. This was the greatest crisis in the history of France. The situation called for a leader. A leader came from the youth—Joan of Arc came and saved France.

Karl Liebknecht, one of the greatest fighters for the organization of Youth, said, "The future belongs to the youth!" We will fulfill our duty to society. We will fight on and march with the proletariat of our class, toward victory—toward freedom—toward justice, away from depression—away from starvation—away from injustice. We will fulfill our obligations—we will!! we must!!!

Source: Isadore Bernick, "The Obligations of Youth Today," handwritten speech in possession of Debbie Bernick. Although the speech is undated, accompanying documents make clear that it was written in April 1932. Special thanks to Bernick's daughter, Debbie, for sharing this document and other biographical materials with me.

24

"Some Vital Problems of Negro Labor" (1935)

FRANK CROSSWAITH

By the 1930s, African Americans made up a growing minority
of the garment industry's workforce and were relatively well
integrated into its unions. For the Caribbean-born labor organizer and socialist Frank Crosswaith (1892–1965), this provided
proof to skeptics within the black community that unions did
not necessarily serve as obstacles to employment and economic
advancement.

In the past a great deal of criticism has been directed against organized labor for its alleged lack of interest in the special problems that face
Negro workers. Much of this criticism, however, came from Negro leaders
who possessed little or no understanding of the structural and functional
nature of organized labor and less sympathy with its recognized aims and
purposes. I speak as one who has definitely identified with the organized
labor movement on both the industrial and political fields for over twenty
years.

To say that organized labor is without blame in these premises would be
similar to assuming the well-known role of the ostrich. However, it is one
thing to be critical of an existing situation and quite another thing to understand the conditions from which that situation emanates.

It is eminently true that race prejudice in varying forms and degrees is
entrenched within the ranks of labor—even as it is interwoven in the fiber
and sinews of American life. Thus, to expect that the Negro can be freely
lynched, segregated, disfranchised and generally maltreated in church, in
school, in workshop, in government service, in public places and elsewhere
while in the labor movement he would immediately be placed upon the
common plane of equality with his fellow union men, is to ignore the influences which economic and social forces, customs, traditions and habits wield
in shaping the psychology and behavior of men. When the general situation

in America—as far as the Negro is concerned—is carefully examined and understood, it is indeed remarkable that there is not more pronounced prejudice openly shown against the Negro by labor organizations.

While we have become accustomed to hear much about the unfair treatment meted out to Negroes in certain unions, we seldom hear, however, about those unions wherein the Negro enjoys equality of treatment with his fellow-tradesmen. Those of us who are in the labor movement know that in the needle trades the Negro worker receives a square deal. These are unions that are generally considered "Socialist unions," such as the International Ladies' Garment Workers' Union, Amalgamated Clothing Workers of America, and others. There are innumerable instances on record where these organizations have literally bent backwards—figuratively speaking—to show a preference to Negro members. In many of the shops and factories where members of these unions are employed, Negro chairmen and chairladies can be found presiding over the destiny of their white fellow-workers although Negroes are in the minority in the union as well as in the particular shop or factory. On the executive boards, appeal boards and grievance boards of these unions sit Negro members, legislating for themselves and their fellows, settling disputes and solving trade problems.

The International Ladies' Garment Workers' Union, with a membership of over 200,000 has recently embarked upon a pretentious educational program for its membership. Among the study courses arranged for this vast army of trade unionists is one in Negro history. This course is more complimentary to Negroes than anything taught about us in any public school in the United States up to the present time. The course is entitled "The Negro in American History" and is calculated to answer factually and favorably the following questions: (1) What part did the Negro play in the development of this country? (2) In Colonial Times? (3) In the American Revolution? (4) In the Civil War and the abolition of slavery? (5) In the rise of industrialism and the winning of the West? (6) In the growth of the American labor movement? (7) In the World War and after? In a union where Negroes number only about seven or eight thousand out of a total of two hundred thousand the healthy effects of this type of education upon the consciousness of the majority should not be underestimated.

At the recent convention of the American Federation of Labor in San Francisco, it was the I.L.G.W.U. which called upon American labor to remove every obstacle that tends to discriminate against Negroes. [. . .] President Dubinsky will be in a more strategic position to fight for equality of opportunity for all workers regardless of race, creed, color or sex. When A. Phillip

Randolph, president of the Pullman Porters' Union, was making his fight for the Negro on the convention floor, he was warmly and enthusiastically supported by President Dubinsky and the other delegates of the I.L.G.W.U.

It appears to me that much of the loose criticism Negro leaders level against organized labor comes mainly from their failure to differentiate between a sound principle and an unsound policy. The principle of trade union organization for working people is sound socially and advantageous.

Abject failure on the part of Negro leadership to appraise adequately and intelligently modern society and to evaluate correctly the influence of economic and social forces upon it, has led these leaders down a precipitous path of uselessness as far as the workers of the race are concerned. These leaders have been stressing work as the goal of the Negro, while they sedulously ignored the only vital reason why people work. We work in order to get wages. With wages we are able to secure the essential material things of life such as food, clothing and shelter. Thus it is obvious that it is not work that is of most importance, but rather the wages we receive for the work we do. Work is therefore the means to an end and not the end in itself. This history of social progress shows conclusively that working people can secure more wages for the work they do as well as reduce the work-day through organized efforts. Instead of recognizing this sound principle and acting upon it, Negro leaders for the most part have been pandering to open shop employers and advising Negro labor to be loyal to such employers.

The existence of race prejudice in the ranks of organized labor is no preventative to Negro labor organizing itself into legitimate trade unions to elevate its wage level and reduce its work-day. Other minority groups of workers in this country have been and still are confronted with problems similar to our own, but these groups faced theirs with intelligence, fortitude, courage and self-sacrifice.

To meet and overcome the prejudice directed against Jewish workers, the United Hebrew Trades was created by Jewish trade unionists; it fights for the Jewish worker on the job and in his union and wields tremendous influence within the councils of A.F. of L. There are also the Italian Chamber of Labor and the Women's Trade Union League. Like the U.H.T., these organizations are used offensively and defensively in the interest of their respective groups. But they not only fight for a square deal for their members; they are ever organizing Jewish, Italian and women workers. They appreciate the fact that "the union is the first step," as President Green[1] says.

The Negro worker needs a United Negro Trades, predicated upon the principles of trade unionism and composed of bona fide Negro and white trade unionists united in opposition to every form and practice of injustice and inequality within and without the limits of the organized labor movement. Such an agency will enable the Negro worker to make invaluable contributions to the cause of labor and social justice.

Source: Frank Crosswaith, "Some Vital Problems of Negro Labor," *Justice*, Sept. 1, 1935, p. 5.

NOTES

1. William Green (1873–1952), president of the American Federation of Labor from 1924 until his death.

25

"Charlatans and Gangsters and Pompous Racketeers" (1938)

JENNIE COHEN

Corruption plagued even progressive, well-managed unions. The following letter of protest against a Philadelphia local of the Amalgamated Clothing Workers of America appeared in *Vanguard*, organ of the anarchist ("libertarian communist") Vanguard Group. No biographical information about the author is known.

Three years ago I went to work at Rosman & Sheer's shop. As a faithful union member I regularly attended meetings of the local. Often I heard Brother Gold, trade manager of Local 25, and Brother Hollander, General Manager, appeal to the workers not to break union regulations against overtime. In my shop they worked three and four hours overtime besides Saturdays. So one Friday I went to the union office to inform the Business Agent, Brother Weiner, as to what was going on. He was out, but an investigating committee was sent and found the shop working full blast. On Monday morning I came to work. The manager of the shop, Morris Kneitel, refused to let me work. He said, "Go to Weiner, he will tell you why." When I went to Brother Weiner to ask for an explanation, he declared, "You started all the trouble, and you yourself will have to take the consequences. I won't do anything for you." I then went to Brother Gold who reinstated me. But things became worse. I was being persecuted. They encouraged some of the women workers to pick fights with me, promising them better working conditions for their dirty work. I was again sent away from the shop. Weiner again refused to do anything for me. I was again reinstated by Brother Hollander.

Realizing that they could not take my job away, they made it unbearable for me. . . . And now comes the climax of this scandalous affair.

A presser by the name of Sam Feldman, works in the shop of Rosman & Sheer. As a member of Local No. 3 he signed an affidavit in which Weiner and the chairman were accused of taking graft, extorting money from him under all sorts of pretenses. I was accused by Weiner of telling the presser to make out his affidavit, I was fired from my job. Weiner told me I was through. When I went to Weiner and asked for my job back, he insulted me in the vilest language. He got himself a woman gangster who threatened me. When I came to Weiner's door this bodyguard was there. She went into Weiner's office, and after coming out she attacked me. I am deprived of earning my daily bread because I was foolish enough to demand that the union live up to its boast of being "progressive" and "democratic," that it be a real union. I dared to interfere with the racketeering of the officialdom. Now I am out of the trade. I appeal to all true friends of unionism to print this protest. I stand behind every statement made. My case is not the only one; countless sincere union members have been subjected to the same, even worse, persecutions. As a matter of principle the facts about the Amalgamated Clothing Workers should be brought before the workers. I challenge any contradiction to the facts stated above. I am willing to submit this case to any impartial tribunal, and I will abide by the decision. Let the charlatans and gangsters and pompous racketeers of the union answer this challenge if they dare.

signed Jennie Cohen

former member Local 25, A.C.W.U. of A.

Source: Jennie Cohen, letter to the editor, *Vanguard*, Apr. 1938, pp. 15–16.

26

"With Nazism We All Are at War" (1942)

J. B. S. HARDMAN

J. B. S Hardman, the adopted name of Jacob Benjamin Salutsky (1882–1968), immigrated to the United States from the Russian Empire in 1908. Between 1912 and 1921, he led the Socialist Party's Jewish Socialist Federation, and for twenty-four years he served as the Amalgamated Clothing Workers' director of education. A highly respected labor intellectual, Hardman delivered this speech to the convention of the Congress of Industrial Organizations.

I rise to speak for the people of my father and my mother, the Jewish people.

The record of Hitlerian atrocity, of the total destruction of the Jewish people in the Hitler held countries, destruction in cold blood and systematically carried out, is more than tragic. It is ghastly.

The Nazis and their camp followers have used Jewish blood to lubricate the wheels of their vehicles, riding to conquest in country after country, to world conquest as they see it in their dreams.

The record is ghastly. The facts I submit come from authoritative sources, the Czech Government-in-Exile, the Polish Government-in-Exile, the Polish underground movement. What's more, the perpetrators of this inhumanity, the Nazis themselves, boast of their murderous achievement.

Between 1933, when Hitler took over in Germany and the outbreak of the war in 1939, 200,000 Jews were massacred in Germany, Austria, Rumania, Hungary, as these countries, one after another, fell under the Hitler yoke. From September 1, 1939 to September 1st of this year, the record shows over 800,000 murders of Jews. Of these, 500,000 were executed and otherwise killed, in Poland. Close to 100,000 Jewish civilians were murdered in pogroms and mass executions in Hungary, Rumania and Slovakia. 300,000 were executed in the Baltic States and part of Nazi-occupied Russia. 8,000 Jewish civilians were executed as hostages in Nazi-occupied France.

This is the record. In the 1,000 days since the war began, 800,000 Jewish men and women were killed, the pace accelerating daily. The tragic average is 800 a day. From thirty to fifty every hour. Each time the clock ticks away the minute the Nazi ax falls upon a Jewish head, a life is taken, and so day-in and day-out, hour-in and hour-out, every minute. I submit the following two quotations, one by the Czech Government-in-Exile. It reads:

> Deportation always occurs at night after a 3-day notice. The transports carry 1000 each. Each person deported must sign a paper in which he surrenders all his property to the Gestapo.
>
> It is now estimated that there is an average of 40 suicides to a transport. Therefore the deportation orders are now given for 1,040 people and when the orders are given, forty graves are dug, and 40 coffins are ordered.

The other quotation is from a statement coming from the Polish underground movement. It reads:

> In the cities of western Poland, Jews were killed by poison gas. Special gas trucks were used that carried 90 persons at a time. The victims were buried in the Subardzki forests. About 1,000 Jews were thus killed daily between Nov. 1941 and March 1942. . . . Altogether the Nazis have now killed about 800,000 Jews in Poland. . . .

This is the record, ladies and gentlemen. I do not rise here to cry, to ask for pity. We know what we are facing. With the peoples, over there in the Hitler-controlled countries, the Jews have no quarrel. With Nazism we all are at war.

We ask for no mercy. We are being destroyed as a people. We want to destroy the destroyers.

Yes, we fight back. Even as this destruction of Jewish men and women and children is proceeding, Jewish men on the United Nations' battle-fronts, are paying with their lives for the privileges of fighting the Nazis. 100,000 of them fell gloriously upon the battlefields of Greece, of Poland, of Russia, of Britain. They fight joyously. No complaint about that. We want our blood to lubricate the wheels of the vehicles upon which the United Nations will ride to victory and return freedom to the world.

We are not alone in this battle. As the Nazis seek to make of destruction and inhumanity a system and a way of life, the peoples under Nazi domination rise to heights of humanity. When Jews in Amsterdam, Holland, were obliged to wear yellow patches on their garments, many Gentiles braved the vengeance of the Gestapo agents and put yellow patches on their own clothes to show sympathy for the Jews and in protest against the Nazis. When in Paris, in Nazi-occupied France, Jews were driven to the railroad stations to be shipped to destinations unknown, French students of the Sorbonne and French workmen rushed to help the Jews carry their meager luggage. They wanted to register their indignation and their sympathy to where each belonged. In the underground movements in the Nazi-occupied countries, the Jews fight as partners and fellow-combatants of the Poles, the Czechs, the French. When the Jews in Poland were put behind ghetto walls and the Gestapo ordered that the death penalty be inflicted on Gentiles who would enter behind the ghetto walls or communicate with those confined there, Polish workmen risked their lives to breach the ghetto walls at night to register their solidarity. On the night of the religious Jewish holiday of Rosh Hashonah, Poles deposited flowers on top of the ghetto walls, to show their sympathy for those behind the walls. When driven by starvation, a Jewish woman or child ventured beyond the ghetto walls, invariably a Polish woman would furtively but helpfully hand a bit of food out of her own terribly limited supply.

We do not despair. We fight back. Our hope lies here in the high court of labor solidarity, in this tribunal of all-inclusive democracy. Not for pity we ask but justice, and we know we will receive it.

It is not feeling between men of various peoples that I am speaking of. The issue isn't whether or not it is right for a Jew to dislike a German, or for a German to hate a Pole, or for an American to distrust a Japanese. I am not speaking of racial preferences or phobias. It is when anti-Semitism is used as an instrument of national policy that danger arises to our common cause of humanity. Let us never forget that when the anti-Semite hits the Semite he also hits his own nation. Anti-Semitism as a national policy is destructive of the Jewish people and of the people on whose behalf it is preached and practiced as well.

I speak here as a Jew and I have no apology to make for my people of origin, the people that has given the world Moses, the prophet Isaiah, Jesus, the carpenter of Nazareth, Albert Einstein, and, yes, Karl Marx. Nothing to apologize for. And I speak as an American, a citizen of the United States by free choice, standing under this flag and happy in the sense of collective democratic security for which the red-white-and-blue stands, the nation that has given the world the legacy of George Washington, Thomas Jefferson, Abraham Lincoln, the living glory of Franklin D. Roosevelt and the American dream of the unknown soldiers of war and industry.

Our side will win. Labor, the redeemer of democracy and justice in the war and hate-torn world, will help make victory certain and the peace lasting.

Source: J. B. S. Hardman, "Our Hope—Labor and Democracy," typescript of speech presented to the CIO national convention, Nov. 12, 1942, J. B. S. Hardman Collection, box 23, folder 7, Tamiment Library, New York University.

.

Part III

Life of the Mind

Socialists believed that workers needed to understand the world in order to change it, and immigrant Jews took this conviction to heart. Thousands of men and women embarked on a quest for knowledge and culture that often impressed outside observers. They became avid readers of newspapers, journals, and books, flocked to lectures, night classes, and public libraries, and frequented cafes and public squares to discuss and debate issues of the day. The passion for learning and intellectual exchange manifested itself most prominently in large cities, where abundant opportunities for education existed. In Chicago, Philadelphia, and New York, immigrants could avail themselves of settlement houses, labor lyceums, union educational programs, bookstores, and public libraries. Supported by a conducive environment and inspired by socialist ideology, urban immigrants created a new secular culture, much of it fostered in the Yiddish language. Yet the future of Yiddish was a subject of debate. Should it survive or give way to English? This question fed into a larger debate over whether Jews as a people should assimilate or maintain a distinct ethno-cultural identity in America. Socialists never reached agreement on these issues, but their arguments animated the intellectual life of immigrant Jewry.

"Their Intense Desire to Study" (1893)

IDA VAN ETTEN

The social reformer Ida Van Etten (c. 1868–1894) spent much time among immigrant Jews on the Lower East Side. In response to growing anti-Jewish prejudice, she penned the following article extolling the attributes of immigrant Jews.

Most men, if asked what class of immigrants they considered the least desirable, would answer, the Russian Jews. There is a preconceived idea that because most of the Russian Jews are dirty, cannot speak the English language, and live closely crowded in unwholesome, ill-smelling tenement quarters, they therefore form an objectionable part of our population. These facts are the chief cause of the popular prejudice against them. To these causes there might be added that vague, indefinite phrase that they do not assimilate with our people. Thus even those who are willing enough to admit our indebtedness to immigration in the past object to Jewish immigrants, saying that the character of our immigrants is not what it was twenty years ago, forgetting that twenty years ago the prejudice against Irish immigrants was as strong and unreasoning as that which now exists against Jewish immigrants. Persons who have once accepted this idea of the Russian Jews, by habitually thinking of them as constituting the lowest dregs of population and by living far removed from any possible contact with them, harden this opinion into a fixed conviction and shut out further inquiry. Although the Russian Jews have now for several years taken an active part in the industrial, intellectual, and civil life of New York, few of its citizens know anything of this earnest, intelligent, and intensely interesting people.

It would clear away many misleading theories to remember that it is not the condition in which the immigrant comes that determines his usefulness, but the power that he shows to rise above his condition; and if the ability to rise superior to adverse condition be a proof of strength of character, we must concede that the Russian Jew possesses this quality in no mean degree.

Centuries of persecution and oppression tend to develop extreme traits of character, some most commendable, others not so praiseworthy. These people possess all the faults of an oppressed people, but they also have the heroic virtues fostered by their oppression. The Russian Jew seems to possess a dual character; to be the best of men and the worst, to practise the meanest vices and the most exalted virtues. He is suspicious, ungrateful, and often treacherous alike to friend and foe, qualities naturally fostered by centuries of tyranny and repression. But on the other hand he possesses, in large measure, the qualities which will inevitably make him a notable figure in the social and political evolution of any country of which he becomes a citizen. From an intimate knowledge of these people, I maintain that they are in many important respects among our most desirable immigrants. [. . .]

The Russian Jews are naturally radicals on all social questions. They have come from a country which represents to them only tyranny and oppression, and social questions have a deep, absorbing, and personal interest to them. Another fact that increases the radicalism of the educated Jews is that, not being an abiding people, they have no strong prejudices in favor of any established party. Thus from the force of circumstances as well as by natural inclination they find their natural and congenial place among the ultraradical workingmen. Thousands of the disciples of Karl Marx may be found among the organized Jewish workingmen. Their intense desire to study and to discuss social questions I have never seen equaled. Scores of great agitation meetings are held weekly on the East Side. A few weeks ago a meeting called to discuss immigration was attended by over six thousand persons, while thousands were unable to obtain admission. A similar call for a meeting issued to native American or to Irish workingmen would probably have brought but a few hundreds.

Almost the first impulse of those who have a cause to champion is to seek the powerful aid of the press, and the Jews quickly recognized this power. In the face of apparently insurmountable obstacles, Russian students with a following chiefly of the underpaid employees of "sweaters" succeeded in founding and maintaining a weekly labor paper of a high order of literary excellence—the "Arbeiter Zeitung,"[1] which has exerted great influence in the struggles of the Jewish workmen. This newspaper is the centre of an agitation which represents great energy and self-denial on the part of its promoters. The editor[2] is a young Russian student who is a remarkable orator in both the Jewish and English languages. Any one who has heard his speeches at the immense meetings which are often held by the Jews in Cooper Union would not be surprised at his influence over them. He was one of the most prominent figures at the recent International Labor Congress in Brussels, where he made an address on the social and industrial condition of the Jewish working class in Europe and America.

The records of the public schools show that the attendance of the Jewish children is more regular than the attendance of the children of any other class and that their standard of scholarship is higher. No sacrifice is considered too great by the Hebrew father and mother to keep their children at school as long as possible. A Jew who cannot read and write his own language at least is the exception. An educational restriction on immigration would have no appreciable effect in excluding Russian Jews.

The Jews are a temperate people, and the saloon is not likely to become an element in their social or political life. Instead of beer or strong alcoholic liquors, they drink enormous quantities of tea and coffee. Coffee-houses are numerous on the East Side and serve as the gathering-places of the Jewish working men and women. A glass of tea with lemon is served with a thin Russian cake for ten cents, and this refreshment, so dear to a Russian, is therefore within the means of the poorest artisan or student. Every night from ten to twelve these coffee-houses are crowded with students and workingmen, many of whom drop in from the numerous trade and agitation meetings which are nightly held in the Jewish quarter. The recreations of a people are commonly the truest indication of their real character. The frequenters of these dingy little coffee-houses are men rough and uncouth in appearance, poorly dressed and often dirty and unkempt, but a lady or a scholar would find nothing offensive in their conversation. They discuss trade matters, political economy, philosophy, the works of Karl Marx, Krapotkine, Tolstoi, Tchernychewsky, and Zola. Almost any Jewish workingman you might chance to meet in these circles would be able to discuss intelligently these authors and their works. This is undoubtedly due to the student influence which so largely predominates in their gatherings. These coffee-houses are often the scene of conversations and discussions which would do credit to a much more ambitious field.

Here, too, you meet the real actors in those Russian tragedies whose ending is usually in far-off Siberia. I remember sitting one evening at a table in one of these coffee-houses, with a young Russian Jew whom I had sometimes met at labor meetings. He was reading a letter. When he had finished he turned to me and said, "It is from my sister in Siberia." When I asked him for what crime she had been sent there, he answered quietly but with a tone of bitter hate in his voice, "Because she studied and taught the others why we were so miserable in Russia." He then told me his sister's sad story.

She was graduated at one of the gymnasiums at the age of sixteen with great honors. She and her brother became revolutionists and for two years devoted themselves to teaching the peasants and others revolutionary doctrines. It became known to the Russian government, and without warning, even without seeing her family, she was sent to Siberia for eighteen years. Her brother escaped to this country. Eight years of her sentence have now passed, and she is allowed, at stated intervals, to write to her friends. He added in a hopeless sort of way, "She has ten years more; she will not live out her sentence." Such stories are only too common on the East Side. Contrast the coffee-houses of the Jews with similar gatherings of American or Irish workingmen in what they call their recreations, and you will understand why the student of sociology looks with greater hope to the Russian Jews. [. . .]

Source: Ida Van Etten, "Russian Jews as Desirable Immigrants," *Forum* 15 (Apr. 1893): pp. 172–182.

NOTES

1. *Di arbeter tsaytung*, see document 9.
2. Abraham Cahan (1860–1951).

28

The Power of Speech and Education (1893)

EDUCATION SOCIETIES

Working-class men and women created numerous self-education societies in cities around the country during the 1890s. In
doing so, they demonstrated the extent to which they had inter-
nalized the values of intellectuals who had become, through
their involvement in labor organizations, political parties, and
the Yiddish press, leaders of the Jewish working class. The following announcements are just two among countless others
that appeared on the pages of radical Yiddish newspapers.

New Haven Educational Club (1893)

The New Haven Educational Club held a banquet specifically for the intelligent public. Comrade Leontieff[1] spoke to our group two weeks ago with
so much success that we decided to invite him to give another lecture on
Sunday, Dec. 17, 3:00 p.m. The gathering and banquet will be only for select
attendees who want to learn something. [. . .] We state this clearly to those
who will perhaps not be able to understand [Leontieff's lecture] because we
are not making this a mass gathering. We have decided to hold a series of scientific lectures only for intelligent people; thus, it would be useless if it were
filled by people who were unable to understand a scientific lecture and who
would just sit there and sleep or yawn. We will, from time to time, also call
large mass meetings.

Source: *Di arbeter tsaytung*, Nov. 7, 1893, p. 3.

Socialist Pamphlet Fund and Workers' Education Group: An Appeal to All Male and Female Workers of New York City (1893)

Our society, the Socialist Pamphlet Fund and Workers' Education Group,
has, in addition to publishing socialist literature in the Yiddish language, also

taken upon itself the task of educating workers through systematic lectures on various elementary branches of science. Considering that [individual] lectures, however useful they may be, cannot achieve as much as a workers' education school, where the teachers can thoroughly listen to and question every student, where each class does not have too many students, and where [the students] stand on the same level of development and knowledge, we have proposed as our goal, our ideal, the establishment of such a school for the Jewish population, along the lines of the workers' schools in Germany and other countries (Sweden, Denmark), which have already brought marvelous results. Since, as of yet, we have not had the means to establish such formal schools, we are doing the same task, but in small groups. We are organizing groups of 10–12 students who want to learn the same subjects, and we are providing them with teachers.

The groups are divided into three parts.

1. Elementary groups, where the students can receive in two lessons a week a popular course on natural science and history and be prepared to enter the next level.

2. Specialized groups in which specific elementary branches of science are taught.

3. Self-education groups, which hold discussion meetings along with lectures by their own members and are responsible for giving beginners, who are embarrassed to open their mouths at a large gathering, the possibility of discussion so as to develop in them the power of speech.

So far, elementary groups have been established specifically for physics, geography, Darwinism, political economy, and history. [. . .]

Source: Di arbeter tsaytung, Dec. 1, 1893, p. 5. Translated by Tony Michels.

NOTES

1. See document 10, note 1.

29

"For That, We Found Time"
(interview; 1965)

PAULINE NEWMAN

Pauline Newman (1890–1986) was the first female organizer for the International Ladies' Garment Workers' Union and a leading member of the New York Women's Trade Union League. In the following recollection, excerpted from an unpublished interview conducted in 1965, Newman describes her path to self-education.

I recall on Saturday nights we'd gather in each other's apartments and try to read English. We were limited, naturally enough, because none of us went to school. We tried to go to school, and then overtime [at work] would interfere. Evening classes, when they were available, were useless because it was a question of attending school or keeping a job. And naturally we chose to keep the job because that meant making a living.

The things we liked most of course were the things that more or less reflected or symbolized our own feelings of conditions and life in general. For example, I recall that we liked Thomas Hood's "The Sound of the Ship." Now, nothing could come closer to the way we felt than that particular poem. We also read and managed an interest in that other one, "The Bridge of Sighs," also by Thomas Hood. Later, we found "The Masque of Anarchy" by Shelley; and of course in addition to that there were the Jewish poets, like Rosenfeld[1] and Edelshtat.[2] They were magnificent in their writing, in their poetry depicting the life of the people in the shop. There was one writer who I got to know later very well, who wrote a thing just called "Sketches," of conditions and of people in the different shops and naturally in the needle industry in New York.[3] He was magnificent, and we loved everything he wrote. For that, we found time. Now, whether all of us found time, I don't know, but I do know that quite a number of us tried to find an interest outside the job.

I also recall that on Sunday morning when we didn't have to go to the shop, we went to lectures. A man called Hugh Pentacost lectured at a place on Sixth Avenue and Forty-Second Street, named Merit Hall. It's no longer there. We would come at eleven o'clock, and Mr. Pentacost would lecture on current events. He was an excellent speaker. He was, as I remember, a philosophical anarchist, and we really didn't discuss his philosophy at all. We would take up current events. We were very much interested in that, and we would go there just as religious people would go to synagogue. We would go there every Sunday except on Sundays that we had to work in the shops.

Later on, some of us got to know about the Socialist Literary Society on the East Side of New York, East Broadway. It was chiefly a young men's club, but some of the young ladies wanted to join. [. . .] I remember the hot debates that went on at the Socialist Literary Society whether to admit women, and finally the women won out. They voted to admit women, so I called a number of young women—one was a law student, one was a dental student, and some of us worked in the shop. We joined the Socialist Literary Society, and there, really, we obtained what we could in the way of education, especially with English literature. The club was very fortunate in obtaining the services of Dr. Henry Newman, no relation of mine, but who was a professor of literature at City College of New York. I think he still is with the Brooklyn Ethical Cultural Society. He was a magnificent teacher. I don't think there are many who can surpass his interest in the students and in the people who came to his classes. And I, personally, shall never forget his kindness and attention. I remember he was teaching us English literature, giving us an idea of what George Eliot and Thackeray and Dickens were about. And he would ask questions to find out whether we really got his point. He would have liked the students to answer. Some of them did, but I always felt that my English was very limited, and consequently I didn't answer. Dr. Newman had the interest, after class, to come to ask me why I didn't answer the questions. I told him I didn't really know enough of the English language to express myself and consequently I thought it better not to reply. Well, that man sat down with me that night and gave me a list of books to read. He was terribly interested in my reading, and I still remember his kindness and attention, because he was a great help to me. Lord knows what I might have read if it weren't for him. [. . .]

I think I must give credit to the Jewish Daily Forward, which I began to read—you see, I knew Yiddish when I came over very well. . . . And by reading the Forward, you contacted the people in groups like the Socialist Literary Society or sometimes a branch of the Socialist Party. Sometimes some of your relatives who already Americanized were able to say, "I'm going to a meeting; you want to come along?" and you came along. And that's how you found an interest in books, because the books you read were of interest. Here a story would illustrate how, if one were interested, one can get information and culture without going to evening school. I remember going home one night from the Triangle Waist Company by way of Houston Street, and on Houston Street were a number of pushcarts. On pushcarts there [they] sold everything: clothes, household goods, candy, groceries, food—everything under the sun and, believe it or not, some old paperback books. I stopped at one of the pushcarts and bought a paperback book for two cents. And it was called—I can't recall what it was called in English, but it was *Great Expectations*. . . . If you had an interest in reading at all, there they were.

Source: Interview with Pauline Newman conducted on Jan. 19, 1965, pp. 9–14, Oral History Collection on the Labor Movement, RG 113, box 4, YIVO Institute for Jewish Research.

NOTES

1. Morris Rosenfeld (1862–1923), one of the most popular Yiddish poets of the late nineteenth and early twentieth centuries.

2. Dovid Edelshtat (see document 7). In the transcription of Newman's interview, the name appears as "Edelstock," but this was certainly a mistake.

3. Newman probably has in mind the *Forverts*'s popular sketch writer Zalman Libin (1872–1955).

30

A Lower East Side Vacation (1903)

BERNARD G. RICHARDS

Bernard Richards (1877–1971), an English- and Yiddish-language journalist and activist in Jewish communal affairs, penned this sketch as part of a series that originally ran in the *Boston Evening Transcript* and later appeared in book form. Here Richards narrates the discourses of a fictional character named Keidansky, "a dreamer, a philosopher, a talker . . . of the Ghetto," in the words of the *New York Times* reviewer (April 18, 1903). The Jewish intellectual had already become a familiar type in writings about immigrant life, but Richards brought a rare insiders' perspective to the English-reading audience.

"Green fields, fair forests, singing streams, pine-clad mountains, verdant vista—from the monotony of the city to the monotony of nature. I wanted a complete change, and so I went to the East Side of New York for my vacation. That is where I have been."

Thus did our friend explain his strange disappearance and unusual absence from Boston for a whole week. For the first time since he came here from New York he had been missing from his home, his regular haunts, such as the cafés, Jewish book-stores and the debating club, and none of those whom I asked knew whither he had betaken himself. The direct cause of his disappearance, explained Keidansky, was a railroad pass, which he had secured from a friendly editor for whom he had done some work. He went on explaining. "I wanted to break away for a while from the sameness and solemnness, the routine and respectability of this town, from my weary idleness, empty labors, and uniformity of our ideas here, so when the opportunity was available I took a little journey to the big metropolis. One becomes rusty and falls into a rut in this suburb. I was becoming so sedate, stale and quiet that I was beginning to be afraid of myself. The revolutionary spirit has somewhat subsided. Many of the comrades have gone back on their ideas, have begun to practice what they preach, to improve their conditions by going into business and into work, and I often feel lonely. Anti-imperialism, Christian Science and the New Thought are amusing; but there is not enough excitement here. Boston is not progressive; there are not enough foreigners in this city. People from many lands with all sorts of ideas and the friction that arises between them—that causes progress. New York is the place, and it is also the refuge of all radicals, revolutionaries, and good people whom the wicked old world has cast out. America, to retain its original character, must constantly be replenished by hounded refugees and victims of persecution in despotic lands. To remain lovers of freedom we must have sufferers from oppression with us. Sad commentary, this, upon our human nature; but so are nearly all commentaries upon human nature. Commentaries upon the superhuman are tragic. New York with its Germans and Russians and Jews is a characteristic American city. Boston and other places are too much like Europe—cold, narrow and provincial. I came to Boston some time ago because I had relatives here—the last reason in the world why any one should go anywhere; but I was ignorant and superstitious in those days. I have since managed to emancipate myself, more or less, from the baneful influences of those near; but meanwhile I have established myself, have become interested in the movements and institutions of the community, and here I am. The symphony concerts, the radical movement, the library, lectures on art, the sunset over the Charles River, the Faneuil Hall protest meetings against everything that continues to be, the literary paper published, the Atlantic Monthly, Gamaliel Bradford, Philip Hale and so many other fixtures of Boston have since endeared it to me and I stayed. Besides, it would cost me too much to ship all my books to New York.

"But wishing a change, I wanted to go to the big metropolis. No, not to the country; not for me those parasitic, pestering and polished summer hotels, where a pile of people get together to gossip and giggle and gormandize and bore each other for several weeks. An accident once brought me to one of these places. I went out to see some friends, and I know what they are. They spend most of their time dressing; these vacationists dress three times a day; the green waist, and yellow waist, the brown skirt and the blue suit, the red jacket, the white hat, and the gray coat, and then the same turn over again; they fill themselves with all sorts of heavy and unwholesome foods brought from the cities; they sit around the verandas and talk all day, never daring to venture into the woods; they do no good to themselves, coming home tired and sick, and they do unspeakable wrong by turning good, honest farmers into parasitic, sophisticated boarder-breeders, and by turning them away from the tilling of the soil. No more of these places for me. Of course, if one could go into the woods and live as simply as a savage for a while it would be fine; but one needs a tent, and I never did own any real estate.

"But this time I wanted a complete change; I wanted something to move and stir me out of the given groove, the beaten path I was falling into, some excitement that would shake the cobwebs out of my brain, so I turned towards the East Side.

"They are all there, the comrades, the radicals, the red ones, and dreamers; people who are free because they own nothing. Poets, philosophers, novelists, dramatists, artists, editors, agitators, and other idle and useless beings, they form a great galaxy in the New York Ghetto. For several years, ever since I left New York, I had been receiving instruction and inspiration from them through the medium of the Yiddish and Socialist press, where my own things often appeared beside their spirited outpourings, and now I was overcome by an overpowering desire to meet them again, talk matters over and fight it all out. There is no sham about the East Side branch of the ancient and most honorable order of Bohemians—the little changing, moving world that is flowing with the milk of human kindness and the honey of fraternal affections, where those who live may die and those who die may live. Here among the East Side Bohemians people feel freely, act independently, speak as they think and are not at all ashamed of their feelings. They have courage. They wear their convictions in public. They do as they please, whether that pleases everybody else or not. They talk with the purpose of saying something. They write with the object of expressing their ideas. They tell the truth and shame those who do not. Hearts are warm because they own their souls. Those who really own their souls will never lose them. As Joseph Bovshover, the fine poet of the East Side has sung:

> 'Beauty hideth,
> Nature chideth,
> When the heart is cold;
> Fame is galling,
> Gold's enthralling,
> When the mind is sold.'

"They all assemble in the cafés, those universities of the East Side, and in these places of judgment all things are determined. Is there a great world problem that puzzles and vexes all mankind? The debaters at one of these tea-houses take it up at their earliest discussion and soon the problem is solved and the way of human progress is clear again. Is there a question that has troubled the ages? Come and spend fifteen minutes on the East Side, and the salvation of humanity will be assured to you. There is so much squalor and suffering and sorrow there that nothing can overcome the optimism of these chosen people. Their incurable faith cannot be shaken even by their religious leaders, and when they become atheists they are the most pious atheists in all the world. But in the cafés the great issues given up in despair by famous statesmen are met and decided upon. The trusts? Are they not paving the way for the realization of Socialism? Not until all the industries have been concentrated by the trusts will the people through the government be able to take possession of them. Otherwise, how in the world will the new régime, for instance, ever organize and take hold of all the peanut stands of the land? You do not understand the question thoroughly if you have not read the articles of I. A. Hurwits in the 'Vorwarts' [*Forverts*]. The future of war? There will be no war in the future. The workingmen of all countries are uniting and so are the capitalists. The international movement is not laboring in vain. Socialism is spreading in the European armies. Every government will have enough trouble in its own land. Others come here and say that every government will have to fight for its own life and will not be able to do anything else. People will take Tolstoy's advice and cease to pay taxes and withdraw their support from the powers that rule. Tolstoy, say some, is a masterful artist, but puerile as a philosopher, a curious mixture of genius and narrow-mindedness, a man, who once having erred, now sins against mankind by denying it the right of erring. The red-haired ragged orator with blue eye-glasses and the face of a Hebrew Beethoven quotes Ingersoll. 'Tolstoy,' said the agnostic, 'stands with this back to the rising sun.' And did not Edward Carpenter say of Tolstoy's book, 'that strange jumble of real acumen and bad logic, large-heartedness and fanaticism—What is art?'

"Ibsen is somber because he is almost alone in seeing the most tragic phases of life, because he feels compelled to treat what all other artists have neglected. Many of his plays are too much like life to be acted, and we go to the theatre only to see plays. One of the listeners speaks of the appreciation of Ibsen in 'The New Spirit,' by Havellock Ellis, and of the analogy that he finds between Ibsen and Whitman. Zangwill places Ibsen above Shakespeare, and more recently he has bestowed great praise upon Hauptmann. Rather strange of Zangwill, who is himself not a realist and has gone in for Zionism, to like Ibsen so much. And who is greater than Ibsen? some one asks. 'Perhaps it is I. Zangwill,' says the cynical, frowzy and frowning little journalist. G. Bernard Shaw is mentioned as a candidate, and his great little book on Ibsenism comes in for a heated discussion. Brandes is quoted, and several of his admirers present go into ecstasies over his works and almost forget the writers whom he has treated. The pale-faced, wistful-eyed poet with the Christ-like face rises high on the wings of his eloquence in praise of the Danish critic's appreciation of Heine, and Brandes is declared to be one of the greatest Jews in the world. What was it Brandes said about Zionism? Zionism, Socialism, and Anarchism come up in turn, and so many trenchant and vital things are said on these subjects. Will the novel pass away? The dramatist—bulky and bearded, impressive and strong-looking, with wonderful piercing eyes—the dramatist is inclined to think that it will. The short story is the story of the future. Long novels give one a glimpse of eternity. By the time you come to the last chapter, conditions have so changed in the world that you do not know whether the story is true to life or not. It is necessarily historical, the long novel is. Old Jules Verne has won the East Side over with the fine words he has said on Guy De Maupassant. Some admirers of Z. Libin say that the Frenchman is too romantic, but on the whole he is the favorite story-writer. 'Yes,' says the Jewish actor, 'De Maupassant writes for all the Yiddish papers'; and in fact all the East Side dailies have for years been treating their readers to his charming tales. He may be imagined to be a constant contributor. Did not an old Israelite walk into the office of the 'Jewish Cry' and ask to see Friedrich Nietzsche? And then the problem of Nietzsche comes up; whether he was, or was not a reaction against, or the opposite extreme from, the meekness of Christianity, the weakness of his time. Wagner's music, Stephen Phillips's poetry, Zola's essay on realism, Maeterlinck's transcendentalism, Gorky's rise in letters, the Anglo-Saxon isolation in literature, Ludwig Fuldas's latest play, all these things are decided upon by people who understand them, more or less.

"I cannot tell you more, but these meetings and these talks at various times and in various places made my vacation on the East Side delightful. Then there were lectures and meetings and social gatherings of the comrades. The sun of new ideas rises on the East Side. Everywhere you meet people who are ready to fight for what they believe in and who do not believe in fighting. For a complete change and for pure air you must go among the people who think about something, have faith in something. Katz, Cahan, Gordin, Yanofsky, Zolotaroff, Harkavy, Frumkin, Krantz, Zametkin, Zeifert, Lessin, Elisowitz, Winchevsky, Jeff, Leontieff, Lipsky, Freidus, Frominson, Selikowitch, Palay, Barondess, and many other intellectual leaders, come into the cafés to pour out wisdom and drink tea, and here comes Hutchins Hapgood[1] to get this education. Each man bears his own particular lantern, it is true, but each one carries a light and every one brings a man with him.

"There was that memorial mass-meeting in honor of Hirsh Leckert, the Jewish shoemaker, who shot at the governor of Wilna, who took his life in hand to avenge a hideous outrage perpetrated upon his fellow-workers by a despicable despot. The Jewish working-people of Wilna organized a peaceful procession, and at the behest of the governor hundreds of them were mercilessly flogged—flogged until they fainted, and when revived, flogged again. Then came this lowly hero, Leckert, and made a glorious ascent on the scaffold. In the afternoon news reached the East Side that Leckert was hanged. The same evening working-people, just out of their factories and sweat-shops, in overwhelming numbers assembled in New Irving Hall, and the fervor and enthusiasm, the sobbing and the sighing, the tear-stained faces and love-lit eyes—the soul-stirring eulogies delivered—I shall never forget it. I tell you no man ever saw anything greater or more inspiring on his vacation.

"Mr. Jacob Gordin gave me a memorable treat, took me to see his latest and one of his best plays, 'Gott, Mensch, und der Teufel.' I have seen many of his works and it is hard to decide which is the best because they are nearly all so good. But this strange story of a Jewish Faust, the pious, saintly Jew who, tempted by Satan's gold, step by step loses his soul and cannot live without it; this wonderful blending of modern realism and supernatural symbolism, this superb summary of man and the new problem of life, the beauty and the strength of the work, is remarkable, to say the least. 'As in times of yore,' says Satan, 'the sons of Adam are divided into Abels and Cains. The former are constantly murdered and the latter are the constant murderers. Gracious Lord, in the new man there dwells the old savage Adam.' Sorry I cannot tell you more about it now, but the last words of the play have been ringing through my mind ever since I saw it.

> 'All must die, all that is and lives;
> Life alone is immortal.
> That only is mortal that desire and strives,
> The striving and the desire immortal.'

"Why," added Keidansky, as a final thunderbolt, "I have gained enough ideas on the East Side to last me here in Boston for ten years."

Source: Bernard G. Richards, *Discourses of Keidansky* (New York: Scott-Thaw, 1903), pp. 199–209.

NOTES

1. Hutchins Hapgood (1869–1944), an influential journalist and author of *The Spirit of the Ghetto* (1902), a classic account of Jewish life on the Lower East Side.

31

"Jewish Working People... Have Lost All Interest in the Synagogue" (1905)

PHILLIP DAVIS

Abandonment of religion was a widespread phenomenon among young immigrant Jews. Although many individuals, including those attracted to socialism, continued to practice Judaism to some extent, total rejection of religion was common. A Boston-based social worker and former labor organizer, Phillip Davis describes the loss of piety he experienced firsthand.

When I came to America, at the age of fifteen, I was fully equipped with a prayer-book, phylacteries, a "four-corners," promising forelocks—with everything, in short, to indicate my strict orthodox training, and to insure its preservation in the "New Wanton World," as America is often styled in Russia. I remember distinctly how cynically my older brother, who brought me here, smiled when he saw me armed with this religious ammunition, ready to go to the synagogue.

"All right," he said, while packing his lunch-box; "if you want to go to a synagogue, I'll take you there. It is on my way to the shop, anyhow. But I doubt whether you will keep this up very long," he added, wistfully.

"How is that?" I asked. "Don't the Jews go to the synagogue here and *davn* (prayo, daily, as they do at home?"

"At home," he said, "Jews are idlers. Here in America they are hard, busy workers. They have no time to pray."

"Could that be possible?" I asked myself, and, as I write now with a better knowledge of existing conditions, I marvel at the breadth of the question then so naïvely put. The question, if answered in the affirmative, meant that here in America it is possible for a Jewish young man to disregard the most sacred object which a father could bestow on his children in the hope that by their constant use the religion of his forefathers might be preserved. Further than this: it meant that in America one may become so occupied as to cease to worship at all, since, traditionally, no Jew may worship without his phylacteries, his "four-corners," etc.

At that time I was quite sure that that was impossible, and for the first six months my conviction was unshaken. Somehow I could find no work, and therefore had ample time to take in even more than three divine daily services, if need be. But at last I got work in one of the old-time sweat-shops of New York, first as a basting-puller, then as a half-baster. From the moment I entered the shop my religious interest began to decline. In a year it was practically nil. My "four-corners" wore out, and were never replaced; my forelocks disappeared; my phylacteries and my prayer-book were in exile. I ceased going to the synagogue, first only on week-days, later on Saturdays as well. In after years I never entered it but twice a year, at the anniversary of my mother's death and during the Day of Atonement.

"Then my brother's prediction had already come true?" you ask. Yes, but note in what way. Had I enjoyed the fullness of life in all its other phases to the exclusion of the religious only, I might have indeed given in to my brother's views. But the fact is that my whole life had suffered the same decline. From the moment I entered the shop until five years thereafter it was actually a blank. I recall nothing which filled its moments from day to day or from year to year. Immediately upon my entering the sweat-shop I seemed to have plunged into a struggle so intense that it absorbed all my energy and simply incapacitated me for any other normal human activity. In the language of Tolstoy's confession, "my life had come to a stop. I was able to breathe, to eat, to drink, to sleep, and I could not help breathing, eating, drinking, or sleeping. But I had no real life in me," because my work consumed it all.

It must be remembered that in these days, 1890–1894, the task system went hand in hand with the sweat-shop. I was a victim of both. I worked from early morning until late at night, Saturdays and Sundays included, for almost five years straight. All I now remember about this period of my life is that it was one of intense labor, sleep, and forgetfulness.

How or when I changed from a half-baster to an under-presser, then to a presser, I cannot tell. I only know that one fine morning during my sixth year in the coat factory I woke up to find myself a full-fledged workman making about $14 a week, sure of my job and proud of my skill. Somehow, mysteriously enough to me, the task system began to disappear, the hours were being gradually shortened, Sunday work was gradually abolished. In short, I emerged at last from a long, bitter struggle as a conqueror—master of myself again and of my time in part, possessor of a little sum of money which I had laid by, a free and independent workman.

Here was the crucial test: Was I, who had at last regained possession of myself, about to revert to my former religious habits, the inheritance of so many generations? I now had the time, I had the leisure. Was I ready to return to my prayer-book and to my phylacteries and re-enter the synagogue? Evidently my brother was in the right, for I *did not* even then. For a year or more I seemed to have relaxed altogether. I went wild after pleasure, amusement, fun. Instinctively, I think, I was trying to make up for lost time. I went to the theater, I struggled to look "sportish," I smoked cigarettes; in short, I was after things, not ideas, whether religious or any other.

Presently I began to shift. My ignorance of English often shamed me in company and was always the cause of great disappointment at the theater. The night school now loomed up before me. I entered it in good earnest; later on I also joined "the Settlement."[1]

Again, I plunged into a new struggle, an intellectual struggle this time, but one far more intense even than the economic, and one which completely barred out any religious activity. English, that stubborn, cruel foreigner's foe called English, physics, chemistry, mathematics, and my manual work, filled all my time, so that from the moment I entered the night school I practically never even thought anything about religion worthy of mention until I left the University of Chicago at the end of my sophomore year, and entered Harvard in 1901. [. . .]

After graduating from Harvard, I had the honor of being elected Organizer for the Ladies' Garment Workers, and the extreme privilege of making an extensive tour throughout the Eastern States, including such centers as Chicago, Cincinnati, Cleveland, Detroit, Baltimore, etc. It was during this trip that I first learned of the true state of Jewish orthodoxy among the workers as a class: how universally they neglected the Bible; violated the Dietary Laws; broke the Sabbath; degraded the holiday; made away with the ceremonies; missed the services; minced their prayers; and, above all, deserted the synagogue. These general signs of revolt against the accepted forms of the Jewish religion indicated a degree of unbelief which, from a religious point of view, assumed striking proportions. To find out how deep-seated this unbelief really was, it was necessary to concentrate attention on any one of those religious institutions and confine the study to a particular place or city. [. . .]

After repeated visits to the greatest and smallest synagogues in New York, it was apparent that, as such, the synagogue everywhere has lost all its meaning to the American Jewish workingman. He hurries by it morning and night on his way to and from the factory without the slightest regard for its former sanctity. The Catholic takes his hat off in reverence on passing his church. The truly orthodox Jew hastily puts his hat on when he finds himself in the shadow of the synagogue. The average Jewish workingman goes past it, or stands idly by, hatless and unconcerned.

East Side writers, reformers, reverends, and radicals—men like A. Kahn,[2] Dr. Blaustein,[3] the Rev. Mr. Masliansky,[4] and Joseph Barondess[5]—in fact, all prominent men on the East Side whom I have consulted—say with one accord: The Jewish workingmen, especially those between the ages of eighteen and thirty-five, have deserted the synagogue. "We all admit the fact," said Dr. Blaustein, "and there is nothing more to say but to admit it." "During the Solemn Days, particularly the Day of Atonement, there is usually a burst of piety among them," declared A. Kahn. "Then they dress up, buy a seat and go to the synagogue. But even this rare visit is made in a perfunctory way. In most cases it is made to please an importunate mother or to appease a petulant wife."

As a rule, the Jewish workingmen stay away from the synagogue, and the more intelligent they are the more consistently they stay away. The Rev. Mr. Masliansky, most favorite of all the East Side Maggidim, or preachers, now preaching at the People's Synagogue of the Educational Alliance, sighed when I put the question to him. "Yes," he said, "religion is in a very bad way here. As for the synagogue, it is a dying institution. The very old, the very orthodox, those who need the synagogue least, are the only people who go there. Yes, these and the mourners," he added, wistfully.

How true the last statement was I had immediate occasion to find out. The Feast of Weeks was at hand. I went the rounds of one of the most prominent Schules in search of a particularly representative workingmen's audience. I found it at the last in the Beth Hamedrosh Hagodel[6] on Norfolk Street, where the preponderance of middle-aged men, mostly workingmen, over the old men fairly surprised me. Presently, however, there was a burst of prayer wrung from the hearts among them. I at once recognized the familiar Kaddish, the prayer for the dead. They were all mourners. These men, I noticed, seldom lingered in the synagogue as the old folks do. They rushed in, offered their prayers (paid the price), and rushed out again. In fact, all workmen, as a rule, enter the synagogues apparently as strangers. They are seldom members of the congregation. They know nothing of how or by whom the synagogue is maintained. Surely they themselves pay very little towards its support. In short, the Jewish working people, as a class, have lost all interest in the synagogue as a religious institution, have practically deserted it.

"How comes it," I asked the Rev. Mr. Masliansky, "that so large a proportion of so pronouncedly religious a people as the Jews traditionally are, should have so completely cut itself loose from the synagogue?" "Read the Jewish Socialist papers, and you will readily see why," he answered. "Every new issue of the 'Forward' and the 'Zuknuft'[7] is a death blow to religion. Each new issue injects another venomous drop of unbelief, until the very heart of religion is poisoned. These Socialists, these men of evil knowledge, instead of helping the immigrant to learn the language and the opportunities of the land, keep stuffing him with a miserable jargon version of political economy, the sum and substance of which is that his poverty is the result, not of his ignorance, but of the 'system,' the so-called Capitalist System, to which all art, literature, morality, and religion are but handmaids. The poor, ignorant workingman is thus made to believe he has discovered his real enemies, gets bitter against the one thing which he has—his religion—and flees from the synagogue."

The Rev. Mr. Jaffe, of the Community of Hebrew Congregations, offered the same explanation. "What more can you expect from so many Anarchistic meetings, with which the East Side is pestered?" he asked.

"I did not know there were so many Anarchists as you imply," I said, "unless you include the Socialists and other radicals."

"Socialists, Anarchists," he said, "they are all alike. They are all atheists."

I spoke to many other religious men; they all had the same view. Invariably the conservatives were blaming it on the radicals. I went to see the radicals.

"Why have the working people abandoned the synagogue?" I asked Mr. Joseph Barondess, the most brilliant labor orator among the Jews of this country.

"Because," he said, "the Jewish synagogue is the most conservative, retrogressive of all churches in America. Its ceremonies are most exacting; its ritual, its liturgy, is foreign, its language is unknown to the masses, its pulpit is barren, its rabbis are sterile. You cannot find one who is progressive enough to say a good word for the cause of labor. Yes, it is unpleasant, very unpleasant, for a Jew to confess, but it is nevertheless true, the Jewish synagogue is a dead institution as compared with the Christian church. With men like Bishop Porter, of New York, Jenkin Lloyd Jones, of Chicago, or Dean Hodges, of Boston, staunch friends of the laboring people, the Christian church may well boast of the workingmen's sympathy. Look at the C.A.I.L. within the ranks of the Episcopal Church, representing a whole army of busy promoters of labor's needs. How many generations will yet pass before the Jewish rabbis [we were speaking, of course, of the Russian Jewish rabbis] will be ready to take up so progressive a work?"

All East Side radicals share Barondess's views. They all lay the charge of the worker's desertion of the synagogue to the door of the extreme orthodoxy of the orthodox.

This fault-finding, with this bitterness against each other, only indicates the keen rivalry which goes on between these two East Side parties—the religious conservatives and the radical atheists. It is evident that the masses of the Jewish workers have turned their backs on the former and are now entirely under the influence of the latter. [. . .]

Source: Phillip Davis, "Making Americans of Russian Jews," *Outlook*, July 8, 1905, pp. 631–635.

NOTES

1. Hull House, Chicago.

2. Abraham Cahan (1860–1951).

3. Dr. David Blaustein (1866–1912), Jewish educator and communal activist. Blaustein was an advocate of aid to the poor and a social reformer who worked to better conditions in immigrant ghettos.

4. Zvi Hirsch Masliansky (1856–1943), popular Yiddish *magid*, or preacher.

5. Joseph Barondess (1867–1928), labor leader and president of the Cloakmakers' Union.

6. Lower East Side synagogue funded by wealthy uptown Jews.

7. *Di tsukunft* (The Future), prestigious socialist Yiddish monthly, founded in 1892.

32

"Peripatetic Philosophers" (1910)

NEW YORK TIMES

Those who visited the Lower East Side and other immigrant Jewish neighborhoods were often struck by the passionate discussions they witnessed in parks, in public squares, and on street corners. The following account, although somewhat condescending, reflects a genuine and widespread fascination with the vibrant intellectual life of the "Jewish ghetto."

There is Scriptural authority for the statement that the ancient Athenians were never content unless discussing some new thing. New York, all Pantheon-less as it is, is in this respect the legitimate successor of the glory that was Greece. It is the talkiest city in the world. There are more new ideas set forth to a benighted universe in Manhattan, Brooklyn, and the Bronx (the Bronx especially must not be omitted) than in any area of similar size on the globe.

Not only does this town of ours follow in the path of the philosophical Athenians, but they have a method of doing it which is taken straight from ancient history. We all know the Greek person who taught his disciples as they walked to and fro in a garden—if there were a classical dictionary handy we would all know where to look him up, so never mind the name.

It was undoubtedly the best way of teaching that had ever been invented. The moment the lecturer became tiresome there was escape at hand, and this prompted not only greater care on the part of the speaker to preserve the interest, but did away with the feeling of hopelessness which dampens the ardor of an audience that is chained to a bench during the pleasure of some irresponsible person. It was a pity the method was ever abandoned, but fortunately it was merely sleeping, not dead, and it has been revived here in New York with the most signal success.

The peripatetic philosopher comes to New York with the flowers that bloom in the Spring. You find him, or her, in all the poorer parts of the city, more or less, but especially in three or four neighborhoods. Little groups of them dot the sidewalk all Summer long, strolling up and down, discussing art, literature, drama, Socialism, Anarchy, woman's suffrage, child labor, the nature of evil, pragmatism, restricted immigration, Milwaukee politics, and any number of other subjects to the number of seventy times seven.

A few years ago the peripatetic philosophers were Russian only, and their one "garden" was East Broadway. East Broadway used to be called the Nevsky Prospect[1] of America for that reason. But now the custom of strolling about and discussing things in the streets has spread elsewhere.

The philosophers of East Broadway have gone northward to Harlem and the Bronx, and even to Brooklyn, while the custom has not been abandoned by their successors on "Nevsky Prospect," and other nationalities are acquiring the habit. Fifth Avenue around 116th Street is even more than East Broadway the happy hunting ground of the peripatetics. From that point down to the Park all philosophers know that the school will meet every fine day in Summer. Another school used last year to walk along Seventh Avenue north from 125th Street.

The Woman Suffrage and Women's Trade Union League[2] people have done much to encourage this custom. The woman and her soap box opened the way for others with ideas on things in general. When the women first began to speak outside of the lower east side, which is pre-eminently the place where everybody minds his own business and you do as you choose, the right of free speech was so far from being a popular ideal that peripatetics had to seek the aid of the police when they wanted to philosophize.

The woman suffrage people tell a tale of a young speaker who was prepared to address the populace for the space of fifteen minutes, and so did, but at the end of the allotted time the crowd was getting ugly and there were no police in sight. She paused, but a tug at her skirt emphasized a distracted whisper from her companion that she had better keep right on and try to prevent an outburst.

She continued, her ideas evaporating as her throat grew husky. Half an hour and the orator paused again despairingly. Another tug and another distracted whisper. "For heaven's sake," muttered the speaker between gestures, "run for the police so I can stop!" At the end of forty-five minutes help appeared and she rested from her labors.

So fully has the idea of using the streets for discussion been accepted by the people in general that the last meat strike on the east side was engineered entirely from the sidewalks. There was not one meeting in a hall all through the women's campaign against the increase in the price of meat. Mrs. Anna Pastor, the mother of Rose Pastor Stokes,[3] organized the strike in the Bronx, and on the lower east side United Jewish Socialist districts managed the affair, doing everything by means of walking up and down with the women they sought to interest.

The Women's Trades Union League uses much the same methods. Their enthusiasts station themselves in the way of a stream of girls pouring out of some great factory. It is a tremendously picturesque sight, the army of girls, coming wearily, worn with work, or running gayly to their playtime, stopping here and there to listen to the plea for union and delaying to walk up and down and discuss. [. . .]

Peripatetic philosophy among the working people, carried on without any idea of making proselytes is especially a Jewish institution. It is not confined to that race, but it flourishes among them.

Any Jew has to struggle hard to keep from being a philosopher, and for a Russian Jew the effort is impossible. So the Jews talk and walk in their several districts, discussing different matters in different places, and passers by may listen or not as they may choose.

If you know what you want to hear talked just tell any Russian intellectual and he will direct you to the exact spot where you will find what you want. The Socialists are prominent in Harlem, the Bronx, and Borough Park, Brooklyn. The peripatetics in those sections, for example, are discussing whether or not the Milwaukee experiment[4] is a success or not. You will hear that it is a fine thing for the cause. You will hear that it is too "Fabian"—and Fabian is in some quarters the last word of damnation. How can we advance when we compromise at every step? says the Bronx. And how can we advance unless we pick and choose our way? retorts Harlem.

Again, how about Briand[5] in France? Is he a statesman or a Judas? And kindly prove it, whatever you say.

Why did they forbid the first of May demonstration in Paris? Anybody can answer that, comrade; the last Ferrer[6] demonstration frightened the bourgeois half to death. Thousands of workmen, organized, disciplined, orderly, singing the songs of the revolution—of course it could not be permitted again.

The Anarchists are always interesting. None need be bored in their company. Their talk runs to such abstract questions as they affect—the Anarchists are pre-eminently the dreamers among the peripatetics, and the topics they discuss are all remote from present-day life.

They have quaint ways of putting things, too. It was at a peripatetic Anarchist meeting that a young man remarked the other day to a woman that he wished he were not a man—a woman merely as a woman was a sufficient asset to the world, "but we men have to be perpetually seeking ideas to justify our existence."

Not all peripatetics are revolutionary. Down on East Broadway the talk turns frequently on art, literature, and the drama.

Do you know Sholem Ash,[7] reader? If you do not you had better acquaint yourself with him before attempting to walk up and down East Broadway with the philosophers. Ash wrote "The God of Vengeance," and he is a great question of dispute on the east side.

And Chaim Zhitlowsky,[8] do you know him? He has an interesting theory about the Hebrew language,[9] and it is discussed these Spring evenings all up and down the sidewalks of that queer country east of the Bowery.

Nor is the Bowery itself without the occasional philosopher. It was not long since that the present scribe walked back and forth before the ten, fifteen, and twenty-five cent lodging houses until after midnight with a few peripatetics who were holding forth on the nature of evil. It would be edifying to repeat what was said on that occasion, but to be quite truthful most of the talk was above the head of the present scribe. There was a lot about Goethe, anyway, and he proved the case of the young man who worked in a sweatshop.

Moreover, can you be a Socialist and a Territorialist? That's a question to settle. Most people say no, but a good many are coming now to say yes, which is queer, because it was only six years ago that a Socialist said: "Oh, what is a Territorialist? Why, a Jew who believes that his people must have a land of their own somewhere soon—a follower of Israel Zangwill." This is a weighty question for East Broadway to discuss on Summer nights, and indeed someday the world may have to stop and listen to what East Broadway has said about it.

There is no need to dwell on the peripatetics who are absorbed in the struggle between the Shund[10] and the literary drama. Their name is legion on the east side. They not only philosophize, but they gather and dispense all important news, such as whether or not Sol Blumgarten,[11] the Hebrew poet, is writing a play and whether Mrs. Kalinsky will come over. There is a group interested in such matters that peripatets in Division Street.

So, you see, you need only to have an enthusiasm and know some one in these circles and you will find your school of philosophy awaiting you on the sidewalk. Considering how the habit has grown in the last two years, together with the fact that the custom is in a high degree practical, there is no reasonable doubt that it will spread.

For who cares, after a hard day's work, to sit in a close room and listen to a discourse, however edifying? And what is more than charming than to stroll about in the open air and think high thoughts in good company?

The rich man has his clubs in which he may discuss Wall Street and such phases of present-day problems as interest him. The clubless poor man has the streets wherein to talk of wages and that part of the social structure which concerns him and his. [...]

Source: "Peripatetic Philosophers of This Many-Sided Town," *New York Times*, May 29, 1910, p. SM11.

NOTES

1. A famous boulevard in St. Petersburg.

2. The Women's Trade Union League was a women's labor union founded by Jane Addams and other prominent women's rights advocates in 1903. The WTUL was crucial in helping to pass a number of significant pieces of labor legislation, including the eight-hour workday and child-labor laws.

3. See document 14.

4. A program of municipal reform implemented by moderate Socialists in Milwaukee and criticized by the party's more radical elements.

5. Aristide Briand (1862–1932), a leader of the French Socialist Party.

6. Francisco Ferrer y Guardia (1859–1909), a Spanish anarchist and pedagogue.

7. Sholem Asch (1880–1957), well-known Yiddish novelist who came to the United States in 1910.

8. Chaim Zhitlowsky, also spelled Zhitlovsky (1856–1943). A seminal figure in the development of modern Jewish politics on both sides of the Atlantic, Zhitlovsky argued that Jews constituted a Yiddish-speaking nation defined by a common culture and should work to develop Jewish communal autonomy in the countries in which they lived.

9. In fact, Zhitlowsky was known for his advocacy of Yiddish, not Hebrew.

10. Formulaic, melodramatic potboilers.

11. Solomon Blumgarten (1870–1927), Yiddish poet who used the pen name Yeoash and was perhaps best known for his translation of the Hebrew Bible into Yiddish.

33

Yiddish Lectures in Philadelphia (1916)

A. FAYNMAN

In 1910, the Arbeter Ring established a national committee to organize lectures and adult classes in cities across the United States. The following report from a local activist describes the successes and shortcomings of a lecture series in Philadelphia. It appeared in *Der fraynd*, the Arbeter Ring's monthly magazine. At the time, the organization counted nearly sixty thousand members.

I want, at the request of the Arbeter Ring's National Education Committee, to give a brief overview of the lectures we have arranged this season.

It is true that we haven't had the opportunity to complete the entire program we worked out. But we have our city's policemen to thank for that because they did not allow us, not even for a single instant, to raise money on Sunday (thereby desecrating the holiness of the day of rest), which we had hoped would enable us to continue the work for the rest of the season. Therefore, we were forced to stop the lectures.

We held nine lectures. The first was by Friend Saul Raskin[1] on "Exilic Motifs and Messianic Motifs in Jewish Art," illustrated with pictures. In spite of the extraordinarily bad weather that evening, more than 400 people came out to the lecture. It was immediately apparent that Raskin's lecture was something new for the average Yiddish lecture attendee. Anxiousness mixed with eagerness. To some, it became clear that everybody, even a worker, should spend a couple of hours in an art gallery, and that a worker, too, is capable of enjoying art—something which some of our intellectuals dispute.

The success of Raskin's first lecture did nothing to diminish the complete failure, if I may, of his second lecture on the topic "Rafoel Nertsekh" by Abraham Cahan. It was supposed to be a popular lecture on the socialist ideal, but it was not interesting and was painfully long for those who were to some extent familiar with the basics of socialism, and if not for the fact that he interrupted the lecture a couple of times with his excellent cartoons (in Raskin's usual fashion), who knows what would have happened with the lecture? No wonder that a large number of attendees left the hall in the middle of the lecture, which also negatively affected the following lectures. The one and only comfort for us is that we are sure that Friend Raskin has lectured on this topic for the last time.

Outstandingly rich in content and interesting was Dr. Syrkin's[2] first lecture on "Modern Yiddish Literature." It is worth noting that before the lecture Friend Kats[3] gave an introduction on "The Effect of Modern Literature on the Development of the Masses," which captured the attention of the attendees. The lecturer led his listeners as if in a library, stopping at every important book, selecting the pearls of Yiddish literature. I did not hear his second lecture on "Jean Juares, August Bebel, and Kier Hardy," but it was relayed to me that it was no less successful than the first.

Very educational for the attendees was A. S. Zaks'[4] lecture on "Darwinism." In large part this was thanks to the pictures he showed, which enlivened the lecture. Some of the attendees have inquired whether we will have more lectures on the same topic, and this shows the great interest elicited by Zaks' lecture. It is understandable why the audience thirsts for knowledge. Coming from a country such as Russia and not having the possibility of becoming familiar with elementary concepts of natural science, it is no wonder that Zaks' lecture brought forth such great interest. The lecture on "The Development of the Socialist Ideal" was less successful, despite the fact that it was no less consistent and learned.

Friend William Edlin,[5] in his lecture "What Education Brings to Every Person," masterly described the divine pleasure of those who possess true education, not the commonplace education of most of the professional "intellectuals." Their education consists only of what they know in their "trade," like any tradesman. The truly educated person, according to Edlin, doesn't need any god or "laws" to protect him; he knows how to protect himself. He himself knows what is "right." "The educated person knows not from race-hatred nor from other such feelings." At the beginning, it seemed the topic wouldn't be successful: who doesn't already know what education can achieve for an individual? Yet those present certainly learned a lot. Edlin's lecture was also interesting in that it described and criticized works by Metterling, Ibsen, and others.

Consistent and interesting were also the lectures (two of them) by Shakhne Epshteyn[6] on "Revolutionary Motifs in World Literature." It must be said that to give a cursory overview of world-literature is only possible for those who are familiar, more or less, with the "world" and who have a conception, more or less, of geography and history so as to know when and where the writers lived and created, and so on. A lecturer cannot explain all of this in one or two hours. And the 800 attendees—the average number of attendees at our lectures—cannot usually expect this.

We want to draw attention to the fact that almost all of the lectures were given in Yiddish on social, political, and contemporary issues, and very few, almost none, were on natural science. Whether this is because we have very few such people in a position to lecture in Yiddish on those questions or whether this is the fault of the organizers, it is certainly not the fault of the attendees. [. . .]

There is one more thing which has been neglected, in my opinion, in our lectures. These are questions of law, government, city government, and the like. It is no wonder why we Jews are so neglectful of things related to our civic duties. We are simply little familiar with them. I am sure that the great number of Jews in America does not know where state law ends and where federal law begins or what the state legislature does and what Congress does. I think that a series of lectures on these questions, naturally by qualified people, would bring more results than a thousand agitational pamphlets and appeals "to become citizens."

One more question, dear editor, and then I am done. Tell me, please, are our Yiddish lecturers really so well versed in all branches of literature and science, subjects which so many of them keep in their "stock" of lectures? Our lecturers will not decline to speak on any topic. This is not at all like the Gentiles, pardon the comparison, among whom each has his own specialty. Don't you think that because of this lack of specialization some of the lectures on "the Jewish street" are so very weak?

Source: A. Faynman, "Iber di filadelfyer lektshurs fun A.R. un lektshurs in algemeyn," *Der fraynd*, Mar. 1916, pp. 15–16. Translated by Tony Michels.

NOTES

1. Saul Raskin (1878–1966), artist, cartoonist, and prolific writer on art and theater. Members of the Arbeter Ring formally addressed one another as "Friend," thereby underscoring the organization's commitment to fellowship and mutual aid.

2. Nachman Syrkin (1868–1924), among the first theoreticians of socialist-Zionism and a staunch advocate for Hebrew over Yiddish, although he lectured and wrote frequently in the Jewish vernacular.

3. Moyshe Kats (1864–1941), Yiddish journalist, literary critic, and lecturer active in the anarchist and territorialist movements.

4. A. S. Zaks (1878–1931), Yiddish journalist, lecturer, and educator, who specialized in natural science and political economy.

5. William Edlin (1878–1947), Yiddish newspaper editor and Socialist Party activist.

6. Shakhne Epshteyn (1883–1945), Yiddish journalist and a leading figure in the Socialist Party's Jewish Socialist Federation. He later became a Communist, active both in Soviet Russia and the United States.

34

"A Language That He Wants to and Must Forget" (1918)

B. SHEYFER

Not all members of the Arbeter Ring agreed with the National Education Committee's policies. Faulting it for paying too much attention to Yiddish and other subjects deemed to be of little practical value, the following letter speaks out in favor of English and a policy of Americanization.

Esteemed editor:

Permit me to say a couple of words about the educational work of the Arbeter Ring.

I think that the work, as now conducted, is wasted. As far as the Arbeter Ring's courses go there can be no discussion. I cannot imagine there is a single member of the Arbeter Ring interested in studying "geology" in Yiddish, if he already knows a world language. The same applies to "political economy" and "physiology." [...] These words are simply foreign. Show me a member of the Arbeter Ring who can pronounce the word "geology" without stammering? In the old country, none of us ever heard such a word. A person who studied in school learned either in Russian or German, or in some cases in Hebrew. But not in Yiddish.

The trouble is this: We consider the average member to be a "greenhorn," and a greenhorn we want him to remain. We teach him "science" in a language that he wants to and must forget—Yiddish. The children around him speak only in English. Everything is in English; but the Education Committee has taken on the task of maintaining the dying language.

Why should we not apply our energies toward Americanizing our members? Why should we not help the natural Americanization process? The government is prepared to help us. Various organizations and other forces want to and will help us.

The Jews boast that they have a natural ability to adapt to every country and to every situation. Why should we now go against the stream? Let us first teach members the language of the land and, after that, other things. For example: the laws of good health, American history, general history, the American form of government. We shouldn't bother with other educational subjects.

As I read in the October issue of *Der fraynd*, a good step is now being made by the Executive Committee, which has started printing tens of thousands of copies of the Constitution in English. Outstanding! And if our un-Americanized teachers are left without teaching positions in the Arbeter Ring, then I can only say what the Americans say: "Why should I worry?!" B. Sheyfer, Buffalo, NY

Source: B. Sheyfer, letter to the editor, *Der fraynd*, Feb. 1918, pp. 29–30. Translated by Tony Michels.

35

"America's Most Interesting Daily" (1922)

OSWALD GARRISON VILLARD

Oswald Garrison Villard (1872–1949), the owner and editor of *The Nation* magazine, belonged to a prominent family of liberal reformers, dating back to the abolitionist William Lloyd Garrison. Villard penned this tribute to the *Forverts* (also referred to by its English name, *Forward*) during its twenty-fifth anniversary year amid a xenophobic political climate in the United States. The article attests to the high esteem in which the *Forverts* was held in liberal and socialist circles outside the immigrant Jewish community.

Which is the most vital, the most interesting, the most democratic of New York's daily journals? If one should ask this question of one hundred New Yorkers and suggest that the answer involved the name of a foreign language newspaper there would be indignant protests. A good many votes would be cast for the *World*, and the *Globe* would doubtless run well. Yet in my judgment the truth is that the *Forward* outshines them all—and the vast bulk of New Yorkers does not know that any such journal exists, much less that it has 200,000 paid circulation. The reason is of course, that it is a Yiddish newspaper and everyone who is not familiar with that tongue must form his estimates of it by looking at it through the eyes of others. That is my plight; but the facts which have come to me for years past about this extraordinary phenomenon in American journalism make it plain that no student of newspaper conditions of today can fail to give it most careful study if only because of one feature.

While others have talked and speculated on the present crass materialism of the American press and its domination by those who profit most by our present economic organization, and have questioned whether this situation can be offset by an endowed journal or one maintained and owned by great groups of workers, a band of men has worked out in New York a cooperative enterprise of much merit with amazing success. For the *Vorwärts*,[1] to use its Yiddish name, does not represent a vision of an ideal toward which laborious and subventioned progress is being made; it is an established money-making concern with a truly extraordinary hold, not only upon the Jewish group in New York City but in other cities as well. I doubt if the publishers of other American journals know much about it. They must have heard vaguely of the superb office building which it has erected on the East Side in the midst of its constituency and they must, most of them, gasp with envy when they hear that its circulation is now 200,000—far beyond that of the *Tribune*, or *Globe*, or *Herald*, or *Sun*! But what must startle them most is the fact that a large part of the net profits of this newspaper go not to the owners or the editors but are under the by-laws of the *Forward* Association distributed among the exponents of the causes to which the *Forward* is devoted.

That, we fancy, must cause uneasy comment on Park Row. "What can you expect of a bunch of foreign Socialists?" is doubtless the usual response. But that hardly covers the case, especially in view of the fact that the editors belong to a race charged with acquisitiveness. Is it possible that when men of the faith of Shylock have the opportunity to line their pockets with huge profits honestly earned, they deliberately deny themselves anything beyond their extremely modest salaries? It *is* possible. During the last ten years the *Forward* has earned one and a half million dollars, of which it has, after providing for its splendid up-to-date plant, donated $350,000 to union labor and to other causes for which it battles. Its assets today are worth more than one million dollars. Often in enterprises like this the profit is distributed in large salaries and expenses; yet the editor-in-chief of this amazing publication, who is perhaps 75 per cent responsible for its success, recently strenuously resisted his colleagues' efforts to advance his salary to a figure which would be scorned by a city editor of any of our English-language morning dailies. But its lower placed workers are well remunerated. Its scrub women receive $37 a week and where the reporters of the English dailies are underpaid the average wage of the *Forward*'s lesser employees is $62.00 a week (two dollars more that the minimum demanded and received by the members of the Jewish Newswriters' Union). Yet that tells only half the story, for the *Forward* is often a most generous benefactor to struggling talent. There have been cases of foreign writers of promise coming to this country without means, who were not only at once placed on the salary-roll but were told that there was no compulsion upon them to write. Genius, in their cases, did not have to labor at all seasons; its product came when the spirit moved.

Is it any wonder that such a journal commands a tremendous following; that thousands of New Yorkers vote regularly as it tells them; that its counsels are accepted by many as beyond question or criticism? Even when one has to find fault with a given policy—as, for instance, its recent attacks upon a Russian relief organization—the dollar motive is not attributed to its conductors. At least I have never heard it so attributed and when there was an investigation during the war of our foreign press an investigator rightly or wrongly testified that the *Forward* was the only foreign language daily in America which could not be bought. Certain it is that the *Forward* is not only clean in its columns, but that it has had a marked effect in improving the manners and morals of the rest of the Jewish papers.

Yet it is bitterly attacked on the East Side as an enemy to Jewish culture and to racial advancement. Why? Well, chiefly because of the colloquial style in which it is written and what is called its vulgarizing of Yiddish. Its editor-in-chief frankly admits that it writes *down* to its public. Here I must introduce this powerful American journalist. He is Abraham Cahan; long a writer of brilliant humorous and pathetic sketches of the Jewish East Side for the old *Sun*, the *Evening Post*, and the magazines; sometimes a remarkable reporter on the *Commercial Advertiser* (now the *Globe*), a novelist, a man of rare understanding of his race and of all human nature; finally, a true American. He was the only one of the group which founded the *Forward* in 1897 who was able to speak English.[2] They decided on a daily to combat the views of Daniel De Leon,[3] whose dream of the coming of socialism seemed to envision a beneficent Messiah imposing it from above, whereas they put their faith in a democratic mass movement. A couple of years of competition forced De Leon's *Arbeiterzeitung*[4] to the wall, although the *Forward* itself progressed slowly enough until the idea of a purely Socialist propaganda organ was abandoned, and Mr. Cahan came to the front making the *Forward* a newspaper first and only secondarily a political instrument. Fortunately for him and his daily, his accession to the editorship was followed in 1903 by a vast increase in the Russian immigration to the United States in consequence of the Kishinev pogroms, by which immigration the *Forward* greatly profited.

Mr. Cahan has been governed by a double standard in dealing with his public. He struck first for popularity; hence he decided to make the writing in his journal so simple that the least intelligent on the East Side could understand it. He not only adopted the colloquialisms of the Yiddish of New York, showing no hostility whatever to the introduction of English words, but employed editors to substitute in the news manuscripts the shortest words possible for more learned ones. In his editorials he dealt with topics of the widest appeal, whenever possible a direct *argumentum ad hominem*.[5] A famous editorial of his urging every mother who read the *Forward* to see that her child took a clean handkerchief to school with him or her illustrates his policy. Over this editorial there raged a storm; East Side intellectuals denounced it as insulting to their people, who, they insisted not only needed no counsel as to handkerchiefs but were quite capable of understanding and appreciating the best language, the purest form of Yiddish. But Mr. Cahan felt that the learning of the learned orthodox Jews was narrow and unsuited to the everyday need of the hundreds of thousand of *Forward* readers.[6] Wherever the whole truth lies, Mr. Cahan may claim that his paper has demonstrated the success of his policy of stooping to the average man.

Mr. Cahan has known, too, how to render his daily of personal service to its readers. In a recent week the *Forward* printed fourteen columns of the names of Jewish America who are being sought by their kin abroad. There is no more striking feature than its letters from readers regarding their personal problems, which letters it answers with advice and sympathy and often with financial aid. Thus a girl suffering from tuberculosis of the throat received $3,000 in quarters, half-dollars, and dollars from sympathetic readers of her letter to the *Forward* asking where she should go for a cure and how she could live during the treatment. Again, there have appeared from time to time extraordinary symposia bearing upon some of the vital problems of the East Side, such as the tragedy of the growing apart of immigrant parents and their rapidly Americanized children. Needless to say that when there is suffering on the East Side, or strikes which affect such masses of the Jewish population as are included in the needle trades, it is the *Forward* to which multitudes look for guidance and leadership as well as for financial aid.

What is the organization behind Mr. Cahan? There is a *Forward* Association of two hundred members, which any member of a trade union or of a Socialist Party may join, the dues being one dollar a year. There is no stock and there are no bonds, but there is a board of management of nine members of which the editor and the manager are members; the editor and manager are elected yearly by this association. Usually the editor's complete control is never questioned; matters of policy may, however, and do occasionally come before the association. Thus there have been two recent meetings of the association to discuss the paper's attitude toward Russia and its policy toward the Jewish labor movement. In both cases Mr. Cahan, the editor, and Mr. Vladeck,[7] the manager, were sustained—they would have resigned had they not been. Perhaps editors should not be so rigid in their views; but their action certainly proves that there is true parliamentary government of this newspaper which is thus conducted cooperatively and democratically as well as without a profit motive. Surely it is not only New York's most interesting newspaper experiment, but America's, for it now has a large office in Chicago and appears daily in eleven cities for each of which there is provided two pages of local news.

What pabulum does this unusual newspaper supply to its followers? Its eight pages of eight columns each (28 or 32 pages on Sundays) offer a variegated bill of fare. Pictures, of course; occasional cartoons; little of crime (about two columns a day); often sensational matter, some say occasionally of questionable taste; extraordinarily valuable letters and correspondence from abroad, together with a great deal of Jewish and labor news, all with Hearst-like headlines. In one week in July it carried 42 columns of letters and cablegrams from its own correspondents in Russia, Germany, Poland, Palestine, Austria, Hungary, and Rumania—throughout the war its foreign correspondents were such men as Longuet in Paris, Breitscheid,[8] Eduard Bernstein,[9] and Kautsky[10] in Germany. In that same week the *Forward* carried 154 columns of serious reading matter and 137 columns which might be termed "light matter," though this does not adequately describe it, for the extraordinary fact is that while the *Forward* writes down to its readers it is printing today by far the best fiction and *belles letters* of any newspaper in America. This is Mr. Cahan's second striking conception for his journal. He has employed an amazing array of remarkable writers whose names are almost unknown to the English-reading public but who are printing real literature in the East Side newspaper.

When I visited Poland in June of this year I traveled from Warsaw to Vilna in the company of a staff writer of the *Forward* and felt as if I were motoring with royalty. For whenever we stopped in a town, if only for a few minutes to get a cup of coffee, someone recognized the man who sat on the front seat with the chauffeur, and in no time at all a crowd gathered to gaze upon him whom I dubbed the uncrowned king of Poland. Sholem Asch, the novelist and playwright, has a following wherever Yiddish is spoken; in several of the towns we passed through his plays were being given; he is known from one end of Germany to the other. And yet our literary world in America hardly knows that this great writer, and American citizen, exists. But Sholem Asch is only one of a group of poets and writers who, like Jonah Rosenfeld, Solomon Levine, and Z. Libin, contribute their sketches and studies of human life, their psychological stories, or their humor to the *Forward* and add to its luster. Best of all, the whole spirit of the paper, though printed in a foreign language, is imbued by a true spirit of Americanism. By that, of course I don't mean the base metal which goes by the name of one hundred per cent patriotism. It is really actuated by the only American ideals of liberty and justice. Hence it was hounded by the Government during the war.

Mr. Cahan's paper, far from working to keep alive a foreign langue in America, is doing everything in its power to make their readers acquire the English language. Recently the *Forward* printed fifty articles on learning English and bound them into a book for general sale. To multitudes of Americans of high intellectuality and poor vocabulary this great newspaper has brought hope and inspiration and an appreciation of the best standards of American life.

Source: Oswald Garrison Villard, "America's Most Interesting Daily," *The Nation*, Sept. 27, 1922, pp. 301–302.

NOTES

1. This is Villard's transliteration of the name *Forverts* and is actually the transliteration the *Forverts* itself used on its masthead.

2. In fact, all the intellectuals involved in the founding of the *Forverts* could speak English well.

3. Daniel De Leon (1852–1914), a Sephardic Jew born in the Caribbean island of Curaçao, migrated to New York in 1874 and became the leader of the Socialist Labor Party in 1890. By the early twentieth century, the SLP had lost membership to the newly formed Socialist Party of America, but De Leon remained active in labor politics and, in 1905, helped to found the Industrial Workers of the World.

4. Villard seems to be referring to the Yiddish weekly *Di arbeter tsaytung* (see document 9).

5. "Argument against the man."

6. Villard seems to misunderstand criticism of Cahan on this point. Criticism of his style of Yiddish had nothing to do with religion or religious learning. Cahan's detractors believed that he demeaned the Yiddish language and held back the development of Yiddish literature and journalism.

7. Baruch Charney Vladeck (1886–1938), former member of the Bund and well-regarded Yiddish journalist and orator. Vladeck managed the *Forverts* from 1918 until his death in 1938. He also served as a city alderman on the Socialist ticket and was a member of the New York City Housing Authority.

8. Rudolph Breitscheid (1874–1944), a leading member of the German Social Democratic Party.

9. Eduard Bernstein (1850–1932), the socialist theoretician of "evolutionary socialism" or "reformism," which held that socialism would be achieved through capitalism.

10. Karl Kautsky (1854–1938), one of the most authoritative Marxist thinkers who upheld orthodox Marxism against Bernstein's evolutionary socialism.

36

"The Strongest Weapons in the Hands of Jewish Workers" (1924)

UNITED JEWISH WORKERS'
CULTURAL SOCIETY

The 1920s witnessed an upsurge of Yiddish cultural activity by activists associated with *Di linke*, the Communist-led segment of the Jewish labor movement. Resisting the general trend in American society toward "100% Americanism," a notion opposed to the maintenance of ethnic identities, radicals in Chicago founded the United Jewish Workers' Cultural Society to develop Yiddish-language education and culture.

Comrades! The United Jewish Workers' Cultural Society has finished its first year of activity.

Twelve months ago the Cultural Society was no more than the sincere wish of a few to bring light and soul into the hardened life of the local Jewish working masses. Now it is the cultural expression of the healthiest part of the Chicago Jewish working class and its grass-roots intellectuals.

Over the course of the past year the United Jewish Workers' Cultural Society has become an important factor in the cultural life of the local revolutionary Jewish workers—*a solidly rooted cultural institution, which now plays a large role in our struggle for a spiritually rich future and the rights of our secular Yiddish culture in America.*

During the entire time of its existence, the Cultural Society has continuously awakened and beckoned the Jewish worker to great, unified, and purposeful cultural action for his own sake, for the interests of the Yiddish language, and for free thought in our culture. You have successfully broken through the wall of indifference toward our cultural problems among many of those who have naively believed that culture, in general, and Yiddish culture, in particular, is a matter for the petty-bourgeois intellectual who has barely a connection to the social-political tasks of the organized Jewish labor movement. The Cultural Society has received approval for its activities, recognition, love, and sympathy from the most significant political, cultural, and mutual-aid Jewish labor organizations in Chicago; even those who have betrayed our cultural interests here in the new country have had to reckon with it.

At the beginning of our second year of cultural work, the United Jewish Workers' Cultural Society may truthfully boast of its accomplishment, *of preparing the warm sentiments needed for tackling our local cultural problems in their full depth and breadth, and for the creation of a beautiful, festive cultural atmosphere in our prosaic working-class life.* This accomplishment will be inscribed in bright colors in the cultural history of American Jewish workers; but it is only the precondition for responsible, ongoing cultural work among the broad Jewish masses.

With strong confidence in our own forces, with redoubled energy, the United Jewish Workers' Cultural Society now enters into the process of building its most important institutions. Those are children's schools, courses for adults, and its own cultural home in the northwest part of the city.

These cultural institutions are the principal parts of the Cultural Society, the basis of every genuine workers' cultural activity; they are the green oases on the dry paths of our workaday lives—the fresh well from which will flow happy belief in our own cultural possibilities; they are the strongest weapons in the hands of the Jewish workers against darkness and slavery; embedded in them is the shining hope and guarantee that we will not be emptied spiritually here in America and will not be left without suitable inheritors for our happy future.

Comrades! We have taken steps to realize the most beautiful dreams of Jewish working-class life. This is a colossally difficult task, which will consume the limited means of the Cultural Society and can only be successfully realized with your help. More so than ever before, we now demand your active participation—your idealism, your warmth and generosity—in our constructive work.

Carry the idea of our education and educational work to your places of work and leisure! Become teachers yourselves, send your children to our schools, and influence others to follow suit. See that our teachings and educational institutions grow in all parts of Jewish Chicago and are able to keep their doors wide open and friendly to every person who thirsts for learning and knowledge!

Make possible the creation of a center, in the northwestern part of the city, for the various undertakings of the Cultural Society and the cultural revival of the local radical Jewish working masses! Carry a brick yourself to this beautiful building for the purpose of sincere friendship, true spiritual entertainment, a pure Yiddish word, and free workers' thought. Buy shares in the center! Distribute them among your friends, in your other organizations!

Become active members of our cultural organization! Fortify the honored position for which the organization has fought in the local Jewish labor movement! Spread its influence among larger circles of our organized Jewish working class and its intellectuals! Lead it, together with us, to the full realization of all its holy and important goals!

Source: Fareynikte Yidishe Arbeter Kultur-Gezelshaft, "Tsu di yidishe arbeter un unzer folkstimlekher-inteligentsia," *Dos naye vort*, Nov. 1924, p. 1. Translated by Tony Michels.

37

The Aims of Workers' Education (1926)

INTERNATIONAL LADIES' GARMENT
WORKERS' UNION

In 1916, the International Ladies' Garment Workers' Union launched a national education program that placed it at the forefront of workers' education in the United States. By 1922, the union's education department spent more than $17,000 annually on classes and lectures for its members. In New York City, the union offered an array of courses in English, Russian, Yiddish, and eventually other languages. The ILGWU's Unity Centers provided courses for lower-level students, while its Worker's University catered to the most serious learners. Its curriculum included courses in literature, drama, poetry, trade-union policies, psychology, and political and social history. More than seventy-six hundred men and women attended classes at the Worker's University in the year 1922–1923. The following statement of purpose and sampling of classes appeared in a brochure published by the ILGWU in 1927.

The function of Workers' Education is to assist in the all-important task of making our world a better place for all. The truth is clear that it is the mission of the workers themselves to abolish the inequalities and injustices which they suffer, and that they can accomplish this only through organization. But it is equally clear that economic strength is much more effective if directed by intelligent, well informed, clear thinking men and women.

The purpose of the educational activities of the I.L.G.W.U. is to provide the Labor Movement with such men and women. The courses arranged by the Educational Department are designed to give the members of the Union those facts of the social sciences which may serve as a basis for sound conclusions, may help create true social and spiritual values, and may help train them for active and successful participation in the Labor Movement, as leaders and workers.

With this in view, our International organized an Educational Department in 1917 and the 1925 Convention authorized an annual appropriation of $17,500 for the following two years.

The members of our union who attend the lectures and courses, learn a great deal about matters connected with their industry, their organization and the Labor Movement. They learn some of the psychologic laws which govern the relations between human beings. They are inspired by the literature which deals with the life, hopes and sorrows of other men and women. But even more important, they learn how workers struggled for many years to get some joy and happiness out of their miserable existence. They learn how unity and solidarity helped their fellow workers overcome persecution and oppression and to succeed finally in winning the improved conditions which prevail today and in raising society to a higher level.

A Sampling of Courses at the ILGWU's Workers' University

Course No. 1. The Place of Workers in History—A. J. Muste.[1]

One of the leaders of the British workers' education remarked some time ago, "History should be the back-bone of the course in all workers' colleges." This would suggest that some workers at least have found a means to read the record of the past, and make it useful in their life and struggles today. Such will be the aim of this course: to survey the past and present life of human beings, especially workers, in our own land and on the other side of the earth, and to see how from it we of today may gain a richer life and more intelligent methods for waging our struggle to attain the goal of all history— the emancipation of the workers.

Course No. 6. Economic Problems of the Working Woman—Theresa Wolfson.[2]

In the organized labor movement the question of women in industry, as a special problem, has often been raised. Two points of view are often expressed. One claims that the interests of men and women workers are identical. The other accepts the fact that women workers are a more or less temporary factor, and therefore, should not be considered. Both these attitudes have seriously handicapped the work of organizing women workers.

A discussion of these problems in the light of experience, as they affect the position of women in industry and in trade unions, will do much toward clarifying a number of issues much befogged by old social and economic prejudices.

Course No. 15. Social Psychology—Alexander Fichandler[3]

Important events occur daily. Some of them have an enormous influence on human history and our personal lives. Most workers, however, accept these more or less uncritically. They read about them in the papers, sometimes discuss them for a little while, forget them and go on living as before.

In this course an attempt will be made to explain such events. Psychology discusses human conduct. It analyzes and explains the fundamental causes which force human beings to act as they do. It attempts to answer such questions as, Why do people fight, why do they cooperate, why do they seek power, why do they follow leaders, why do they make sacrifices for ideas, why do they fear, etc.

Course No. 17. Social Tendencies in Modern Literature—By B. J. R. Stolper[4]

Yiddish both as a language and a literature, has made extraordinary strides in the last thirty years. It has risen to the dignity of a skillful, powerful, subtle instrument smoothly moulded by fine literary craftsmen. The coldest logic, the warmest sympathy, the most delicate imagery and music, the most fine-spun metaphysics of the race find Yiddish as a language peculiarly adequate to express every turn of mood or thought.

This course will take up Yiddish dramatists, poets, novelists, critics: names like those of Peretz, Sholom Asch, Mendele Mochor Sphorim, Sholom Aleichem, Jacob Gordin, Spektor, Ignatoff, Shomer, Raboi, Mani Leib, H. Leivick, Reisen, Yehoash, Opatoshu, Morris Rosenfeld, Bialik, Niger, Vipper, Frug, Eliashev, Hirschbein, Pinski, etc.

Of Modern Italian writers, very few, apparently, have managed to pass into international currency over the border of their own country. Of those, D'Annunzio, Leopardi, Carducci, Benedetto Croce, Fogazzaro, Anna Neri will be examined for what they are worth in expressing the literary tendencies of their racial genius.

Among the Spanish craftsmen, the work of Echegaray, Benavente, Alarcon, Galdos, De Ayala, and Martiniez will be discussed.

Source: ILGWU Educational Department, box 10, folder 1, Kheel Center, Cornell University.

NOTES

1. A. J. Muste (1885–1967), prominent socialist, labor educator, pacifist, and ordained minister in the Reformed Church of America.

2. Theresa Wolfson (1897–1972), economics professor at Brooklyn College. Her primary area of study and activism was around women's labor organizing and discrimination against women in the workplace.

3. Alexander Fichandler (1879–?), director of the education department of the International Ladies' Garment Workers' Union. He wrote numerous pieces on economics and the psychology of the labor movement.

4. B. J. R. (Benjamin John Reeman) Stolper (1886–1974), scholar and advocate of progressive education.

Sexual Relations from a Communist Standpoint (1928)

N. GLASS

Kalman Marmor (1876–1956), a prolific cultural historian and educator in the Communist movement, received the following query regarding marital infidelity. Although infidelity was not unknown to eastern European Jews, the letter indicates a shift in morality regarding sex and the new role played by radical intellectuals as moral arbiters.

Dear Comrade K. Marmor!

We, a group of comrades, turn to you with a request to clarify for us the following question: what is Communist morality regarding married life? Is a couple, legally married or not, obligated [to be faithful] to one another? [. . .] Is it moral, from a Communist standpoint, to have sexual relations with one person when one is bound to another? Should one's conscience play some role in such a case? Does one side, which wants to be freed from the other, but cannot because of various reasons, have a right to engage in sexual relations with a stranger? Can a man or woman have relations with his or her friend's wife or husband without a bad conscience? Would it be foolish or smart for one to disclose to the other the relations one is having with another? We would like you to answer all of these questions—and we would like it if you answered in a private letter.

With comradely greetings,

N. Glass

Youngstown, Ohio

Source: N. Gles [Glass] to Kalman Marmor, Feb. 15, 1928, Kalman Marmor Papers, RG 205, folder 463, YIVO Institute for Jewish Research. Translated by Tony Michels.

"Sow the Field of Yiddish Cultural Tradition" (1939)

UNITED COUNCIL OF YIDDISH WOMEN'S
READING CIRCLES OF DETROIT

Yiddish literary clubs for women began appearing in cities around the United States and Canada during the 1910s. In
addition to reading works of literature, members of these clubs
engaged in various efforts on behalf of Yiddish writers and publications. The expansion of reading circles indicates the important role played by women in the development of Yiddish literary culture and secular education. The following excerpt from a
longer report provides an unusually detailed portrait of wom-
en's Yiddish cultural activism. Its author takes pride in the organization's success in bringing together groups from across polit-
ical-ideological boundaries, a rare instance of nonpartisanship.

At this difficult time, our hearts, wills, and might have been
strengthened to withstand adversity and, with persistence, to build and
establish a healthy, productive Jewish life. This persistence has also intensified our desire to study, to learn the Yiddish language and its literature, and
to bring the "Yiddish word" into homes where it is now unfamiliar.

It is truly wonderful that just at this distressing moment, the Jewish
woman and Jewish mother take an interest in the Yiddish word, eagerly
taking to Yiddish literature and familiarizing themselves with Yiddish cultural production. What's especially gratifying is how the Jewish woman and
mother are organizing themselves culturally and how they have successfully
avoided the interparty wrangling that usually dominates the "Jewish Street."

There are twenty-five reading circles and study groups in Detroit, and
they are all connected to each other in a communal organization: The United
Council of Yiddish Women's Reading Circles of Detroit. Through the Council the reading circles have become a cultural force, an organization that
holds an honorable place in Detroit Jewish life. The Council is a place where

people turn for different cultural activities. Through the Council it has been possible to bring speakers and writers from afar. Since the Council tolerates all perspectives, from the political right and left, and advances no political differences of opinion, and since with it all partisan quarrels are avoided, the Council has been able to organize lectures with different speakers who visit our city. The hundreds of reading-circle members are encouraged by the Council to attend all lectures.

The Council facilitates different cultural activities occurring in the city. It helps spread the Yiddish book and creativity to Jewish homes, as well as an atmosphere of love for and nearness to the Yiddish word and Yiddish education.

The council was established in May 1934, initially with only four reading circles, and we note here the four with which the council was organized: a reading circle from the Sholem Aleichem Folk-Institute, a reading circle from the Pioneer Women, a reading circle from the Workmen's Circle, and the group from the Free Society. The other reading circles that then existed refrained from the Council, some out of mistrust, others out of distaste. The constitution upon which they worked at the first meeting was designed to avoid all that was partisan; this has always been protected and not diminished at all.

The Council was organized late in the year, but it immediately set to work and arranged a lecture with Mr. Kazhdan on the theme of "Sholem Aleichem and the Child." The lecture was well attended by the majority of reading-club members. The proceeds were given to TSYSHO[1] of which Mr. Kazhdan was a representative.

Composition of the Council

Now, at the fifth anniversary of the United Council, we can report that all reading clubs that currently exist in Detroit are part of the Council, and we have quite a few gains and accomplishments.

There are now twenty-five reading clubs in the United Council: three from the Workmen's Circle [social democratic] schools, three from the Sholem Aleichem Folk-Institute [Yiddish cultural nationalist], six from the Pioneer Women [socialist-Zionist], six from the International Workers Order [Communist], one group from the Free Society [anarchist], three unaffiliated groups, and three reading groups from Windsor.

The Pioneer reading groups, the reading groups from the International Workers Order, and the reading groups from Windsor are connected in a separate council. But at the United Council they exist as unique reading groups; unity and harmony dominate all aspects of our work.

Lectures, Symposia, Classes

Beginning in the 1935 season, the Council organized a symposium on Sholem Asch's *Tehilim-Yid* [lit. "Psalm-Jew"]. The symposium, in which Mr. Haar and Radin participated, was conducted in a very festive manner at decorated tables.

During the fifth year, the Council used every opportunity when a guest speaker was in town to organize a lecture for our membership. Previously we had lectures from the following writers and speakers: H. Leyvik, Sh. Niger, Perets Hirshbein, Abba Gordin, William Nathanson, Kadya Molodovsky, Dovid Pinsky, B. Y. Bialostotsky, Leah K. Hoffman, Dvora Marant, Sandler, Sultan, Shteynberg, Dr. Mayzl, Melekh Ravitch, Kazhdan, Gingold, Rudolph Roker, Sh. Yanovksy, Alterman. We already had several lectures by Leyvik, Niger, Hirshbein, Molodovsky, Pinski, Bialostotsky, almost every time they visited our city.

Aside from the aforementioned speakers, the Council organized lectures with the following local cultural activists: Drobler, Bercovitch, Haar, Radin, Korman, Finklshteyn, Morris, and Radinki. Others besides those mentioned also participated in symposia on different literary themes.

Aside from these lectures and symposia, the Council also organized courses for our members. The courses were on history (Mr. Haar) and on the history of Yiddish literature (Mr. Bercovitch).

General Gatherings

The Council also organized general gatherings of all reading-club members. These gatherings usually took place at decorated tables and included singing. At these gatherings a few members would appear on stage: one with a reading, another with a recitation, one with a lecture, another with an original work, poem, or story. At the gatherings, members would also report on their reading club's activities, and this is how we would all become acquainted with the work of each specific reading club and also how we became closer friends with each other. These gatherings stimulated the work of and strengthened unity among the different strands.

The Council also celebrated traditional and national holidays and International Women's Day.

The Yiddish Book

The United Council accomplished much in the area of promoting the Yiddish book. It's especially worthwhile to note that it popularized the book *Mendele* from Sh. Niger, the collections of Leyvik and Opatoshu, "The Song of My Bones" from Kadya Molodovsky, and a book of poems from B. Y. Bialostotsky. The Council influenced the city library to acquire new Yiddish books and encouraged our women to bring Yiddish books into the library. The Council was also active in the effort toward a Yiddish library in Detroit, which, unfortunately, has not yet materialized.

Other Cultural Activities

The Council participated in fund-raising that took place in the city on behalf of different cultural institutions like YIVO, TSYSHO, Tanakh Publications, etc. The Council also supports the Teacher Seminary, Workers' University, *Kinder-Zhurnal*, etc. We also joined and participated actively in the cultural division of the Jewish Council.

Midwestern Body

The success of the Detroit reading circles' harmonious and communal work led us to the idea that perhaps we could join with and forge a kind of bond with the reading circles in other cities, especially with the nearer cities in the Midwest like Chicago, Cleveland, etc. We made several visits to the conventions of the Yiddish Culture Society in Cleveland and Detroit. At these conventions were also representatives from the reading circles, and we had a communal meeting about this topic. Unfortunately, for a variety of reasons, we have not yet succeeded in our efforts.

We have not, however, given up on the idea, and we hope that in time we will succeed in creating a central body of all reading circles in the Midwest.

In closing my report, it is with joy that I am able to highlight all these attainments: from a composition of four reading circles, the United Council is now made up of twenty-five reading circles from Detroit and nearby Windsor—and it has been a significant factor in Yiddish cultural life. To spite our enemies, we Jewish women and mothers will continue to sow the field of the Yiddish cultural tradition and, with the power of the Yiddish word, take a stand against and overcome all evil and adversity.

Source: Adele Mondry, *Yidishe froyen leyenkrayzn in Detroyt* (Detroit: Fareynikte Konsil, 1939), pp. 6–8. Translated by Alisa Braun.

NOTES

1. Yiddish acronym for Di Tsentrale Yidishe Shul-Organizatsye (Central Yiddish School Organization), founded in Warsaw in 1921 by members of the Bund and left-wing social-ist Zionists. TSYSHO established a network of secular Yiddish schools for children in Poland.

40

"The Responsibility of English-Speaking Jewish Intellectuals" (1946)

NATHAN AUSUBEL

Nathan Ausubel (1898–1986), contributing editor to the Communist literary journal *New Masses*, authored numerous books on Jewish culture, most famously *A Treasury of Jewish Folklore* (1948). His essay here, originally published in the Communist-affiliated monthly *Jewish Life*, reflects a new interest in Jewish culture among left-wing, English-speaking Jews following the Holocaust. Ausubel broke with the Communist Party in the early 1950s.

Among many educated Jews today, Jewish culture is treated like an unwanted "poor relation." When "important" guests, such as the cultures of other nations, arrive and are ceremoniously entertained in the parlor "the poor thing" is obliged to slink away and hide itself in the kitchen.

This attitude is more widespread than one would be led to think. It is perfectly understandable in the case of the bourgeois assimilationists. They have a cowardly compulsion to deny, ignore, or gloss over their Jewish origin because the stock of their identity has very low market value on the fascist exchange. Vulgar opportunists, they shamelessly betray themselves and their people even when there is no pressing necessity to do so. But it is baffling why so many Jewish liberals and "Marxists" take such a philistine attitude toward their people's culture. Perhaps this may be explained by the fact that vain individuals are frequently forced to justify their ignorance by glibly despising what they don't know. Or perhaps it is an expression of a deep-seated neurosis, of a morbid fear of being identified with something that might further accentuate their social inferiority in the anti-Jewish capitalist world. No amount of buttressing with tortured arguments, which they well-pepper with misapplied, misquoted and misunderstood citations from Marx, Lenin, and Stalin, can successfully explain it away. . . .

Who hasn't heard and marveled over these arguments from the bourgeois assimilationists on the "left"? Except that in their raisonne they employ glittering but spurious Marxist terminology one could just as well mistake them for their assimilationist brothers on the right. . . . There are the same old slanders and snobberies.

"What! Yiddish a language! I thought it was a jargon. . . . You mean to tell me it has a fine literature! . . . You advise me to interest myself in Jewish culture; do you want me to go back to the ghetto? . . . Isn't Jewish culture, synagogue culture? I am a materialist—do you want me to turn to religion? . . . If I absorb myself with Jewish culture won't I be a Zionist then? What an idiotic contradiction! I'm a Marxist and an internationalist, not a synagogue Zionist and a nationalist!"

This is not the place to examine these slanders and misconceptions in order to refute them. The individuals who mouth them are neither good Marxists nor truly cultured people. A true Marxist cannot be a *cultural anti-Semite* or any other variety of anti-Semite. The mark of a cultured person is a hunger for universal knowledge, a humanist approach to the intellectual creations of mankind. Nothing that concerns the free spirit of man is alien to him, for it is this very spirit which aspires to a finer and more just life that is the hope of the world. Therefore, whether he knows it or not, the Jewish intellectual assimilationist with Marxist pretensions has drunk deep and dangerously from the poisoned well of the anti-Semites. And if there is anything more frightening and unspeakable than a non-Jewish anti-Semite it is a Jewish anti-Semite. There is no loathing so horrible as self-loathing, no betrayal so final as self-betrayal!

In all fairness to the educated progressive Jews on the left, it must be said that the great majority of them are not to be included in the above dismal category which I have made to serve as a whipping post merely to point more drastically [to] the danger and the hideousness of cultural anti-Semitism. The average intellectual person of Jewish origin who has identified himself with the worker's cause is honest and courageous in his thinking. The worst that may be said of him is that he has been either ignorant of or indifferent to this people's creative riches. His is a fault of omission rather than of commission, although in its effect one sometimes can be just as harmful as the other. Much of his negative attitude towards the problem is due mainly to an ideological confusion and sloppy thinking: he erroneously associates Jewish culture with nationalism and religion. At the same time he unwarrantedly glorifies assimilation as the immediate goal of socialism, a fundamental error of which the communist Jews in the Soviet Union are not guilty.

It is the urgent duty of all thoughtful Jewish men and women to examine their attitudes toward their Jewishness and Jewish culture. If they are uninformed, they must learn. Ignorance of one's people's intellectual creativeness is inexcusable at all times, particularly in these cataclysmic days. How is it possible for one to have an intelligent understanding of *oneself* without knowing the history and culture of one's people? One who is unacquainted with Jewish history cannot properly understand its nightmarish experiences in the slaughter-house of Hitler Europe. Nor can one have the slightest inkling of the moral resources on which the Jewish people has drawn in the time of its greatest agony without knowing of the wonderful tradition of individual and social ethics in Jewish life.

We usually speak of culture as if it were an ornament, a decoration of intellectual distinction to be worn in one's lapel like a rosette of the Legion of Honor for all the world to see and admire. It is supposed to set us apart and above the "rude" hoi poloi and flatter our snobbishness and self-esteem like the iridescent feathers that adorn a peacock. But culture as the expression of the urgent social drive of a people seeking a progressive course in civilizations is a concept despised in the capitalist world. Even many of us, who take pride in our Marxist-Leninist understanding, are sometimes pretty obdurate in holding on to the moldy thesis that culture is solely the private concern and aspiration of the individual. Somehow the basic truth eludes us that when culture is devoid of collective striving and social content it becomes *culture in a vacuum*. It is then sterile and intellectually without meaning or purpose. And this equally holds true of Jewish culture.

Intellectual Jews in our time have been seared by the universal Jewish tragedy which they have seen unfold so-to-speak before their very eyes. Even if it were desirable it is no longer possible for a Jew to play the chameleon. No amount of assimilation can abstract him from his Jewishness. Hitler fascism slaughtered one-third of the Jewish people and broke the bodies and spirits of other millions. Reaction in America, a fascist wolf disguised in democratic sheep's clothing, is now making hideous the air of our country with its Jew-baiting.

The liberal and communist Jew is, in an important sense, a leader in his community and helps form public opinion which he is so desirous of channelizing into constructive, progressive action. He would like to take common action with all Jews and all decent Americans in fighting anti-Semitism. He has learned much from the terrible mistakes made by the German Jews so many of whom watched the growth of the Nazi incubus with smug equanimity, who deluded themselves with the thought that anti-Semitism was a separate and static problem without any connection with the life and death struggle of society against the most murderous, reactionary movement in all history.

But again the inescapable looms up that, before one can act, one must have clear and correct ideas. Such understanding one cannot draw from thin air. In order to become fully effective in fighting our native fascism of which anti-Semitism is the deadly poison-gas, in order to know how to cope with the many ramifications of the Jewish problem which demand urgent attention, the progressive Jewish intellectual in America must devote himself to an earnest study of the Jewish masses, their history, culture and folk-life. This study will not only enrich him as an individual, make him understand himself as a Jew better, but will give him a clearer historic perspective with which to analyze the most pressing problems of our time. And since all ideas lead to action, the correct ideas based on knowledge will lead him to take correct and effective action.

In 1937 delegates from twenty-two countries gathered in Paris at the First World Jewish (Yiddish) Culture Congress (YCUF) in history. They concluded that Jewish culture created in the Yiddish language is a true people's culture since a majority of the Jews today employ Yiddish as their mother-tongue. The Congress issued a manifesto highlighting this historic truth.

"Jewish (Yiddish) culture cannot be separated from the Jewish people, from its broad working-masses. The more firmly its forces are united the more luxuriant will bloom the Jewish people's culture, and the stronger its capacity to survive."

How much broader the view, deeper the understanding, and more upright the approach were those of the non-Jewish Romain Rolland towards the objective of this people's conference on Jewish culture in Yiddish than of many Jewish "progressive" intellectuals in America. These spoke Yiddish in their childhood but, nevertheless, turned from it later with the scorn of ignorant Pharisees. In his greetings to the delegates Rolland wrote:

"Jewish intellectuals, our comrades—an old intellectual of France presses your hand! . . . Let us draw closer to the bond between the people of Rabelais, Montaigne and Voltaire, and the people of Karl Marx and Spinoza. . . . All those who are fighting for justice and for the progress of mankind know that the finest sons of the Jewish people have always been found in the vanguard of this struggle. Justice and righteousness, the quintessence of the living conscience of the Jewish people, have always appeared like the two sun-rays that flashed from the forehead of Moses."

Since the occasion of the first Congress of Jewish Culture in Paris the Jewish people of Europe have lived through the most cataclysmic experience in all their history. They are now binding up their wounds, hushing their grief, and courageously turning their hands to the rebuilding of their broken lives. We Jews in America can no longer live in blind ostrich isolation from other Jews. Now more than ever the same destiny that lies in store for them is awaiting us. Whether we will it or not our unity with them is inescapable, complete and final. Our common problems and needs drive us inexorably to act together for our preservation. And one of the most effective instruments of our self-defense as well as of social progress is our Jewish culture, whether culture in Yiddish, in English, in Hebrew (non-nationalist), or in any other language.

Once more the Jews of the world are preparing for an international Congress on Jewish Culture. As in 1937 there will take place a prior Congress of Jewish Culture in the United States projected by the American Division of the YCUF.

The responsibility of English-speaking Jewish intellectuals in the working class movement toward the American Congress on Jewish Culture cannot be shirked by them any longer. Although, at the present time, the majority of Jews in the world employ Yiddish as their chief cultural medium, it is also undeniable that in the United States there has been slowly emerging a progressive Jewish culture in English. As yet this culture is in its infancy, but it must be encouraged and helped to develop in a socially constructive and energetic way. The Jewish youth of America largely speaks English and can only be influenced at present by a Jewish culture in English. But this does not mean that there must be created an artificial barrier between Jewish culture in Yiddish and *Jewish culture in English*. They must be considered in the same relation to each other as the right hand is to the left hand; both belong to the same living organism of American Jewry, and they must be coordinated in *unified* action by the same needs and understanding.

Source: Nathan Ausubel, "Jewish Culture," *Jewish Life*, Dec. 1946, pp. 10–12.

Part IV

The Russian Revolution

The overthrow of the czar on March 15, 1917 (February, according to the Julian calendar) caused immense joy among American Jews, many of whom had direct familial and political ties to Russia. Yet the Bolshevik seizure of power six months later bitterly divided Jewish socialists, as it did socialists worldwide. After an initial period of enthusiasm, many Jewish socialists turned against the Bolshevik government, outraged by its repression of political opponents. Social democrats and anarchists were the first to see Soviet Russia as a new form of dictatorship, an abomination of the socialist ideal. Yet many Jews, and not only Communists, remained enchanted by or, at least, sympathetic to the Soviet revolution. From the perspective of its sympathizers, Soviet Russia had elevated the working class to a position of power, stamped out anti-Semitism, and fostered a Yiddish cultural renaissance. Was the Soviet Union a workers' paradise or a totalitarian hell? No question proved more contentious, capable of dividing families, friends, and the Left as a whole.

41

In Honor of Red Sunday (1906)

NEW YORK TIMES

The 1905 Russian Revolution captured the attention of immigrant Jews and Americans broadly, setting off a flurry of political debate and fund-raising activity on behalf of the major revolutionary parties. Jewish socialists continued to commemorate the events of 1905 even after the revolution's collapse.

The first anniversary of "Red Sunday," of Jan. 22, 1905, when thousands of Russian workingmen were shot down in St. Petersburg while endeavoring to submit an appeal to the Czar, was celebrated in New York yesterday.

Between 5,000 and 6,000 Polish, Roumanian, German, and Russian Jews gathered at Rutgers Square, in East Broadway, and to the step of the "Marsellaise" marched through the lower east side up to Union Square, where they assembled to hear half a dozen speeches denunciatory of the Czar and to adopt resolutions calling for Russian freedom.

There had been expectations that at least 50,000 men and women would participate in the parade, but the threatening weather kept the number down. There was no lacking in enthusiasm, however, and as the parade filed through its three or four miles of march its decorations of red were met with cheers. [. . .]

There were 1,000 women in line carrying all sorts of emblems and transparencies, and a dozen bands enlivened the march. The men and women carried red banners or ribbons and wore bouquets of carnations. [. . .]

Some of the transparencies read:

"Proletarians of all countries unite."

"Long live the Jewish Bund's struggle for rights."

"Workingmen unite in all countries."

"Hurrah for Socialism."

"Down with anti-Semitism."

"Heroes of St. Petersburg, Odessa, Lodz, and Warsaw, we honor you on this side of the Atlantic."

The first division of the parade was under the command of Grand Marshals Shapiro and Golden and comprised members of the various labor unions of the east side. It included, among others, the members of the United Hebrew Trades. The second division was under the command of Assistant Marshal Lewensohn and included the Bundist Society and the Socialist Revolutionaries of Russia. The third division embraced the Workmen's Circle and twenty-five branches of organized labor, the membership of which included many women. The female contingent consisted mainly of members of the Ladies' Cloth, Hat, and Cap Makers, the Dressmakers' Union, and the Lady Tailors' Union.

As the parade lined up before the cottage in Union Square half a dozen speakers gathered to address it. The crowd was so large that two overflow meetings were held. Jack London and "Mother" Jones had been scheduled for addresses, but did not appear. An American flag was unfurled, and then black and red banners were waved. The gathering cheered.

Ex-Mayor Chase[1] was the first speaker. He said that the gathering had appeared as citizens and workingmen to register a protest against the Czar, against plutocracy, and against absolutism. "We are here," he declared, "to demand Socialism in the United States and to give notice that we will not stand for any bloody Sundays in the United States."

Abraham Cahan, editor of The Forward, said: "The next ruler of Russia will be named 'Workingman,' and not 'Romanoff.'"

Meyer London,[2] Alexander Jonas,[3] Dr. Pollack, Dr. Schillowsky,[4] and B. Feigenbaum[5] also addressed the meeting. The resolutions adopted expressed sympathy with the people of all nationalities of Russia who were struggling for liberty. The massacre of the Jews and autocratic government were denounced, and the repeal of our extradition treaty with Russia was demanded.

Several persons were slightly injured during last night's parade. While the line was turning from Houston Street into Avenue A a horse attached to a peddler's wagon, driven by David Brownstein of 310 East 102d Street, became excited at the fireworks, and plunged into the crowd on the corner, slightly injuring Annie Bloom, a sixteen-year-old girl; Blanche Gardner, 17 years old; Morris Christ, 27 years old, and Herman Kalamar, 19 years old. [. . .]

Source: "Red Sunday Parade Was a Mild Affair," *New York Times*, Jan. 23, 1906, p. 6.

NOTES

1. John C. Chase, former Socialist Party mayor of Haverhill, Massachusetts.

2. Meyer London (1871–1926), prominent labor lawyer and activist, elected to Congress on the Socialist Party ticket in 1914, 1916, and 1920.

3. Alexander Jonas (1834–1912), German-born journalist and socialist leader.

4. The author means Dr. Chaim Zhitlovsky, then in New York City as an emissary of the Party of Socialist Revolutionaries.

5. Benjamin Feigenbaum (1860–1932), popular Yiddish journalist and socialist propagandist in New York City.

42

Leon Trotsky on Second Avenue (memoir; 1944)

LOUIS WALDMAN

Leon Trotsky (1879–1940) spent ten weeks in New York City between January and March 1917. A powerful writer and orator, he loomed large in New York's socialist circles. After Czar Nicholas II abdicated his thrown, Trotsky left the United States for Russia and eventually achieved international fame as the commander of the Red Army. The labor lawyer Louis Waldman (see document 16) published this recollection four years after Trotsky's murder by a Soviet agent in Mexico City.

Back in 1917 the Café Monopole, at the corner of Second Avenue and Ninth Street in downtown New York, was the hub of the social life of the East Side intelligentsia. Flowing ties, odd costumes, variegated beards and silver-topped walking sticks, set the habitués of this hangout apart from their more conservatively attired fellows. Teachers, journalists, actors, ex-actors, would-be actors, painters, and sculptors constituted for the most part its colorful clientele. Unpublished writers rubbed shoulders with recognized literary lions. They gossiped and chattered; but most of all they argued. They sat at their tables consuming enormous quantities of Russian tea and lemon and stared and were, to their undisguised satisfaction, stared at in turn.

Men and women of every conceivable political complexion gathered here: single taxers, Marxists, Veblenites, Revisionists, Kropotkinites, Fabians, syndicalists and pacifists. There they sat throughout the night destroying and reconstructing entire social systems.

In the rear of the café card games and betting were in constant progress. Waiters carried on a check-discounting and money-lending business which, rumor had it, ran into fabulous figures. A waiter by the name of Aladar, dirty and flatfooted, shuffled his shrewd and knowing way from table to table, fawning on well-to-do customers and storing up a vast accumulation of nickels and dimes which he expected as his right for obsequiously placing a glass of water on the table. It was said that Aladar owned an entire block of tenements of the East Side as a result of his "banking" activities at the Monopole. European visitors declared with a touch of nostalgia that it was only at the Monopole that they found the kind of life they had known in the cafés of Paris, Vienna, and Budapest.

Into this veritable League of Nations one evening in January 1917 came one whom we later knew to be Leon Trotsky. And although he was the man who with Nikolay Lenin, many months later was to share the rule over a hundred and sixty million people who inhabited one-sixth of the earth's surface, at that time his entrance failed to stir a ripple of interest.

I remember Trotsky in those days as a man with an unusually broad and high forehead topped by a tempestuous shock of black hair. Behind the thick lenses of his pince-nez flashed eyes of magnetic and restless power. His petulant and sensual mouth was partly concealed by a large drooping mustache and his dark goatee beard created a triangle of face which was otherwise round. There was nothing of the peasant or the worker about the man. He was an intellectual with a nervous system pitched to the highest degree of tension.

I confess that, had we sensed the role he was ultimately to play in destroying one tyranny and laying the foundations of another equally destructive of the peace and happiness of the Russian people, we might have listened more attentively to the doctrines which he preached in those days. But, outstanding though Trotsky may have been in appearance, there were other personalities at the Monopole who seemed to outshine him. And looking back, I remember him as simply another café seer and pundit. However, as time went on, he collected a small coterie of disciples, all of them Russian, a handful of revolutionary asteroids revolving around a star of the first magnitude. Occasionally I would stand a few minutes listening to the Russian political émigré. His favorite theme at that time was denunciation of "the abhorrent, the almost depraved social-patriots," as he invariable referred to the Social Democrats. Of all the species of political fauna, none was lower, none more contemptible, none more dangerous to the interests of Trotsky's working class than the Socialist who defended his country in time of war. Ruthless industrialists, strike-breaking employers, conniving munitions manufacturers, and reactionary politicians were not nearly as hateful in Trotsky's eyes as the merest soft-spoken moderate Socialist. He loathed men like Hillquit[1] and Vanderwelde,[2] head of the Second International, with more intense hatred than he felt toward J.P. Morgan or the Czar. Shaking his finger at me one evening, he declaimed: "Yes, the victorious proletariat will know how to deal with you social-patriots." [. . .]

The Labor Temple, on Second Avenue and Fourteenth Street, was a popular radical meeting place for the district in those days and one day when Trotsky was scheduled to speak there, having heard that he was a brilliant orator, I dropped in to watch him perform. I found his platform technique remarkably effective. He had an extraordinary sense of the dramatic which, together with an excellent stage presence and rich choice of language and a masterful use of invective, combined to give him complete mastery over an audience. However, for all its dynamic brilliance, I found his speech barren of all original thought and substance. He stood on the platform with an annotated copy of the *Communist Manifesto* and after reading a paragraph launched into an inspired explanation of its meaning, as he saw it. Now and then he departed from the main thread of his argument to excoriate with wit and irony, those whose opinions differed by so much as a hair's breadth from his own. This speech was heavily laden with mytho-mechanical, Communist jargon which later came to dominate the speech of American radicals for nearly two decades. He spoke of the masses, class struggle and historical necessity. The expression "the masses" was then a term new to most of us in the Socialist movement. We preferred to say "labor" or "workers." But Trotsky's term was sufficiently vague and flexible to include all workers and non-workers, intellectuals, middle-class dilettantes and Park Avenue vicarious revolutionists who, when animated by propaganda and inflamed by hate, would, on the basis of "historical necessity," overthrow the existing form of society and install Trotsky and his fellow Communists in power. [. . .]

"The class struggle is class war," shouted Trotsky by way of interpreting the words he had just quoted. "There can be no compromise between the capitalist class and the working class!"

Cleverly twisting the sense of Marx's and Engel's phrase "the class struggle," the phrase became "class war" and later on its character was broadened to mean *civil war*. In this way Trotsky read into the text precisely what he wanted to find there. This technique of reading into Marx whatever suits one's own purpose was not unique with Trotsky. In this he was typical of all Communist and some Socialist leaders even to the present day.

Trotsky was active in the Russian Socialist Federation. The power and tendencies of this and other foreign language federations affiliated with the Socialist Party soon became manifest when America was faced with the issue of war.

Because the American Socialists were not subjected to the same historical pressure as their European contemporaries, the party was a pacifist island in a belligerent ocean. To European Socialists, the outbreak of the war came as a sudden, staggering blow. The question that faced them was whether or not they would stand with their respective countries in this international crisis. The traditional anti-war position of Socialists in the United States was subjected to no such point-blank demand. Nearly half of the country's Socialist voters had supported President Wilson rather than their own candidates in the belief that the country would be kept out of the war. While American Socialists would have followed the example of their European colleagues in resisting invasion, actual or threatened, no such alternative was presented to them, because the war in 1917 involved no threat of invasion to the United Sates. Since American participation in the war involved the sending of an expeditionary force to Europe, the traditional Socialist pacifism asserted itself, augmented by the attitude of the foreign language federations. These federations took little part in the domestic political life of the party. But they were to play a major role in the party crisis which was precipitated by the war and continued as a result of the Bolshevik Revolution in Russia.

This conflict came to a head at a Manhattan party membership meeting at Lenox Casino on March 4, 1917. The Russians, Ukrainians, Lithuanians, Germans, Poles, and other foreign language groups were there in full force. Of these groups, none except the Germans had ever before played a substantial role in the party.

A committee had been appointed to formulate instructions for the delegates to the forthcoming St. Louis convention. Two specific tendencies were evident in its report. One called for out-and-out resistance to the government's war policy, even if this involved civil war; while the other, sponsored by the majority, called for a forthright statement against war, but placed our position strictly on American lines, to be expressed exclusively in the tradition of American parliamentarism. Leaders of the group which favored the former course were led by Trotsky, Santeri Nuorteva,[3] a Finn, and Louis C. Fraina.[4] The Trotsky-Nuorteva-Fraina faction called upon members of the party "to resist all efforts at recruiting by means of mass meetings, street demonstrations and educational propaganda, and by other means, in accordance with Socialist principles and tactics." Needless to say, the question of Socialist principles and tactics would, when the proper time arrived, be interpreted by Trotsky and his associates. The minority resolution also called for strikes against the mobilization of industry during war time.

This was the stormiest meeting I ever witnessed in a long career of stormy meetings. Two chairmen had to surrender their posts because they found it impossible to maintain order. Fist fights kept breaking out in the hall as partisans of opposing factions split into little sub-meetings, without benefit of parliamentary procedure to abate their passions. Trotsky was the leader of the faction which opposed the government's policy even if it led to civil war, while Hillquit directed the tactics of the moderates.

When I was finally granted the floor I stated my position as follows: "Martyrdom should not be imposed on anyone by the fiat of this meeting or the Socialist Party. Should the country declare war, should the draft become law, neither this meeting nor the Socialist Party could stop the war nor stop the draft by resolutions or otherwise. Is it democratic for this meeting, composed overwhelmingly of men over military age and those who because of non-citizenship are not subject to the draft, to tell our American young men to resist the draft even at the risk of being shot? There is a vast difference between objecting to a proposed law and disobeying one that has been enacted. It is against American and Socialist tradition to tell others to do what one is not called on to do himself. Our young men will obey the draft law."

As I sat down, Trotsky, who was sitting in front of me, turned and sneered: "Chauvinist!"

I had, in the eyes of this implacable revolutionist, committed the unpardonable crime of asserting that there was something in our American tradition which was worthy of respect. A few days later he disappeared into the international underground and when he next emerged he was a world figure.

Source: Louis Waldman, *Labor Lawyer* (New York: Dutton, 1944), pp. 63–68.

NOTES

1. Morris Hillquit (1869–1933), born in Latvia, was an activist in the early Jewish labor movement, a founder of the Socialist Party in 1901, and a prominent attorney. Hillquit represented the party's moderate or "centrist" element, but contrary to the impression given by Waldman, Hillquit opposed the United States' entry into World War I.

2. Emile Vandervelde (1866–1938), leader of the Belgian Labor Party and president of the Second (or Socialist) International from 1900 to 1918.

3. Santeri Nuorteva (1881–1929), former member of the Finnish parliament, leader in the American Socialist Party's Left Wing, and a founder of the Communist Labor Party, which in 1920 merged into the Communist Party. Fearing deportation for his activities on behalf of the Bolshevik Revolution, Nuorteva emigrated in 1920 and assumed several important posts in the Soviet government.

4. Louis C. Fraina (1892–1953), an Italian immigrant, played an important role in the founding of the Communist Party. He moved away from the party during the 1920s and, under the name Lewis Corey, became a highly regarded economist and best-selling author during the 1930s.

43

"These Glad Days of Russian Freedom" (1917)

KATHERINA MARYSON

The czar's downfall put immigrant Jewry in a state of near euphoria. The Yiddish writer and anarchist Dr. Katherina Maryson, writing from her sickbed, expressed delight in the following letter to her friend and confidante, Anna Strunsky Walling.[1]

Dearest Anna,

In these glad days of Russian freedom my thoughts were with you many times. [. . .] It was Thursday afternoon March 15. I lay in bed racked by a crunching pain in the back; my throat was sore and my heart beat irregularly under the stress of fever. [. . .] Suddenly, Jay[2] came in and beaming with joy held out before me an evening edition of a newspaper with large headlines reading: Revolution in Russia, Czar abdicates, etc.

Throat, back and heart were obliterated, I felt calm at first, took in the news as a matter of fact, and soon after, like a miser dreaming of hoards of gold, began to fear that the thing will vanish. More newspapers were brought in during the evening, and the next day and the next. Not flowers decorated my sick room, but many editions of various papers surrounded me, all telling the glad tidings, the realization of the dreams of our youth. Yes the thing is real and permanent. Friends came in, friends called up. Nothing but greetings and rejoicing and congratulations.

The feeling is of a mother rejoicing and worrying over the arrival of a long expected baby. Will the infant survive all the trials of babyhood? Will it grow to maturity? And again the joy that it is here, it has come.

I wrote a letter to one of my sisters yesterday; I finished addressing it with the word "Russia" and gazed at it long and lovingly. "Russia." I wanted to write the word "Libre" after it. It seemed so natural. Today I went out for a short stroll in the street, the first time after my illness. I looked at the people, at the streets, at the newsstands. Are they the same? Why, how so! Russia's free. Yes, we cannot express the thousands of emotions and feelings filling us to overflowing. A brighter spring is coming, a happiness never felt before.

The thing which mars the happiness slightly is the war and my great hope is that it will soon come to an end.

I send my love to you and all of yours, I hope you are well in these wonderful days that have come to us.

Yours
Katherina

Source: Katherina Maryson to Anna Strunsky, Mar. 20, 1917, Anna Strunsky Walling Papers, box 9, folder 15, Manuscripts and Archives, Yale University Library.

NOTES

1. Anna Strunsky Walling (1879–1964), Russian-born socialist and writer whose marriage to William English Walling, a wealthy Protestant American from a prominent southern family, drew much attention. Strunsky and Walling were among the founders of the National Association for the Advancement of Colored People in 1909. Strunsky Walling was a close friend and confidante of Maryson's.

2. Jay Maryson (1866–1941), Katherina's husband and a prominent Yiddish writer involved in Jewish anarchist and Yiddish cultural nationalist circles.

44

New York Socialists Contribute to Chaos in Russia (1917)

NEW YORK TIMES

The prominence of individual Jews in the new Bolshevik government drew much comment from observers in the United States and Europe. Some went so far as to accuse Jews of having masterminded the revolution as part of a worldwide political conspiracy. While the following report does not indulge in such anti-Semitism, it exaggerates the role played by Jews in Soviet Russia.

That some of the radicals who went from New York to join the Bolsheviki in Petrograd may have violated the passport regulations of the United States was alleged in a statement issued yesterday by the American Alliance for Labor and Democracy,[1] of which Samuel Gompers[2] is the head. The statement identified some of the men who have gone from New York to Russia as being leaders in the radical socialist movement here and linked their going to Russia with the so-called People's Council,[3] a pacifist organization, with headquarters in the city.

That there is a direct line of communication between the Bolsheviki in Petrograd and radicals in New York was one of the allegations made by Robert Maisel,[4] Director of the Alliance, who said that the plight into which the Bolsheviki had led Russia was a justification of the stand of many former leading Socialists in condemning the pro-German activities of some of the present Socialist leaders.

"New York Socialists have contributed in no small share to the present chaotic state of affairs in Russia," said the Alliance's statement, "and if reports that reach this office are true, there is reason to believe that the passport privileges of this country have at least been abused in that connection.

"It is interesting to learn who are some of the prominent leaders of the Bolsheviki, and to learn their past connection with the element in the Socialist Party of New York that corresponds most closely to the Bolsheviki in Russia.

"For example, S. Epstein,[5] former organizer of the Ladies' Waist Makers, and editor of their journal, now is a Bolsheviki organizer in Russia. J. Voskow, former organizer of one of the Jewish painters' unions, now is a Bolsheviki organizer in Moscow. J. Shubin, a former New York Jewish newspaper man of strong Bolshevist tendencies, left this country on Nov. 7, carrying, so he boasted, important documents from the so-called Workmen's Council here to the Bolshevist leaders in Petrograd. It also is reported that he carried letters from one of the newly elected Socialist officials here. Dr. Max Goldfarb,[6] former labor writer on the Forward, also is in Russia.

"These are only a few of the more prominent ones. There have been hundreds who have gone to Russia from here, many of them with the deliberate intention of helping the Bolshevist movement. Of course, Trotzky's[7] own relations in New York are well known.

"All of these people were heavily influenced by the Germanic Socialist doctrine of which Morris Hillquit is the leading exponent in America and which is a perversion of true socialism and a denial of true internationalism. It is dominated by the German conception, which is metaphysical in the extreme and which, when not consciously German, plays into the hands of Germany as effectively as though it were consciously operated for the German Government.

"This is excellently illustrated by the dictatorship of Lenine[8] and Trotzky, who declare themselves the proletariat, denying to the actual proletariat any rights whatever, just as the German Emperor might declare himself the State.

"This inter-relation between the Bolsheviki of Russia and of New York simply goes to prove the similarity of types, regardless of locality, and to disclose the German origin of the whole movement, due in large part to the German domination and coloring of the Socialist philosophy.

"This is also why the Socialist Party in America, under its present leadership and with its present Germanized philosophy is a menace to our own country, and because it is a menace to our own country is also a menace to our war program and to the cause for which we fight. Until the Germanic metaphysical conception is taken out of the American Socialist movement it will continue to be a pro-German menace and must be regarded as such by true Americans."

Source: "Say Radicals Here Back Bolsheviki," New York Times, Nov. 30, 1917, p. 3.

1. The American Alliance for Labor and Democracy (AALD), an organization established by Samuel Gompers and other labor leaders to foster support for World War I. AALD leaders feared that pacifist organizations would stir unrest among workers in crucial wartime industries; especially worrisome were Jewish immigrant workers in New York's garment industry, whom the AALD most closely associated with radical, anti-American political leanings. The government-sponsored Committee on Public Information funded many AALD initiatives, including propaganda campaigns and public rallies.

2. Samuel Gompers (1850–1924), British-born Jew and president of the American Federation of Labor (AFL) almost continuously from its founding in 1886 until his death in 1924. Gompers also served as president of the American Alliance for Labor and Democracy (AALD) from 1917 to 1919.

3. The People's Council for Peace and Democracy (alternately known as the People's Council of America for Peace and Democracy or simply the People's Council) was founded in 1917, on the eve of World War I. It was less an organization than it was a movement for peace, with members including socialists, liberals, and labor radicals. In addition to opposing U.S. involvement in World War I, the People's Council spoke out against wartime repression, including the Espionage Act, a piece of legislation that outlawed a broad array of political dissent, including antiwar speech and writing, during the war.

4. Robert Maisel, prowar socialist and director of the American Alliance for Labor and Democracy from 1917 to 1919.

5. Known in Yiddish as Shakhne Epshteyn, see document 33, note 6. Between 1919 and 1921, Epshteyn, a former member of the Bund, was an official in the Bolshevik Party's Jewish Commissariat and editor of party publications in Russian and Yiddish. In mid-1921, the Third (or Communist) International sent Epshteyn back to the United States to help organize the Communist movement among Jews there. He continued to travel back and forth between the United States and the Soviet Union over the years.

6. Max Goldfarb, a former member of the Bund, became a high-ranking official in the Red Army and, later, the Communist International. He was expelled from the party and executed in 1937.

7. See document 42.

8. Vladimir Lenin (1870–1924), leader of the Bolsheviks and chairman of the Council of People's Commissars, the highest position in Soviet politics, in 1917; he remained in power until 1922, when a stroke forced him to resign from political life.

45

"The New Man" (1921)

MOISSAYE J. OLGIN

Essayist, educator, and scholar Moissaye Olgin (1878–1939) was the foremost Jewish Communist during the 1920s and 1930s. Although originally opposed to the Bolshevik seizure of power in the fall of 1917, Olgin soon became an ardent admirer of Soviet Russia and eventually a member of the American Communist Party. An important turning point was Olgin's six-month visit to Russia in 1920–1921, on which he reported and lectured extensively in Yiddish and English. Olgin published a series of articles in *The New Republic* that contributed to the sympathy many American liberals felt toward the Soviet experiment. At the time, Olgin was regarded as an authority on Russian politics and literature.

[. . .] Perhaps the most striking feature of the new man is intrepidity. All those doubts, queries, forebodings which torture the old intelligentzia are unknown to him. His philosophy is quite definite, the philosophy of economic materialism. His social conceptions amount to a firm conviction of the possibility and feasibility at the present moment of a socialist state in all the modern countries the world over. His dislike of the bourgeoisie is not the fruit of altruistic emotions but it is part of his nature. He is not aware of theoretical profundities. He cares little for religion. He is decidedly of this life and this time and has an unusual appetite for the enjoyment of things that are.

His intrepidity is carried into the realm of practical affairs. The new man approaches unknown difficulties with a boldness and vigor which spell success. He assumes that there is nothing on earth or heaven that a man with general intelligence and great willingness cannot learn in a brief time. He does not refuse to occupy a position whose duties are foreign to him. He is convinced that what looks baffling at first sight will become clay under his hands upon nearer acquaintance. Sometimes he is mistaken. But he is difficult to dishearten. He would easily recognize an error, he would retract when need be—a trait closely related to the lack of obligations towards an all embracing and subtle theory—but he would not give up. The thing must be done at whatever cost—is his slogan.

It follows that the new man has an obstinacy unknown to the intelligentzia of the former period. His working capacity is larger. His endurance is equal to his physical strength. We call it self-sacrificing spirit. In his eyes it is work that must be done. Overtime after eight hours of crushing labor in the mills, late hours of exhausting activities in governmental departments, sleep in the mud of the fields at the front in warfare with the foreign invaders, travel in overcrowded, unclean box-cars on official errands, attendance at meetings and committee sessions in cold, unfriendly rooms after a day's fatiguing work, does not seem extraordinary to him and does not dismay him as it does the intellectual of the older style. The new man is of a stronger fibre. He enjoys activity where the old intellectual enjoyed brooding.

The new man feels responsibility for the existing order. It is *his* state and his order. Whereas the old intelligentzia always had to look at revolutionary ideas either "from the standpoint of the worker" or "from the standpoint of the peasant," the new man looks at the revolution and its achievements from his own standpoint. He makes no compromise and therefore has no reason to shirk his duties. He has won a victory and wishes to retain his superior position. This is why he does not blame anybody when he does discover an error committed. He has no respect for traditions, for written laws, for constitutional guarantees, for refinements of the legal mind. Traditions cannot hamper a man who has but yesterday appeared on the surface of a brand new world. Written laws have no sanctity to a fighter who has just thrown on the scrap heap a staggering volume of written laws accumulated these three hundred years and who has in a whirl created a new set of laws to work with. Legal reasoning is in sharp contrast to the character of a man of practical action. To the new man, the idea that law is "man made" is as natural as it is natural for a workman to throw away a tool and grasp a better one when work must be speeded up. *My* country, my power, my responsibility, my law—is the article of faith of the new man, to the despair of the mystic philosopher and the jurist.

The new intellectual is ordinarily good-natured but he can be grim. He has regard for the personality of others but he can be implacable to his foes. His attitude toward the old intelligentzia is that of envy and contempt. He envies the ease with which it handles ideas quite beyond his reach. He envies accumulated theoretical and practical knowledge. This is perhaps a more corroding feeling than the envy formerly aroused in him by material luxuries. The intelligentzia is, to his mind, a group of bourgeois monopolists who, on the shoulders of the people, attained to heights of knowledge and experiences sorely needed for the workmen's republic. He despises the intelligentzia for its lack of sympathy with the new order and, wherever he can, he makes it feel his domination. When he makes the old intelligentzia give instruction in the new schools, the training grounds of the new intelligentzia, he is animated by the same spirit of revenge which he experienced when he made the manager of an old private firm conduct affairs in favor of the people. "To break the cultural monopoly of the bourgeoisie" is to him one of the greatest aims of the revolution.

The avidity of the new man for knowledge is unquenchable. His prowess in overcoming material and mental difficulties is amazing. Not only things immediately necessary for his practical activities absorb his interest. He makes it his business to take as much as he can from the old culture created by the bourgeoisie. In a way, he passes through the same stages of development that were passed by the intelligentzia long ago. He greedily reads the classics. He is fascinated by productions of Shakespeare, Molière and Schiller. He goes to picture galleries where romantic painting makes the strongest appeal to his imagination. He packs the Moscow art theatre of which the fastidious intelligentzia speaks as of an art stage long passed. He crowds lecture rooms and evening courses. All this he does not without effort, but with a virile determination and a great deal of sacrifice.

In his private life the new man is close to the ordinary workman. His house may be cleaner and his speech dotted with foreign words of which he does not always know the exact meaning, yet essentially he is a worker. He shuns no physical labor. He certainly has no contempt for physical labor. He has no contempt for the man of the masses. He speaks his language perfectly, and in time of crisis he can deal with him more easily than any representative of the other classes. On the other hand, he does not eulogize over the "poor people." He knows their faults are his own. Sometimes he has in store for a harsh word which they take from him more placidly than from anybody else. In fact, he is sometimes too eager, too vociferous; he often overreaches himself in administrative zeal, but this is an old general trait of a temperamental, imaginative nation, as is its bent toward too much control and, consequently, an abundance of red tape in public affairs. With all this, the new man is an undaunted optimist. Hasn't he gained a whole world, and isn't it true that he had to lose nothing but his chains?

The new intelligentzia is vitally interested in increasing its number. Public schools and secondary schools will yield a new crop of men only in years to come. Meanwhile, national affairs cannot be delayed. The Soviet government has created a great number of schools to train new functionaries. Chief among them are the workers' facilities attached to each university, giving two years' training courses for young workmen and peasants which will enable them to pursue university studies. The Communist party schools and colleges give earnest instruction in sociology and economics and prepare the students for administrative work. The officers training camps ("courses for Red commanders") give to tens of thousands of workmen and peasants not only specific military knowledge but also a general knowledge and, in some of them, a working knowledge of engineering, chemistry, railroads, business administration. The schools of the labor unions prepare union officials. The cultural resources of the entire country, the libraries, museums, lecture halls, theatres, musical forces are all at the disposal of those new breeding places of the new leaders of Russia.

When Russia emerges from the present crisis into a more stable and comfortable mode of living, its spiritual life will have assumed a totally new aspect.

Source: Moissaye J. Olgin, "The Type Which Rules Russia," *The New Republic*, Sept. 28, 1921, pp. 133–135.

46

Communism and Freedom of Speech (1925)

WORKERS' (COMMUNIST) PARTY; ROGER BALDWIN AND EARL BROWDER

In 1925, Raphael Abramovich (1880–1963) a leader of the Bund and the Russian Social Democratic Party (then based in Germany) came to the United States on a speaking tour. Abramovich hoped to draw attention to political repression in Soviet Russia and to raise money on behalf of political prisoners. At the behest of the Communist International in Moscow, the American Communist Party—then officially named the Workers (Communist) Party—attempted to break up Abramovich's lectures. Its disruptions prompted an exchange of letters between the American Civil Liberties Union's director, Roger Baldwin, and the Communist Party's acting executive secretary, Earl Browder, about the party's position on freedom of speech.

The Workers (Communist) Party Initiates a Campaign against Raphael Abramovich

Minutes of the Secretariat (Jan. 17, 1925)
 Present: [Alexander] Bittelman,[1] [Max] Bedacht,[2] [Earl] Browder[3]
 Abramovich Campaign
Communication from the CI [Communist International] advising of Abramovich visit to United States for purpose of launching propaganda against Russia, and outlining counter-campaign.
 Motion by Bittelman:
Program to combat the counter-revolutionary mission of the emissary of the Second International to the U.S., Mr. Abramovich.
 In view of the fact that the mission of Mr. Abramovich [. . .] is to carry on a campaign for moral, financial, and political support against the Soviet

Republic, against the international unity movement of the trade unions, and against the Communist International:

Taking also into consideration that such a campaign will serve as a rallying center in the U.S. for all black, yellow, and reactionary elements against the progressive and militant sections of the American labor movement, and that such a concentration of reaction will undoubtedly strengthen the present capitalist offensive against labor; therefore be it

Resolved: (1) That the C.E.C. [Central Executive Committee] issue a call to the American working class, exposing the mission of the Abramovich conspiracy of the enemies of the working class.

(2) That we carry on an intensive agitation in our press thru mass meetings, pamphlets, and leaflets against the Second International, the Russian counter-revolution, and against the mission of Abramovich under the general slogan:

not a cent of money, not an ounce of support, to the agents of international imperialsim and servants of "open shopper" dawes.[4]

(3) That we immediately familiarize the leading comrades of the party with the mission of Abramovich and with our policy as the first step towards preparing the party for its task.

(4) For this purpose conferences shall be arranged in the following cities: New York, Philadelphia, Boston, Buffalo, Cleveland, Pittsburgh, Detroit, Minneapolis–St. Paul. In all these cities the conferences shall include District Committees, city committees, T.U.E.L.[5] workers, and representatives from each branch; in New York [and Chicago] shall be added Federation officers and editorial staffs of papers.

(5) Since the activities of Abramovich will be carried on mainly among the Jewish, German, and Russian workers, and will touch also the Esthonian and Caucasion, therefore the CEC instructs the respective language sections immediately to circularize their memberships in preparation for the campaign.

(6) Special committees to carry on the work shall be formed in New York, Philadelphia, Boston, Buffalo, Cleveland, Pittsburgh, Detroit, Chicago, Minneapolis, St. Paul, and Los Angeles. These committees shall consist of one representative each from the D.E.C., C.C.C., T.U.E.L., Jewish, German, Russian, Esthonian, Armenian, sections. These committees shall be organized by the DOs [District Organizers] and shall elect secretaries whose names and addresses shall immediately be transmitted to the national office.

(7) The CEC appoints Com. Alexander Bittelman as national director of this campaign to supervise and direct the activities of these committees.

(8) The conferences provided for shall be addressed by the national director of the campaign.

(9) The national director shall be authorized, in cooperation with the Educational Committee, to prepare a program of pamphlets to be published in this campaign.

Adopted Draft of appeal approved and ordered sent to all party papers.

Source: Minutes of the Secretariat of Workers' Party, Jan. 17, 1925, Records of the Communist Party of the United States in the Comintern Archives (Fond 515), microfilm edition compiled by the Library of Congress and the Russian State Archive of Social and Political History, reel 31, delo 471, Tamiment Library, New York University.

Roger Baldwin to Earl Browder (March 3, 1925)

Dear Earl:

We have a complaint from our friends in Pittsburgh that members of the Workers Party attempted to break up a meeting addressed by Dr. Abramovich in the Labor Lyceum on March 1st, by throwing bricks and other missiles through the windows of the meeting hall where 1200 persons were seated. Six of the disturbers were arrested.

Knowing the record of previous interferences with Dr. Abramovich's meetings, we have no doubt that these persons are correctly described as members of the Workers Party or sympathizers, and that they have been inspired by the official attitude of the Workers Party as expressed in the Daily Worker.[6] It is intolerable that the Workers Party should solicit and accept aid in its own efforts for the right of free speech and free assemblage and to deny it to its opponents. I cannot understand how the Party can continue to talk about free speech, to sponsor the organization of the Labor Defense Council, to retain William Z. Foster[7] on our National Committee, and at the same time to approve of such tactics as these.

Our Executive Committee looks for a prompt disavowal on the part of the officers of the Party of these tactics and a definite pronouncement in favor of allowing Dr. Abramovich or anyone else to hold meetings on private property in peace. The outside limits of making your protest against Dr. Abramovich should be heckling at meetings and expressions of disapproval of what he has to say. Any attempts to break up his meetings by mass action in the audience, by throwing missiles or the like are utterly unjustified on the part of those who are demanding for themselves the rights of free speech and assemblage. Either the Workers Party will have to continue its agitation for these rights without soliciting or accepting the help of liberals outside, or if it does solicit or accept that help, the Party must indicate some respect for the principle it invokes.

We shall look for an early reply and we request your careful attention to this request made on behalf of the organization officially.

Very truly yours,
Roger Baldwin
Director

Source: Roger Baldwin to Earl Browder, Mar. 3, 1925, Records of the Communist Party of the United States in the Comintern Archives (Fond 515), microfilm edition compiled by the Library of Congress and the Russian State Archive of Social and Political History, reel 34, delo 510, Tamiment Library, New York University.

Roger Baldwin to Earl Browder (March 11, 1925)

Dear Earl:

[. . .] Your party members have raised an exceedingly embarrassing and critical issue by their attacks upon the Abramovich meetings and particularly by the interference in a meeting at Town Hall, New York City, last Monday night, presided over by Norman Hapgood[8] at which the subject of the political prisoners was discussed. The local party officials objected to our discussing the prisoners in Russia and particularly to one speaker, B.C. Vladeck.[9] They also objected to my discussion on the same issue and it was only with difficulty that I got through my speech. Mr. Vladeck was unable to speak at all against the constant uproar which lasted fifteen minutes until the meeting was adjourned. The uproar was directly caused by the Workers Party members under the leadership of Ludwig Lore[10] and Juliet Poyntz,[11] both of whom had come to see me in advance of the meeting and had warned me that such a demonstration would be made.

This went far beyond the limits of any proper protest and raises the issue which we both must face. [. . .]

I do hope the Party will see its way clear to a policy consistent with your own demand for free speech.

Sincerely yours,
Roger Baldwin

Source: Roger Baldwin to Earl Browder, Mar. 11, 1925, Records of the Communist Party of the United States in the Comintern Archives (Fond 515), microfilm edition compiled by the Library of Congress and the Russian State Archive of Social and Political History, reel 34, delo 510, Tamiment Library, New York University.

Earl Browder to Roger Baldwin (March 12, 1925)

Dear Baldwin:

In reply to your communications of March 3rd and 11th, the Central Executive Committee of the Workers Party of America makes the following statement:

As we foresaw, the demand for "free speech" on behalf of Mr. Abramovich, enemy of the workers' government of Russia, has turned into a fight, not for free speech, but to slander and discredit Soviet Russia—to assist the capitalist governments of the world to intimidate the workers and prepare for new warfare against the stronghold of the world's workers.

No other conclusion is possible when we see the *New York Times* jubilantly making common cause with the friends of "free speech." We are not surprised that the capitalist papers suddenly throw open their news columns to you, and even their editorial pages, for you are rendering their owners a great service. You are being placed in a position of sponsoring the lies which they have been unable to make the workers of America believe.

You demand that the Communists shall grant free speech to Abramovich. But we are not the ruling party in America. We have not closed Mr. Abramovich's halls. We have not jailed his supporters and beaten them up in meetings. No! These very things have been perpetrated upon us. The Workers Party is a persecuted political organization of the conscious workers, fighting every day for its very life against the combined forces of the capitalist government, its lackeys, and the misleaders of labor. In spite of our comparative weakness in numbers and power, however, we are strong in our position as the only champions of the interests of the workers and their protectors against the political poison of the Abramoviches.

We have not only the right but also the duty to raise loud protest against the activities of Abramovich, tool of imperialism. You yourself have twice definitely stated your opinion that the workers are entirely in order in "heckling at meetings and expressions of disapproval of what he has to say." That is precisely what the workers have attempted to do at the Abramovich meetings. There would therefore seem to be no need of any conflict between you and us. But because the Abramovich agents have themselves physically attacked Communists, have beaten them up with weapons inside the meetings, have used the capitalist police systematically, and have thrown dozens of Communists into jail *for the crime of heckling and expressions of disapproval*—you, instead of protesting against this outrageous abuse of workers, appeal to us to protest "free speech." It is a most astonishing thing. It is senseless unless what you are really asking of us is to drop our political struggle for the interest of the workers against the treasonous Abramoviches.

Abramovich has completely failed to sway any considerable portion of the workers to his purpose. But it seems that he has succeeded in entangling some liberals, making them into tools (we hope unconscious ones) in the hand of the bitterest enemies of Soviet Russia and the militant workers of America, in the hands of the *New York Times*, of Abramovich's Second International which stinks to high heaven with the stench of [. . .] corruption and murder and imprisonment of workers thruout Europe, and of American and world imperialism. That is the meaning of the formation of the so-called "International Committee for Political Prisoners." It is a weapon directed against Soviet Russia, and if Roger Baldwin does not know it, at least Vladeck and the *New York Times* do.

You have known for some time that there is an international organization that is doing tremendous work in the interests of the prisoners of capitalism thruout the world, the International Red Aid, represented at this time in America by the I.W.A. You received a letter from its secretary, Rose Karsner, some weeks ago, which also states the position of the Workers Party. In that letter you have been offered an opportunity to cooperate with the American Section of the I.R.A. in securing relief for the victims of capitalism abroad. Every intelligent and sincere friend of political prisoners is cooperating in the work of the International Red Aid, which has done immeasurable service in this field. Your new "committee," whatever the purpose of some individuals in it, will not result in helping the prisoners. And that is not its real purpose—it is intended as a weapon against Russia and when it has served that purpose we venture to predict that it will be allowed to quietly die.

The Workers (Communist) Party of America and the sympathetic workers grouped around it in the International Workers Aid and kindred organizations, is the only organized body in America that has always and everywhere done its utmost to protect the victims of imperialist persecution, not only in America, but thruout the world. What assistance has been given from America to the hundreds of thousands of victims of European reaction and imperialism has been organized and led by the Communists. We will continue this task, along with the kindred task of fighting against the servants of the white terror, the Abramoviches, and will not be swerved from the struggle by threats or trickery.

We call upon every worker and poor farmer and every sincere enemy of capitalist oppression to rally to the International Red Aid for effective support of the victims of capitalist reaction thruout the world.

Central Executive Committee
Workers Party of America
Earl Browder
Acting Secretary

Source: Earl Browder to Roger Baldwin, Mar. 12, 1925, Records of the Communist Party of the United States in the Comintern Archives (Fond 515), microfilm edition compiled by the Library of Congress and the Russian State Archive of Social and Political History, reel 34, delo 510, Tamiment Library, New York University.

Roger Baldwin to Earl Browder (March 14, 1925)

Dear Earl:

Thank you for your letter of March 12 to which I replied by wire today, as you will note by the enclosed. I trust we may have your reply on Monday for our committee. But I want to make our position clear so that at least there will no misunderstanding between us, even though we have to do business by the unsatisfactory means of long distance correspondence.

Your letter, as I stated, failed to answer the single issue with which we are concerned, namely, whether the Workers Party asserts its right to break up meetings which it disapproves, while demanding the right of peaceful assemblage for itself. We are not at all concerned with the character of the meetings which you break up. Those issues are entirely aside from our job in behalf of freedom of opinion. Your reply avoids that issue altogether and endeavors to inject into the situation the struggle between various factions in the radical movement and between capital and labor.

We are just as much concerned, for instance, for the right of Catholics to condemn birth control, as we are for the right of Margaret Sanger[12] to advocate it. We are just as much concerned with the right of the Ku Klux Klan to hold meetings on private property unmolested, as we are with the right of the Knights of Columbus to hold peaceful meetings to attack the Ku Klux Klan. Similarly, we are advocates of the right of socialists and communists to hold meetings attacking each other, if they choose, so long as the meetings are not interfered with. The common practice of heckling, booing, hissing, of course, are perfectly legitimate. We have never questioned them. What we do question is the effort of one group to break up another group's meeting either by organized mass action in the audience or by violence. That the Workers Party has been guilty of these latter practices is proven beyond all argument. If the Socialist Party has also been guilty of them, we would condemn them equally. But your Party has not called our attention to any such instances, while the Socialist Party has. We shall be just as prompt and vigorous to take up any complaints from you as we would from them. And you know it from our record. There has never been an occasion when the Workers Party appealed to us for help of any sort when we have not gone to the front for them.

As a matter of fact, the present difficulty is largely due to the position we would be put in if we did not protest against your interference with meetings. We would properly be regarded as an ally of the communist movement, a defender of their activities, sitting silent when the communists violate the very rights for which they invoke our help.

You will thus see the impossibility of the position you force upon us when you break up by force the meetings either of Dr. Abramovich or of such meetings as that held in the Town Hall last Monday. The revolutionary issues which you describe as involved do not concern us at all. Attacks on Soviet Russia, if you choose to regard the discussion of political prisoners there as such, are just as legitimate as your meetings honoring the Russian revolution, and should be just as free from interference.

If you will look at this matter dispassionately from the point-of-view of the practical conditions we face in the United States today, I am confident you will agree that the Party is in an indefensible position, demanding help from persons outside in your struggle to get your rights, and at the same time denying those rights to others. Just try to look at it from our point-of-view, with our record of absolutely impartial and non-partisan campaigning year in and year out for the past eight years for the rights of all persons attacked. The Workers Party and the Civil Liberties Union would of course disagree as to the philosophy of free speech. You regard it as a means to an end. We regard it as an end in itself. Nevertheless, William Z. Foster sits upon our National Committee just as does Charney Vladeck, whom the Workers Party so bitterly opposes, and just as do scores of other persons whose economic philosophies would clash.

We ask you to give this matter your further and most careful attention, for we want to continue serving you in your struggle, and yet your present position and activities against peaceful assemblage make it exceedingly embarrassing and difficult to do so.

Sincerely,
Roger Baldwin

Source: Roger Baldwin to Earl Browder, Mar. 14, 1925, Records of the Communist Party of the United States in the Comintern Archives (Fond 515), microfilm edition compiled by the Library of Congress and the Russian State Archive of Social and Political History, reel 34, delo 510, Tamiment Library, New York University.

Earl Browder to Roger Baldwin (March 19, 1925)

My dear Baldwin,

[. . .] As we made clear before, we are vitally concerned in protecting the workers in their right to heckle and demonstrate disapproval of such [counterrevolutionary] propaganda.

As to the specific issue of the Town Hall meeting: We are in possession of the facts of the case reported by our comrades, according to which the Workers Party members in New York did not organize themselves to break up the meeting, but to demonstrate disapproval of the attack against Soviet Russia launched under cover of an appeal for political prisoners.

Our understanding of the facts of the case is that heckling and demonstration was the limit of tactics of the Workers Party members at the Town Hall meeting. It is the opinion of the Central Executive Committee that the comrades in New York did not, as you assume, endeavor to break up the meeting. What they did and what the policy of the Party approves, was to demonstrate against the attempt to turn the issue of working class prisoners under capitalist governments into a weapon against Soviet Russia.

Fraternally yours,
Earl Browder

Source: Earl Browder to Roger Baldwin, Mar. 19, 1925, Records of the Communist Party of the United States in the Comintern Archives (Fond 515), microfilm edition compiled by the Library of Congress and the Russian State Archive of Social and Political History, reel 34, delo 510, Tamiment Library, New York University.

Roger Baldwin to Earl Browder (March 21, 1925)

Dear Earl,

[. . .] The trouble with the Party's position is that you say one thing on paper and do another in fact. You defend the conduct of the local Workers Party at the Town Hall meeting as heckling and protest, when as a matter of fact, it was an organized effort to keep Vladeck from talking.

All you fellows know perfectly well that at the various meetings we have been discussing, the Party was out to prevent the speakers from talking at all. Your members boast of this in private conversation although in your public statements you deny it. Honesty is one of the commendable virtues of most Communists. Why don't you do some plain speaking on this matter? We won't get anywhere by dressing up bad situations in nice words.

I want all you fellows to believe us very deeply concerned in regard to this matter and profoundly distressed that the Party should have raised such an issue. It is bad judgment and poor tactics and you put your friends outside in a very difficult position. I hope that the Party can see its way clear to answer our former letter in a way that will settle this whole matter to our mutual satisfaction.

Sincerely yours,
Roger Baldwin

Source: Roger Baldwin to Earl Browder, Mar. 21, 1925, Records of the Communist Party of the United States in the Comintern Archives (Fond 515), microfilm edition compiled by the Library of Congress and the Russian State Archive of Social and Political History, reel 34, delo 510, Tamiment Library, New York University.

NOTES

1. See document 3.

2. Max Bedacht (1883–1972), a German-born founder of the Communist Party, USA. During the 1940s, Bedacht served as head of the International Workers Order, a multiethnic fraternal, insurance, and mutual-aid organization with a membership peaking at two hundred thousand.

3. Earl Browder (1891–1973) was a high-ranking Communist leader. He served as general secretary of the party during its most successful period between 1934 and 1945.

4. General Dawes, a bank president in Chicago who wrote an approving report of the Dawes Act, the war-reparations payment plan implemented by Charles W. Dawes (no relation to General Dawes) following World War I. Communists claimed the plan would enslave the German working class to the Morgan Bank.

5. The Trade Union Educational League, a national association of militant trade unionists associated with the Communist Party.

6. The Communist Party's English-language daily newspaper, founded in 1924.

7. William Z. Foster (1881–1961), veteran labor organizer and, for a lengthy stint, general secretary of the Communist Party.

8. Norman Hapgood (1868–1937), prominent journalist and social reformer.

9. Baruch Charney Vladeck (1886–1938), a former member of the Bund in Russia, immigrated to the United States in 1908. A prominent Yiddish lecturer, journalist, and Socialist Party activist, Vladeck served as manager of the daily *Forverts* for two decades, was elected to the New York City Council in 1917 and 1937, and was, in 1934, the founding president of the Jewish Labor Committee. He was a staunch critic of the Communist Party and the Soviet Union.

10. Editor of the highly regarded, German-language *New Yorker Volkzeitung*, Ludwig Lore (1875–1942) was a leading figure in the German-immigrant left and the Workers' (Communist) Party.

11. Juliet Poyntz (1886–1937; also spelled Pointz) was a founding member of the Communist Party USA and an organizer in the International Ladies' Garment Workers' Union. She defected from the Communist Party in 1936, after witnessing Stalin's purges while in the Soviet Union. Shortly after her return to the United States, Poyntz disappeared; it was widely believed that she was kidnapped and executed by Soviet agents in the United States (see document 49).

12. Margaret Sanger (1879–1966) was perhaps the most famous birth control advocate in the United States in the early twentieth century. Focusing primarily on working-class women and the connections between contraception and working-class empowerment, Sanger established the nation's first birth control clinic in Brooklyn, New York, and campaigned around the country for the repeal of restrictive laws on contraceptive information and devices.

47

A Revolutionary Returns (1929)

NOKHUM KHANIN

A former member of the Bund in Russia, Nokhum Khanin (1885–1965) was an experienced revolutionary by the time he immigrated to the United States in 1912. He rose through the ranks of the Socialist Party's Jewish Socialist Federation and, in 1921, became head of its successor organization, the Jewish Socialist Farband. In the late-1920s Khanin journeyed to the Soviet Union and sought out former comrades and friends, as described in the following travelogue.

I had a very close friend in New York years ago. When the split between the Left Wing and Right Wing in our movement happened, he became a Leftist.[1] He never belonged to the Communist Party, but he was friendly toward it, attended its gatherings, gave money, in a word, helped in all respects. He worked as a dentist and earned very well. In 1922, he decided to take his wife and child back to Russia. Before leaving he came to say good-bye to me. I pleaded with him: "Motl, don't go!" But he didn't listen. He gave me only one answer: "I want to help build socialism in the country where socialism is being built, and I'm going there."

I had almost completely forgotten about Motl. I did not even know where he was. When I was in the city N., I met one of my old party comrades. An hour before my departure, he asked me, "Have you seen Motl while you were here?" I soon found out where he was; I took a carriage and ran off to the office where Motl was an employee. Entering the office, I spotted Motl handing a client something. When Motl was done with the client, I approached him. When he noticed me, he became pale, he stared, tears welled up, and cried out: "Nokhum, what are you doing here? How did you get here?" Motl had become thinner over time and, it seemed, shorter too. The clothes he wore were very poor. Holding his hand in mine, I asked him: "Motl, how are you, how's life?" And with the irony, gall, and bitterness that fate had dealt him, he answered: "Nokhum, I am building socialism." I could not speak to Motl any further. Our hearts understood one another. I had to run to the train. I shook his hand, said goodbye, and left."

Yosl was once the leader of the Bund in our city. He was the son of very wealthy parents. He had received an excellent education, and not only did he become the leader of the Bund in our city, but also became a prominent speaker and journalist. His father was a very strict orthodox Jew, and he was very unhappy that his Yosl had befriended poor tailors and cobblers. His mother, a simple Jewish woman, loved Yosl and idolized him. All of our meetings, secret meetings, used to take place in Yosl's house.

I was a regular visitor to his place. His mother was always interested in me. She always used to listen to what I had to say about the working class [. . .] and how Yosl was prepared to do everything he could for it, even sit in prison and go to Siberia. And she probably saw in me that Worker about which Yosl spoke so much.

Today, Yosl is a prominent Communist. When I came to the city where Yosl's parents live, I decided to go to Yosl's mother. His father was already dead. Yosl now lives in Moscow. When I entered the house, Yosl's mother immediately recognized me. She stared at me; her eyes filled with amazement and she cried out:

"Look, it's Nokhum! Where have you been all this time? In Russia there was such a tumult, such a scene, and you, Nokhum, for whom the whole tumult was made, you disappeared, you were nowhere to be seen the entire time." I answered that I was in America and I've come from there now. Quietly and modestly she said: "So you're a happy man. You haven't had to go through what all of us have gone through."

She asked me to sit and treated me to tea. She began inquiring about how I live, how people generally live in America. Afterward, she said to me in a very good-natured tone with a kind smile, full of grace and motherly love: "Nokhum, do you remember when you and Yosl used to declare a strike in the city, and all the businesses used to close? You used to tell me two days before the strike would happen, and how I should go buy everything, so I wouldn't be lacking anything at home. You used to know everything back then. Tell me, Nokhum, seeing as you know everything, how long will this take?"

By "how long will this take" she meant the Bolshevik regime.

I started laughing and said, "What are you saying? I'll tell you this about Yosl! Yosl is such a devoted Communist, he'll never forgive you for such a question." She said to me in the same calm tone, "And what do you think?

Yosl doesn't want the same? Yosl won't be happy when all this ends? Do you think it's good for Yosl to lead such a hard life? He, too, lacks everything. So, how long do you think he'll be able to endure?"

Mariashe lived in "Blote,"[2] once the poorest part of the city. There lived the discarded, the poorest of poor people: drivers, haulers, and just common folk without work. No work was too difficult for them, but they never had any work. The Bund arose from "Blote." We used to have our meetings there, in our illegal headquarters. We were sure the simple residents of "Blote" would never betray us. We had our headquarters at Mariashe's place for a long time. Mariashe's husband was a worker in a tobacco factory. They were just married. She knew that we were "unkosher" people, but that did not bother her. She used to look out for us as if she had eyes in the back of her head. When I used to leave the Bund's headquarters, Mariashe would collect all the printed papers and hide them so they wouldn't be discovered by anybody. Mariashe never enlisted in the movement, never even attended a meeting, but she related to us with a certain respect. Her heart told her that we were the defenders of "Blote," that we sacrificed ourselves for its poor people. We would eventually make it so that Mariashe would have an easier and better life.

When I came to the city where Mariashe lived, I remembered her and went off to find out if she still lived there, if she was still alive. When I came to the house, I found out that Mariashe no longer lived in "Blote," but on the main street in what was formerly one of the richest houses in the city. I went there.

I knocked on the door and Mariashe opened it. She recognized me. With the greatest joy she swung open the door and hugged me like a good, old comrade. Mariashe had become frightfully old. She had six children and they lived all in one room. The room, in what was once a fancy house that looked onto the main street, was very neglected. The windows were old, broken; entire pieces were torn out of the ceiling. The two beds, which stood by the sides of the room, were old, poor. In the middle of the house stood a table with a couple of broken chairs. On the walls hung pictures of the country's prominent Communist leaders. The walls were partially pasted over with Communist slogans.

Mariashe asked me to sit, immediately warmed up tea, and we both sat at the table, talking about the past and the present. Mariashe spoke about things she had no conception of in the old days. She spoke about wars, about Lenin, even about Trotsky, with whom she did not agree. Mariashe still could not read and write, just as before. But all of her children are Communists, and she constantly hears talk about national affairs, world affairs. Her house has become a school where she listens to everything the Communists have to say. When I asked her how she survives, whether she's happy, if she's content, Mariashe said this:

"We live very poorly, we lack bread, we lack clothing. We are eight people in the family. There isn't anywhere to sleep properly. We sleep three people in a bed. Two children sleep on the floor. My husband, Berl, is old. He can't get any work. Yet I'm happy because the rulers are doing everything they can so the workers can live better. And if we're living poorly it is not their fault. When we used to live in 'Blote' nobody cared for us. Our children lied around in the street. We didn't even have the opportunity to send them to Talmud Torah.[3] Everybody looked at us residents of 'Blote' with contempt. We were hated. We used to feel ashamed to walk on the city's main street because we were poor. We went around ragged. We're also poor and ragged now, but we can go wherever we want. Nobody is ashamed of us. My children go to school; they're learning. They're being made into decent human beings, educated. And, therefore, all of my children are dedicated Communists. Those who used to live on the main streets now live in 'Blote' and they're now hated, like we used to be hated. Now *we're* the ones ashamed of 'Blote.'

"I and my husband"—she continued—"have nothing at this point to expect from life. We're old already. We will live another five, ten years. But our children will be happier than us. And I now live with joy from my children. I am not a party member," she tells me, "but I am entirely with the Bolsheviks because they are our friends. They care for the poor; they want to make us into decent people. I know that many poor people are unhappy with the Bolsheviks because they live harder now than in the past. But they are not '*soznatelne*' (not "conscious," in Communist jargon), they don't know that the government wants to make them happy.

"If I could go with my six children to my brother in New York, where they earn a good living, I'd surely do this. But you can't get into America, and there is nowhere else to go. We must remain here and suffer. And if we have to be here, it's better that we have a Bolshevik government."

There are many such mothers who live for the happiness of their children, but who themselves are unhappy. In Russia, they're called "for-the-sake-of-their-children Bolsheviks."

It used to gladden me when I would encounter people in old Russia who were happy even in their unhappiness; who cheered themselves up with future happiness. Their happiness also used to warm me a little. When a small spark of joy would come my way, it used to feel so good. In today's Russian life, though, you will find very few people who can gladden you and give you cheer.

I was once in prison with him in Warsaw. He belonged to the Polish Socialist Party, even though he was a Jew. The Bolshevik Revolution drove him to Siberia, where he was exiled. After returning to Russia, he became a member of the Communist Party. Now he is a Soviet official. He is regarded in his city as one of the most dedicated Communists.

I met him accidentally in that city. He invited me to his house. He's now a father of six children, beginning with a fourteen-year-old daughter and ending with a child of four. He lives in three nice rooms in a house that used to belong to a rich Russian businessman. Inside, the rooms were quite well decorated, and it was pleasant to sit there.

From our chats he could easily surmise I am not a Communist. He was dressed quite ordinarily, poor according to our American standard of dress. But the clothes of his wife and children looked completely different. When I asked him where one could buy such pretty clothes, like his children's, he explained he bought them in Germany. Several years ago, he served in the foreign commissariat. He was a courier. He used to travel from country to country to inform Russian ambassadors about things the government did not want to send via written messages.

Such officials can cross Russian borders quite freely and bring in what they want. In Europe, America, or Asia they are allowed to live very generously. They stay in the best hotels, wear the best clothes, and eat in the best restaurants. They must not report to the Communist parties in whichever country they are in so as not to attract the slightest suspicion. Naturally, when he used to travel home to his family, he would bring clothes from Europe, and they still wear the clothes he once brought from abroad.

Now, he has been transferred to another post and has to live in Russia. Since he was accustomed to a life of luxury in Europe, it was very difficult for him to live in Russia. He longs to return to a post as a "traveling courier."

But there are a lot of Communists interested in the post of "traveling courier." What people won't do to attain such a post! When a person is given a Communist mission in Europe somewhere, he's the happiest man. And my old Polish Socialist Party, now Communist, friend still hopes he will succeed in being promoted to his old position, which he lost due to party politics. He lives in a Communist country, built on Communism, and yet longs for a trip to the capitalist countries so that he and his family can snack on a little something made by capitalist production in bourgeois countries.

I belonged to the Jewish Socialist Federation[4] with Yankl. He came to America in the same year I did, but he could not adapt. He worked in various trades and mastered none of them. Being a child of rich parents, he hadn't worked his entire life. And he did not want to work here. He went hungry in America and he studied along the way. When the Russian Revolution broke out, Yankl had just become a student in a New York college. He decided to leave college and travel to Russia. He traveled as far as Charbin, China, but could not go further. He returned to America and spent his years here until 1922. He was a member of the Socialist Party, but, in 1921, he left the party along with the Jewish Socialist Federation. A short time later, Yankl again departed for Russia, where he became an official in the foreign affairs commissariat.

I had long forgotten about Yankl. In the city where Yankl now lives I had troubles with my foreign passport, and I had to take care of the matter in a division of the foreign commissariat. Entering the office, I took my place in line, waiting until my turn came. In the office were a lot of old people, whose children were in America and were now bringing them over.

When my turn came, the official very politely greeted me and, before he answered my request, began questioning me about America. It didn't bother him that there were people behind me who had been waiting impatiently for hours. I became uncomfortable with the fact that he was holding me up and holding up others because of that. When the official finally took care of my issue, he said it would take four, five days to clear up.

I could not stay in the city any longer. I had to leave. And here was this official saying to me that I must remain another five days. I began to ask, complain, look for excuses as to why I could not stay, why I needed to depart. The official told me that he could not do anything, and that I should go to the director's office. I knocked on the director's door and he immediately shouted, "Come in!"

When I opened the door, I saw Yankl sitting there. I let out a shout, "Yankl!" With his pleasant smile, he shot back, "Don't shout, you scoundrel, close the door!" I closed the door, entered, and hugged him, and he began asking how was it that I came there, to the foreign ministry. I explained. He calmed me down and said he would solve the problem for me. And he soon began inquiring about what kind of impression Russia made on me.

Before I gave him my impression I made a small preface. "Listen, Yankl," I said, "I've been in Russia thirty days already. In the first few days I didn't have any fear. I conducted myself very freely. I thought that if I were to be arrested, I'd be held ten, fifteen days, but I'd be released. Now I'm on my way home and I don't want to be arrested. If you're a good guy, and I can be straight with you, I'll tell you everything." He immediately assured me, "Don't be a child, talk to me as freely as you can."

I told him everything I saw: poverty, despair, unbearable housing, factories operating on deficits, peasants who neglect their fields, the failure of the Communist economy. He heard me out and said to me in Russian: "But you're still a socialist and you want to see socialism realized in Russia! So, you should forget the bad things you saw and remember only the good."

I answered Yankl that if at least 60 percent of what I saw was good, then I'd forget the other 40 percent. And even if I didn't see anything good in the current moment, but had the slightest hope that Russia would crawl out from its desolation and want, and that the bitter present in Russia would lead to a better tomorrow, then perhaps today's bad wouldn't bother me. But the economic situation in Russia is not getting better; it is growing worse from day to day. That which is bad today becomes even worse tomorrow, so how can I forget the bad today?

To that I received no answer from Yankl.

To the city of D. I traveled to see an old friend, Beylke. I had been active in the Bund with her. Today, she is uninvolved in politics, but the most interesting people in town, both Communists and non-Communists, gather in her home. All of my old comrades meet at her place in the evenings; they sit until four in the morning and discuss Russia and America; they recollect the past, and so on.

One night, around twelve, as we sat steeped in conversation, there was a knock on the door. The son of my old comrade went to the door, opened it, and someone asked him if he could see me. I went toward the door; I took a look—it was Leybl! I ran over to him and hugged him like a good, old comrade. But Leybl stood cold and kept his eyes lowered, as if he had committed a crime.

After a short pause, Leybl said to me: "Beylke didn't say anything to you about me?" I answered no. He asked me further: "Can I go with you into a different room? I have an important thing to speak with you about."

We both went into a separate room.

But before I continue with this story, I must tell you who Leybl is.

I met Leybl twenty-five years ago in a factory where the Bund had sent me to organize. When Leybl—the child of poor parents who never had a happy day in his life because he had to work hard from his earliest youth—heard a socialist speech for the first time at a Bundist gathering, he became an enthusiastic Bundist. Leybl saw his liberation in the Bund, his defender, the force that would stick up for him. The Bund gave substance to Leybl's poor, discarded life. From that point on, Leybl was our staunchest man; he took part in all the Bund's dangerous work. Everyone loved him for his simplicity, his sincerity, and his naïve, childlike innocence. When I left D., Leybl was the only person who wept at my departure as he bid me farewell.

Twenty-five years have passed since that time. I have met many Leybls in my life and they have disappeared from my horizon. I had long forgotten Leybl.

Now, as I walked into a separate room with Leybl, all the past events connected to our heroic work, and with Leybl's idealism, became refreshed in my mind.

Leybl took off his cap and sat down. His hair was now speckled with gray, his face wrinkled. Leybl had become old. He seemed tired, his eyes dull. After a short while Leybl said to me:

"I thought Beylke had told you everything about me, but if not, I'm pleased. I will tell you.

"After the 1905 revolution, the Bund in our city went into decline. The largest number of activists and the masses, too, went off to America; a terrible right-wing reaction set in throughout the country, the number of arrests were very large, those who remained in the city began to avoid us, yet the Bund's work continued in the city until 1910. When everything collapsed I was tired, disappointed, alone.

"I got married, children were born, my life took on new meaning. I became a devoted father to my children. I became so settled in my family life that when the second revolution came in 1917, it couldn't stir me up or pull me in. I worked in the same factory. I didn't even go to the meetings that were held legally.

"Later came the Bolsheviks, and I remained completely passive and indifferent. Many of the Bolsheviks who worked with me at the factory, those who knew I was once an active Bundist, used to chide me often for not becoming a member of the Communist Party. But I was indifferent to their reproaches.

"In 1926 I received a summons to report to the Cheka.[5] The Cheka's name used to cause a shudder among the people of our city. When I received the summons I trembled from head to toe, but I couldn't be helped. I went at the appointed hour. I entered the room where you have to wait, took a look around, and there, sitting and waiting, are Beylke and Libe, two former Bundists who received the same summons.

"When we were called in, we were ordered to sign a declaration that we, former Bundists, recognized the Bund as a counterrevolutionary organization, whose activities were once harmful, whose goals were bourgeois-nationalist, and so on.

"All three of us refused to give our signatures. They tried to convince us, but it didn't help. We refused. Then we were released.

"Two years later, I received a second summons. I went. And Beylke and Libe were there again. This time we were called in one by one; they threatened, but we remained stubborn. Beylke and Libe were released, but not me. The guy in charge from Cheka showed me a written order addressed to the factory where I worked, stating that I should be let go because I'm not loyal to the Soviet government. When I saw the order I was left frightened, despondent.

"You don't know, Nokhum, what this means!" Leybl said to me. "To lose your job at a factory here means to be sentenced to hunger, to death. Out of mercy to my wife and children I signed the declaration. Beylke and Libe could remain steadfast because they were housewives, so they couldn't be thrown out of the factory. My declaration was printed in all the Yiddish and Russian newspapers in our region. I was ashamed to show myself to Beylke and Libe, to my old comrades. I felt like a traitor to my beautiful, happy Bundist youth. When I found out that you're here, I decided I must see you and tell you that I am not guilty, that I did not voluntarily commit the betrayal, that the Cheka forced me to spit in my own face."

Leybl's sad tone and his sad story cast a gloom, a fright, on me. I saw anew his past childlike innocence. Here was honest Leybl, so pained that he was forced against his will to sign a declaration which insulted him. I calmed Leybl and comforted him. Late at night, Leybl left me.

When I departed from the city the next night, Leybl came to the train station to say goodbye. When he held my hand in his, he asked, "Will better times ever come to us?" What could I say to him? How could I answer?

Amid the great tragedy of Russia there is so much comedy that it calls for a second Sholem Aleichem who could make readers laugh through their tears. In the city of B. I looked for one of my old comrades, whose address I didn't know. I looked for him in the neighborhood where he lived three years ago, according to his last letter to me. I remembered the street but not the address, and so I walked from house to house and asked about an old comrade named Levin. Levin himself I have never seen, but I knew his wife Basye. Finally, someone pointed out a house where a Levin lives. I knocked on the door, and a young man with lengthy hair and a black shirt opened the door in front of me. I asked him if his wife was named Basye. "No," he answered. But, he said, he has a sister named Basye, and without asking he gave a shout, "Basye!" Basye came out. It was indeed Basye, but not *the* Basye. I explained to him that this is a mistake; this is, evidently, a different Levin. I explained further that I am from America, looking for an acquaintance named Levin, who doesn't know me, but I know his wife, Basye. As soon as he heard I'm an American, he wouldn't let me go. He asked me about relatives in America; he asked about the workers' movement, about the social revolution; and I sensed during the conversation that the person speaking to me was a Communist. As we spoke, we walked into a room. The entire wall was covered with pictures of Communist leaders. Among the pictures, those of Lenin and Trotsky, which hung next to one another, stood out. Seeing Trotsky's picture, I said to him in jest: "How did it occur to you to hang a picture of Trotsky? He's unkosher." He answered me, "You know, the struggle with Trotsky is an internal struggle; sooner or later, it will be worked out. So why should I remove his picture? When there's reconciliation, I'll only have to hang the picture again back where it was." There was no jest in his tone. He sincerely believed that removing Trotsky's picture would be a wasted effort because change was going to come. "It'll get worked out," as we say in America.

Source: Nokhum Khanin, *Soviet Rusland: Vi ikh hob ir gezen* (New York: Farlag Veker, 1929), pp. 211–226. Translated by Tony Michels.

NOTES

1. The reference here is to the factional splits in the Jewish Socialist Federation, the Yiddish-speaking section of the Socialist Party between 1919 and 1921. The JSF split into two factions in September 1921. The "left-wing" faction eventually merged into the Communist Party; the "right-wing" faction remained loyal to the Socialist Party and named itself the Jewish Socialist Farband.

2. Yiddish for "mud."

3. A communally funded Jewish school at the elementary level.

4. See note 1.

5. The Soviet secret police, established in 1917 but reorganized as the GPU in 1922. Khanin's use of the name "Cheka" is therefore anachronistic.

48

Building Communism in the Ukraine (interview, 1981–1982)

MAX GRANICH

Born on New York City's Lower East Side, Max Granich (1896–1987) was the younger brother of Michael Gold, a leading Communist literary critic and author of the popular novel *Jews without Money* (1930). Between 1930 and 1946, Granich worked as the chauffer to Earl Browder, the Communist Party's general secretary. The following account of Granich's 1931 trip to the Soviet Union is taken from his previously unpublished memoir.

I arrived in Leningrad on December 1st, 1931. There were winter skies in Leningrad, you have an everlasting mid-night there during that period, so in wandering the streets, wet with snow, slushy, no lights, no store fronts lit so you look in the windows to see what they were selling and we saw cheeses but no foods and in another shop it looked like second hand clothes. But you saw shabby poverty in the streets, the buildings and the people, because in 1931 they were suffering a famine period and this was the end of the first five year plan and all the food products and production was exported to pay for their machinery. It was a dim and depressing [city] that we stepped into. I stepped into something else. I was not an intourist subject so they did not take care of me and actually I had to beg my way from the boat to get into the city and the question was where do I sleep. I couldn't speak a word of Russian so one of the workers on the ship who was also a traveler and said "look, I've got a room, come up and sleep with us" and I slept on the floor that night in my clothes and the next day I took the train to Moscow. In Moscow, I made contact immediately and started to work. The letters of introduction from Mike[1] were people who were writers, working on international literature at the time. One woman was an English expert following all English writers and writing articles about them for the magazine *International Literature*. She was very active in helping me because she admired Mike. She managed to get me a job in an automobile factory there as assistant production manager. Anna Louise Strong[2] was to do this kind of liaison work for the incoming Americans; to help them get a place to live and jobs. I didn't know her, I met her later on. And much later she talked about building a house on our farm in Vermont. It was fortunate that she didn't because she was difficult to get along with, she was so imperialist. In fact, her arrest in the Soviet Union came about because as a friend of Stalin's she refused to accept the order that no foreigner could travel on the trans-Siberian Railroad at that particular time as they were probably doing something special. She got a certain distance up the line where she was arrested and sent back to Moscow. She provoked this entire action.

In Moscow I visited the sites, Lenin's Tomb in particular, which I never got to see because the lines were too long. I got well acquainted with a Russian engineer who came to America early for an education in engineering and when the Russian Revolution broke he went back to the Soviet Union. He was a revolutionary even before he returned to the Soviet Union. He was a personal friend of Earl Browder's and had dinner there once a week. And I really got to know him in Moscow. He was also the translator for the first trial of the English engineers who established a number of power stations in the Soviet Union. Sam Kogan was the translator and after the first session I questioned him and he said they were lying so much that they were blushing while answering. They were accused of sabotage and you could see the guilt written on their faces. They had established good engineering power plants but then what they did was brought out one or two Russians in the plant to do their dirty work. What happened was this: there were about 6 plants established, one plant would break down for repairs because something happened. All kinds of things could happen like putting sand in a flute, it would cause trouble etc., so that would mean replacements and shut down. Then when two or three of these plants started breaking down the Russians started looking into the matter and after making thorough checks they discovered the guys who were doing the dirty work and the Russians confessed that they had taken money from the Britishers. It was a deliberate scheme on the part of the company, part of the anti-communism to make the operation costly and break down. The Englishmen were arrested, tried and found guilty. Then international politics got involved and some restitution was made and the engineers were expelled from the country.

Kogan was working for a sub-rock crushing plant to build railroads. [. . .] He told me to examine the blueprints, this is while I was still in Moscow. So I spent a week doing this and some of it seemed repetitious. I went to Sam and he told me that I was just to follow the blueprints. I didn't know until later that he too knew that the plans were wrong. These were German plans that the Russians worked over and 2 of the 10 engineers who saw the plans refused to sign them and Sam was one of the two. Later, the other engineer who refused to sign was picked up as a Trotskyite. And then they realized that Sam had also refused to sign and O.K. these prints and he was also picked up, and arrested. This was in 1933.

Browder came over about this time and we thought he would go to bat for Sam because they had been good friends in America. Actually, Browder didn't lift a finger in his behalf. Browder was protecting his own secure position and that didn't include someone who was accused of Trotskyism. Sam spent three years in Siberia and returned and he was a slight man and the hardships of Siberia living with poor food, there was practically no food in this famine period and he was a broken individual and lived about 6 more months. Sam was never a Trotskyite, never. His revolutionary integrity was profound in this man's make up, and I knew this well.

Anna Louise Strong was put in jail once for three days and when she came out she said her great fear was what they might do to her. But they so terrorized her and she feared the K.G.B. and she left for the States and never went back to the Soviet Union. That fear was prevalent, it was tangible, you could almost touch it and yet on my railroad job at Magidigorsk I had occasion to find some piping. And in order to get the pipes I needed I had to get permission from the K.G.B. and I got permission and later on when I traveled back this same man was on the train and we had a nice conversation going back. This was a train that had three levels of bunks in each car and a box car and the peasants would bring their bundles into the car and occupy a level. It was freezing cold outside and they had stoves going in the car and it was hot and steamy and this K.G.B. man got me a seat by yanking a peasant out of the way.

The job I was doing was the instillation of all the equipment in a rock crushing plant. We had a 10 ton rock crusher to drop into a pit 21 ft. below ground and that was a big chore, because I had been sent the wrong size wrench. I figured out a way to do it with railroad ties and we gradually went down 21 feet and got it in place. It was one helluva job.

I did everything on that job to protect the workers in spite of some of the wrong equipment that was sent to us.

When I left that job at a farewell talk that I was making to the 40 workers a young man got up and said he had been on a number of jobs in the Soviet Union and in one of the jobs he saw 7 men killed by somebody's carelessness and this was a job that was much more dangerous and no one was hurt because our boss really cared about our safety. [. . .]

Since I was a model worker, a farmer we helped wanted to reward me and all we had to eat at that time was a bowl of soup with black bread and a dumpling in the soup. That dumpling must have been made out of weed seeds and tasted like no grain I had ever tasted in my life and as I was eating it I was getting indigestion but being a foreigner and our host trying to please me and being very rewarding for what I had done and insisted on another and I suffered thru half of it to show my appreciation and that was all I could take. The next day when we went to work I was just useless. Actually, I developed dysentery in the Ukraine, I was so weak and I would come to work and lay on a board and make sketches as to what had to be done, and Ilia, my assistant, handed out the sketches to each group and we accomplished the job.

I projected 70 odd rock crushing plants around the Soviet Union. I worked on the first pair and there were two more in the works at the same time. All four of these were wrong because of the process I objected to at the beginning and the others were just as bad.

The one in the Ural mountains was [a] monster of a plant and when we had completed one half of it that was stopped because the original geological survey was incorrect and we were putting the plant on the wrong mountain. And it would have been prohibitive. Whether it was inefficiency or stupidity or plain carelessness, I don't know it may have also been the fear of questioning a superior. But these were costly mistakes. [. . .]

I came back to Moscow after Siberia because the job was stopped. And I was given another job by the same Trust. They had a feeder line of trucks to load and unload box cars from the railroad to take the materials to the villages and out of the 30 trucks they had only 3 were operable all the time. The trucks were always breaking down. I was introduced to the manager of the place, a Tartar, and then I didn't see him for weeks on end. He just left the workers to their own devices. So I went around to the workers asking why the failure of so many trucks and the one thing I learned quickly was that the springs were manufactured on the place and just couldn't take the bad roads. So I went to the country blacksmith, a man who had a forge and knew how to work iron and we would have steel plates ¼ thick and then we would try to forge them and bend them to shape. And actually [after] the first bump the truck hit the steel just flattened out. So the blacksmith had a constant job of hammering out steel springs. I went to a German-Russian Institute there where they were teaching about steel. I asked them if they would make springs for us out of steel and we couldn't pay them but we could pay them in transportation and they agreed. I came back and told the blacksmith to send our model springs over to the German-American Institute. Well, for the first time in a month and a half I saw my boss the Tartar and he came at me and said "who the hell are you to give orders around here?" And I said "you haven't been here even to talk to" and he exclaimed he'd been a party member for 13 years and "who are you? Just an American worker to come here." I left and went to see Sam, and told him the situation and he said "you know Manny, no foreigner could have an official position to do what you're doing." And I said, "I know what I can do, I'm going home" and that's when I left the Soviet Union. There was no sense in my trying to buck that kind of ignorance. [...]

The difficulties in the Soviet Union manifested [themselves] in different ways; in fact when I came back from Siberia I was advised to sleep on my shoes or they might be stolen. And when I bought a garland of onions where there was a great shortage in Moscow, I also slept on those for three nights. The tensions of Soviet living at the time created a lot of neurotic youngsters under the pressure of doing their jobs and being a good soviet citizen. The lines in the food shops were very long and time and again before you would reach the counter they would be out of food so you traveled from shop to shop to try to get food. It was hardship, hardship and hardship plus the friction of people under such pressure in their jobs alone. You would hear of all kinds of difficulties of even two people working in the same office and it was constant.

Two youngsters I knew there at the particular period committed suicide. I saw enough though in the Soviet Union that when I returned to the States I joined the Communist Party. Because key workers in different plants, workers I saw and talked to had a vision of what the future could be and that they did own the factory they worked in. [...] I got the feeling that the people were hopeful.

Source: Max Granich, "Political Awakening," c. 1981–1982, Oral History Transcript, Grace Maul Granich and Max Granich Papers, box 1, Tamiment Library, New York University.

NOTES

1. Granich's brother, Michael Gold (1894–1967).

2. Anna Louise Strong (1885–1970), left-wing writer and journalist. During the 1920s and '30s, Strong lived half of each year in the Soviet Union, where she reported on various issues having to do with the Bolshevik state and, especially, Soviet women.

49

"G.P.U. Intrigues in America" (1938)

VANGUARD

Anarchists, though small in number by the 1930s, ranked among the most vocal opponents of Soviet Communism. The following editorial warns against Soviet agents operating in the United States and exposes their possible involvement in the disappearance of Juliet Poyntz, a trade-union activist and former Communist leader. Poyntz's disappearance remains unsolved to this day.

That the G.P.U.[1] maintains its spies in foreign countries has been known to many, but it was generally assumed that their main activities centered upon the tasks of informing on and denouncing each other or keeping track of the latest Moscow line. But several occurrences in the past few years have revealed the astonishing and horrible fact that the Stalinist octopus has extended its tentacles far beyond the courtroom walls and the G.P.U. dungeons of Moscow. Its human victims are seized on the shores of Geneva, on the Barricades of Barcelona, even on the streets of New York, and transported to the inky black hell of the "Socialist Fatherland." No more can any revolutionist or truly honest liberal sit back complacently and view the degenerate regime from the distance. Once safety from Moscow was measured by the distance from that unhappy paradise. Today we are faced with the astonishing fact that no one anywhere, who is too well-informed, is safe from Stalin's international gangsters.

The recent case of Robinson-Rubens and the disappearance of Miss Juliet Stuart Pointz reveal the methods of the G.P.U.; how the Moscow trials are prepared, how witnesses and "confessions" may be obtained and how undesirables are disposed of.

Stalin prepares his trials not only with the purpose of disposing of enemies, shifting blame to the shoulders of unfortunate rivals, future and past, for the mistakes of his regime, but with the view also of influencing foreign policy and setting the stage for military alliances. It is no secret that he fervently hopes for such an alliance with the U.S. against Japan. If the foreign office cannot do it, then maybe the G.P.U. can? The intrigue apparently involves a cooked-up Japanese plot against America and the unfortunate confessors will be the Fascist agents of Japan—the Robinson-Rubens couple.

But the facts that have been revealed have exploded the well laid plans of the bureaucracy. Many months ago the Soviet government let it be known that they were seeking for a Robinson couple. The couple obliged and arrived at Moscow, leaving America as the Rubens and coming into the U.S.S.R., for the benefit of the G.P.U., as the Robinsons. That they were G.P.U. agents, being sacrificed may be incontrovertibly shown:

They applied for birth certificates in the name of long dead children and used an address on 17th St., N.Y., which was the hangout of Stalinists and G.P.U. agents. They obtained their passports thru the intervention of one Sharfin, a member of Section 15, Bronx C.P. [Communist Party]. The passports were received in care of Helen Ravitch, also a communist in the Drama Travel League, who is the wife of Dr. S. Bernstein, personal physician to William Z. Foster, communist leader, and to the Stalinist I.W.O.[2] The G.P.U. got them faked passports—and their friends described them as "communists." Mr. Alfred Bingham, editor of *Common Sense*, has received a letter from a close friend of Mrs. Rubens who was a fanatical communist. Mrs. Rubens participated in communist unemployed demonstrations and was hauled into court for her activities. And to add the appearance of authenticity to the trial the couple visited the West Coast where Japan would presumably have its interest centered and saw the sights of Mexico so that Trotzky could be implicated. Thus the plot was laid. The conduct of the Soviet authorities offers further evidence. First came the denials and the affirmation of the arrest. After much pressure and delay an "interview" was guaranteed to the American *attaché*, in which Mrs. Rubens refused American aid. But to Moscow's dismay, the woman has definitely been established as an American citizen, and as a result the case was investigated by the U.S. government.

Juliet Stuart Pointz' disappearance has not received the attention from the press nor from the radicals and "liberals" that it should have. Why are the latter silent about her? Where is Juliet Pointz?

Startling circumstantial evidence indicates that Miss Pointz was either kidnapped or lured to Russia from New York by agents of the G.P.U.

The woman was an outstanding Stalinist leader, for years serving as a connecting link between the American Communist Party and Moscow. Miss Pointz held an important position in the G.P.U. and when her loyalty to Stalin waned a short time ago, the bureaucracy feared she would disclose some of the secret methods of Moscow. Juliet Stuart Pointz disappeared on or about June 5th, 1937. *Her disappearance aroused no public interest on the part of the Communist Party. A high official of the Party even denied that she was known to the Party!*

Associated with Miss Pointz in her G.P.U. activities were several other agents who could probably shed much light on her disappearance. One [was] George Mink, late Philadelphia taxi driver and petty crook, latter G.P.U. chief in Barcelona, under the name of Alfred Hertz, carrying a faked American passport. Mink had been named as the assassin of Camilo Berneri and Barbieri by Carlo Tresca[3] on the basis of conclusive evidence presented by our comrades of the C.N.T.-F.A.I.[4] in Spain. Miss Pointz was seen with Mink as late as 1936 in Moscow. Another G.P.U. agent who was in the company of Miss Pointz *the week of her disappearance* and an ideal man to do the "job" because he had known her for many years, (it was he who had first introduced her to the Communist Party) was Schachno Epstein, former editor of the Communist Yiddish daily, *Freiheit*.

Before the Russian Revolution, Epstein was an editor of *Gerechtigkeit*, the Yiddish organ of the International Ladies Garment Workers union. Miss Pointz was then employed in the same union and the two were intimate friends. When the revolution broke out Epstein went to Russia, joined the Communists to save his neck and was sent back to America as Joseph Berson. Later he became editor of the *Freiheit*. In two or three years he was recalled to Russia. As it happens to anyone in the Russian system who can be of use, accusations are made, confessions given and, before this modern era of mass murder, exile and recantation, would usually be the sequence of events. Thus Epstein was denounced as a Trotzkyite and after a short period of exile he became an agent of the G.P.U. as the price for his liberty and life, ready to do whatever they bid, just as the unfortunate Robinson-Rubens couple.

Miss Pointz returned from Moscow in 1936 disillusioned and therefore dangerous to the Party. It is only natural that her life long friend, Epstein, should be given a new "job." He was seen in her company by several persons just prior to her disappearance.

On August 17th, 1937, Epstein sailed from America on the "Queen Mary." He told Julius Hochmah, general manager of the Dressmakers Joint Board of the I.L.G.W.U., who was traveling in the same boat that he was going back and forth from Russia to keep valid his American Citizenship status as Schachno Epstein. The list of passengers published by the "Queen Mary" showed no such name. It is a fact that he was traveling under the name of

Stone—with a false passport. (Stone was on the list.) In the Jewish circles of the United States where he worked he is also known as Stone. The day that Carlo Tresca appeared before the Grand Jury, *The Jewish Daily Forward* published the name of Schachno Epstein in connection with the Pointz case. It seems that the *Forward* is not afraid of any comeback from Epstein. One of the editors of that paper has stated that a leading member of the Communist Party has told him that the charges in connection with this matter are true and that the facts are known in Communist Party circles in New York City.

Where is Juliet Pointz? That the government is not much concerned we can clearly see and understand. That the Communist Party doesn't evince any interest in her disappearance can have but one explanation. But that thousands of liberals, radicals and organizations like the American Civil Liberties Union and its director Roger Baldwin should have no word of protest is abominable. The safety of the outspoken anti-Stalinists is at stake. Shall Stalin be permitted to extend the terrors of his G.P.U. even to the shores of America? The labor and liberal world owes itself an answer to that question. What shall that answer be?

Source: "G.P.U. Intrigues in America," *Vanguard*, Apr. 1938, pp. 11, 16.

NOTES

1. The Soviet Union's secret police from 1922 to 1934.

2. International Workers Order, a multiethnic fraternal order affiliated with the Communist Party.

3. Carlos Tresca (1879–1943), Italian-born anarchist who spoke out against fascism in his home country of Italy and, later, against Soviet totalitarianism. His assassination in 1943 is believed by many people to have been politically motivated.

4. A confederation of anarchist-syndicalist trade unions in Spain.

50

Fighting Stalinists and Chasing Girls (memoir; 1965)

PAUL JACOBS

The conflict between Communists and followers of Leon Trotsky was among the most bitter in the history of American socialism. While Communists greatly outnumbered their opponents and enjoyed backing by the Soviet Union, Trotskyists viewed themselves as the true standard-bearers of the Bolshevik Revolution. With characteristic irreverence, Paul Jacobs (see document 5) recounts the hothouse atmosphere inside the Trotskyist movement during the 1930s.

All of the headquarters looked alike and had the same general atmosphere. On the wall hung large pictures of Marx and Engels, sometimes flanked by photos of Rosa Luxemburg and Karl Liebknecht, the martyrs of the 1918–19 German revolution. But the places of honor on the walls of our headquarters were always reserved for a picture or drawing of Lenin and one of Leon Trotsky. We called Trotsky the Old Man, using the phrase not to refer to his age but to the place he held in our consciousness as the commander of our forces.

The drabness of the rooms (they were always ugly, always painted in the mud-brown color that landlords use to cover up the dirt of an endless procession of tenants who come and go with monotonous regularity) was lightened with posters, first about the German parties fighting the Nazis, later for the Spanish Civil War. Alongside the wall at the back or side of the room a literature table held the pamphlets written by the theoreticians of the movement—Marx, Engels, Lenin, and Trotsky—and these could be looked at and purchased for ten cents or a quarter by neophytes like me. On the table, too, were copies of the organization's newspaper, its monthly magazine, and the mimeographed bulletins put out by the various other branches or committees. And during the internal factional fights, which at that time were beginning to engross the attention of all the Trotskyists, the detailed and to me very bewildering political documents of the contending groups could be picked up from the literature table, to be argued over during meetings or over cups of coffee as we adjourned to sit in a nearby cafeteria.

Folding chairs were always kept along walls of the headquarters and brought out for the meetings. Up front at a table the branch chairman conducted the business of the meetings. One corner always contained a hand-operated mimeograph machine and an old typewriter used to cut the stencils for it. And everywhere there were ashtrays, for all of us seemed to smoke so much that by the end of each meeting a blue-gray haze hung over the badly ventilated rooms.

The routine of the meeting was a reasonably fixed one. We would drift into the hall at roughly the time the meeting was scheduled to begin, greeting each other as "comrade," a salutation I used very self-consciously at first until it ultimately became a familiar part of my vocabulary. We stood or sat in little circles, perhaps looking over the new literature or discussing the latest change in someone's political position. Often a comrade would bring a "sympathizer" or "contact" to the meeting to be introduced to the other members. A subtle distinction existed between these two categories, relating to the degree of involvement in the movement. A contact was someone rather new to either the movement or the organization, who had shown some definite sign of interest but was still an unknown quantity. A sympathizer was a person more definitely committed to the group but unwilling or unable, usually for personal reasons, to take the final step of joining and accepting the discipline imposed on members.

Soon after I moved from the stage of being a contact to the status of sympathizer, and then on to actual formal membership, I discovered that being a Trotskyist in New York during the thirties was something akin to having leprosy during the Middle Ages. We were hated and despised by almost every other political group, we were political pariahs, always on the defensive against the vicious onslaughts of the Stalinists, who had taken over control of the world communist movement and its periphery of front organizations. And since the popular front became a successful tactic of the Communist party in 1935, the party influence over liberal organizations grew so great that we Trotskyists ended up as political outcasts.

But in a way, I think, we also glorified this role, for the isolation forced on us nurtured the attitude that we were the chosen ones, the true martyrs of the Revolution, the only pure inheritors of the Bolshevik tradition established by Lenin and Trotsky during the glorious days of the Russian Revolution.

Our pariah status and defensiveness had another consequence: Trotskyists were the best educated, politically, among the socialist and revolutionary groups. Because we had no long native tradition to sustain us, as did the members of the Socialist party, and no powerful motherland to look to, as the Communists did to the Soviet Union, we were thrown completely back upon our own resources and our intelligences to defend the correctness of our line. This meant that a young Trotskyist like me not only was supposed to study constantly what was happening in the world, but, equally important, was expected to know the complete history of the Russian Revolution in some detail and be able to argue, in a loud voice, about what had happened in China in 1927, in Bulgaria in 1919, in France in 1934, and even sometimes in America.

So out of necessity we became experts, prodigies, the Townsend Harris[1] boys of the revolutionary movement, able to quote the line and page in Lenin or Marx that justified the Trotskyist view of the world. [. . .]

For years Trotskyists were devils incarnate to the Communists, the horrible boogie men out of their childhood. Most Communists believed the lies they were told about the Trotskyists, and they acted on those beliefs with all the fervor they could muster. If they did have any doubts about Trotskyist villainy, they learned quickly to suppress them, lest their whole life pattern collapse. (The most pathetic of the ex-Communists are those who had to hear Khrushchev say it before they finally conceded, grudgingly, the truth about what the Trotskyists had maintained all along about the Moscow trials. However I have never heard of one of them coming now to an ex-Trotskyist and apologizing in any way for the personal lies and slander they spread.)

As part of my education as a Trotskyist, I learned to despise the Communists as ignorant, slavish followers of Stalin, people who betrayed the revolutionary tradition over and over again in the interests of Soviet foreign policy. "Our line's been changed again" we sang at all our parties as a popular parody of the Communist positions; the song described in hilarious detail the flip-flops made by the American Communists to keep up with the sometimes sudden changes in the policies of the Soviet Union. And I know a girl from a Trotskyist family who as a child was brought up believing that the name of the Soviet dictator wasn't just Stalin but "Stalinthebutcher," always shouted as one word, and a curse word at that.

We had bitter political fights within the Trotskyist group, too, often conducted in pretty abusive terms, but always a sharp distinction was made between such quarrels within the family, so to speak, and those we had with the Stalinists. [. . .] And so, slowly over the months I learned that although the Ohler-Stamm minority faction of the Trotskyists, to which I belonged, denounced the Cannon-Schachtman majority group, and while later Ohler broke with Stamm and Cannon split with Schachtman, all of them believed the Stalinists to be permanent betrayers of the revolution.

These factional fights were always going on within the Trotskyist organization, often leading to splits and the formation of new groups. The process was a form of political mitosis as each splitting group in turn gave birth to another split, but there was one important difference between body cells and Trotskyist factions; in physical life, division is a process of growth, while among the Trotskyists the over-all number of members remained fixed even as the number of groups proliferated, which meant that each new one was even smaller than its parents. The issues which brought about these solemn splits were extremely complicated even for the politically sophisticated comrades, and so were usually completely incomprehensible to me, a neophyte. I couldn't understand the issues at the time, for I was still learning the differences between "democratic centralism" as the Trotskyists used it and as a Stalinist description. I was trying out a wholly new and bewildering vocabulary and at the same time pretending to a degree of political sophistication far above my capacities. But despite my real ignorance of the issues, I represented a vote in my branch, for once a comrade was accepted into membership, the assumption was that he was immediately as capable of making political decisions as any of the old-timers who had been in the movement for years.

My becoming an Ohlerite, as members of the Ohler-Stamm group were called, was less related to the superior revolutionary merits of the group's position than to geography. In the branch of the Spartacus Youth League to which I was assigned because of where I lived, the Ohlerite group was in the minority, and I have never liked majorities. Then again, it may simply have been that the Ohlerites in my branch were nicer to me than were the Cannonites. Anyway, the only sharp recollection I have of this fight, which engrossed the complete attention of the organization for months, is one of Max Schachtman, the witty opposition leader, demolishing Ohler in a memorably succinct speech delivered late one night at a crowded meeting hall in lower Manhattan.

The meeting was held at the climax of the faction fight, when it seemed certain the organization was moving toward a split. Ohler, an undistinguished-looking man who spoke in an even dull monotone, never raising or lowering his voice, had been talking for more than two hours when finally he wound up with what, for him, was a stirring peroration: "Do you want our party to be nourished on the right breast of opportunism or the left breast of revolutionary Marxism?" he asked, and took his seat on the platform.

As Schachtman stood up to deliver the attack of the majority, he looked around the jammed room and shrewdly estimated the inability of the comrades to absorb any more vocal punishment. "Comrades, to be perfectly frank with you, comrades, I don't really care whether our party is nourished on the right breast of opportunism or the left breast of revolutionary Marxism, just so long, comrades, just so long as it's not nourished on another organ for which God intended a different purpose." A roar of laughter went up from the hall, Max impishly stared at Ohler and then sat down as the meeting broke up. A few weeks later the split did take place and the Ohler-Stamm group organized its own party, the Revolutionary Workers League, proclaimed to be the only true interpreter of Marx, Lenin, and Trotsky.

But despite the continuous splits that divided the Trotskyists—always, the splitters assured each other, on questions of the highest principles—all the groups maintained a loose amorphous common identity. If the Ohlerites gave a party, the Marlenites—all seven of them—came. The leader of the Marlenites was Marlen, of course, who had constructed his party name from the first syllables of Marx and Lenin. I have no idea, any longer, of what esoteric differences separated the Marlen group from the other Trotskyists, but they must have been important ones to him and his immediate family, who made up the bulk of his group.

Yet despite the sharp political differences that separated us from the Communists we were culturally dependent upon the Communists and their web of peripheral and supporting organizations, for the American Trotskyist movement had no folk-singing groups, no foreign-language associations, no fraternal orders, no hiking clubs, no classes in drama, nor any of the varied other activities which made the "What's Doing" column in the *Daily Worker* so long every day.

The "What's Doing" column was an important part of our daily reading, even though we were Trotskyists. If we wanted to see a movie about the Russian Revolution, we had to go to the Cameo Theatre on Fourteenth Street, where we would sit in the balcony, cracking sunflower seeds with our teeth, and giggle at the more blatant examples of Stalinist propaganda. Sometimes, as when the screen showed a Russian girl falling asleep to dream of a luminous fatherly Stalin tossing her baby high in his arms and chucking it under the chin, we would laugh—but always surreptitiously, lest some of the Stalinist faithful in the downstairs section hear us and come up to start a fight. But we thrilled at the heroics in Eisenstein's *Potemkin* and, no matter how often I saw it, the scene in *Chapayev* when the Red Army finally overcomes the White Russians always sent shivers through my body. So, too, when the proletarian heroes, the union members and organizers, rushed out onto the stage in the last scene of the plays presented by the New Theatre League at the old civic Repertory Theatre, I responded just as viscerally as did any Communist.

Occasionally, if we were really daring, we would go to a social event sponsored by a Young Communist League branch or a Communist party front group. The trick was to find such an event far enough away from our normal area of activity to prevent the likelihood of being recognized as Trotskyists. Then, we would try to make it with the YCL girls, pretending to be potential sympathizers of the group and always hoping that the evening would end up in bed. Of course there was a risk, for if a Trotskyist was recognized at a Communist social event, he was almost certain to be shoved around, and possibly even beaten.

But the party hopping was always pretty dull, for almost always the YCL girls turned out to be nice Jewish girls with thick legs and bad skins. Even worse, most of them had the same ideas of virtue held by nice Jewish girls who weren't in the movement. The only place that offered a reasonable chance of willing Communist girls, or so I was told, was a Communist camp near New York called Nitgedaiget.[2] There, if you were foolhardy enough to risk a week end and could successfully pass yourself off as a party sympathizer, you might end up in someone else's sleeping bag or bunk, discussing the terrible Trotskyists.

Source: Paul Jacobs, *Is Curly Jewish? A Political Self-Portrait Illuminating Three Turbulent Decades of Social Revolt, 1935–1965* (New York: Atheneum, 1965).

NOTES
  1. An elite public high school in New York City.
  2. Yiddish: "not worried."

51

The Murder of Ehrlich and Alter (1943)

THE NEW INTERNATIONAL

The New International represented an unusual perspective on the American Left. The journal, published by the Workers' Party (founded in 1940), celebrated the Bolshevik Revolution and its leaders, Vladimir Lenin and Leon Trotsky, yet condemned Stalin's Russia as a totalitarian country dominated by a new bureaucratic ruling class. One of the many Soviet crimes denounced by *The New International*—and by virtually all segments of the anti-Soviet Left—was the execution of Henryk Ehrlich and Victor Alter, leaders of the Bund in Poland.

The Stalinist crimes against the international labor movement have not ceased with Hitler's invasion of Russia. Nor has the preoccupation with the greatest war in Russian history eliminated murder as a political weapon in the labor movement by the infamous regime of Cain Stalin. This was once more brought to light with the announcement, a few weeks ago, that Henryk Ehrlich and Victor Alter, leaders of the Jewish Workers Party of Poland,[1] seized by the GPU when the Red Army invaded Poland, were secretly executed as agents of Hitler's Gestapo!

The mystery of this case was cleared up when William Green, president of the American Federation of Labor, announced to the press that, in response to his inquiries over an extended period of time, he was informed by the Russian Ambassador, Litvinov, of the execution of the two Jewish socialists. Green had, on the "advice" of the State Department, kept this information to himself. War exigencies, don't you know!

Following Green's announcement, many things were disclosed, all of them pointing to the utter perfidiousness of the Kremlin regime. A mere chronological detailing of the circumstances following the arrests are sufficient to properly assess the nature of this latest Stalinist frameup.

Ehrlich and Alter were seized four years ago. Their arrest undoubtedly was one of the results of the Hitler-Stalin pact. They were "left" social-democrats who, throughout their lives, retained adherence to the general principles of Marxism. They were confused centrists rather than revolutionary internationalists. But, guided by their own concepts of the socialist struggle, they were in direct conflict with Stalinism and all that its reactionary nationalist doctrines signify. Ehrlich's and Alter's attempt to organize resistance in Warsaw to the German invader and their general anti-fascist activity in that particular period, led to their incarceration by the GPU. Furthermore, they were arrested as part of Stalin's policy to destroy the whole pre-war Polish labor movement as inimical to his interests.

The announcement that Ehrlich, a member of the Labor and Socialist International, and Alter, a member of the executive committee of the Trade Union Congress, were arrested by Stalin, led to the formation of many international committees to seek their release. In this country, a committee headed by William Green, Philip Murray,[2] Dr. Albert Einstein and Raymond Gram Swing,[3] repeatedly intervened without result. Wendell Willkie,[4] while in Moscow, pleaded in vain with Russian officials for their freedom. The intervention of Eleanor Roosevelt and countless other personages brought not the slightest concession from Stalin's hangman.

Material aid was sent to Ehrlich and Alter, but there was no visible evidence that the food and money ever reached their proper destination. It was quite possible that they were already executed when this aid was sent. Certainly they were already dead while many pleas for their release were made. But the Kremlin, by calculated silence, gave no sign as to the fate of its prisoners.

The first release which announced the execution of Ehrlich and Alter stated that they were murdered more than a year ago. This was later denied by Litvinov, who volunteered the information that they were executed only four months previous to the information given in a letter to William Green. No one will really know exactly when the deed was done. But that can only shed light on the cynicism of the murderous regime as it is reflected in their particular case. The thing to be remembered is the deed itself.

The execution of Ehrlich and Alter followed the typical GPU pattern. According to Szmul Zygielbojm,[5] one of the leaders of the Jewish Workers Party of Poland, and a member of the Polish National Council, they were kept in prison for nearly two years without formal charge and with no apparent disposition of their case. In July, 1941, six weeks after the German invasion of Russia, they were court-martialed under the charge of "working for the forces of international fascist reaction." It was under this charge that they were first sentenced to death. While awaiting execution in the death cells of Moscow and Saratov, they were informed that their death sentence had been commuted to ten years' penal servitude.

But, in September, 1941, following the signing of the Polish-Russian pact, they were released with apologies of the government. A terrible mistake had been made, said the agents of the GPU. The charges against them were false! Ehrlich himself had described what happened following their release. They were given residence "in the best hotel and a complete set of clothes, and were placed under medical care. Most important of all, we were assured that the action taken against us was a mistake and that our collaboration in the fight against Hitlerism is a necessity both with regard to the interests of the USSR and to those of the Jewish nation and Poland."

Following their release and the apology, the Kremlin sought their services. A Colonel Wolkowsky of the Commissariat of the Interior, proposed to them that they should organize in Russia a Jewish committee to fight Hitlerism on a world scale. Ehrlich and Alter agreed to this since, in general, they found themselves sympathetic to the Russian war against Germany.

According to their agreement with the government, Ehrlich was to act as a chairman of this committee, Alter as secretary, and a Russian artist named Nichoels as vice-chairman. The head of the GPU, Beria, invited Ehrlich and Alter to a special conference at which they discussed the work of this committee. The latter were then invited to send their material and proposals to Stalin, which they did. It was necessary to do this, they were advised, in order to get official sanction from the "good father" in the Kremlin.

But, according to Stalin, it was after their release that they began agitating for a peace with Hitler!—at the very time they were being wined and dined in Moscow and in the midst of the organization of the previously mentioned Jewish committee to fight Hitlerism! And at the very time that they were presumably agitating for this peace, they were evacuated, together with all other government officials and workers, to the temporary capital of Kuibyshev.

Last December, according to the latest evidence, they were called to pay a visit to the Commissariat of the Interior. They never came back!

Why then were Ehrlich and Alter murdered? The reasons are several, although it is impossible to know all the facts at this time. Stalin was taking revenge on two anti-Stalinist socialists! Stalin is preparing for the seizure of Poland if the United Nations are victorious in the war. Ehrlich and Alter, by their past, are committed to an "independent Poland," which, whatever its character, Stalin is determined to prevent. Their murder was, therefore, insurance for the future. It was a political murder.

In an effort to make the execution more palatable, it is necessary for Stalin to besmirch these two men, to create an amalgam. Thus, Ehrlich and Alter, two Jewish labor and social democratic leaders, are linked to Hitler and the German Gestapo! The *Daily Worker*, following the lead of its GPU master, called them "pro-Nazis." One can expect almost any day that the "intuitionist" ex-Ambassador Davies, as William Henry Chamberlain called him, will include this incident in a revised edition of *Mission to Moscow* and in the motion picture version of the book. To complete the "realism" of this charge, he might even show that Ehrlich and Alter received money from the Gestapo in a synagogue. This is all that is needed to complete the Stalinist frameup against these two men.

Ehrlich and Alter, leaders of a movement and a people which have been butchered by the Nazi barbarians, opponents of fascism to their last days were murdered by Stalin on the charge that they were German agents. Need anything more be said?

Source: "Murder as a Political Weapon," *The New International: A Monthly Organ of Revolutionary Marxism*, Mar. 1943, pp. 69–70.

NOTES

1. I.e., the Bund.
2. Philip Murray (1886–1952), president of the Congress of Industrial Organizations.
3. Raymond Gram Swing (1887–1968), popular radio journalist.
4. Wendell Wilkie (1892–1944), lawyer and prominent member of the Republican Party.
5. On May 12, 1943, Szmul Zygielbojm (1895–1943) committed suicide in London in protest against the indifference and inaction of the Allied powers toward the Nazi extermination of the Jews.

52

The Soviet Union Reappraised (1956)

JEWISH LIFE

In February 1956, Soviet Premier Nikita Khrushchev delivered a four-hour speech to the Communist Party Congress detailing crimes committed by Joseph Stalin. This led to the publication of an article in Poland's Communist Yiddish daily denouncing Soviet anti-Semitism and the suppression of Yiddish culture. The American Yiddish Communist daily *Di morgn frayhayt* reprinted the article, and a translation soon appeared in *Jewish Life*, a monthly magazine published under the Yiddish daily's auspices. Thus began a long, painful process of reevaluation and self-reflection among Jewish Communists. In 1958, *Jewish Life* reorganized itself as *Jewish Currents* and moved away from the Communist Party.

The wiping out of Soviet Jewish culture, confirmed in the past few months, horrified us. The revelations also impose obligations upon us. Why did this magazine in the past eight years fail to raise questions concerning the shutting down of Jewish cultural institutions in the Soviet Union? Why did we not suspect foul play in the disappearance of leading Soviet Yiddish writers?[1] Why did we not detect the anti-Semitism injected in the Prague trial?[2]

Answers to these questions constitute our form of apology to our readers for having failed them in these important respects.

We feel sorrow and resentment—but these are not enough. Understanding and perspective are just as necessary. What is the significance of the injustices against the Jews in the Soviet Union for the continuing fight for peace, which is central for all people? What are the prospects for a revival of Jewish culture in the Soviet Union?

To regard these anti-Semitic manifestations in isolation from the evil condition of which they were one expression would be a distortion. For not only were the crimes committed against Jews. Other nations and nationalities also suffered from the one-man rule that afflicted the Soviet Union for some 20 years. These manifestations, so harmful to the East European countries, were profoundly anti-socialist in character, for they violated socialist principles of democracy and equality.

The leaders of the socialist countries are taking steps not only to repair whatever damage can be remedied, but also to avoid recurrence of these evils. Our anguish and anger do not blind us to the efforts made during the past three years to uncover the malignant growth on a state that is advancing the cause of peace and equality of peoples. The disclosures by the socialist countries themselves of anti-national and undemocratic practices are signs of the determination to prevent a recurrence of the evils exposed.

But why were we so insensitive to anti-Semitism as to ignore or to deny outright the reports published in the press about measures taken against Jews and Jewish culture in the Soviet Union in the five years before 1953?

It is true that no authentic information from any original socialist source was forthcoming. We did know, however, that all Jewish cultural institutions in the Soviet Union outside of Birobidjan[3] were closed down after 1948 and that the flow of literature from Soviet Yiddish writers ceased. This should have been enough to arouse insistent questions that should have been expressed and pressed. For such drastic cutting off of cultural expression could not be justified. If, as we privately speculated, some Jewish writers may have violated Soviet law, could this have justified the wiping out of a whole culture? The answer is obviously no. It should have been apparent then and expressed publicly. The reasons why this wasn't done will be discussed later.

Again, why did we not perceive that the campaign against "cosmopolitanism," which was directed preponderantly against Jews, was a thinly disguised form of anti-Semitism? Most people suppose that the idea of "cosmopolitanism" was thought up recently in the Soviet Union. But it was in fact a leading idea of the Russian revolutionary democratic literary critic V. G. Belinsky in the mid-nineteenth century. He polemicized against Russian writers of his time who slavishly looked for inspiration to foreign literature as their model and held their own national literature in contempt. This concept was applied in the Soviet Union during the cold war to polemicize against those who were according to the critics, in their writing, expressing pro-imperialist attitudes in the cold war. Critics of "cosmopolitanism" maintained that such writing became an instrument in the United States' attempts at world economic and political domination.

Speaking for ourselves, we were not acquainted with the content of the writings against which this accusing in the Soviet Union was leveled. We could not therefore judge the validity of the charge. But it should have been clear that the predominance of Jewish names in this campaign and the use of Jewish-sounding names in parentheses were anti-Semitic in intent and effect. It is not a matter of pride to us that we did not share in protests but rather tried to explain away the practice.

This magazine erred also in its treatment of the Prague trial of the Slansky[4] group in November 1952. We categorically denied that any anti-Semitism was involved. That we were mistaken has now been proved by the Czech government itself. While the Czech government in April confirmed the validity of the Prague trial, it pointed out several illegitimate aspects of it.

On May 12, the *N.Y. Times* reported a Czech radio broadcast by Premier Siroky stating that Slansky's chief crime was that he used the "cult of personality" to create a special police organization, independent of the Communist Party, for his own purpose and that Slansky had been guilty of "bourgeois nationalism."

Premier V. Siroky said on April 13 that in addition to the falsity of the charges concerning "Titoism," "certain manifestations of anti-Semitism" had been wrongly injected into the trial. Siroky maintained that the distinction between anti-Semitism and anti-Zionism was valid but he declared that the prosecutor in the case was wrong in bringing out that most defendants were Jewish (*N.Y. Times*, April 14).

Designating defendants as being "of Jewish origin" was undoubtedly an anti-Semitic device. In the interrogation of defendant Bedrich Geminder the charge of "cosmopolitanism" because he could not speak Czech without an accent was certainly an anti-Semitic thrust. Sidney Gruson reported (*N.Y. Times*, April 27) that an article in the Czech trade union paper *Prace* admitted that, in Gruson's interpretation of the article, "a wave of officially inspired anti-Semitism swept Czechoslovakia" after the Prague trial. "We went so far," said the author of the *Prace* article, "as to blame people not only for their own sins but also for sins committed by someone belonging to a certain group"— that is, to the Jewish people.

From the Soviet Union, too, there have been intimations of criticism for the criminal treatment of Jews and other nationalities. The *N.Y. Times* reported from Moscow (April 14) that an article in the journal *Voprosi Historii* (Problems of History) recalled Lenin's condemnation of anti-Semitism as "alien to the spirit of the proletariat" and his campaign against "Great Russian chauvinism." The article pointed out that "serious errors in the leadership of the party and country in the post-war period" had resulted in deviations in carrying out "Leninist nationalities policy."

These Soviet acknowledgements of anti-Semitism and of crimes committed against Jews and other peoples are highly significant. They indicate that these crimes were part of an effort to undermine and destroy socialism. They were in no way consonant with socialism. On the contrary, these crimes were contrary to socialist policy toward nationalities and constituted a great danger to socialism itself.

We have sketched some of the grave delinquencies of this magazine. Why, then, did this happen?

Our disbelief of charges of anti-Semitism in socialist countries was based on our belief that the basic socialist policy of equality of nations made highly improbable the brazen violations charged. Like many others we knew that the tsarist "prison house of nations" had been dissolved in the Soviet Union, that formerly oppressed and backward nations had in an incredibly short time developed into modern states and had achieved equality. [. . .]

More specifically, it was well known that all barriers to equality for the Jewish people had been demolished in the Soviet Union. Anti-Semitism itself was outlawed. Educational and vocational opportunity was opened to all Jews. Jews played an important role in Soviet life at all levels and in all fields. Yiddish culture itself flourished. Yiddish literature, theater, schools, and press blossomed in a land where Jews had been ghettoized and oppressed for centuries.

When all this was suddenly stopped in 1948—and this we, like everyone else, knew—it was hard for us to believe that this earlier policy had been discarded. But we had no authentic information beyond the bare fact that the institutions had been shut down. We should have suspected foul play and made a noise about it. Our confidence in the Soviet nationalities policy led us to disbelieve that charges of anti-Semitic intention had a valid basis.

There was another reason why we tended to disbelieve the press reports about anti-Semitism in the Soviet Union. They seemed to us to be, and often were, used as a means of heating up the cold war and of intensifying the anti-communist, anti-democratic, anti-peace hysteria that flourished in our country in those bitter years.

We were fortified in this position by the baseless rumors and downright misrepresentation that accompanied these reports. One of the most brazen of these misrepresentations was the false charge that a cartoon in the Soviet satirical magazine *Krokodil* had in 1949 used the word "*Zhid*," Russian equivalent of our "kike." The truth was that this word in *Krokodil* was the

Russian transliteration of the name of Andre Gide, French writer, in a cartoon lampooning "cosmopolitanism." *Newsweek* actually shadowed over the "Andre" in its reproduction of the cartoon in order to bolster the charge that the epithet "Zhid" was used. Instances of misrepresentation could be multiplied from the files of our magazine, where we often exposed such crude falsifications.

The role of the Soviet Union in saving hundreds of thousands of Jews during the war by evacuating them to the East was scandalously misrepresented by professional anti-Soviet writers. The decisive part played by the Soviet Union and other socialist countries in gaining passage of the UN resolution on the establishment of Israel and in arming Israel to defend itself against the Arab invasion was played down or misrepresented in the interests of the cold war.

Since expounders of the cold war were using reports of the anti-Semitism to further their dangerous aims, we did not wish to do anything that could seem to range us on the side of the enemies of peace. We were not resourceful enough to develop means of inquiry and protest that would have clearly distinguished us from the enemies of peace. We misguidedly held the view that to question the policy of the Soviet Union or to protest its results would harm the cause of peace. We now realize that in fact the cause of peace would have been strengthened, had we followed a more independent and courageous path.

We have stated the causes of our failure to perceive the anti-Semitism that occurred in socialist countries in recent years: we had no authoritative information; we had blind faith in the nationalities policies of the Soviet Union; the provable misrepresentations in some reports of anti-Semitism led us to the extreme of questioning the truth of all of them; and the cold war use to which these reports were put led us to reject them as part of the incitation of world war.

These reasons help to explain but not to excuse our failure to protest the anti-Semitism revealed in some reports and activities that should have been apparent to us.

Yet, the revelation of anti-Semitism and suppression of Jewish culture in the Soviet Union should not distort our understanding of the large degree of freedom gained by Jews under socialism. Jews did win the right to live where they pleased, to equal opportunity in jobs, education and religion. This freedom was gravely undermined by some anti-Semitic elements in the socialist countries and full recovery of these rights is still to be reached. For some years Jews in the Soviet Union suffered from intimidation and anti-Semitism and Yiddish culture was all but obliterated in the Soviet Union. Yet equality of all nationalities is so basic to socialist principles that these crimes were finally admitted by the Soviet leadership itself, and correction undertaken.

It was because socialist theories of equality were basic, however, that anti-Semitism had to be practiced by innuendo and indirection and never directly or overtly. For even while Jews in the USSR were intimidated by the anti-Semitic acts, the socialist policy of equality continued to operate and to be enunciated.

Jack Raymond reported in the *N.Y. Times* (April 15) that 50,000 Jews live in Kishinev, the city of the frightful pogroms early in this century. "An important post-war change in the situation of the Jews," wrote Raymond, "stressed by city officials and confirmed by Jews here, was that they no longer live in a ghetto-like community but are scattered throughout the city. Jews are no longer limited to the old vocations of trade and tailoring. Now Jews can be found side by side with others doing construction and industrial labor."

In addition, information has reached us, which we have published in this magazine, that gives promise of a revival of Jewish cultural activity in the Soviet Union. We have noted that numerous programs of Yiddish songs and writing have been performed in past months in all centers of Jewish population. Yiddish songs have been broadcast on the Moscow radio. About 60 Yiddish writers are active and preparing their work for publication. And for the first time in some years a greeting signed by 14 Soviet Yiddish writers was received in April by the third annual conference of the Jewish Social and Cultural Association of Poland in Warsaw.

Despite these signs of recovery and the revelations gradually being unfolded about crimes against Jews and others in the socialist countries during the period when the security police were above the law, much still needs to be ascertained.

With respect to the Prague trial, the situation is not yet wholly clear. Even if the trial is valid, as Czech authorities maintain, precisely how does this case differ from those of Lazlo Rajk in Hungary and Traicho Kostov in Bulgaria, both of which have been declared as frame-ups by their own governments? The same type of confessions were presented at the Prague trial as in these cases. Further, which defendants in the Prague trial, most of whom were Jewish, were actually guilty and which innocent?

Does the reported release of the three Slansky co-defendants, Arthur London, Vavro Hajdu and Evzan Loebl, mean that they were innocent or not? Other witnesses at this trial who were themselves tried and imprisoned, such as Edward Goldstuecker, former Czech ambassador to Israel, have been released. Who was guilty and who was framed? What is the situation regarding Mordecai Oren, a leader of the Israel Mapam[5] Party who was implicated in the Prague trial, and sentenced to 15 years, and was just released? To what extent have the charges against the Zionist movement made in the Prague trial been sustained by the recent review of the case? We believe that these questions should be answered by the Czech government.

The shocking information concerning the anti-Semitic closing down of Jewish cultural institutions in the Soviet Union and execution of leading Yiddish writers came in a statement from Poland (see our May issue). Why has no word on this terrible series of events come from the Soviet Union itself? We believe that it is incumbent upon the Soviet government to make known through its own channels the full truth about the crimes against the Jewish culture and the Jewish writers. The world is entitled to know just who was affected, what exactly did happen in this series of events, who was responsible and what punishment has been meted out to the perpetrators of these crimes. Even at this late date too much is obscure. And obscurity harms the cause of peace.

At the same time, we believe that the radical turn of events in the Soviet Union in the past three years and especially in the past few months indicate that the genuine socialist national policy will be resumed.

We expect to observe the resumption of Jewish cultural activity in the Soviet Union in accordance with the socialist principle of the right of nationalities. We hope the government will actively encourage the Jews in re-establishing a Yiddish press and theater and any other forms of cultural expression the Soviet Jews themselves may desire. Whatever degree of integration Soviet Jews have reached up to now, numbers of them desire cultural expression in Yiddish. This is attested by reports of crowded and enthusiastic audiences for concerts of Yiddish song and poetry held in the past months in many Soviet Russian and Ukrainian cities. So long as such an audience exists, socialist policy requires satisfaction of this desire.

The correction of the violations of the rights of Soviet Jews is further demanded in the interests of peace. For with such remedial action socialist countries not only fulfil the socialist policies that were permitted to be violated, but they also make a contribution to peace. The removal of this justifiable grievance will greatly facilitate the unification of all the forces laboring for peaceful so-existence.

Source: "Review and Reappraisal," *Jewish Life*, June 1956, pp. 3–7, 30–31.

NOTES

1. The author refers here to Stalin's execution of prominent Soviet Yiddish writers, artists, and political leaders who were associated with the Jewish Anti-Fascist Committee. The killings occurred between 1948 and 1952 and culminated in the death of at least fifteen Jewish cultural figures on August 12, 1952.

2. The Prague Trial, also known as the Slansky Trial after the primary defendant, Czech Communist Party general secretary Rudolf Slansky, occurred in 1951. It is widely considered to have been a purge, orchestrated by Stalin, of many of the prominent Jews from the Czech Communist Party, as eleven of the fourteen defendants in the trial, including Slansky, were Jews. Slansky and ten others were executed after being coerced into pleading guilty to the charge of conspiring against the Communist Party.

3. Birobidjan (also spelled Birobidzhan), a town in the Soviet far east, which Stalin designated as the administrative center of the Jewish Autonomous Republic in 1934 as an alternative Jewish homeland to Palestine.

4. See note 2.

5. Hebrew acronym of the United Workers Party, a socialist-Zionist party sympathetic to the Soviet Union during the late 1940s and 1950s.

The Question of Zionism

If there is a political issue from the nineteenth century that remains controversial to the present day, it is Zionism. In the Jewish labor movement's early years, most socialists were opposed to Zionism, viewing it an impractical scheme, a violation of internationalist norms, a diversion from the class struggle, and an accomplice of imperialism. However, attitudes began to shift with the arrival of socialist-Zionists in the early 1900s. Socialist-Zionists argued that Jewish workers were burdened by a dual oppression, both national and economic in character, and they therefore needed to struggle for two goals simultaneously: liberation of the proletariat through the overthrow of capitalism and liberation of the Jewish nation through the creation of a socialist Jewish homeland. An increasing number of leftists grew to appreciate Zionism, if not embrace it outright, from the 1910s forward. Escalating cycles of violence against Jews in Europe played a major role, as did the growing practical achievements of socialist-Zionists in Palestine. This is not to say that opposition diminished. The most vociferous, best-organized foes were the Communists, who condemned Zionism as a tool of British imperialism. Beyond the Communist movement and even within the Zionist movement, lively debates took place. Did Zionism cause harm to the Arabs? Could it solve the problem of anti-Semitism in the Diaspora? Was it consonant with socialist principles? Debate over these and similar questions continued until World War II, when most leftists, profoundly shaken by Nazism, concluded that Jews indeed required a homeland and this could be achieved without obstructing the national aspirations of Arabs. The Soviet Union's short-lived support for Jewish statehood in 1947 and 1948 prompted Communists to reverse their previous opposition and join the emerging pro-Zionist consensus. Not until the Six Day War in June 1967 did the question of Zionism reopen and grow more acrimonious over subsequent decades.

53

"The Whole Thing Is Ridiculous" (1906)

JACOB MILCH

Like many of the Jewish labor movement's pioneers, Jacob Milch (1866–1945) opposed Zionism and other varieties of left-wing Jewish nationalism making their presence felt in the United States during the early years of the twentieth century. His critique here originally appeared in the Yiddish monthly *Di tsukunft* and was reprinted in English translation in the *International Socialist Review*, a Marxist journal associated with the Socialist Party.

The newest stream of Jewish immigration, driven to these shores by the waves of the Russian Revolution, and its counterpart, the atrocious massacres of Jews, has brought in its wake an undercurrent of new ideas and ideals which of late has excited the interest of the Jews in their old homes.

As a result the little world in the so-called Ghetto is teeming with new life, new aspirations, new problems and new hopes.

Until recently the intellectual life of the great East Side of New York was absorbed mainly in social questions of a general nature, or, to be more correct, in Socialism.

To be sure no great event of contemporary life escaped the philosophic mind of the East Side, neither did the inhabitants thereof forget their unfortunate brethren at home, but all these were, so to say, secondary questions. The great problem which has moved the heart of the East Side was Socialism. The victories and defeats of the proletariat in any part of the world were of greater importance to them than the victory of the Japanese at Port Arthur, or any like event.

This has now been changed to a great extent. The general spread of socialist thought throughout Russia, the deathly struggle now raging between the entire Russian people and the despotic regime, and the cowardly outrages perpetrated against the Jews by the "Black Hundreds" organized and supported by the bureaucracy for the purposes of combating the revolution—all these have made their imprint upon the psychology of the Russian Jews and gave impetus to the organization of innumerable parties, the consequence of which is a mosaic of theories and movements which have for their end the establishment of an independent Jewish state on the one hand and the social revolution on the other. With the newest immigration these theories have now been transplanted to our shores and the little Jewish world was beset by a host of new parties of different descriptions and denominations; we have now Zionists and Territorialists, Zionist-Socialists and Socialists-Territorialists, Poalei Zion (Workingmen-Zionist), Socialist Revolutionary Territorialists, etc. And it goes without saying that each has its own theory, which is of course the only true one, with its own newspaper and party organization; and it also goes without saying that everlasting discussions, squabbles, quarrels and all sorts of friction is the order of the day.

Upon a close examination we find that these theories and movements, notwithstanding their high-sounding and unpronounceable names, all emanate from, and are very much connected with, the old fashioned Zionism, are indeed only variations of the same. Our accounts must therefore be settled, first of all, with Zionism proper. [. . .]

It is not within the province of this short work to point out all the shortcomings of political Zionism. Besides, the subject has been thrashed out so many times there is hardly any new word to be said about it. At best I can only repeat some of the objections that are being made against it, and this I shall do here only to the extent absolutely necessary to the understanding of our discussion.

Zionism, or rather, Zionists, though starting from a common point—the persecution of the Jews, and reaching the same conclusion—the necessity of establishing an independent Jewish state, are nevertheless divided and subdivided among themselves as to the reason and ultimate aims of their movements. We shall here touch upon the two main divisions only, namely, the "Materialistic" and the "Idealistic."

Materialist Zionism deals mainly with the economic conditions and necessities of the Jews, while the Idealists take for their text the spiritual side of the Jews—the Jew not as an individual but as a nation. The one seeks to acquire the holy land for the purpose of improving the economic condition of the Jews as a nation, while the other refuses to consider this side of the question, claiming that with regard to the question of bread and butter the Jew can work out his salvation in exile. What he most needs, they maintain, is an "intellectual center" where he would be enabled to develop his national genius, to preserve the national "self" which each nation possesses and has a right to preserve. The author of this latter Zionism is Asher Ginsburg, better known as Ahad Ha'am.[1]

Both these factions, as can be seen, are one as to the cardinal point, namely that the Jews are a separate nation; that neither their sojourn in so many different countries, among so many different peoples for almost twenty centuries, nor the various political institutions, nor the degree of civilization of those countries and peoples, has in the least affected or impaired their character as a nation; that they are being persecuted just because of this peculiarity of theirs; that they have, nevertheless, suffered greatly in their economic development, according to the one, and in their intellectual progress, according to the other.

The materialist Zionists have in a great measure already received an answer from life itself. They found, to their great discomfiture, that Palestine is not to be had, and, on the other hand, that the Jews would not go there if it were to be had. Out of the one and a half million souls that have shaken off the dust of their native land for the last twenty years, only a very small portion migrated to the "Yiddish"[2] land, a goodly portion of which have since left in disgust. And this in spite of the financial aid they received out of the Rothschild funds. Moreover, this immense mass of emigration has not in the least diminished the Jewish population in Russia. This fact alone should have sufficed to convince the Zionists of the futility of their efforts. It should have proven to them that the Jewish problem is not to be solved by emigration; that a whole nation can not, will not, emigrate on account of an imaginary prosperity in a semi-barbarous land where their forefathers of two thousand years ago lived, or out of devotion to ideals, no matter how sublime they may be; that it is rather the immediate necessities, and, to a certain extent, political oppression, that will put the wandering stick in the hands of a great number, and that, consequently, the place of destination would be decided upon by the chances it offers to new comers to win bread and shelter.

This fact alone, I repeat, should have been sufficient to show the Zionists the impossibility of their scheme. Unfortunately such "minor" considerations do not enter the mind of Zionists. Cause and effect seem to have no meaning for them. They reckon little with the cold facts of life, and they listen only to the voice of their mind and desires—the result is, therefore, usually disastrous to them.

But when the facts become so obvious that even the blind can see them, they take refuge in reasoning somewhat like this:

"We know perfectly well," they say, "that all the Jews can not emigrate; it is in fact not at all desirable they should. It is not desirable, for instance, nor necessary, for the Jews of England, France or North America to emigrate. The Zionist movement is mainly for the benefit of the Russian and Roumanian Jews, and even from those counties it is not necessary they should all emigrate. What we are after is a center, a home, somewhere, for a portion of the nation. There are many foreigners to-day living in Russia without being molested because they have somewhere a fatherland with a government to protect them. So would the persecution of the Jews cease if they had a country somewhere."

In an article entitled "Zionism or Socialism" in Number 6 of "The Jewish Worker,"[3] Ben Ahud[4] brings out some remarks which are worthwhile reproducing here. After having shown that Zionism is a dream at best; after having shown that the whole of Palestine is neither sufficiently large in area to hold, nor does it possess the fertility of soil to support, a population of ten millions; that in addition, the Jews could not prevent non-Jews from immigrating to their country, were it ever sufficiently developed industrially to invite foreign immigration; after having pointed out that it would take at least fifty years for two or three millions of Jews to emigrate to the new land, in which time the depletion would be made good by new births—after having shown this, Ben Ahud continues:

"It is true some of the Zionists think that so soon as the Jews will have established their own government, even the smallest, the other nations would refrain from persecuting those that will have remained in exile, because they would all know that there is a Jewish state which would protect its children, that there is a nation which would fight for their brothers. . . . How puerile! It is only to laugh at such expectations. The great majority of the Jews will have remained with such great naval powers as Russia, Germany, Austria, France, England and the United States of America, and these first class naval powers shiver in their boots at the sight of the Lilliputian "Yiddish Land." They would be frightened to death at the news that the representatives of the "Yiddish Land" in Congress assembled have adopted a resolution protesting against Russia for the expulsion of the Jews from Moscow; against Austria for mistreating the Jews in Galicia; against Germany for not admitting Jewish girls to the profession of teachers, against France for the massacres of Jews in Algiers, etc. Did Russia shrink from oppressing Germans in the Baltic provinces in the face of Germany with its large and modernly equipped army, with its great influence in European politics? Would this same Russia treat its Jews with more consideration because somewhere in Asia existed a little Jewish country under the suzerainty of the Turkish Sultan? . . .

"It can thus be seen in that the plan of Dr. Hertzel,[5] should it ever be realized, could not in any way ameliorate the sufferings of the Jews.

"A good portion of the Jewish bourgeoisie would make capital out of the scheme; a small portion of the Jewish workingmen would get a chance to sell their labor power, as they do everywhere. This is the best of the sum total of the whole Zionistic movements. And with such empty, worthless dreams they try to avert the thoughts of the Jews from their real needs at home!"

So far Ben Ahud [has had this to say] as to the argument of the materialist Zionist about a Jewish center to infuse respect for the Jews in exile.

Not much better showing can the argument of an intellectual center make for the "idealist" Zionist, those who try to save the souls of the Jews.

This twin brother of the "materialist" commits the same error, but in a different way. The "materialists" who speak of the economic backwardness forget the economic surroundings of the Jews, and the economic impossibility of their scheme. The "idealist" again, trying to save the Jewish "spirit," forgets to consider the nature of this spirit. They talk much of the Jewish genius, of the intellectual culture, and they forget that the Jewish "spirit" is not "Jewish" at all; that if the intellectual side of a nation can be developed, modified or mutilated under specific social and economic environments—and there can be no doubt about that—then the Jewish nation has undergone such an evolution for almost two thousand years under exceptional circumstances, and that the results of this evolution cannot be erased because a million or even two million people will emigrate to a semi-barbarous country which once upon a time belonged to their ancestors. The point is very often omitted by our newly baked nationalists.

The truth of the matter is that we can speak of a Jewish nation in the spiritual sense only, because in the sense of a political or social unit the Jews are surely no nation. But this intellect, this spirit, manifested in a special Jewish form (if there be such a thing) is the product, not of the Jewish land, but of the exile, nay, it is because of it! What forms the Jewish culture would have assumed had they lived on their own soil all this time, what shape it would assume should it again settle independently on its land, or any other newly acquired territory is a matter of conjecture. The Jew of to-day is the Jew of the diaspora. His culture, his civilization, his "spirit," is therefore not Jewish, but western. It is therefore pure nonsense to speak of a Jewish "spirit" that can thrive on the soil of Palestine only. Furthermore, there are many arguments in support of the theory that the Jewish nation, such as it is, is a "nation" in exile only. There are probabilities that the Jews would not have retained their religion and the purity of the race, a thing the Zionist puts much stock in, had they remained in their land. No ruling nation preserved its purity in the same degree as the Jews. The ruling nations usually assimilate with others, either through conquest or immigration. The Jews in their own land were not exempt from such influences. Their language they had lost long before their independence, so much did they mix with the heathen by intermarriage, their very religion was much neglected.

The exile alone united them; in exile the form of their religion developed and crystallized; in exile they stopped intermarriages. The exile then developed the peculiarities of Jewism. If we are therefore to speak of a Jewish nation as an intellectual unity we cannot separate it from the exile spirit. It is utterly incomprehensible how this evolution of twenty centuries can be done away with.

Add to this that the Zionists of all shades admit that the great majority of the Jews will remain where they are at present and the whole proposition of an "intellectual center" becomes ridiculous. A million, at the best two millions, of the poorest and humblest Jews will emigrate to a semi-savage country. At the best it will take tens or even hundreds of years until they will be able to procure a decent livelihood by tilling the soil and doing all kinds of manual labor. And this handful of Jews somewhere in Asia or Africa is to become the intellectual and spiritual guides of the ten or more millions that remained under the intellectual influence of European and American civilization, with its famous universities and libraries, museums and laboratories, literature and theatres; with its highly developed art and technic with its newspapers, etc. Is this not puerile? Is this not ridiculous? Jerusalem in intellectual competition with Paris, London, New York, or even Warsaw. Uganda, or another wilderness in Africa to compete with Heidelberg, Oxford, Yale or Columbia as teachers. Jaffa racing with the British Museum, or the Paris [Library], or even the New York Library.

It is only to laugh!

Turn Zionism or Territorialism as you may, the whole thing is ridiculous. But the worst was yet to come.

Before Zionism had time to stand firmly on its feet, before it was able to make the first step, it was already clear to every observer that besides its external deformities it is subject to an incurable, chronic, internal sickness.

At the time when Zionism made its great efforts social life in Russia took its usual course. Industry, with the aid of foreign capital, had been greatly developed, and along with it grew the proletariat and class consciousness.

The Revolutionary movement progressed immensely, and the Jew did not only not keep aloof from it, he, on the contrary, was found in the front line, and these circumstances helped to tear asunder the Zionist movement. The proletarian Zionist opened his eyes; the working man and his exploiter met face to face and the sweet dream of a united nation was at once scattered to the winds. The united and undivided Jewish "nation" was divided into two hostile camps.

The proletarian Zionists did not, however, awake altogether; they only awoke for a minute, turned on the other side and began to dream again. Would they dream quietly to themselves we could leave them alone. The trouble with them is that they speak out in their dreams and produce much noise.

We must, therefore, disturb them from their pleasant dream.

Source: Jacob Milch, "New Movements amongst the Jewish Proletariat," *International Socialist Review*, Dec. 1906, pp. 354–363.

NOTES

1. Asher Ginsburg (1856–1927), who wrote under the pen name Ahad Ha'am ("One of the People"), was the foremost proponent of cultural Zionism. He advocated for the use of Hebrew as the "national" language of the Jewish people and believed that Zionism's grounding in Palestine would transform Judaism in the Diaspora from a culture centered on religious practice to one based on secular, humanistic values. In the original text, Milch spells Ginsburg's pseudonym as "Akhad Haam," which is no longer the common spelling.

2. In this sense, "Yiddish" means "Jewish," that is, the Land of Israel.

3. Organ of the Bund, published in Yiddish as *Der yidisher arbeter*.

4. Pseudonym of Chaim Zhitlovsky. In the following decade, Zhitlovsky shifted to a qualified pro-Zionist position.

5. Theodore Herzl (1860–1904), Hungarian-born writer and the father of political Zionism. Herzl believed that Jews had no hope of combating anti-Semitism in Europe; rather, they must create a new homeland for themselves—ideally in Palestine. His phrase "If you will it, it is no dream" became a slogan of the Zionist movement.

54

"The Jewish Militant" (1906)

In 1906, the socialist-Zionist party Poale Tsion began publishing the weekly *Der yidisher kemfer*. Its statement of principles, excerpted here, was probably written by the newspaper's editor, Kalman Marmor, later an important figure in the Communist movement.

[. . .] The Jewish militant faces a difficult struggle to liberate the Jew from his dual suffering as both a Jew and a human being. Even so, he will break down the walls of the old ghetto and those of the new ghetto,[1] and unite with freedom fighters of all nations to struggle for the equal rights of all people, regardless of sex, color, and nationality, and for the humanization of all people and their unification in one large family of peoples—humanity! The motto of all militants is, "In struggle shall your freedom be achieved!" And "If I am not for myself, who will be?" Every person must fight for his own freedom. Working-class freedom will be attained by the militant worker, women's emancipation by the militant woman, and Jewish freedom by the Jewish militant.

The Jewish militant is a Zionist-Socialist.

He is a Zionist because he is a Jew—a devoted child of Israel—and Zionism is the *only* means to free the Jewish people from its national suffering.

He is a socialist because he is a proletarian—an organic part of suffering humanity—and socialism is the *only* means to liberate humanity from its social suffering.

The Jewish militant is not a Zionistic socialist. [. . .] There is no such thing as a Zionistic socialism, just as there is no such thing as a Jewish socialism or a Russian, Polish, or Lithuanian socialism. Socialism is international, an international means to improve and beautify human life and, ultimately, to liberate it completely from all social suffering. And if socialism becomes dependent on various national forms, then only the form changes; the content remains and must remain *international*.

The Jewish militant is also not a Socialistic Zionist. The Zionist movement is a national movement to liberate the entire Jewish nation regardless of where and under which political and economic conditions various Jewish national communities find themselves today.

The world is divided between nations—therefore the Jewish militant wants to have *his* national rights, *his* voice heard in parliaments of other peoples; every people has its own land, and therefore the Jews want to have their own land, the Land of Israel. Other peoples speak various languages; thus, the Jewish people wants respect for Yiddish and recognition of Hebrew. Every people has its own literature and art; thus, the Jewish militant wants his people to have its own literature and the Jewish artist to create as a son of the Jewish people.

The Jewish militant, therefore, walks hand in hand with the nonsocialist Zionists regarding all Jewish national questions and diverges from them when it comes to social questions. And, likewise, the Jewish militant walks together with nonnationalist socialists regarding all social questions and diverges from them when it comes to Jewish national questions.

If the Jewish people had its own country, then the Jewish militant would be a socialist internationalist, rather than a Zionist, because he could be most useful to humanity from the position of his own national soil. But as long as the Jewish people is dispersed throughout all corners of the world, the Jewish militant has within himself a divided soul, two souls, and he must be more than a socialist among fellow socialists and more than a Zionist among fellow Zionists.

Source: "Der yidisher kemfer," *Der yidisher kemfer*, Mar. 30, 1906, p. 4. Translated by Tony Michels.

NOTES

1. It is not clear what the author means by "the new ghetto," but he could be referring to poor immigrant enclaves, such as the Lower East Side, often described as ghettos.

55

Zionism and Transnationalism
(1916)

RANDOLPH BOURNE

Born into a middle-class, Protestant family, Randolph Bourne (1886–1918) was one of the leading lights of Greenwich Village's radical bohemia. Influenced by Jewish intellectuals who rejected the idea of American society as a "melting pot," Bourne put forward the notion of a "transnational America," in which ethnic groups would persist and maintain ties to their countries of origin, thereby contributing to a cosmopolitan American national culture. Zionism, according to Bourne, provided the best example of transnationalism at work.

Before the American people at the present time there are two ideals of American nationalism, sharply focused and emphasized by the war. One is that of the traditional melting-pot, the other is that of a co-operation of cultures. The first is congenial to the ruling class, the nativist element of our population; the second appeals, however vaguely, to the leaders of the various self-conscious European national groups which have settled here. The idealism of the melting-pot would assimilate all Europeans, as they are received into the American social and economic scheme, to a very definite type, that of the prevailing Anglo-Saxon. For however much this desire may be obscured, what the Anglicized American prophets of the melting-pot really mean shall happen to the immigrant is that he shall acquire, along with the new common English language, the whole stock of English political and social ideals. When they attempt to judge how far any group has been Americanized, it is by this standard that they judge them.

The effect of the melting-pot ideal is either to influence this Anglicizing, or to obliterate the distinctive racial and cultural qualities, and work the American population into a colorless, tasteless, homogenous mass. With large masses of our foreign-born of the second generation this latter process is far advanced, and the result is that cultural pointlessness and vacuity which our critics of American life are never weary of deploring. Both effects of the melting-pot idealism, I believe, are highly undesirable. Both make in the long run for exactly that terrible unity of pride, chauvinism, and ambition that has furnished the popular fuel in the armed clash of nationalism in Europe. To preach a pure and undiluted Americanism with the spectacle of suicidal Europe before us is to invite disaster and destruction. American idealism is face to face with a crucial dilemma. Cultural self-consciousness, concentrated, inspiring vigor of intellectual and personal qualities such as the French possess, for instance, is the most precious heritage a nation can have. Yet apparently this intense national feeling leads straight into chauvinistic self-assertion, into conflict with other nationalisms, into a belligerency which drags the world down in mutual ruin. Who can doubt that, if we ever obtained this homogenous Americanism that our Rooseveltian prophets desire, the latent imperialism of our ruling class would flame forth and America would follow the other States in their plunge to perdition? America's only hope is in the development of a democratic and pacific way of life. We have an opportunity at last to try to make good that old boast of our being a model to the nations. We can at least make the effort to show that a democratic civilization founded on peace is a possibility in this portentous twentieth century. [. . .]

If America is to be nationalistic without being chauvinistic, we need new conceptions of the state, of nationality, of citizenship, of allegiance. The war, to my mind, has proved the utter obsolescence of the old conceptions. Even without the war the old conceptions would have been obsolete. For the development of backward countries, the growth of population in Europe, the demand for labor and colonists in all parts of the globe, the ease and cheapness of travel, have set in motion vast currents of immigration which render impossible the old tight geographical groupings of nationality. The political ideas of the future will have to be adjusted to a shifting world-population, to the mobility of labor, to all kinds of new temporary mixings of widely diverse peoples, as well as to their permanent mixings.

The Jews have lost their distinction of being a peculiar people. Dispersion is now the lot of every race. The Jewish ghetto in America is matched by the Italian, by the Slavic ghetto. The war will intensify this setting in motion of wandering peoples. The age-long problems of Jewish nationalism have become the burning problems of other dispersed nationalities. America has become a vast reservoir of dispersions. The adjustment which the Jew has had to make throughout the ages is a pattern of what other nationals have to make today. From their point of view, the same dilemmas of assimilation and absorption, of cultural and racial allegiance, beset them. In the new country they have often the same alternatives of disintegration or subnational life. To the intelligent and enthusiastic émigré from the Teuton or Slavic or Latin lands, it seems no more desirable that his cultural soul should be washed out of him than it seems to the Jew. America puts to him the same problem of becoming assimilated to New World life, of meeting his new political freedom and vague expansion of economic opportunity, without becoming a mere colorless unit in a gray mass. And the immigrant puts to America the problem of finding a place for him to make his peculiar and whole-hearted contribution to the upbuilding of the America which is still in process of creation. The problem of the Jew in the modern world is identical. As a Jew has said, "The modern world sets the Jew the problem of maintaining some sort of distinctive existence without external props of territorial sovereignty and a political machine; the Jew sets the modern world the problem of finding for him a place in its social structure which shall enable him to live as a human being without demanding that he cease to be a Jew."

If then this co-operative Americanism is an ideal which meets at once the demands of a native American like myself who wishes to see America kept from militarization and feudalization, and also the demands of the foreign immigré who wishes freedom to preserve his heritage at the same time that he co-operates loyally with all other nationals in the building-up of America, I believe we shall find in the current Jewish ideal of Zionism the purest pattern and the most inspiring conceptions of trans-nationalism. I used to think, as many Americans still do, that Zionism was incompatible with Americanism, that if your enthusiasm and energy went into creating a Jewish nation in the Orient, you could not give yourself to building up the State in which you lived. I have since learned that however flawless such a logical antithesis would be nothing could be falser than this idea. This dilemma of dual allegiance must be solved in America, it must be solved by the world, and it is in the fertile implications of Zionism that I veritably believe the solution will be found.

To the orthodox Jew, I presume the ideas clustering about the founding of Zion will seem only the realization of age-long Jewish hopes. To me they represent an international idealism almost perilously new. They furnish just those new conceptions that I said this new American idealism would need. Indeed my own mind was set working on the whole idea of American national ideals by the remarkable articles of Dr. Kallen[1] in *The Nation* last year, and the very phrase, "trans-nationalism," I stole from a Jewish college mate of mine who, I suspect, is now a member of your Menorah Society[2] here.

The idea is a Jewish idea, and the great contribution of Jewish intelligence in America I conceive to be to clarify and spread these new conceptions.

It may be daring of me to assume that the Jew, with his traditional segregation, his intense fusion of racial and religious egoism, will contribute hopefully to the foundations of a new spiritual internationalism. But has it not always been the anomaly of the Jew that he was at once the most self-conscious of beings—feels himself, that is, religiously, culturally, racially, a being peculiar in his lot and signally blessed—and yet has proven himself perhaps the most assimilable of all races to other and quite alien cultures? Which is cause and which effect? Is he assimilable because he has had no national centre, no geographical and political basis for his religion and his mode of life, or has he not had his Jewish nation because he has been so readily assimilated? Is it not just this in the Jewish personality that has piqued and irritated and attracted other peoples, that it is at once so congenial and so alien? And can we not connect the so very recent flowing of the hopes of Jewish nationalism with the fact that Zionistic ideals now for the first time seem to be making towards internationalism? They move in line with the world's best hope. For as I understand it, the Jewish State which Zionists are building is a non-military, a non-chauvinistic State. Palestine is to be built as a Jewish centre on purely religious and cultural foundations. It is not to be the home of all the Jewish people. Zionism does not propose to prevent Jews from living in full citizenship in other countries. The Zionist does not believe that there is a necessary conflict between a cultural allegiance to the Jewish centre and political allegiance to a State. [. . .]

If this interpretation of mine is correct, then the modern world, and above all America, needs these Zionist conceptions. What I mean by co-operative Americanism—that is, an ideal of a freely mingling society of peoples of very different racial and cultural antecedents, with a common political allegiance and common social ends but with free distinctive cultural allegiances which may be placed anywhere in the world that they like—is simply a generalization of the practical effect of the Zionist ideal. I see no other way by which international sympathy may be created and the best human expressivenesses and distinctive attitudes and traits preserved. And if the Jews have been the first international race, I look to America to be the first international nation.

Groups of identical culture must find some way of leading a national life that is neither belligerently egoistic like the hectic nationalism of Europe nor sub-national like that of the Jews of the Russian Pale. The American ideal must make possible such an ideal national life within our own country if the people who came here are to be enriched and enriching. [. . .]

If I take this Zionism, which seems to me to contain the best current Jewish idealism, as a pattern for American trans-nationalism, I may unwittingly be doing it injustice. It will seem to you that I have ignored the religious aspect, and I have perhaps unknowingly caricatured its political conceptions. But I am looking at Zionism from the outside and not from within. My interest is in the question how far do Jewish ideals contribute to that larger internationalism of which America might be the exponent? There is very real danger that a reactionary idealism may force a fatally narrow patriotic spirit upon us. In new conceptions, such as those which this Jewish idealism seems to contribute, I see our salvation. The Jew in America is proving every day the possibility of this dual life. To clinch one's argument one would need no other evidence than the figure of Justice Brandeis,[3] at once an ardent Zionist and at the same time an incomparable American leader in economic and social reconstruction. And what shall we say of the younger generation of Jewish intelligents, which includes such men as Felix Frankfurter,[4] Horace M. Kallen, Morris R. Cohen,[5] Walter Lippmann?[6] The intellectual service which such writers are doing us with their clarity of expression, their radical philosophy, their masterly fibre of thought, can hardly be over-valued. Their contribution is so incomparably greater than that of any other American group of foreign cultural affiliations that one can scarcely get one's perspective. A large majority of this younger generation is, I understand, Zionist in its sympathy. Yet that Jewish idealism has not in the least vitiated their peculiarly intimate insight into American problems, their gift of picking a way though the tangled social and economic maze. In their light we all see light. They are my last proof of the practicability of the co-operative American ideal. And they suggest that an ardent Zionism involves the responsibility for an equally ardent effort for that progressive democratic reconstruction in America which is the ideal of all true Americans, no matter what their heritage or trans-nationality.

Source: Randolph Bourne, "The Jew and Trans-National America," *The Menorah Journal* 2 (Dec. 1916): pp. 277–284.

NOTES

1. Horace Kallen, "Democracy versus the Melting Pot," *The Nation*, Feb. 18 and 25, 1915, pp. 190–194, 217–220. Kallen (1882–1974), a professor of philosophy, advocated "cultural pluralism," the notion that immigrants in America should retain their cultural heritage, including language, while still being loyal American citizens who contribute to the entire American culture.

2. Bourne refers to the Intercollegiate Menorah Association, publisher of *The Menorah Journal*.

3. In 1916, President Woodrow Wilson had just named Louis Brandeis (1856–1941) the newest justice on the U.S. Supreme Court, where Brandeis served until 1939.

4. Felix Frankfurter (1882–1965), liberal lawyer and a justice on the U.S. Supreme Court from 1939 to 1962.

5. Morris R. Cohen (1880–1947), influential philosopher and legal scholar, taught at City College of New York, the first free public institution of higher learning in the United States. Cohen did much to secure CCNY's reputation as the "proletarian Harvard."

6. Walter Lippman (1889–1974), one of the country's foremost political commentators and author of influential studies on media bias and public opinion, among other topics.

56

"Should We Change Our Stance toward Zionism?" (1918)

HERTS BURGIN

In November 1917, Great Britain issued the Balfour Declaration in support of a Jewish homeland. What had previously seemed fantastic now appeared plausible, thus prompting some socialists to reassess their previous opposition to Zionism. In response, Herts Burgin (1870–1949), veteran journalist and author of the first comprehensive history of the Jewish labor movement, reasserted the orthodox view that socialism and Zionism could not be reconciled.

We are living in a time of confusion, just like the generation after Babel. We doubt accepted truths. We reappraise old values.

It is understandable that we are reappraising the values whose worth has in recent times been somewhat shaken. But in our devastating critique we even dare to take on those truths whose value has not at all changed.

We have in mind here our stance toward the Zionist movement.

Our main argument against the Zionist movement is that it is a nationalist, not class-based, movement. It is an example of petit-bourgeois, not proletarian, struggle.

And it remains as such even now. Still, one notices in some socialist circles an inclination to revise our stance or, in any case, to pose the "revision-question" as part of our program.

Why? Because Zionism is now not just a pure utopia; it already has a small basis in reality. It happened while the whole time we were against Zionism mainly because we considered it an empty dream.

It is true that Zionism is no longer an empty dream. Although it is still far from the real thing, it is more or less possible, though of course not to the extent that its proponents assert.

But let us consider whether the gains of realized Zionism are so great that because of them we should risk the interests of the socialist movement.

What are the main gains we can expect from a realized Zionism? The chief gains consist of the fact that through the realization of Zionism, the Jewish Question will be solved.

First of all, let us note that the Jewish Question does not exist anymore, not since Tsarism was destroyed in Russia. The Jewish Question was mainly a question about the Jewish lack of rights in Russia. This lack of rights used to compel Jews to flee to other countries and therefore raised the Jewish Question in these other countries.

Now, since the denial of rights in Russia has disappeared, the Jewish Question as a matter of course also disappeared.

This does not imply that the question of relations between Jew and non-Jew no longer exists in European countries and in America. We don't mean to imply that with the abolition of laws against the Jews, hostility toward Jews in Russia has also been eliminated, as it has in other countries. No, unfortunately, they still look and will in the future everywhere look askance at the Jews. Because the tragedy of the Jews is that they are among the nations of the world as a grown-up among small children. Because of their thousands-year-old history and mainly because of their thousands-year-old suffering, they have learned better than anyone how to adapt to surrounding conditions. They have succeeded where others have failed. And that has made those around them jealous.

This is an unavoidable tragedy allotted to the Jews by History, and the Jew must carry around this tragedy until the bitter end, when the reason for jealousy will disappear, that is, when competition will disappear (wherein the Jew is particularly troublesome for his neighbors). And this, again, will only be possible when the socialist order is introduced. Only then and not sooner. If it were possible to gather the scattered Jewish people from the four corners of the world and transfer them entirely to the Land of Israel, we could expect that this jealousy would disappear within the capitalist order. But since the most fervent Zionists do not posit that all of the Jewish people, or even the majority, will move to Palestine, millions of Jews will still remain in Russia, western Europe, America, etc. and the leftover millions will suffer from the jealousy, just as before.

Also, when people say that the realization of the Zionist plan will solve the Jewish Question, they mean the Jewish Question as it exists in Tsarist Russia and, through it, in other lands. And just as Jews were granted rights in Russia, the Jewish Question will be solved.

But let us concede that the Jewish Question is still in its former full bloom and blossom—we cannot see how their own home in Palestine will solve the

Question. Will the Jews then be secured from harm? What sort of worth will a little land by the Jordan have in the eyes of great states? China is a great state, but still the Chinese cannot be citizens here. Japan is a world power, but when California found it necessary, it passed a terrible law against the Japanese.

But, they say to us, what harm could it do?

Let's consider whether it will really *not* do any harm. If it would be a matter of "platonic" feeling, of sympathy, we could be satisfied with the answer that it "will not cause harm." But the question of changing our stance is not just a question of our sympathy but of our practical work. If we change our stance, we would have to include Zionism in our program of activity. We would also have to become socialist-Zionists. We would not succeed by awakening the worker in the Jew; we would also have to awaken the Jew in the worker.

In our field of activity, we would have to include the Jewish people in its broadest sense. As Zionists, we would have to bend the class struggle before the Jewish bourgeoisie; as socialists, we would have to bend working-class unity before this same bourgeoisie. We would be "two-faced," a kind of "Jekyll and Hyde." In the case of a conflict between class interests and national interests, we would feel lost, constrained, and would not be faithful to the worker *or* the Jew.

As a consequence, our practical work on behalf of the class struggle would not produce any results.

It thus appears that "it can definitely cause harm"; our movement, the socialist movement, will only suffer from a change in our perspective. It will suffer to the extent that the class struggle will be weakened by it. [. . .]

The class struggle exists and will exist as long as the capitalist order exists. And in this regard nothing has changed. [. . .]

Class struggle still remains the only path to socialism. Socialism is already no "empty dream" but something that can quickly be realized. And, if so, it behooves us now more than ever before to develop the worker's class consciousness.

A change in our stance toward Zionism will only lead to a certain dulling of the worker's class consciousness.

But, they tell us, the non-Jewish socialists have made firm resolutions in favor of Zionism. Why should we, Jewish socialists, do otherwise?

Those who put forth this argument forget a small point: for the socialists in other nations of the world, Zionism only requires sympathy; for us, however, it requires half our soul, which we need for our socialist cause.

Sympathy we can give. We do not deny that the Zionist movement strives toward an ideal, but its ideal is not ours.

There are many things with which we sympathize, but we cannot take them on as ours.

The bottom line is this: with a healthy head, you shouldn't crawl into a sick bed.

Source: Herts Burgin, "Zoln mir endern unzer shtelung tsum tsienizmus?," *Forverts*, May 14, 1918. Translated by Alisa Braun.

57

"The Pogroms in Palestine" (1929)

THE FORVERTS

In August 1929, widespread violence broke out in Palestine following an incident in which Muslim groups protested the terms
of Jewish use of the Western Wall. Tensions escalated and led
to public demonstrations and murderous attacks against Jews—
Zionists and non-Zionists alike—in cities and towns such as
Jerusalem, Hebron, and Safed. The *Forverts* condemned the
violence in the following editorial.

The pogroms against Jews in Palestine have taken on the character of a bloody catastrophe. Murderous attacks by Arabs against Jews have
occurred several times in recent years. The hateful mood, which has recently
been incited against Jews in Palestine, is also known. But nobody had imagined that such a fire of blood and hatred would break out in the Land of
Israel. Nobody had imagined that such would be possible under English rule
and in a land where the Jewish population consists entirely of a creative, constructive element.

It will still take time for all the facts behind the catastrophe to be thoroughly investigated and determined.

The most important questions for everyone who reads about the bloody
events are these: Where did the Arabs get their weapons? Who provided
them with ammunition? It is clear that they were organized, carefully organized. This was not a sudden, mass outbreak. In certain cases the pogromists
used cunning means, "strategic" means, to be able to more easily break into
Jewish neighborhoods. There were people who thought through all of this,
carried out all of this; people who provided the weapons; people who led the
attacks; people who worked out strategy.

The political situation in Palestine and the general politics around Palestine is so muddled that it is easy for each side to interpret the facts as they suit
him. Opponents of a Jewish Palestine find justification for the Arab pogromists in the fact that Jews held a demonstration by the Western Wall; oppo-

nents of the current English government say the pogroms happened because there were not enough soldiers in and around Palestine to keep order; countries which are against the British Mandate in Palestine cast blame on Britain's general policies in the Middle East; and so on. Every side in this great political muddle finds a justification for itself finds in the Jewish misfortune, and an accusation against its opponents.

But what are the dry facts?

There was a conflict between the Arabs and Jews over the Western Wall, over whether or not Jews should have certain rights there. The conflict, of course, consisted of words, claims, and arguments. Both sides appealed to the British government in Palestine. The government took a position in favor of the Arabs. The Jews were not pleased, and they organized a demonstration, a demonstration that consisted entirely of verbal demands, which they considered right and just.

And at the demonstration the Arabs responded with a bloody attack on a Jewish family. The bloodbath began therewith. Jews spoke and Arabs stabbed.

A little later a second instance very similar to the first happened. Jews again held a demonstration, a funeral demonstration, carrying the body of the murdered young boy to his eternal rest. And during the demonstration Jews were beaten by the police, which consisted mainly of Arabs.

And afterward the fire truly blazed. Armed Arabs began murdering right and left. They attacked defenseless neighborhoods, yeshivas, private residences, stabbing and shooting young and old, women and men.

Of course, the Arabs would not have responded so bloodily, so murderously, against Jewish demonstrations if they were not incited earlier. Above all, therefore, the blood of the Jewish victims falls on the heads of all those who incited Arabs against Jews in all the years since Jews began to build up Palestine.

The inciters have been diverse. There are fanatical Christians who cannot stand the idea that the birthplace of Jesus should become a Jewish country. There are fanatical Muslims who fear that the Jews in Palestine would defile their holy sites. There are groups, both Arabs and Englishmen, with specific economic interests, which have come into conflict with the economic policies of the Jewish colonists. There are just plain anti-Semites, who are always prepared to incite against Jews. And, finally, there are Communists, who, in the interests of world revolution, have incited the Arabs against the British government as an imperialist country, against the Zionist organization as an imperialist assistant to England, and, perforce, against all Jews who have come to the Land of Israel as a result of the Balfour Declaration.

And, speaking of all the inciters, one must mention regretfully the British government, which has never done anything to reconcile the interests of the Jews with the Arabs, to bring the two elements of the population closer together. The British government has known over all these years what is going on in Palestine. They have seen how the kindling has accumulated, how the powder keg has grown larger. And not only did it not take the necessary steps to avoid a catastrophe, not only did it not take care to prevent a spark from falling into the power keg, but when the catastrophe came, it did not have the means to stop the misfortune. The greatest bloodshed took place days after the first pogrom broke out, and had the British government at least prepared the necessary forces to stop the pogromists, many of those who perished would today be among the living.

There is no economic basis for opposition between Jews and Arabs in Palestine. The interests of both elements, their economic interests, coincide. Jews are helping to build the country; they are bringing new possibilities to the Arab population. Therefore, economic interests dictate that both elements should live together harmoniously and peacefully and work together harmoniously and peacefully.

The hatred between Jews and Arabs has been incited—incited partly by religious fanatics and partly by political provocateurs. And because the outbreak happened through incitement, and because it required religious and political provocations, one can hope for better relations in the near future. Only hatred stemming from economic conflict, from economic opposition, can be called a natural conflict. All others are artificially made. And as soon as the forces that provoke and incite are abolished, the hatred will disappear.

We want to hope that the new government in England, the Labor government, will adopt a different policy in Palestine, not a policy of looking on with indifference, while the coexistence of the two races in Palestine becomes destroyed, but a policy of helping to bring together the two peoples in close, friendly relations, for their own interests and for the interests of building up the country.

Source: "Di pogromen in Palestine," *Forverts*, Aug. 27, 1929, p. 4. Translated by Tony Michels.

58

A Revolt of the Oppressed Arab Masses (1929)

DI MORGN FRAYHAYT

Di morgn frayhayt, like the *Forverts*, originally described the riots in Palestine as "pogroms," implying they contained an unjustifiable, anti-Semitic character. However, due to pressure from the Communist Party leadership, the newspaper changed its position and described the disturbances as a warranted uprising against imperialism. Over the ensuing days and weeks, the newspaper escalated its rhetoric and organized anti-Zionist rallies, touching off a furious reaction in the immigrant Jewish community.

The Zionists and Jewish nationalists and chauvinists of all kinds led a demonstration yesterday on the streets of New York as a protest against the events in Palestine. Against whom did the Jewish nationalists protest? What have they demanded?

The Zionists, the longtime agents of British imperialism in Palestine, are looking to present the events in Palestine as an outbreak of "half wild Arab bandits, which . . . have in one week destroyed and ruined that which has taken many years for the Jews to build"—so writes the Zionist bourgeois newspaper *Der tog*.[1]

They have protested, that is, against wild pogromists; they have demanded that the British authority in Palestine adopt means to put down the pogrom.

But has a pogrom taken place in Palestine—a pogrom in the sense of a bloodbath, which a ruling people makes against an oppressed people?

All the reports which come from Palestine are strongly censored and do not tell the truth about the events in Palestine, but it is difficult even for the capitalist newspapers to hide the fact that in Palestine a revolt of the oppressed Arab masses is taking place against British imperialist rule. Surely this is a revolt of the unconscious masses, which are being misled on a false road. But the Arab masses are not to blame for this.

Who are the ones truly guilty for the bloody events in Palestine?

Guilty, first of all, are the agents of British imperialism in Palestine, the Zionists.

For the Arab toiler, the Zionists are the unmitigated enemy. He cannot see British imperialism with its silent interests in Palestine, Arabia, India, Egypt, and so on. But he does see Zionism, which has driven him from his land. He sees the Jewish capitalist, which has planted orange plantations on his land and exploits him, the former owner of the land, in a merciless way.

The oppressed Arab toiler sees the Jewish labor fakers, the leaders of the Jewish labor federation,[2] the Palestine section of the Amsterdam International,[3] which leads a boycott agitation against him, the leaders that have mobilized the Jewish workers to tear away the Arab workers' morsel of food. This labor faker is, for the Arab toiler, the embodiment of the conqueror, the culprit in his difficult, bitter situation.

The kindling, which has over the course of years gathered among the Arab masses against the Jewish imperialists in Palestine, is now being utilized by the Arab landowners, the effendis, for their own interests. They, the effendis, exploit the Arab toilers no less than the Jewish capitalist colonists do. And national and religious hatred is an old, proven means of the ruling classes. Through incitement of religious superstition, the attention of the masses is diverted from their own exploitation. The Arab landowners and clerics have hoped to establish their own power over the misguided masses.

And guilty is the British MacDonald government, which uses the slogan "divide and rule" in all countries that find themselves under the yoke of British imperialism. The MacDonald government hoped that a little Arab and Jewish blood would give it the opportunity to establish its feet more strongly on the oppressed Arabs of Palestine.

But the imperialists have unleashed forces that they can no longer control. The events in Palestine have taken on a character of a mass revolt against imperialist domination. The masses struggle instinctively against all of their exploiters.

The current struggles in Palestine should be transformed into a struggle against British imperialism and its servants. An independent workers' and peasants' Palestine for the masses of Palestine, for both Arabs and Jews—this is the correct demand, which the Communists in Palestine put forward.

This evening in Irving Plaza Hall, the Jewish workers of New York will protest against the Jewish and British imperialists, the true guilty ones in the bloody events in Palestine. They will express their brotherly support for the Palestine Communists in their struggle for an independent, workers' and peasants' Palestine for all toilers, Jews and Arabs.

Source: "Kegn vemen protestirn?," *Di morgn frayhayt*, Aug. 28, 1929, p. 4. Translated by Tony Michels.

   1. An independent, liberal New York–based Yiddish daily.
   2. The editor is referring to the Histadrut, an umbrella organization of unions and cooperative ventures.
   3. The International Federation of Trade Unions, based in Amsterdam. The federation had a social democratic orientation.

59

"Jew and Arab" (1934)

HAYIM GREENBERG

Hayim Greenberg (1889–1953), editor of the socialist-Zionist
weekly *Der yidisher kemfer* and its sister publication *Jewish
Frontier,* was one of the most respected Zionist intellectuals in
the United States. In this article, written after a trip to Palestine,
Greenberg argues that while Zionist settlement has helped to
raise the standard of living of Palestinian Arabs, it has engen-
dered a loss of Arab dignity. This loss, Greenberg concludes, lies
at the root of the conflict between Zionists and Arabs.

In Palestine I asked myself many times have I told the truth about
Palestine? Was I justified in claiming for years that we have not harmed the
Arabs economically; that the Arabs were better off with us than without us?

I made no scholarly study of the question. For that I had neither the time
nor the specialist's knowledge. However, while traveling about the country—
visiting towns and villages, houses and hovels, observing women and children—I came to an inescapable, no longer theoretical conclusion: the closer
an Arab settlement lay to the zone of Jewish colonization, the better fed and
better housed were the inhabitants. The houses cleaner and larger, the trees
were more numerous. The stores more elaborate. The children were friend-
lier; Arab boys on bicycles and Arab-owned automobiles were seen more
frequently. The reverse was also true. The farther an Arab village was situated from a center of Jewish colonization, the more dirt and mud were visible; the larger the number of blind wrecks—men in rags and women in tat-
ters. The hungry, bare-foot children suffered from sick, inflamed eyes; their
camels were scrawny, the donkeys undersized—desert creatures without the
romance of the desert.

I discussed the subject with Jews, Englishmen and working-class Arabs
with whom I had occasion to chat several times. The Jews confirmed my
observation. The Englishmen brought dozens of additional examples; the
Arabs made no denials whenever questions of fact, and not diplomacy were

involved. Jews who had lived in the country almost half a century and had a romantic weakness for the Arabs, agreed with me. They agreed that the general well-being of the Arab had been increased, even though they were profoundly shocked to hear that friends had reproved me for driving with an Arab chauffeur from Haifa to Tel Aviv, or that a little Jewish boy in Jerusalem had called out "Arabi asur," "the Arab is forbidden," when I was about to get a shoe-shine from an Arabian bootblack.

Today the Arabs have more and better paid work; they have easier and humaner working conditions. No such change would have been possible without Jewish colonization. English officials, outwardly ultra-courteous, furnished me with handfuls of material which demonstrated how influential Jewish colonization had been in raising the economic standard of the Arab. However, to discourage me, they would say evasively: "But that's not the problem; that's not the difficulty in Arab-Jewish relations." When I finally urged one such Englishman to speak up, he took out a fresh cigar, muttered what might have been "you know" or "I'll tell you," and proceeded to tell me something of his family troubles. His mother and elder brother lived somewhere in Australia. Their only income was a meager pension from the English government, not enough to keep body and soul together. He, the Jerusalem official, had to support both because the older brother was a ne'er-do-well who spent his days at tennis. Two years ago he had passed a bad check. If not for the help of the Jerusalem brother, he would have been jailed. "And you can imagine," said the English official, "that he never so much as sends me a card! Furthermore, this only brother of mine is my bitterest enemy and would be happy to hear that a Bedouin's knife had dispatched me. He eats my bread but the good-for-nothing doesn't wish to be beholden to me. Marxists, they tell me, believe only in economic motives. How idiotic! The lowest of the low seeks dignity above all else. If he doesn't get it, he is prepared to destroy the whole world. I have told you a story. You can deduce the moral."

True enough, an old story with an old moral. Cain and Abel—economically equal! Had they been what the Englishman called "Marxists" they could have lived in peace—the one with his sheep; the other with his fields. But Cain also wanted his "dignity"—that God should smile when he laid his sacrifice on the altar. An old story—Joseph and his brethren; Isaac and Ishmael; Jacob and Esau. The Esau problem is not simple. Richard Beer Hoffman in his dramatic poem, "Jacob's Dream" has revealed the full tragedy of being Esau. "Give me a pot of lentils: I am hungry. Take the birthright for the pottage." But after the mess of pottage has been eaten, the hunger stilled, one is a man again. "I want my birthright too." Jacob seeks to persuade Esau that he does not need the birthright; that the difference between Jacob and Esau is not the difference between greater and lower, but merely a difference in kind. But Esau is not persuaded—he wants what the Englishman calls "dignity"— the birthright for himself and for his children.

Is this the crux of the Arab-Jewish problem? My Englishman's knowledge of Nietzsche is slight: he has probably never heard of Alfred Adler, but I feel that he is right. Intuitively, he has grasped the essentials of the question. There are probably no absolute Jacob natures or Esau natures. The "Nordic" theoreticians are pathologically obsessed with the notion of superiority. Probably one is cast for the role of Jacob or Esau not so much because of spiritual differences as because of historic conditions. Nevertheless the time comes when Esau rebels against his state. If he cannot have the birthright, he does not want Jacob to have it either—or else, let Jacob have it at a distance so that Esau's eyes will not grow sick with envy.

Lenin understood this when, in the years of military communism, he bestowed a sense of "superiority" on the wretched Russian worker. The Russian proletarian was hungry and cold. Instead of a pot of lentils, Lenin gave him a vision of a pot of meat in times to come. For years the worker's chief gratification came from the new aristocratic rank he had secured during the revolution. Hitler, too, understands the secret. He intoxicated all German youth with a sense of "superiority" to erase the Esau stigma. Germany may have to forgo the pot of lentils for years, but as long as the young men can march along the streets and believe that they are not inferior to France and that Europe is terrified, all is well.

One can prove to an Arab in Palestine that he has lost nothing through Jewish colonization. One can show him all the advantages that have accrued to him; one can persuade him that in the future he will profit still more from Jewish immigration. He will understand and agree, but the Esau-worm will, nevertheless, gnaw at his heart. The mess of pottage is conceded, but where is the birthright? "Jacob says that he will not lord it over me. I believe him; I believe that he will not wish to lord it, that he will respect my rights—but his very existence is a violation of me, because Jacob reminds me, even through his benefactions, that he is Jacob and I am Esau—at any rate—Esau for the time being."

Perhaps the problem of Jewish-Arab relations belongs to the realm of psychology rather than economics or politics. We must have good economists and diplomats in Palestine. Our life with the Arabs, however, demands the presence of competent social physicians. The labor movement, above all, must discover the therapeutic measures which will heal the sore spots in the relations between Jew and Arab.

Source: Hayim Greenberg, "Jew and Arab," *Jewish Frontier*, Dec. 1934, pp. 23–24.

60

"Give Up the Illusion of Building a Jewish Homeland" (1936)

SAMUEL WEISS

A member of the Central Bureau of Jewish Socialist Branches of the Socialist Party, Samuel Weiss published the following critique of Zionism in response to the Great Arab Revolt that raged in Palestine between 1936 and 1939, Weiss opposed Zionism, but nonetheless called for open Jewish immigration to Palestine, contrary to the demand of Arab nationalists and many left-wing anti-Zionists. Weiss's piece was one in a series of discussion articles that appeared in the *American Socialist Monthly*, the official theoretical organ of the Socialist Party.

The present situation in Palestine is the result of the three-cornered conflict between Jews, Arabs and English imperialism, a conflict of some years, and one which is growing steadily more severe. The situation must be considered in the light of the historic background from which the conflict began. The main forces responsible for that conflict must be defined and effort made toward a solution of this problem. [. . .]

The old Roman motto, "divide and rule" is practiced in a complete form by English Imperialism in Palestine.

In consonance with this strategy the chauvinistic impulses of the Arab and of the Jewish masses are constantly kept at high pitch, so that at the slightest provocation the Holy Land becomes a battle-ground between Jews and Arabs.

English Imperialism finds fertile soil in the strategy of the "Effendi" and Zionists. On the one hand, the "Effendis" have material economic interest in stirring a fighting spirit among the Arabian population against the Jews, in order to wipe out the class-consciousness which might take concrete form in a demand of the poor land-less "felachs" for an agrarian reform which would satisfy their hunger for soil at the expense of the rich landowners.

The agitation against the Jews and the cementing of Pan-Arabic tendencies finds fertile soil in Zionism. Zionism, in accordance with its illusion of building a homeland for Jews in Palestine, is constantly pursuing the policy of taking over the economic positions of the native population. Zionist institutions which buy new land for new Jewish settlements are often forced to evict the poor "felachs" for whom the piece of land is often the only means of a livelihood.

The "Histadrut,"[1] an organization of Jewish industrial and field laborers, has conducted a chauvinistic campaign against the employment of Arab labor by Jewish enterprises and colonies, a systematic campaign that Jewish factory and landowners should employ exclusively, Jewish labor only.

Even though Jewish colonization creates new industries in Palestine, fills in swamp-lands, and raises the cultural standard of the population, which is to the advantage of the Arabian population, the policy of the Zionist organizations, including the "Histradrut," must however, lead to the creation of a hostile relationship between the Jewish and Arabic working masses. This relationship creates a condition in which the Arab considers the Zionist colonization and immigration a danger to his own interests.

The Arabian masses feel that the small Jewish minority, supported by hated English imperialism, is about to conquer their lands.

The tactics of Zionism, and its component sections, brought about a condition through which the Arabian ruling classes are diverting the Arabian struggle for emancipation. Instead of conducting that struggle with a clear vision of liberating themselves from English imperialism, they are directing it against the Jewish population. This struggle takes on the grotesque form of pogroms and hooligan excesses, which must be condemned by every socialist. The Arabic masses instead of being incited against the Jewish masses should be educated in the interests of mutual understanding between both nationalities instead of being stirred up against each other.

The present situation in Palestine which finds expression in a system of terroristic acts against the Jewish population, burning of Jewish fields, uprooting of planted trees, etc., have their causes and grow out of the above mentioned relationship. Even should order be restored through negotiation or by English military force and the Arabic general strike be terminated, as long as the relationship between the Jews and the Arabs remains as it is now, without any basic change, the uprising will constantly be repeated.

As Jews and socialists, we must at the present moment, warn against the continuation of the chauvinistic policies of the Zionists of all kinds in Palestine. Immigration to Palestine which is the result of the growing reaction in Poland and Germany must be utilized for the peaceful up-building of the land and be a constructive force for those Jews, who, through economic boycott and oppression, have been driven out of these countries. In no case, should this immigration be utilized to deepen the chasm between the Jews and Arabs in Palestine.

Not English bayonets, but a serious understanding between the Arabian and Jewish working masses will make it possible for the Jewish minority in Palestine to live in peace and enjoy the fruits of its labors.

Mutual unions of Arabian and Jewish workers, both industrial and agricultural, built on the principle of class-struggle against the mutual exploiting forces, will be the best answer to the "divide and rule" policy of the British imperialism and against the chauvinistic propaganda of the "Effendis" and the Zionists.

The "Histadrut," as the organization of thousands of Jewish workers in Palestine will, in the interests of these masses, have to draw a line between themselves and the policies of general Zionism, and give up the illusion of building a Jewish homeland in Palestine. This illusion is not only responsible for the chauvinistic policy against the Arabians, but it is also responsible for its orientation on the Hebraic culture that makes the "Histadrut" looked upon with disfavor by the Yiddish-speaking masses in the whole world.

The Jewish problem in Palestine, just as in Poland, in Roumania and America, can only be solved through a joint struggle of the working masses in each country, against reaction, against anti-semitism and fascism and for the establishment of a socialist society. As Socialists we should basically be for:

1. Free immigration in Palestine, just as we are for such free immigration the world over.

2. Recognition of the rights of the Jewish minority in Palestine to live and enjoy all privileges that are to a free citizen in a civilized country, including the right of the Yiddish language, just as we are for the recognition of these rights for the Jewish minorities throughout the world.

3. The creation of a form of government autonomy, which should embrace proportional representation and should be based on democratic principles.

4. The building of a Socialist Party as the vanguard for the carrying out of Jewish and Arab working class unity.

Source: Samuel Weiss, "Statement on the Present Situation in Palestine," *American Socialist Monthly*, Aug. 1936, pp. 17–19.

NOTES

1. The Histadrut, or the General Federation of Workers in the Land of Israel, was a socialist labor organization founded in 1920. Its intent was to support economic development and workers' rights in Palestine, as well as to encourage Jewish immigration to Palestine and to nurture Jewish culture. Shortly after its founding, the Histadrut began to reach out to Arab workers in Palestine, publishing a periodical in Arabic in 1925 and organizing Arab-Jewish trade unions in specific government industries.

61

Jewish Upbuilding Is Revolutionizing Palestine (1939)

BEZALEL SHERMAN

Bezalel Sherman (1896–1971), a prolific sociologist of American Jewry who wrote in English and Yiddish, published this defense of Zionism as a revolutionary, antifascist force. It appeared in the Socialist Party's journal, *Socialist Review*, at the tail end of the Great Arab Revolt.

[. . .] Since 1920, the Jewish community in Palestine was subjected to four pogrom-attacks—each more violent than the preceding one. Now, if we have learned anything from Jewish history, we learned this: no pogrom occurs in any country whose government does not want it to occur. Surely, British imperialism, which rules over a quarter of the globe, could find a way to cope with the small terrorist bands in Palestine, especially when the Palestinian Jew is not at all ready to be slaughtered without a fight.

The pogroms were never unexpected. The air was charged before each attack. There was ample time to take precautionary measures. But the government did nothing. If it did not actually instigate or encourage the pogroms, it is certainly guilty of criminal negligence—negligence which gave the terrorists the right to claim that the Government was with them. The Peel Commission[1] was quite outspoken on this point. It publicly made the charge that the Palestinian government failed to give Jews the protection to which they were entitled.

Every pogrom resulted in a commission being appointed to determine its causes. And the report of every commission led to some new restriction of Jewish immigration and endeavor in Palestine. In the intervals, the government would sometimes relent in the enforcement of the restrictions without, however, repealing them. They were held as a sword over the head of the Jewish population.

Whenever there was a clash of interest between Arabs and Jews, the government sided with the first. At the same time it tried to appease the Jewish population by granting it some minor concession. It has enacted laws which, in effect, rewarded the terrorists for their attacks on Jews, and attempted to offset by overlooking slight violations of the same laws by Jews.

But England has not overlooked something that Zionist leadership has failed to notice for a long time, namely—the coming into being of an Arab nation. She realized that new methods would have to be applied if her rule over the Arab lands was to continue. Before the war, there were only Arab tribes, scattered over a number of countries and forever quarreling with each other. British promises of Arab political independence have certainly contributed to the Arabs' enlisting under the English flag. But after reading the memoirs of T. E. Lawrence, organizer of the "Arab Revolt" against Turkey, one cannot escape the conclusion that British gold played an even more decisive role. The support of the Arab chieftains was simply bought and paid for.

But the situation changed. In the first place, the Arabs who entered the war as tribes, came out of it a people, even if only in embryo. In the second place, a new bidder for Arab cooperation appeared on the scene: Hitlerism-Fascism. A number of Arab states were born. In Palestine, Jewish activity has given accelerated tempo to the process of Arab social differentiation, bringing in its wake a process of Arab national consolidation. Arab land-owners and their servants—the Muftis and intellectuals—put themselves at the head of the national movement in order not to be swept out of power by the social awakening of the Arab toiling masses. Hence the ultra-reactionary character of the Arab Nationalist Movement. Hence, too, the close relationship between the movement and Hitlerism.

That the Arab National Movement has, from its very inception, assumed an anti-Jewish character goes without saying. Jewish settlement spelled the death-knell of the very system upon which the economic and social power of the Arab leaders rested. And they could no more be expected peacefully to accept Jewish development in Palestine than could the French aristocracy be expected to make peace with the French bourgeoisie at the time of the Great Revolution.

England was not unmindful of the *objective* danger of the Arab National Movement eventually turning against herself—and she tried to curtail its direction. By catering to the anti-Jewish sentiments of the incited Arab mobs, she hoped to prevent, or at least to retard, the development of the movement into an anti-imperialist force.

This explains why the English government tolerated the pogrom-activities of the Effendis (Arab feudalist land-owners). Here we also find the explanation for the fact that the government always supported the most reactionary leaders and helped to crush all opposition emanating from more liberal Arab groupings.

British maneuvers in international affairs have also had repercussions in Palestine. To a certain extent British policy in Palestine has become a barometer by which could be ascertained the social climate of the world. Whenever international liberalism gained the upper hand, Jewish effort in Palestine was allowed to proceed unfettered. However, in times of reactionary tides, a pro-Arab policy was pursued by the English Government. Is it any wonder, then, that the "White Paper" coincides with the policy of "appeasement"?

The lines are now becoming visible. On one side we have the Arab nationalist movement headed by fascist elements who are desperately trying to check the cultural and economic growth of Palestine in order to retain an obsolete system. On the other hand there is Jewish upbuilding which is revolutionizing the country. Between them stands England, trying to strike a balance by giving the loaf to Arab reaction and some crumbs to the Jews. She occupies the same position in the world at large; standing between democracy and fascism, feeding bread to the latter and stones to the first.

But what of Zionism and what stand must Socialists now take in relation to it?

A correct answer to these questions is possible only on the basis of the following considerations:

1. To many Jews Palestine represents the glory of their national past. To others it represents a normal national future. But to the vast majority of the more than a quarter of a million Jews who have immigrated into Palestine in the past ten years, and to many more hundreds of thousands of Jews who are waiting for a chance to enter Palestine,—that country means the only escape from an unbearable present. They are not carried to Palestine on the wings of national aspirations or social ideals; they are driven thither by the most brutal persecution in modern history.

2. Socialists must evaluate events and processes from the point of view of their effect on the play of social forces. A movement is progressive if it advances the cause of social liberation; it is reactionary if it is detrimental to that cause.

Proceeding from these considerations, [. . .] it is the duty of true socialists to support the Jewish upbuilding in Palestine.

Source: Bezalel Sherman, "British Policy in Palestine," *Socialist Review*, Sept.–Oct. 1939, pp. 19–20.

NOTES

1. The British government appointed the Peel Commission (headed by Earl Peel, a former Conservative minister) in 1936 to investigate the causes of the Great Revolt and of the "Palestine problem" more generally. The Commission eventually (in 1937) recommended the termination of the British Mandate in Palestine and advocated for the partitioning of Palestine into a Jewish state, an Arab state, and a residual British-controlled area around Jerusalem, with a corridor to the coast at Haifa. The plan was quickly rejected by the British government.

62

"The Jewish Problem Will Be Solved as Soon as the Jews Again Become a Normal Nation" (1943)

ARTHUR ROSENBERG

The historian Arthur Rosenberg (1889–1943) was a former member of the German Communist Party's Central Committee until his expulsion in 1927. He subsequently became a democratic socialist and a Zionist. After Hitler's ascension to power in 1933, Rosenberg fled Germany and settled in New York City. The following article argues that the problem of anti-Semitism can only be solved by the establishment of a Jewish homeland. It appeared in *Youth and Nation*, organ of the socialist-Zionist youth organization Ha-Shomer Ha-Tsair.

Certain benevolent people like to ask us: "Why do you bother us with the so-called Jewish question? After the fall of Fascism and the victory of Democracy (or Socialism, or Communism) everything will be all right. The Jews will enjoy equal rights with everybody else and will no longer constitute a special problem."

The victory of Democracy (or Socialism, etc.) can achieve much and improve many things, but it will not produce one major result, i.e., the abolition of existing nations of mankind. To have a hope that one day all the nations of the world will disappear and that all men will enter one big international family, is a fine and noble one, but it has little chance of fulfillment during the next five hundred years. During our own generation and the forthcoming, a Democratic or Socialist world will be divided among the old historical nations: there will be English and French and Chinese and Jews.

It is true that after the fall of Fascism the relation of the different nations to one another can be much improved, that the gangster rule can be abolished, and reasonable, peaceful agreements can be concluded. The nations of the future might use humanitarian methods, especially if they are under the leadership of organized labor, but nations will continue to defend the right of their members to eat and to work. Therefore, the Jewish problem will not disappear in the most auspicious future.

Our benevolent friends might perhaps deny the fact that the Jews are a nation, and they might claim that the Jews are only a religious group. This is the most foolish argument that can be used in any discussion of the Jewish problem. The large majority of the Jews today, the Jews of Eastern and oriental origin, have never lost any of the attributes of a normal nation: they have their own language, their own culture (not only religion), their own manners of life, and they constitute a separate economic and social body.

But what was the position of the emancipated and assimilated Jews of Central and Western Europe before Hitler? [. . .]

During the whole history of the Jews it has never happened that any considerable group of Jews was successfully assimilated to another nation. It so happens too that the instances of individual cases of perfect assimilation is smaller than people usually believe. [. . .]

If somebody should prophesy today that Fascism would fall in the next year and after it would follow one full century during which all the governments of the civilized world would be pro-Jewish, we would regard such a prophet as a fanatic optimist. Nevertheless, we have had a century of this kind of history: namely the period from the Great French Revolution to the Dreyfus case during which time practically all the governments and the public opinion in Central and Western Europe and North America were pro-Jewish. In this period the Jews had all the opportunities of a free development and the result was the most dreadful breakdown in Jewish history. Every historical and social study of the Jewish problem confirms the truth of the national and Zionist outlook. The futile longing for assimilation can only result in the moral and physical degradation of the Jews.

The Jewish problem will be solved as soon as the Jews again become a normal nation, in their own country and that can only be Palestine, a nation composed of productive men and women and that means a Labor Palestine. No modern system of Socialism or Communism would be able to abolish the national distinctions that exist. Internationalism does not intend to abolish nations, but rather to educate them to an honest cooperation. There is, therefore, not the smallest contradiction between the Socialist ideal of the Jewish worker and the Jewish youth and their national program.

By concentrating again on Palestine, we Jews turn away from Europe and America and become an Eastern nation once more. This fact has very great implications for the present time for this war will have as one of its results the emancipation of Asia from rule by the White Man. The Jews will have to prove to the other future free nations of Asia and especially the Arab nations, that they are no appendix to any "white imperialism," but brothers in Asia. A workable compromise between Jewish Labor in Palestine and the toiling Arab masses will safeguard the Jewish national future.

Source: Arthur Rosenberg, "The Jewish Nation and Socialism," *Youth and Nation*, June 1943, pp. 11–12.

63

The Final Emancipation of the Jews Is the Struggle for Socialism (1946)

ERNEST MANDEL

Ernest Mandel (1923–1995) was born in Frankfurt, Germany, to Polish-Jewish parents and raised in Belgium. During Nazi Germany's occupation of Belgium, Mandel was imprisoned in a concentration camp for his resistance activities. He wrote the following article in French as the concluding chapter to *The Materialist Conception of the Jewish Question*, a treatise composed in 1942 by the Belgian Trotskyist Abram Leon, who perished in Auschwitz in 1944. In the decades after World War II, Mandel became an influential theorist of revolutionary Marxism in Europe. The selection here appeared under the pseudonym "Ernest Germain" in the American Trotskyist journal *Fourth International* at a time when British rule over Palestine was growing increasingly untenable.

The development of anti-Semitism, the result of definite social and historic causes, is producing the spread of Zionist nationalism among the despairing and declassed petty bourgeois Jewish masses. The brutal equalization of Jews of all strata in the extermination camps sharpened nationalism even among Jewish workers, in the degree that international solidarity remained too weak on the part of the workers of other nations. It is up to those who find themselves in a favored position as compared with the Jewish workers to take the leadership now and bring about freedom of immigration into their countries for their survivors. This is the best way to win the Jewish workers from the Zionist utopia.

If thousands of Jews in Europe are now demanding the right to migrate to Palestine, the primary reason for this is that the doors of the rest of the world are closed to them. It is also the product of the incredible persecutions of these past years and of the relative passivity of the world proletariat. [. . .]

In the past the Zionists counted, even during the war, upon the support of British imperialism. In reality, the latter "merely uses the Jews as a counterweight to the Arab threat, but does everything to raise difficulties for Jewish immigration." No one today can doubt the exactness of this analysis. At the moment when the position of the British empire in the Arab world—decisive link between India and the Mediterranean—is threatened at one and the same time by American imperialism and the Soviet bureaucracy, it is a matter of life and death for the City [London] to have the Arab factor on its side. Inevitably British concessions to the Jews will tend to diminish, not increase. Neither in the name of "justice," nor in that of "past promises," nor because of the terrorist threats, will the British risk losing their control of the Suez Canal and of their last oil fields. [. . .]

This consequently indicates the immediate duty of the Palestinian workers' movement: to integrate itself in the overall workers' movement of the Middle East against British imperialism. An obstacle on the road to unity of the Jewish and Arab proletariat, Zionism at the same time bars the road to this integration, and prevents the concentration of all Palestinian working class forces around the slogan: *Immediate and complete independence for Palestine! Immediate withdrawal of all British troops! Election of a Constituent Assembly by direct and secret vote!* All intermediate formulae, such as the "binational state," represent at bottom only the refusal to give up a nationalist position in favor of the general interests of the proletariat and will rebound directly against their authors.

Only a position by the vanguard of the Jewish workers calling for Palestine independence will allow it in the next stage to pose the question of Jewish immigration to the Arab workers in a sovereign Palestinian Assembly. Only the Arab masses, once they are freed from the imperialist yoke, will have the right to decide whether or not they are opposed to the immigration of Jewish workers. [. . .]

[. . .] The problems which are posed before Jewry, like those which are posed before humanity, demand such radical solutions and are so urgent that no one dares any longer to seek refuge behind a propaganda for temporary palliatives. But all those who still continue to call revolutionists illusory thinkers will find, if they have not already done so, that there is no illusion worse than an expectation of viable solutions from a regime which is no longer able to introduce improvements in anything except machines for death.

The ordeals through which humanity has just passed have stultified many minds and paralyzed many wills. The petty bourgeoisie and especially the intellectuals have been the most affected. Those who were in the habit of thinking of the world as "rational" are themselves losing their reason in face of such irrational decay. But it is not these skeptics who will determine the fate of humanity. The will to struggle of the working masses of the entire world has already affirmed itself more mightily than ever during the year which has followed the end of hostilities. It is upon this will to struggle of the proletariat that the vanguard must fix its hopes and growth.

As the most sorely wounded, the Jews have especially allowed themselves to be carried away by the psychosis of despair and demoralization, which has been further sharpened by the specific social structure of this people. But in a few years, the immediate effects of the nightmare will disappear. The collapse of Palestinian hopes will become obvious. Whereas for the moment there exist only negative poles which repel each other, by that time the positive pole, that of the international revolutionary proletariat, will have already confirmed its attractive force with striking victories. Since we have no reason to doubt the fate of humanity, let us also not doubt that the Jewish working masses, after passing through a series of disappointing experiences, will recognize that their future is indissolubly linked with that of the proletariat and the revolutionary movement and that they will again, as in the past, take an important place in this movement, and will owe their final emancipation to a devoted struggle for the cause of socialism.

Source: Ernest Germain [Mandel], "Jewish Question since World War II," *Fourth International* (Apr. 1947): pp. 109–113.

64

Jewish National Aspirations Are Not a Violation of Marxist Principles (1947)

ALBERT GLOTZER

Born in Russia and raised in Chicago, Albert Glotzer (1908–1999) was a founder of the Fourth International, the league of revolutionary Marxist parties loyal to Leon Trotsky and opposed to the Moscow-based Third International. Glotzer broke with the Fourth International and its American affiliate, the Socialist Workers Party, in 1940 to help found the Workers' Party, a Marxist organization hostile to the USSR. The following response to Ernest Mandel, who is referred to throughout as "Germain" (see document 63), appeared in the journal of the Workers' Party. Glotzer's critique did not represent the party's official position, only that of members sympathetic to the creation of a Jewish homeland.

The reaction of the official Fourth Internationalist organization to the Jewish question and the problem of Palestine in the new situation produced by Hitlerism and the war is a measure of their incapacity to free themselves from outlived theories and political positions. This results in a dreary reaffirmation of old ideas and programs accompanied by the repetitious explanation that "there is no reason to change our position" since "there is nothing new in the situation." Thus it is the same with the Russian question, the national question and the Jewish question. For the most part, these organizations, most notably the Socialist Workers Party[1] in the United States, have remained virtually silent on the Jewish question. The silence is not wholly accidental; it is a reflection of policy. [...]

Germain's essay, which marks one of the first efforts of the official Fourth International to speak somewhat concretely on the Jewish question, is distinguished by its utterly detached and abstract approach to the problem, but which is characteristic for its unquestionably correct interpretations of parts of an old Marxist position which has little to do with life today. [...]

This article can be summarized briefly: The Jews of Europe have undergone almost unhuman suffering; this is due to the nature of capitalism. But the Jews are not alone in this suffering. Other peoples, other national minorities are faced with the same or similar prospects of extermination or near-extermination. This is a symbol of the decay of capitalism. There is no hope for these people except in the victory between now and the future, but . . . oops, sorry . . . that can't be helped, you know. That's capitalism for you. The Jews, despite this grim prospect, must not allow themselves to be emotionally worked up by the fact that six, seven or eight millions of them have been wiped out in Europe! [. . .]

Germain characterizes the experiences of the Jews as a symbol of the fate of humanity in general and as the product of a sick society. And he adds: "The tragedy of the Jews is only the herald to other peoples of their coming fate." The correctness of this generalization has a strange ring: the expression of sympathy for the Jews seems constantly to be apologized for and qualified by the observations that their sufferings are socially and historically conditioned, as if that in some way mitigates the condition of this people.

Thus, after describing the unrelieved horrors of the Jews, Germain is under compulsion to write: "Alongside of five million murdered Jews are sixty million victims of imperialist war. The barbaric treatment of the Jews by Hitlerite imperialism is only an extreme expression of the barbarism of the general methods of imperialism in our period. As against the Jewish deportations we now find the deportation of millions of Germans from Poland and Czechoslovakia."

What is the point of these comparisons? To show the Jews that there is nothing unique in their position in European society today? But that is silly, for the conditions which the Jewish people face *are* unique. While it is true that Germans have been deported from Poland and Czechoslovakia, undergoing severe suffering in the process, the comparison ends at that point. For these Germans return to their own nation, however divided it may be under conditions of military occupation. They may return to friends and relatives. They do not remain in concentration camps where their families and friends had been exterminated by the hundreds of thousands and millions. They do not return to a hostile country which hates them.

Chancing the charge that I do not have real feelings for the sixty million victims of the imperialist slaughter, I still say that the comparison made by Germain is false. The Jews were not merely victims of an imperialist war; they were the victims of a social and political program of German fascism serving its big business masters, and would have faced the same extermination whether there was a war or not.

But is there not some special point to Germain's observation? Yes, there is. It is to affirm by commission and omission there is really nothing unique in the position of European Jewry, no special problems created by their homelessness and landlessness. [. . .]

Where does this bring us? To Germain's blind alley: the Jews cannot live in Europe. They must leave. However, there is no place for them to go. The brutality of the conditions they experience daily and their homelessness has resulted in their universal desire to go to Palestine. Therefore we are for opening the doors of the whole world—five continents no less. Africa included—but . . . not Palestine! Why not Palestine? According to Germain:

> 1. From an economic point of view, Palestine and the whole Middle East will suffer terrible devastation in the coming world economic crisis. That means no future for the Jews there.
> 2. From the "socio-economic" point of view, "the forces opposing this immigration have a crushing superiority over the Palestinian Jews and over world Zionism."

But from an economic point of view, the whole world will suffer just as severely from the coming world economic crisis, and from the "socio-economic" point of view, the populations of other countries are just as opposed to the migration of the Jews as the Arab nationalists. No matter. This does not deter Germain and his co-thinkers from demanding the right of the Jews to enter *those* countries. And so we find that the slogans for the right of free immigration for Jews to all countries and to the five continents did not, in Germain's mind, mean complete *free* immigration, and to *all* countries.

Are the Arabs right in opposing Jewish immigration? If the demand for free immigration is a correct democratic, socialist slogan, shouldn't revolutionary socialists issue it despite the opposition of the Arabs and try to convince, not to opposite it? Is there any special merit in criticizing only the reactionary positions of the official Jewish organizations and to say not a word about the reactionary feudalistic concepts of the Arab chieftains? On our part, we have made our severest criticisms of official Jewish policy, but we have not lost sight of the false attitude of the Arab rulers whose opposition to immigration has a strong reactionary base and coincides in part with British imperialist policy. For the truth is that the British use both Jews and Arabs with varying success.

And yet the fate of the Jews is sealed. The continued existence of bourgeois society will mean not merely the extermination of the Jews in Europe, but over the whole world, and especially in the United States. Can anything be done about it? No, not really, for "the only way out which still remains open to humanity is at the same time the solution of the Jewish question." Worse than that, "the peculiarities of Jewish history have only determined a special subordination of the future of this people to the outcome of the unfolding social struggles." Only the Jews? And other peoples? Apparently not. In *this* case, the Jews *are* unique, says Germain. For them there really is no hope unless socialism comes and quickly, too. [. . .]

Only dogmatic and schematic thinking could produce such abstractions on the current Jewish question. [. . .] The Jewish problem today is so different qualitatively from the past, that it is almost entirely a new one demanding new solutions. [. . .]

All one has to do is to examine the real world of today to see how clearly different it is, how completely insecure is the position of the Jews now. Is it an exaggeration to say, after more than ten years of Hitlerism in a decaying world characteristic for its social degeneration, that the existence of the Jews is as perilous in 1947 as it was in 1940? The virus of anti-Semitism has spread to all borders and has infected nations and peoples whose relative tolerance was conspicuous in former years. The truth is that the Jews have no place in Europe to live. They cannot return to their old homes and resume their former occupations. They are for the most part, the few hundred thousand European Jews who are left, inhabitants of former concentration camps in an atmosphere polluted with the stink of crematories, dungeons and fresh-dug graves. A person would have to be thick-skinned indeed not to feel the depths of despair which have seized hold of the Jewish population of the world, especially those who remain in Europe today.

Out of the cemetery in which the remnants of European Jews now temporarily reside has come a mass desire for emigration to Palestine, a desire which took almost spontaneous form. Why Palestine? Why not the United States, Australia, South America, England or France? The principal reason, as Germain himself admits, is that none of these countries will permit the entry of Jews or other displaced persons. In these circumstances, the Jews have, in fact, only one place to turn to that offers them some realistic prospect of salvation, namely, Palestine. Without going into a discussion now as to all the reasons why emigration to Palestine is justifiable, let me cite an important reason for it. More than one-third of the population of Palestine, who are Jews, want their fellow nationals to come there. The weight of persecution has created a deep bond of solidarity between European and Palestinian Jews. Palestine can absorb these several hundred thousand European Jews and offer them a haven in a world whose doors are closed to them. In a way it is an answer to the disgusting, hypocritical sympathies expressed for the Jews by the United States, Great Britain, Russia and the leading powers of the UN who are using the Jewish question as a political football in the new imperialist struggle for world domination.

To recognize the validity of these national aspirations for survival among Europe's Jews is not a violation of Marxist principles. On the contrary, to deny them would reveal not only an obstinate misunderstanding of everything that Lenin wrote on the national question, but a failure to understand what has happened in Europe in the past twenty-five years.

Source: Albert Gates [Glotzer], "The Jewish Problem after Hitler," *The New International* 13, no. 7 (Sept. 1947): pp. 206–210.

NOTES

1. Founded in 1937, the Socialist Workers Party was the official U.S. branch of the Trotskyist Fourth International. The SWP did not often address the specific plight of Jews in Europe; rather, the organization predicted that a worldwide Marxist-led revolution would follow World War II and would solve the problem of anti-Semitism through the defeat of capitalism and imperialism.

65

Israel and the World Struggle for Peace and Democracy (1948)

ALEXANDER BITTELMAN

In 1947, the Soviet Union unexpectedly reversed its traditional opposition to Zionism and called for the creation of a Jewish state, alongside an Arab state, in Palestine. The American Communist Party changed its position accordingly. Veteran Communist leader Alexander Bittelman (see document 3), who oversaw party work among Jews during the 1940s, articulated the following case for Israel in the party's monthly journal, *Political Affairs*. Although the Soviet Union reverted to an anti-Israel position in the early 1950s, elements within the American Communist Party, especially within its organized Jewish sector, remained sympathetic to the Jewish state.

The emergence of the state of Israel at this time is of considerable international significance. For the Jewish people this marks a great milestone in its history.

It can be safely assumed that the struggles of the Jewish masses against national discrimination and for equal rights in countries where Jewish communities suffer from anti-Semitic persecutions and inequality, will become intensified and strengthened because of the rise of Israel. Depending upon the degree of influence which the anti-imperialist and labor forces in Israel will be able to exercise upon the policies and development of the new state, Israel may in time become a very important factor in the struggle for national liberation and for peace throughout the Middle East.

The struggle for the independence and territorial integrity of the new Jewish state is part of the general struggle for peace, national independence, and democracy. It is also a struggle for the liberation of the Arab peoples from British and Anglo-American imperialist domination. It is a fight to prevent the imperialists and warmakers from turning the Middle East into a major base of military operations in a new world war.

It is necessary to say at this point that the anti-imperialist forces of the world, the peace forces headed by the Soviet Union, have played a decisive part in enabling the Jewish people of Palestine to attain their own state. This must be said now, not only because many leading Zionists tend to forget it, but especially because the fate of Israel as an independent and democratic state—its very existence—is inextricably bound up with the progress and success of the anti-imperialist and peace camp.

It is necessary to say further that Communists generally have played a very important part in the emergence of the Jewish state at this time, and that the American Communists have made serious contributions to the struggle for Israel.

In this fight we were guided by the fact that there lived in Palestine two peoples, not one—an Arab people and a Jewish people—and that the principle of national self-determination required that each of these two peoples be given the right decide for itself the kind and form of national existence it wanted to have.

Some comrades had difficulties for a while in seeing that the Jewish people in Palestine had the right to self-determination. The source of these difficulties was the inability to recognize that the Jewish people in Palestine was not just an aggregation of so many immigrants or children or immigrants, but that, in the course of recent history, a Jewish community had arisen which had begun to develop all the characteristics of a nation—and every oppressed nation is entitled to the right to self-determination. This applied equally to the Arabs of Palestine whose community also began to develop the characteristics of a nation. That is why the anti-imperialist forces, including the Communists, are the only consistent supporters, and now the best fighters, for the United Nations decision of November 29, 1947, which calls for the setting up of two independent and democratic states in Palestine—a Jewish state and an Arab state.

Another source of difficulty for some comrades in recognizing the progressive nature of the struggle for Jewish statehood in Palestine *in the present period*, as distinct from the time when there were no progressive forces interested in and capable of realizing it, was the fact that Zionism—bourgeois nationalism—was the original political movement championing the establishment of a Jewish state in Palestine.

Here the misapprehension was twofold. First, there was a lack of realization that historically the bourgeoisie was the leading force in the rise of many nations and states, in the period when the bourgeoisie was still capable of progressive actions. The fact that it was the Jewish nationalist bourgeoisie which originally raised the political demand for a Jewish state could not in itself—abstracted from the concrete historical conditions—invalidate the progressive nature of the demand. Moreover, these comrades did not grasp the fact that the fight for the right to national self-determination even today, in the imperialist era, is of a general democratic character and not of a socialist character.

The demand for a Jewish state in Palestine *in past periods* was not utopian and reactionary because bourgeois nationalists were leading the fight for it. The demand was utopian and reactionary because there was no Jewish nation in Palestine and no progressive forces internationally interested in and capable of realizing this demand.

Secondly, there was the lack of understanding that in the imperialist era it is the working class and its Marxist party that are capable of leading a consistent fight for national self-determination and freedom. Who is it, if not the working class, led by the Communist Parties, that is now rallying the people of Western Europe to resist the enslavement by Wall Street imperialism and to defend the national independence of their countries? And who is leading the fight for the national freedom of China? Again it is the working class, led by the Communist Party of China, that is building the alliance with the peasantry, the middle classes and all other anti-imperialist forces, and that is leading the fight for national freedom.

There was also a certain lack of understanding that Communists can—and must—carry on the fight for the national independence of their peoples not as bourgeois nationalists but as working-class internationalists. It is in the nature—the class nature—of bourgeois nationalism to tend to narrow down the fight, to vacillate between imperialism and anti-imperialism, to mistrust the working class and to seek to prevent its emergence as the leader of the national struggle for independence and, consequently, as the leader of the nation in the struggle for socialism. All this makes bourgeois nationalism highly inconsistent and wavering in the fight of the people for their national freedom. It produces tendencies of capitulation to, and compromise with, imperialism and strengthens the efforts of the reactionary forces in the Zionist movement to betray the national liberation fight completely.

But the nature of working-class internationalism is qualitatively different. It is consistently anti-imperialist and seeks the complete overthrow of imperialist domination. It bases itself upon the working class and all the other democratic forces of the people and seeks to make the working class the leader of the fight. It looks for allies internationally among the consistent anti-imperialist forces, the forces of peace, democracy, and socialism, the camp headed by the Soviet Union. It links up the fight for national liberation with the historical struggle of the exploited masses of the people for social liberation. It wages the fight for national freedom in such a way as to make it a stage in the struggle for socialism.

Inability to see clearly that the fight for Jewish statehood in Palestine can and must be carried on by Communists not as bourgeois nationalists but as working-class internationalists, was in part responsible for the temporary difficulties of certain comrades in recognizing the progressive nature of this struggle in the present period. This same inability to distinguish clearly enough between the bourgeois-nationalism and working-class internationalist policies in the struggle for the Jewish state has been and continues to be a source of errors and weakness of a bourgeois-nationalist nature in our own midst.

Communists aim to help bring about the broadest coalition of democratic and anti-imperialist peace forces, including Jewish bourgeois nationalists, to help Israel defend its independence, democracy, and territorial integrity. But in this broad coalition movement, Communists exert all their efforts to advance the working class to positions of leadership and to help the movement rise to the levels of ever greater anti-imperialist consistency—to the struggle to undermine the power of the monopolies. In other words, Communists fight and work in this broad coalition as working-class internationalists and not as bourgeois nationalists. This is one of the major conclusions that can be drawn from the application to this question of the draft resolution of the National Committee for our coming Party convention.

Consequently, we must view the fight for Israel in its broadest aspects. It is a fight for national freedom and independence. Why? Because Anglo-American imperialism threatens at present both the territorial integrity and national sovereignty of the new Jewish state, using for this purpose the so-called "truce" resolution of the United Nations and its "mediator." It is an anti-imperialist fight for peace because it aims to prevent Anglo-American imperialism from turning the Middle East and Israel into a strategic bridgehead for Wall Street's new world war. It is a fight for the liberation of the entire Middle East from imperialist domination and oppression—from the rule of the oil monopolies and their political agents.

In other words, we must see the fight for Israel as an organic part of the world struggle for peace and democracy, and we must so wage it. This means that the fight for Israel requires a struggle against the Truman Doctrine and Marshall Plan, against Wall Street's imperialist expansionism, against Wall Street's pro-fascist offensive upon the democratic liberties of the American people at home. It means, finally, that the fight for Israel can and will be won decisively and completely only by joining it with the fight of the camp of anti-imperialism and democracy headed by the Soviet Union. [. . .]

Source: Alexander Bittelman, "The New State of Israel," *Political Affairs* 17, no. 8 (Aug. 1948): pp. 720–730.

Recommended Reading
on Jewish Radicals

Cassedy, Steven. *To the Other Shore: The Russian Jewish Intellectuals Who Came to America.* Princeton: Princeton University Press, 1997.

Frankel, Jonathan. *Prophecy and Politics: Socialism, Nationalism, and the Russian Jews, 1862–1917.* Cambridge: Cambridge University Press, 1981.

Fraser, Steven. *Labor Will Rule: Sidney Hillman and the Rise of American Labor.* Ithaca: Cornell University Press, 1993.

Gittelman, Zvi, ed. *The Emergence of Modern Jewish Politics: Bundism and Zionism in Eastern Europe.* Pittsburgh: University of Pittsburgh Press, 2003.

Glazer, Nathan. *The Social Basis of American Communism.* New York: Harcourt, Brace & World, 1961.

Glenn, Susan A. *Daughters of the Shtetl: Life and Labor in the Immigrant Generation.* Ithaca: Cornell University Press, 1990.

Howe, Irving. *World of Our Fathers: The Journey of the East European Jews to America and the Life They Found and Made.* New York: Harcourt, Brace, Jovanovich, 1976; New York: NYU Press, 2005.

Jacobs, Jack. *On Socialists and "The Jewish Question" after Marx.* New York: NYU Press, 1993.

Katz, Daniel. *All Together Different: Yiddish Socialists, Garment Workers, and the Labor Roots of Multiculturalism.* New York: NYU Press, 2011.

Kossack, Hadassah. *Cultures of Opposition: Jewish Immigrant Workers, New York City, 1881–1905.* Albany: SUNY Press, 2000.

Laslett, John H. M. *Labor and Left: A Study of Socialist and Radical Influences in the American Labor Movement, 1881–1924.* New York: Basic Books, 1970.

Lederhendler, Eli. *Jewish Immigrants and American Capitalism, 1880–1920: From Caste to Class.* Cambridge: Cambridge University Press, 2009.

Liebman, Arthur. *Jews and the Left.* New York: Wiley, 1979.

Mendelsohn, Ezra, ed. *Essential Papers on Jews and the Left.* New York: NYU Press, 1997.

———. *On Modern Jewish Politics.* New York: Oxford University Press, 1993.

Michels, Tony. *A Fire in Their Hearts: Yiddish Socialists in New York.* Cambridge: Harvard University Press, 2005.

Orleck, Annelise. *Common Sense and a Little Fire: Women and Working-Class Politics in the United States, 1900–1965.* Chapel Hill: University of North Carolina Press, 1995.

Parmet, Robert D. *The Master of Seventh Avenue: David Dubinsky and the American Labor Movement.* New York: NYU Press, 2005.

Rischin, Moses. *The Promised City: New York's Jews, 1870–1914.* Cambridge: Harvard University Press, 1962.

Index

AALD. *See* American Alliance for Labor and Democracy

Abramovich, Raphael: Baldwin for, 230–31, 234–37; Browder against, 232–34, 236; free speech issues related to, 230–31, 234–35; intentions of, 228–29; resolutions against, 229–30

ACLU. *See* American Civil Liberties Union

ACWA. *See* Amalgamated Clothing Workers of America

Addams, Jane, 67–69, 69n2, 178n2

African Americans: Crosswaith for, 140–43, 143n1; economics for, 121–22; education for, 122; goals for, 120–23; Harrison, H., as, 100, 102n3; history of, 141; ILGWU for, 141–42; Jewish Americans for, 7–8, 17–18; Jewish labor movement for, 7–8; Ku Klux Klan and, 128, 234; in Los Angeles, 121–23; politics for, 121–22; pride for, 120; against trade-unionism, 140; trade-unionism for, 140–42, 142n1

Ahad Ha'am. *See* Ginsburg, Asher

Allison, Charles L., 131–32

ALP. *See* American Labor Party

Alter, Victor: aid for, 265, 267nn2–4; arrest of, 265, 267n5; execution of, 264–67; framing of, 267; for Poland, 264–67, 267nn1–5; release of, 266

Altgeld, John Peter, 47n4

Amalgamated Clothing Workers of America (ACWA), 18, 24n60; broad agenda of, 8; Cohen, Jennie, against, 144–45; hope from, 133

America: Anglo-Saxon, 288–89; secret police in, 254–57, 257nn1–4; socialists

in Europe compared to, 216–18, 218n3; social patriots in, 215; tradition of, 218. *See also specific organizations*

American Alliance for Labor and Democracy (AALD), 221, 223nn1–2

American Civil Liberties Union (ACLU), 257. *See also* Baldwin, Roger

American Communist Party: camp of, 263, 263n2; Democrats related to, 16; divisions within, 10–11, 126; field work in, 126–28; Jews in, 10, 15, 23n36, 23n49; in unions, 10. *See also specific communists*

American Communist Party membership: of Finnish immigrants, 10–11, 23n35; of Jewish immigrants, 10–11, 22n34, 23n35; of Polish immigrants, 22n34

American Federation of Labor, 9, 40n2, 133–34, 223n2

Americanism: co-operative, 290–92; in *Forverts*, 189–90; melting-pot as, 288–89; Zionism with, 291–92

Americanization: labor and, 36; tradition or, 68–69

American labor movement: Great Upheaval in, 25; Jewish leadership for, 8–9; Labor Day for, 124–25. *See also* Jewish labor movement; Labor movement meeting

American Labor Party (ALP), 16–17, 24n56

American Left, 12, 19; Jews' influence on, 17, 24n60

American Socialist Monthly, 308–10

American socialist movement, 21n24; German immigrants and, 2–3, 222; Jewish immigrants for, 5–7

Anarchism, 3, 25, 34, 66–67; *Di fraye arbeter shtime*, 93, 94n1, 124; Italian immigrants and, 6, 21n18; membership and, 21n18; socialism or, 38, 46. *See also* Haymarket Square; *specific anarchists*

Anti-fascism, 17–18

Anti-Semitism: in Depression, 11–12, 23n36; internationalism of, 325–26; Jewish culture and, 205–7; Lenin against, 270–71; nationalism from, 319; Nazism as, 146–48; Prague Trial as, 268, 270, 273–74, 275n2; Russia's revelation of, 274; against socialism, 271; Zionism and, 316–19. *See also* Arab violence; Hitler, Adolf; Russian anti-Semitism

Appeal to Reason, 3–4

Arab National Movement, 313–14

Arabs: Britain for, 300, 312–14, 320; dignity of, 306–7; Hitler compared to, 313; imperialism and, 308–9, 315n1, 320, 324; nation for, 313–14; rights of, 310; self-determination of, 328; well-being of, 304–5

Arab violence: Britain and, 300–302, 308–10, 312–14; as class struggle, 301–2, 308–10; from Communists, 299–300; demonstrations and, 299; exploitation for, 302; against Histadrut, 302, 303n2; immigration and, 309–10; inciters for, 299–300; misdirection of, 309; against oppression, 301–2, 303nn1–3; as pogroms, 298, 300–301, 312; politics of, 298–300; strategy behind, 298; understanding and, 309–10

Arbeter Ring (Workmen's Circle), 2, 18; description of, 135; English education from, 183–84; for Kentucky miners, 135, 136n1; Yiddish lectures from, 179–81, 181nn1–2, 182nn3–6

Asch, Sholem, 177, 178n7, 189, 201

Ashley, Jessie, 101

Assimilation: diaspora and, 289–90; Jews and, 291, 317

Ausubel, Nathan, 204–8

Baldwin, Roger, 257; for Abramovich,

230–31, 234–37; Browder and, 230–37; on free speech issues, 230–31, 234–35; for honesty, 236–37; impartiality of, 234–35

Balfour Declaration, 294

Barondess, Joseph, 171–73, 173n5

Barrett, James, 24n60

Beardsley, John, 131

Bedacht, Max, 228, 237n2

Belinsky, V. G., 269

Ben Ahud. *See* Zhitlowsky, Chaim

Berkman, Alexander, 43–44, 47n3, 95–96

Berkowitz, Isidor, 132

Bernick, Isadore, 137–39

Bernstein, Eduard, 189, 190nn9–10

Berson, Joseph. *See* Mink, George

Better America Foundation, 129–31, 132n1

Bingham, Alfred, 255

Birth control: capitalism and, 105, 107–8; child labor and, 106; costs of, 105; against God, 105–6; poverty related to, 104–5; Reitman for, 101, 105, 108n3; Sanger, M., for, 108n2, 234, 238n12; Sanger, W., for, 105, 108n2; science and, 106–7; socialism and, 107

Birth Control League, 101

Bisno, Abraham, 25, 27; on Haymarket Square, 35–36; on Spies, 33–34. *See also* Labor movement meeting; Manufacturers; Workingman's Educational Society

Bittelman, Alexander, 14–15, 25, 49; contradictions within, 53–54; on demonstration, 55–57; for Israel, 327–31; mother of, 53–54, 57. *See also* Bund

Blaustein, David, 171, 173n3

Blumgarten, Solomon, 177, 178n11

Bolshevik Party, 221–22, 223n5, 242

Bondi, August, 19n1

Bourne, Randolph, 288–92, 292n1, 293nn2–6

Bovshover, Joseph, 164

Brandeis, Louis, 292, 293n3

Breitscheid, Rudolph, 189, 190n8

Briand, Aristide, 176, 178n5

Britain: for Arabs, 300, 312–14, 320; Arab violence and, 300–302, 308–10, 312–14; against oppression, 301–2, 303nn1–3;

in Palestine, 298–302, 308–10, 312–14, 315n1, 320; Peel Commission of, 312, 315n1

Browder, Earl, 228, 237n3, 251; against Abramovich, 232–34, 236; Baldwin and, 230–37; for heckling, 232–33, 236; against imperialism, 233–34; against slander, 232

Buhle, Paul, 18, 24n64

Bulgaria, 273

Bullard, Arthur. *See* Edwards, Albert

Bund (Alliance), 5, 20n12, 282, 285n3; enrollment in, 51–53; loyalty to, 246–47; secret meetings of, 49–51; violence towards, 264–67. *See also* Russian Communists

Burgin, Herts, 294–97

Cady Stanton, Elizabeth, 113, 119n2

Cahan, Abraham, 154–55, 179–80; *Di arbeter tsaytung* from, 91–94, 94nn2–4, 154. See also *Forverts*

Cannistraro, Philip, 21n18

Capitalism, 37, 83; birth control and, 105, 107–8; Holocaust related to, 323; labor and, 33–34; for Russian Communists, 243–44

Caren, Arthur, 102

Catholics, 72

Chase, John C., 212, 213n1

Children: birth of, 63–64, 69n3; education of, 129–32, 242, 248n3; labor for, 60, 62–66; as second generation, 11–14. *See also* Birth control; Education

Cilano, Cosmo, 114

Civil Liberties Union, 131

Class struggle, 37, 97; Arab violence as, 301–2, 308–10; goals of, 83–84; imperialism and, 329; wages and, 33–34; Zionism and, 294

C.N.T.-F.A.I., 256, 257n4

Cohen, Jennie, 81, 144–45

Cohen, Lizbeth, 8

Cohen, Morris R., 292, 293n5

Communists: Arab violence from, 299–300; for coalition, 330; internationalism of, 329; Trotskyism and, 260, 262–63;

at Union Square, 102. *See also* Russian Communists

Comstock, Anthony, 108n1

Comstock Law (1873), 104–8, 108nn1–3

Congress of Industrial Organizations, 146–49

Conservativism: Better America Foundation from, 129–31, 132n1; synagogues and, 172–73

Contractors, 28, 89

Corey, Lewis. *See* Fraina, Louis C.

Corruption: of elections, 111–14; in Unions, 144–45. *See also* Anti-Semitism; Secret police

Crosswaith, Frank, 140–43, 143n1

Cultural pluralism, 291, 292n1

Culture. *See* Jewish culture

Czechoslovakia, 146–47; Prague Trial, 268, 270, 273–74, 275n2

Darcy, Sam Adams (Samuel Dardeck), 81, 126–28

Davis, Phillip, 168–73, 173nn1–7

Dawes, General, 229, 237n4

Debs, Eugene V., 3, 7

De Leon, Daniel, 187, 190n3

De Maupassant, Guy, 166

De Meyere, C. F., 131–32

Democracy: Russia without, 52; social, 3, 215; before socialism, 52–53; victory of, 316. *See also specific organizations*

Democrats, 16

Demonstrations: Arab violence and, 299; for Labor Day, 125; in New York City, 91–92; Red Sunday parade, 211–12, 213nn1–5; in Russia, 55–57; violence at, 56, 299

Denning, Michael, 18, 24n64

Depression: anti-Semitism in, 11–12, 23n36; Jacobs and, 76; youth and, 138

Detroit, Michigan, 199–202

Deutscher, Isaac, 12

Diaspora: assimilation and, 289–90; idealist Zionism and, 283–84; protection in, 282–83

Diner, Hasia, 8

Discrimination: from Histadrut, 309. *See also* Anti-Semitism; Racial discrimination

Donnenfeld, Harry, 112–13, 119n1

Dubofsky, Melvyn, 5

Economics: for African Americans, 121–22; Jacob and Esau in, 305–6; Marx and, 304–5; in Palestine, 300, 304–5, 324

Edelshtat, Dovid, 87n1, 159, 161n2; background on, 86; on Haymarket Square memorial, 86–87, 87n2; on Most, 87, 87n3; on Schewitsch, 87, 87n4

Edelson, Beckie, 101–2

Edlin, William, 180, 182n5

Education, 38–40; for African Americans, 122; of children, 129–32, 242, 248n3; in English, 183–84; for Granich, 250; from ILGWU, 194–96, 197nn1–4; of Jacobs, 71, 73–74, 77–80; of Jewish workers, 84–85, 157–58, 170; New Haven Educational Club, 157; for Newman, P., 159–61, 161nn1–3; from New York's East Side, 164–67; night school for, 65–67; of Russian Jews, 155; for Russia's new intelligentzia, 226–27; from Second Avenue University, 114–15; on sexual relations, 198; for socialism, 37, 55, 57–58, 151; strolling and, 174–76; in Trotskyism, 260–61; for wives, 94, 94n4; for women, 160, 175–76, 195–96, 197n2, 199–202, 203n1; in Yiddish language, 196, 197n4, 199–202, 203n1. *See also* Second Avenue University; *specific organizations*

Edwards, Albert (Arthur Bullard), 130, 132n1

Ehrlich, Henryk: aid for, 265, 267nn2–4; arrest of, 265, 267n5; execution of, 264–67; framing of, 267; for Poland, 264–67, 267nn1–5; release of, 266

Eight-hour day, 30, 40n2, 55

Elections: ballot mutilation in, 112; corruption of, 111–14; intimidation at, 112–14; polling places for, 111–12, 116–17; Socialist Party and, 3, 111–19, 119nn1–2; Stanton Blatch and, 113; of Waldman,
116–19. *See also* Second Avenue University; *specific political parties*

Election law: ballots and, 117; disregard for, 111–13, 117–19; gangsters and, 117–19

Employers: contractors as, 28, 89; Knights of Labor with, 31; organization by, 133. *See also* Manufacturers

English language, 187, 190n2, 208; education in, 183–84

Epshteyn, Shakhne, 180–81, 182n6, 222, 223n5

Epstein, Schachno, 256–57

Erlich, Henryk. *See* Ehrlich, Henryk

Esau, 305–6

Espionage Act, 223n3

Europe, 124; Holocaust in, 146–48, 323. *See also specific countries*

Fascism, 17–18, 316–17. *See also specific fascists*

Faynman, A., 179–81, 181nn1–2, 182nn3–6

Feigenbaum, Benjamin, 212, 213n5

Ferrer y Guardia, Francisco, 176, 178n6

Fichandler, Alexander, 196, 197n3

Finland: immigrants from, 6–7, 10–11, 21n21, 23n35; radicalism and, 11, 23n35

Flynn, Elizabeth Gurley, 100, 102n2

Forverts (*Forward*), 2, 90n1; Americanism in, 189–90; against Arab violence, 298–300; content of, 188–89, 190nn8–10; finances of, 186–87; Marshall for, 109–10; preservation of, 110; service of, 188; structure of, 188–89, 190n7; Villard for, 185–90, 190nn1–10; wages at, 186; World War I and, 109

Foster, William Z., 24n60, 230, 237n6, 255

Fourth International, 322, 326n1

Fraina, Louis C. (Lewis Corey), 217, 218n4

France, 148; French Revolution, 37; nationalism of, 289

Frankfurter, Felix, 292, 293n4

Fraser, Steve, 18

Freeman, Joshua, 18

Free speech issues, 230–31, 234–35

Frey, John, 9–10

Frick, Henry Clay, 47n3, 95–96

Gallagher, Leo, 131
Gangsters: election law and, 117–19; poverty and, 116, 118; Second Avenue University and, 116, 118; in unions, 144–45. *See also* Secret police
Garment workers, 20n9, 88–90, 90nn2–4
Garvey, Marcus, 120
Geminder, Bedrich, 270
Germaine. *See* Glotzer, Albert; Mandel, Ernest
German immigrants, 80n2; American socialist movement and, 2–3, 222; anarchism from, 3; German-speaking Jews related to, 20n6; as Socialists, 6. *See also* Jacobs, Paul
Germany, 146–48
Gide, Andre, 271–72
Ginsburg, Asher (Ahad Ha'am), 281, 285n1
Glass, N., 198
Glazer, Nathan, 15
Glenn, Susan, 20n9
Glotzer, Albert, 15; background on, 322; against Mandel, 322–25; on Zionism, 322–26, 326n1
Goldfarb, Max, 222, 223n6
Goldman, Emma, 65–66, 105, 108n4; Berkman with, 43–44, 47n3; Greie with, 46–47; New York City arrival of, 41–42; Solotaroff and, 42–43, 47n2. *See also* Birth control; Pastor Stokes, Rose
Goldstuecker, Edward, 273–74
Gompers, Samuel, 221, 223nn1–2
Gordin, Jacob, 167
G.P.U. *See* Secret police
Granich, Max, 253nn1–2; appreciation for, 251–52; background on, 249; education for, 250; hospitality for, 249–50; work of, 250–53
Great Upheaval, 25
Green, William, 142, 143n1, 264
Greenberg, Hayim, 304–7
Greie, Johanna, 45–47, 48n5
Gruson, Sidney, 270
Guglielmo, Jennifer, 21n18

Hall, Bolton, 101

Hapgood, Hutchins, 166, 167n1
Hapgood, Norman, 231, 237n8
Harding, William, 7
Hardman, J. B. S. (Jacob Benjamin Salutsky), 146–49
Harrison, Carter, 45
Harrison, Hubert, 100, 102n3
Haymarket Square (1886), 40n3, 47n4; Bisno on, 35–36; Greie on, 44–46; memorial for, 86–87, 87n2
Haywood, William ("Big Bill"), 100, 102n1
Hebrew language, 73
Herrick, William, 15
Hertz, Alfred. *See* Mink, George
Herzl, Theodore, 283, 285n5
Hill, Joe, 100–101, 103n4
Hillman, Sidney, 18–19
Hillquit, Morris, 88, 90n1, 222; Waldman and, 215, 218n1
Histadrut: Arab violence against, 302, 303n2; discrimination from, 309; role of, 311n1; Zionism and, 310
Hitler, Adolf, 146–47; Arabs compared to, 313; as imperialism, 323; Jacobs and, 76–77; status and, 306
Hoffman, Richard Beer, 304–5
Holland, 147
Holocaust, 146–48; capitalism related to, 323
Hospitality, 249–50
Housing, 36, 50, 60, 63, 70
Howe, Irving, 12
Hull House, 63, 67–68, 69n2
Hungary, 273

Idealist Zionism: diaspora and, 283–84; for intellectual center, 284; Jewish culture and, 283–84; materialist Zionism compared to, 280–81
ILGWU. *See* International Ladies Garment Workers' Union
Immigration: Arab violence and, 309–10; nationalism and, 289; to Palestine, 314, 319, 324–26; for progress, 163; socialism for, 310, 314. *See also specific countries*

Imperialism: Arabs and, 308–9, 315n1, 320, 324; Browder against, 233–34; class struggle and, 329; Hitler as, 323; internationalism and, 329–31; Israel and, 327–31; nationalism and, 289, 329–30

Independence, for Palestine, 320, 327

Industrial Workers of the World, 99–100, 102n1, 103n4

Ingerman, Anna Amitin, 94, 94n3

Intercollegiate Menorah Association, 290, 293n2

International Federation of Trade Unions, 302, 303n3

Internationalism: of anti-Semitism, 325–26; of Communists, 329; imperialism and, 329–31; of socialism, 286; Zionism as, 291

Internationalists, 5

International Labor Congress, 154–55

International Ladies Garment Workers' Union (ILGWU), 4, 18, 24n60; for African Americans, 141–42; broad agenda of, 8; education from, 194–96, 197nn1–4; hope from, 133; Labor Day for, 124–25; successes of, 134

International Red Aid, 233

International Workers Order (IWO), 15, 24n52, 255, 257n2

Irish immigrants, 6

Israel: Bittelman for, 327–31; bourgeois nationalism and, 328–30; imperialism and, 327–31; self-determination in, 328. See also Palestine

Israel Mapam Party, 274, 275n5

Italian immigrants, 6, 21n18

IWO. See International Workers Order

Jacob, 305–6

Jacobs, Paul, 14, 26, 258; background on, 70; childhood of, 70–71; Christianity and, 72; Depression and, 76; education of, 71, 73–74, 77–80; on extracurricular activities, 74; Hitler and, 76–77; Jewish identity for, 73, 75, 77–78; Judaism of, 71–73, 75; language and, 73–74, 77–78, 80n2; politics for, 76–77; rebellion of,

75–76; SYL for, 79–80; for YCL, 76, 78–79, 263; for YCL girls, 263

Jews: in American Communist Party, 10, 15, 23n36, 23n49; American Left influence from, 17; assimilation and, 291, 317; Communist Party membership of, 22n34; extermination of, 146–48; jealousy about, 295; as nation, 317–18; nationalities compared with, 289–90, 323; Nazis and, 146–48; socialism for, 4, 325; as workers, 84–85, 157–58, 170. See also specific nationalities

Jewish Americans: for African Americans, 7–8, 17–18; fears of, 75

Jewish Communism, 23n35

Jewish Communist Party membership, 22n34

Jewish culture, 18, 24n64, 151; anti-Semitism and, 205–7; films as, 262–63; idealist Zionism and, 283–84; of Jewish militants, 287; Kallen and, 290–91, 292n1; Marxism and, 204–6; misconceptions of, 204–6; poetry as, 164; revival of, 271, 273; United Jewish Workers' Cultural Society, 191–93. See also Education; Yiddish language

Jewish identity: changes regarding, 14–15; for Jacobs, 73, 75, 77–78; of second generation, 12–14; of Trotsky, 13, 14; Yiddish language for, 207–8

Jewish immigrants, 20n6; for American socialist movement, 5–7; prejudice against, 153; second generation compared with, 11–12. See also Russian Jews

Jewish labor movement: for African Americans, 7–8; diversity within, 2; Jewish socialism from, 1–4; loyalty of, 7; origins of, 1–2; size of, 2; in social reform movements, 18–19; transnational context of, 4–5

Jewish organizations: German-speaking Jews related to, 20n6; individual Jews compared with, 19n1. See also specific organizations

Jewish People's Fraternal Order, 15

Jewish Question, 84–85, 325; disappearance

of, 295, 316–17; Zionism and, 295–96
Jewish radicalism: Finish radicalism
    compared with, 11, 23n35; militants in,
    286–87, 287n1; 1950s and, 19. *See also*
    specific radicals
Jewish socialism: ethnicity of, 12–13; from
    Jewish labor movement, 1–4; longev-
    ity of, 7–8; non-Jewish socialism and,
    13, 13–14. *See also* Newspapers; *specific*
    organizations; *specific socialists*
Jewish Socialist Federation, 239, 244, 248n1
Jewish women, 20n9. *See also specific*
    women
Joan of Arc, 138–39
Jonas, Alexander, 212, 213n3
Judaism: Christianity compared with, 172;
    of Jacobs, 71–73, 75; Reform, 72–73, 75;
    socialism as, 25, 52–54; without syna-
    gogues, 170–73; without worship, 168–73

Kallen, Horace, 290–91, 292n1
Karpeloff, Ester, 129–32
Kats, Moyshe, 180, 182n3
Kautsky, Karl, 189, 190n10
Kazin, Alfred, 13
Kentucky miners, 135, 136n1
Khanin, Nokhum, 246–48; background on,
    239; capitalism and, 243–44; empathy
    with, 239–40; honesty from, 245; meet-
    ings for, 241; red tape for, 244; trust for,
    240–41
Klehr, Harvey, 23n36
Knights of Labor: for eight-hour strike, 30,
    40n2; employers with, 31; membership
    in, 30–31; misunderstanding with, 31–32;
    negotiations from, 31
Ku Klux Klan, 128, 234

Labor: Americanization and, 36; capital-
    ism and, 33–34; for children, 60, 62–66,
    106; at home, 28–29; housing for, 36;
    workday length for, 31–32
Labor Day, 124–25
Labor movement meeting: assembling for,
    27; complaints at, 28; against contrac-
    tors, 28; fears at, 28; innocence about,

30–31; manufacturers and, 30; about
    slack, 28, 40n1; spokesmen from, 29;
    spontaneity of, 27, 30; for strike, 29–30;
    violence and, 29
Labor union: description of, 40; Working-
    man's Educational Society for, 39–40.
    See also specific unions
Lang, Lucy Robins, 25; background on, 59;
    education for, 65–67; father of, 59–62;
    honors for, 67–68; work for, 62–66
Language: English, 183–84, 187, 190n2, 208;
    Hebrew, 73; Jacobs and, 73–74, 77–78,
    80n2; Zhitlowsky and, 177, 178nn8–9. *See*
    also Yiddish language
Law: Cahan for, 109–10; Comstock, 104–8,
    108nn1–3; for elections, 111–13, 117–19;
    The Tombs and, 90, 90n4. *See also* Hay-
    market Square; Prague Trial; Stromberg,
    Yetta
Lawrence, T. E., 313
Leckert, Hirsh, 166–67
Lederhendler, Eli, 4, 20n9
Lee, Algernon, 114
Lenin, Vladimir, 16, 222, 223n8; against
    anti-Semitism, 270–71; picture of, 258;
    status and, 306
Leon, Abram, 319
Leontieff, Comrade. *See* Moisseiff, Leon
The Liberator, 13, 14
Libin, Zalman, 159, 161n3, 166
Liebknecht, Karl, 139
Lincoln, Abe, 51
Lippman, Walter, 292, 293n6
London, Meyer, 212, 213n2
Lore, Ludwig, 231, 237n10
Los Angeles: African Americans in, 121–23;
    Communist "criminals" in, 129–32,
    132nn1–2
Louis, Ed, 100
Lovestone, Jay, 16

Magazines and journals: *American Socialist*
    Monthly, 308–10; *International Socialist*
    Review, 279; *The Jewish Daily Forward*,
    257; *Jewish Life*, 268; *The Jewish Worker*
    (*Der yidisher arbeter*), 282, 285n3;

Magazines and journals (*continued*)
The Liberator, 13, 14; *The Nation*, 8,
129–32, 132nn1–2, 133–34; *The New
International*, 264–67, 267nn1–5; *Party
Affairs*, 327–31; *Socialist Review*, 312–14;
Di tsukunft, 172, 173n7; *Youth and Nation*,
316–18
Maisel, Robert, 221, 223n4
Maison, Mark, 17–18
Mandel, Ernest: background on, 319;
Glotzer against, 322–25; for Palestine
socialism, 320–21
Manufacturers: competition over wages
from, 32; labor movement meeting and,
30; shops of, 34–35; unions and, 32–33
Marlenites, 262
Marmor, Kalman, 198
Marriage, 67; sexual relations and, 198;
wives, 94, 94n4
Marshall, Louis, 109–10
Marx, Karl, 57; class struggle for, 97;
economics and, 304–5; as prophet, 97;
Shiplacoff for, 97–98; for spiritual life,
98; Trotsky on, 216
Marxism: Fourth International, 322, 326n1;
Jewish culture and, 204–6; nationalism
with, 322–26
Marxist-Leninist parties, 16
Maryson, Jay, 219, 220n2
Maryson, Katherina, 219–20, 220nn1–2
Masliansky, Zvi Hirsch, 171, 173n4
*The Materialist Conception of the Jewish
Question* (Leon), 319
Materialist Zionism: diaspora protection
in, 282–83; idealist Zionism compared
to, 280–81
May Day, 124
McCormick Harvester Works, 35, 45–47
McKinley, William, 66
Meyer, Gerald, 21n18
Michel, Louis, 81, 120–23
Milch, Jacob, 279–85, 285nn1–5
Militants, Jewish, 286–87, 287n1
Miller, Louis, 88, 90n1
Mink, George (Joseph Berson, Alfred
Hertz), 256

Mintz, Bella, 129–32
Moisseiff, Leon (Comrade Leontieff), 93,
94n1, 157
Morality, 198
Most, Johann, 41, 47, 87n4; background
on, 47n1; Edelshtat on, 87, 87n3; speech
of, 44
Mother: of Bittelman, 53–54, 57; of Strom-
berg, 131–32; as teacher, 138
Murray, Philip, 265, 267n2
Muste, A. J., 195, 197n1

The Nation, 8; "Communist 'Criminals' in
Los Angeles," 129–32, 132nn1–2; "Unions
with Brains," 133–34
National Association for the Advancement
of Colored People, 220n1
Nationalism: from anti-Semitism, 319;
bourgeois, 328–30; of France, 289; immi-
gration and, 289; imperialism and, 289,
329–30; Marxism with, 322–26; World
War I and, 289. *See also* International-
ism; Zionism
Nazis, 146–48. *See also* Hitler, Adolf
Nearing, Scott, 114
New Left, 19
Newman, Henry, 160
Newman, Pauline, 159–61, 161nn1–3
Newspapers, 10; *Di arbeter tsaytung*, 91–94,
94nn2–4, 154, 187, 190n4; *California
Eagle*, 120; *Daily Worker*, 230, 237n6, 262,
267; *Di fraye arbeter shtime*, 93, 94n1,
124; *Die Freiheit*, 47; *The Jewish Daily
Forward*, 257; *Justice*, 124–25; *Di morgn
frayhayt*, 301–2, 303nn1–3; *New Yorker
Volkszeitung*, 87n4; *Di nyu-yorker yidishe
folkstsaytung*, 83–85; *Der tog*, 301, 303n1;
Vanguard, 144–45, 254–57, 257nn1–4;
Di varhayt, 90n1; *Der yidisher kemfer*,
286–87, 287n1. *See also* Forverts; New
York Times
New York City, 4, 162–63; Café Monopole
in, 214–16; East Side, 164–67, 279; 1892
demonstration in, 91–92; Goldman's
arrival in, 41–42; Second Avenue in,
214–18, 218nn2–4. *See also* Second

Avenue University; Union Square
New Yorker Volkszeitung, 87n4
New York Times, 162, 233; on Jewish phi-
losophers outdoors, 174–78, 178nn1–11;
on New York socialists in Russia, 221–22,
223nn1–8; on Prague Trial, 270; on Red
Sunday parade, 211–12, 213nn1–5; on
Russian anti-Semitism, 270–71; on Rus-
sian Jews' freedom, 273
Nuorteva, Santeri, 217, 218n3

O'Carroll, "Wild Joe," 101–2
Ohlerites, 261–62
Olgin, Moissaye J., 224–27
Oren, Mordecai, 274

Palestine: discrimination in, 309; economics in, 300, 304–5, 324; Histadrut for,
302, 303n2, 309–10, 311n1; immigra-
tion to, 314, 319, 324–26; independence
for, 320, 327; liberalism related to, 314;
Russia for, 327–28; self-determination
in, 328; socialism for, 317–18, 320–21;
welcome from, 325–26; Western Wall in,
298–99. *See also* Arabs; Britain
Party Affairs, 327–31
Pastor Stokes, Rose: background on, 104;
against capitalism, 105, 107–8; against
Comstock Law, 104–8, 108n1
Peddlers, 59–60
Peel Commission, 312, 315n1
People's Council for Peace and Democracy
(People's Council), 221, 223n3
Poale Tsion, 286–87, 287n1
Poland, 189; Ehrlich and Alter for, 264–67,
267nn1–5; Holocaust in, 146–47; Zygiel-
bojm for, 265, 267n5
Polish-American socialists, 21n24
Polish immigrants, 22n34; as socialists, 6,
21n17
Politics: for African Americans, 121–22;
of Arab violence, 298–300; for Jacobs,
76–77
Poverty: birth control related to, 104–5;
farmers and, 127–28; gangsters and, 116,
118; Ku Klux Klan and, 128; of Russian

Communists, 241–42, 245, 253
Power: of capitalism, 83; of women, 67–69.
See also Imperialism
Poyntz, Juliet (Juliet Pointz), 231, 238n11;
secret police against, 254–57, 257nn1–4
Prague Trial, 268, 270, 275n2; releases
from, 273–74
Progressive Women's Society, 93, 94n1

Racial discrimination: Ku Klux Klan, 128,
234; pride despite, 120–22; in unions,
140–43
Randolph, A. Phillip, 141–42
Raskin, Saul, 179–80, 181n1
Raymond, Jack, 273
Red Sunday parade, 211–12, 213nn1–5
Reed, John, 78
Reform Judaism, 72–73, 75
Reitman, Ben, 101, 105, 108n3
Religion, 57–58; birth control and, 105–6;
Christianity, 72, 172. *See also* Arabs;
Judaism
Richards, Bernard G., 162–67, 167n1
Rischin, Moses, 2
Robinson-Rubens couple, 254–55
Roosevelt, Franklin D., 16
Rose, Ernestine, 19n1
Rosenberg, Arthur, 316–18
Rosenfeld, Morris, 159, 161n1
Russia: without democracy, 52; demon-
stration in, 55–57; hardship in, 253;
hospitality in, 249–50; internationalists
in, 5; Jewish homeland and, 269, 275n3,
277, 327–31; labor unrest in, 54–55; mis-
takes in, 251–53; New York socialists in,
221–22, 223nn1–8; for Palestine, 327–28;
sabotage in, 250–51; Socialist-Zionists
in, 5; Zionism and, 5, 327–31. *See also*
Arbeter Ring; Bund; Stalin, Joseph
Russian anti-Semitism, 270; anti-cosmo-
politanism as, 271–72; ignorance about,
268–72; Jewish culture revival against,
271, 273; Jews' freedom despite, 272–73;
Russia's revelation of, 274; Yiddish writers' murders as, 268–69, 274, 275n1. *See
also* Prague Trial

Russian Communists: capitalism for, 243–44; hope for, 246, 248, 253; innocence of, 239–41, 246–48; poverty of, 241–42, 245, 253; red tape from, 244; secret police against, 246–47, 248n5

Russian Jews, 51; at coffee-houses, 155–56; education of, 155; freedom of, 273; intensity of, 154; persecution of, 155–56; prejudice against, 153; for press, 154; qualities of, 153–54; radicalism of, 154. *See also specific Russian Jews*

Russian Revolution, 209; Maryson, K., for, 219–20, 220nn1–2; parade for, 211–12, 213nn1–5; Zionism and, 285

Russia's new intelligentzia: avidity of, 226; education for, 226–27; intrepidity of, 224–25; obstinacy of, 225; against old intelligentzia, 225–26; responsibility of, 225; as workers, 226

Salutsky, Jacob Benjamin. *See* Hardman, J. B. S.

Sanger, Margaret, 108n2, 234, 238n12

Sanger, William, 105, 108n2

Scabs, 89–90, 90n3

Scab shops, 89, 90n2

Schachtman, Max, 261–62

Schewitsch, Sergius, 87, 87n4

Schlesinger, Benjamin, 9–10

Schneiderman, Emma, 131–32

Second Avenue University: education from, 114–15; gangsters and, 116, 118; heckling at, 115, 118; Nearing for, 114; Stanton Blatch for, 114; subjects of, 115; violence at, 115–16, 118; Waldman for, 114–16

Second generation: Jewish identity of, 12–14; Jewish immigrants compared with, 11–12

Secret police: in America, 254–57, 257nn1–4; Robinson-Rubens couple as, 254–55; against Russian Communists, 246–47, 248n5

Sexual relations, 198

Shachtman, Max, 16

Sherman, Bezalel, 312–14, 315n1

Sheyfer, B., 183–84

Shiplacoff, Abraham, 97–98

Shoeworkers, 49–50

Shub, David, 8–9

Sinclair, Upton, 129–32, 132nn1–2

Slansky, Rudolf, 270, 275n2

Slansky Trial. *See* Prague Trial

Slogans, 91

Social democracy, 3, 215

Socialism: anarchism or, 38, 46; anti-Semitism against, 271; birth control and, 107; class struggle for, 37; democracy before, 52–53; education for, 37, 55, 57–58, 151; for immigration, 310, 314; internationalism of, 286; for Jews, 4, 325; Judaism and, 25, 52–54; for Palestine, 317–18, 320–21; Trotskyism and, 78–79; without Zionism, 296–97, 320

Socialists: in America compared to Europe, 216–18, 218n3; American, 216–18, 218n3, 221–22, 223nn1–8; Finnish immigrants as, 6–7, 21n21; German immigrants as, 6; Italian immigrants as, 6; from New York in Russia, 221–22, 223nn1–8; Polish-American, 21n24; Polish immigrants as, 6, 21n17; World War I and, 109–10, 216–18; Zionism and, 314. *See also specific socialists*

Socialist Labor Party, 6, 40n4, 91

Socialist Literary Society, 160

Socialist Pamphlet Fund, 157–58

Socialist Party: elections and, 3, 111–19, 119nn1–2; election victories of, 3, 117–19; Nearing for, 114; origins of, 3; union control by, 4

Socialist Review, 312–14

Socialist Workers Party (SWP), 322, 326n1

Socialist-Zionists, 5; Poale Tsion as, 286–87, 287n1

Social patriots, 215

Solotaroff, Hillel, 42–43, 47n2

Soviet Union. *See* Russia

Spartacus Youth League (SYL), 79–80

Spies, August, 33–34, 40n3

Spiritual life, 98

Stalin, Joseph, 254–55; criticism of, 264–65;

murders by, 268, 275nn1–2; for Russia's
Jewish homeland, 269, 275n3
Stanton Blatch, Harriot: election and, 113;
for Second Avenue University, 114
Starr, Ellen Gates, 69n2
Stokes, James Graham Phelps, 104
Stolper, B. J. R., 196, 197n4
Strikes: for eight-hour day, 30, 40n2; of
knee-pants workers, 88–90, 90nn1–4;
labor movement meeting for, 29–30;
meeting about, 33–34; picketing and, 36,
40n3; results from, 51–52; scab shops in,
89, 90n2; scabs in, 89–90, 90n3; violence
and, 35–36, 90; votes for, 33; workers'
wives for, 94, 94n4. See also Haymarket
Square
Stromberg, Yetta: conviction of, 131; flag
from, 130–31; mother of, 131–32; teach-
ings of, 130
Strong, Anna Louise, 250, 251, 253n2
Strunsky Walling, Anna, 219–20, 220nn1–2
Sunshine, Charley, 100
Swing, Raymond Gram, 265, 267n3
SWP. See Socialist Workers Party
SYL. See Spartacus Youth League
Syrkin, Nachman, 180, 181n2

Ten Days That Shook the World (Reed), 78
Thomas, Norman, 16, 78, 80n3, 102
Tobacco work, 62–63, 65–66
Tolstoy, Leo, 165
The Tombs, 90, 90n4
Trade Union Educational League, 24n60,
229, 237n5
Trade-unionism: for African Americans,
140–42, 142n1; demonstration of, 91–92;
for knee-pants workers, 88–90; practi-
calities of, 9; for shoemakers, 49–50. See
also specific organizations; specific unions
Tradition: of America, 218; Americaniza-
tion or, 68–69. See also Judaism
Transnationalism: Jewish labor movement
context and, 4–5; Zionism and, 288–92,
292n1, 292nn2–6
Tresca, Carlos, 256, 257n3
Trotsky, Leon, 248; description of, 215;

Fourth International for, 322, 326n1; Jewish identity of, 13, 14; on Marx, 216; on
New York City's Second Avenue, 214–18,
218nn2–4; pictures of, 258; against social
patriots, 215; speech of, 216
Trotskyism: attitude towards, 259; Bernick
for, 137; Communists and, 260, 262–63;
education in, 260–61; factionalism
within, 260–62; headquarters for,
258–59; ignorance about, 261; literature
of, 258–59; meetings for, 259; membership in, 259; Ohlerites in, 261–62; socialism and, 78–79

UHT. See United Hebrew Trades
Unemployment, 61
Unions: American Communist Party in,
10; with brains, 133–34; corruption in,
144–45; gangsters in, 144–45; manufacturers and, 32–33; racial discrimination
in, 140–43. See also Trade-unionism;
specific unions
Union Square, 91–92; assembly at, 99–100;
Communists at, 102; Flynn at, 100,
102n2; Haywood at, 100, 102n1; rallies
at, 99; speakers at, 100–102, 102nn2–3,
103n4; violence at, 101–2
United Hebrew Trades (UHT), 2; committee from, 88–90, 90n1; purpose of, 142
United Jewish Workers' Cultural Society,
191–93
United Mine Workers, 136n1
United Nations, 147
United Workers Party, 275n5

Vacations, 163
Vandervelde, Emile, 215, 218n2
Van Etten, Ida, 153–56
Vanguard, 144–45, 254–57, 257nn1–4
Vaynshteyn, Bernard, 88–90, 90nn1–4
Villard, Oswald Garrison, 185–90,
190nn1–10
Violence: towards Bund, 264–67; at
demonstrations, 56, 299; against Frick,
95–96; to Kentucky miners, 136n1; labor
movement meeting and, 29;

Violence (*continued*)
    at Second Avenue University, 115–16,
    118; Stalin's murders as, 268, 275nn1–2;
    strikes and, 35–36, 90; at Union Square,
    101–2. *See also* Arab violence; Haymar-
    ket Square; Holocaust
Vladeck, Baruch Charney, 188, 190n7, 231,
    237n9

Wages: class struggle and, 33–34; competi-
    tion over, 32; at *Forverts*, 186; for knee-
    pants workers, 89–90
Wald, Alan, 17, 24n64
Waldman, Louis, 81; background on, 111;
    election of, 116–19; heroism of, 112–13;
    Hillquit and, 215, 218n1; for Second
    Avenue University, 114–16; on Trotsky,
    214–18, 218nn1–4; victory of, 117, 119
Walling, William English, 220n1
Waltzer, Kenneth, 16–17
War: cold war, 271–72; World War I,
    109–10, 216–18, 289
Weiss, Samuel, 308–10, 311n1
Wilkie, Wendell, 265, 267n5
Wilson, Woodrow, 293n3
Wisotsky, Isadore, 99–102, 102nn1–3
Wolfson, Jennie, 129–32
Wolfson, Theresa, 195–96, 197n2
Women, 20n9, 263; education for, 160,
    175–76, 195–96, 197n2, 199–202, 203n1;
    gathering of, 94, 94n4; marriage and,
    67, 94, 94n4, 198; mothers as, 53–54, 57,
    131–32, 138; as orators, 175; as peddlers,
    59–60; power of, 67–69; pregnancy and
    childbirth for, 63–64; rights for, 119n2;
    voluntary societies for, 93–94, 94nn1–5;
    as wives, 94, 94n4. *See also* Birth control;
    specific women
Women's Trade Union League, 175–76,
    178n2
Workers: garment, 20n9, 88–90, 90nn2–4;
    interconnectedness of, 83; Jews as,
    84–85, 157–58, 170; of knee-pants, 88–90,
    90nn2–4; Labor Day for, 124–25; leisure
    for, 170; replacement of, 34; Russia's
    new intelligentzia as, 226; shoework-

ers, 49–50; of tobacco, 62–63, 65–66;
    wives of, 94, 94n4. *See also specific
    organizations*
Workers' Party, 322
Workers' (Communist) Party, 126, 128n1.
    See also Abramovich, Raphael
Workingman's Educational Society: for
    labor union, 39–40; meeting about,
    37–38
Workingwomen's Society, 93–94, 94nn2–3
Workmen's Circle. *See* Arbeter Ring
World War I: *Forverts* and, 109; national-
    ism and, 289; socialists and, 109–10,
    216–18

Yanovsky, Shoel, 124–25
YCL. *See* Young Communist League
Yiddish language, 14, 51, 178n11; culture
    and, 191–93, 207–8; education in, 196,
    197n4, 199–202, 203n1; Jacobs and,
    73–74, 77–78; for Jewish identity,
    207–8; lectures in, 179–81, 181nn1–2,
    182nn3–6; Zhitlowsky for, 178nn8–9.
    See also Newspapers; Russian
    anti-Semitism
Young Communist League (YCL), 14–15,
    26; girls in, 263; Jacobs for, 76, 78–79,
    263; SYL compared with, 79–80
Young Pioneers, 137
Young Workers League, 126–27
Youth and Nation, 316–18

Zaks, A. S., 180, 182n4
Zametkin, Adele Kean, 93, 94n2
Zametkin, Michael, 88, 90n1
Zhitlowsky, Chaim (Chaim Zhitlovsky)
    (Ben Ahud), 212, 213n4; language and,
    177, 178nn8–9; Zionism and, 282–83,
    285n4
Zionism: Americanism with, 290–92;
    anti-Semitism and, 316–19; as bourgeois
    nationalism, 328–30; class struggle and,
    294; co-operative Americanism and,
    291–92; emigration from, 281–82; against
    exiles' persecution, 282–83; futility of,
    281–83; Glotzer on, 322–26, 326n1; Herzl

for, 283, 285n5; Histadrut and, 310; as internationalism, 291; Jewish Question and, 295–96; Milch against, 279–85, 285nn1–5; questions about, 277; reality for, 294–95; Russia and, 5, 327–31; Russian Revolution and, 285; selectivity in, 282; Sherman for, 312–14, 315n1; socialism without, 296–97, 320; socialists and, 314; Socialist-Zionists, 5, 286–87, 287n1; stance on, 296–97, 322–26; sympathy for, 296–97; transnationalism and, 288–92, 292n1, 292nn2–6; Weiss against, 308–10, 311n1; Zhitlowsky and, 282–83, 285n4. *See also* Socialist-Zionists

Zionist factions: agreements among, 281; idealist Zionism, 280–81, 283–84; materialist Zionism, 280–83

Zygielbojm, Szmul, 265, 267n5

About the Editor

TONY MICHELS is the George L. Mosse Associate Professor of American Jewish History at the University of Wisconsin, Madison. He is the author of *A Fire in Their Hearts: Yiddish Socialists in New York* (2005).